Shrine of the Morning Mist

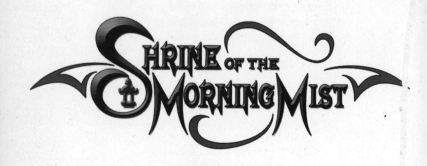

Volume 1

by
Hiroki Ugawa

Shrine of the Morning Mist Vol. 1
created by Hiroki Ugawa

Translation - Jeremiah Bourque
English Adaptation - Hope Donovan
Retouch and Lettering - Bowen Park
Production Artist - Erika "Skooter" Terriquez
Cover Design - Louis Csontos

Editor- Bryce P. Coleman
Digital Imaging Manager - Chris Buford
Managing Editor - Lindsey Johnston
VP of Production - Ron Klamert
Editor-In-Chief - Rob Tokar
Publisher - Mike Kiley
President and C.O.O. - John Parker
Chief Creative Officer and C.E.O. - Stuart Levy

A 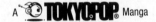 Manga

TOKYOPOP Inc.
5900 Wilshire Blvd. Suite 2000
Los Angeles, CA 90036

E-mail: info@TOKYOPOP.com
Come visit us online at www.TOKYOPOP.com

ISBN: 1-59816-343-4

First TOKYOPOP printing: May 2006
10 9 8 7 6 5 4 3 2
Printed in the USA

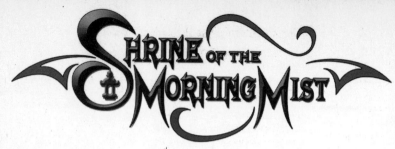

SHRINE OF THE MORNING MIST

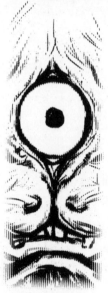

"When you can no longer tell what is real and what is illusion, do not despair. But know that soon a Time of Trials will begin, when a Great Eye will stare at you from over a mountain of corpses..."

(from Inou's Heisei Monster Tales: Mystery of the Haired Giant)

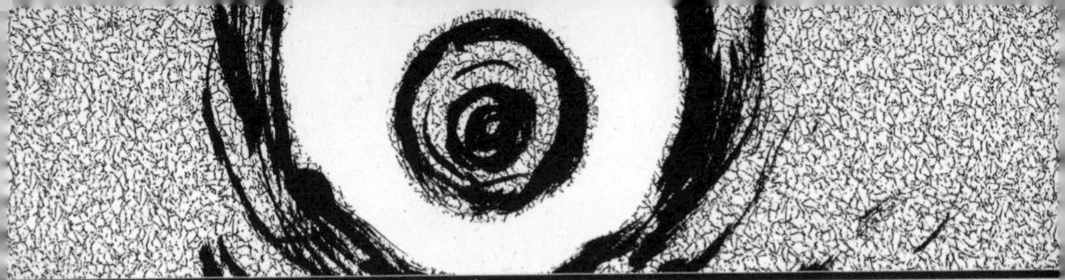

Contents

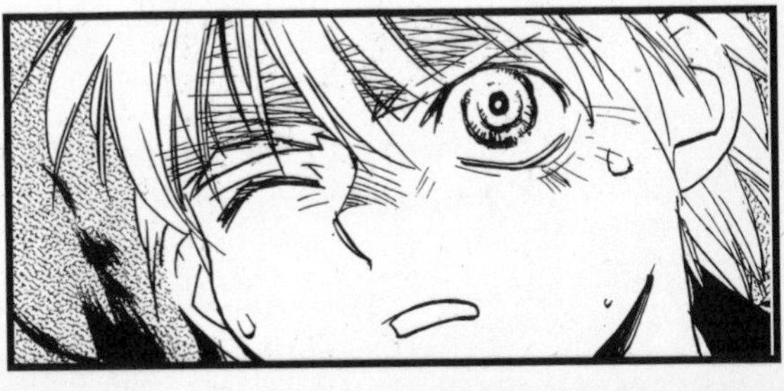

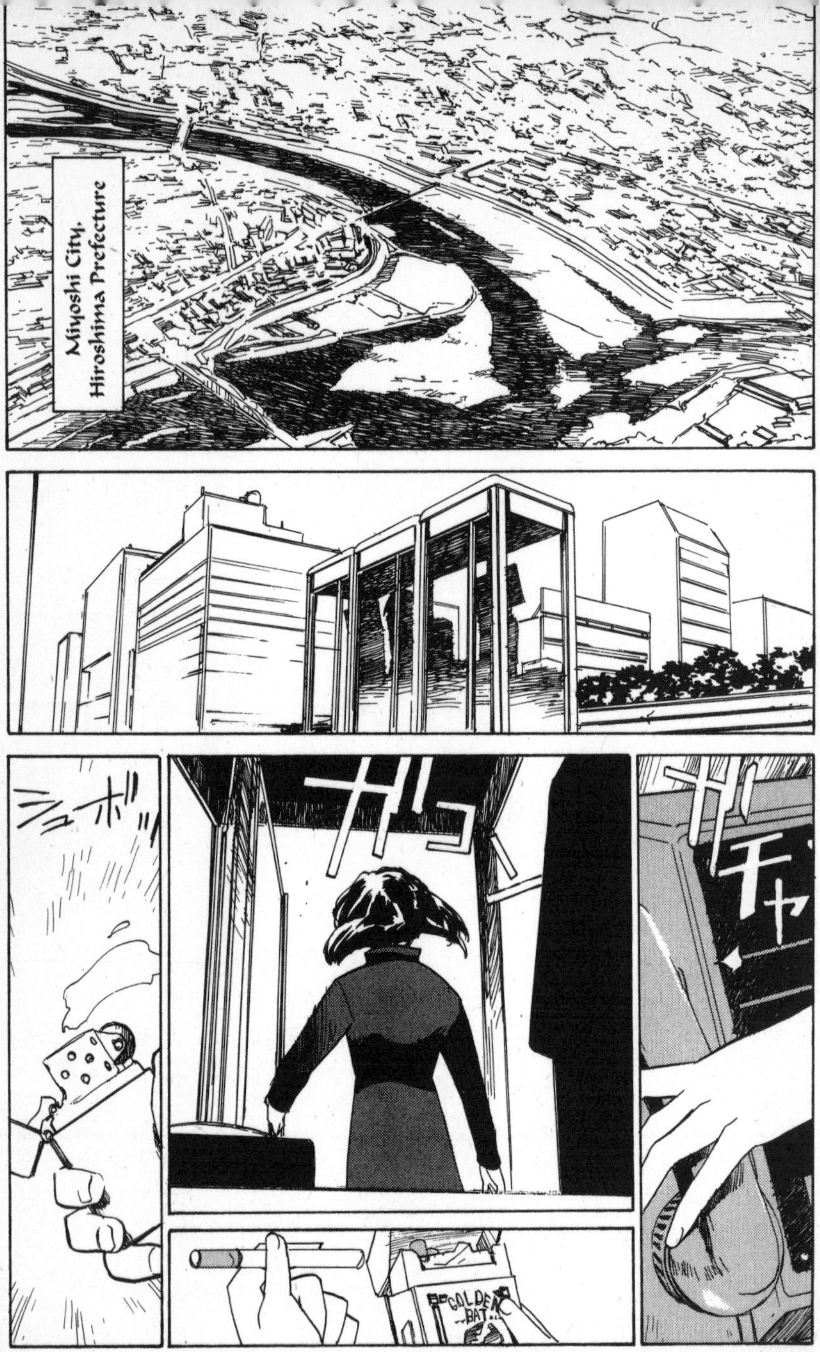
Miyoshi City,
Hiroshima Prefecture
ガチャ
ガコッ
GOLDEN BAT
シュボッ

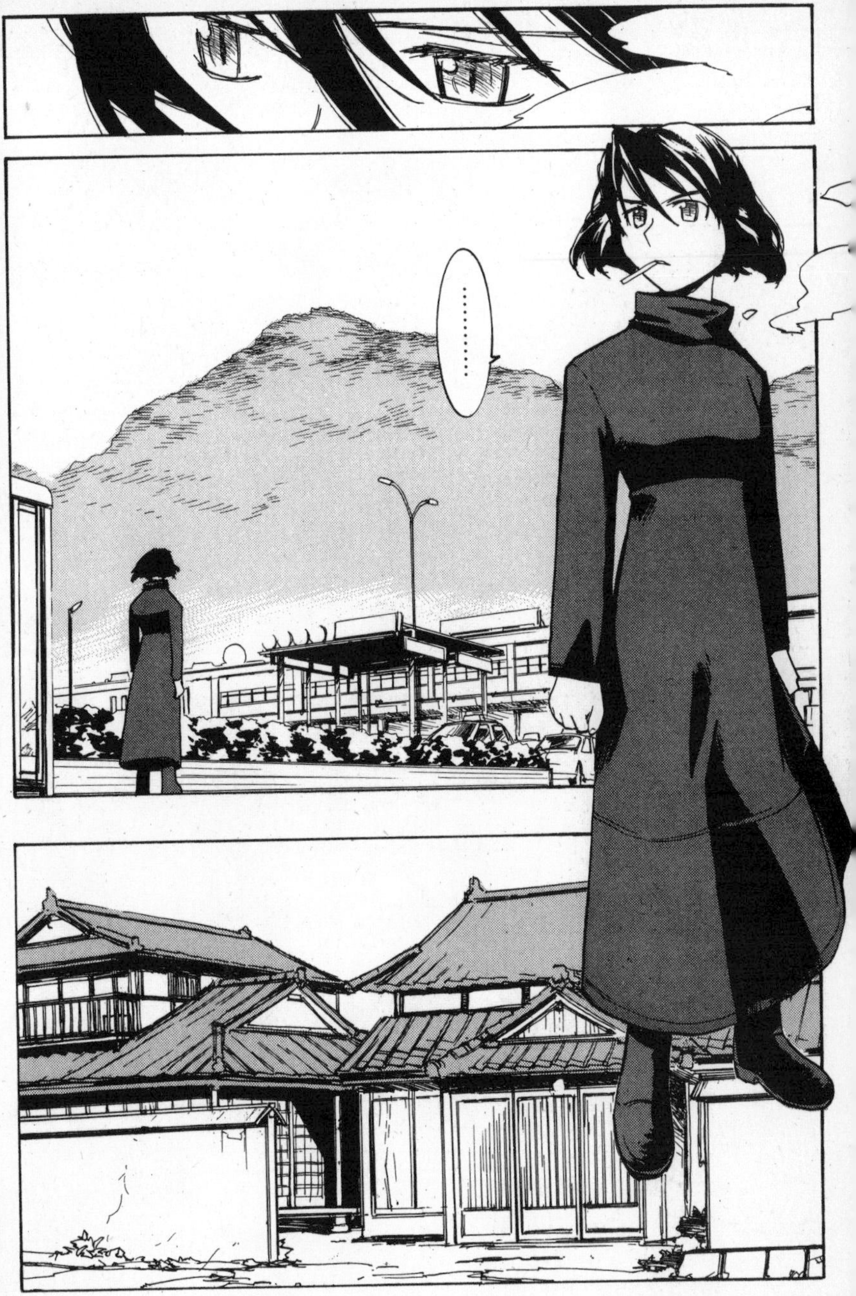

……

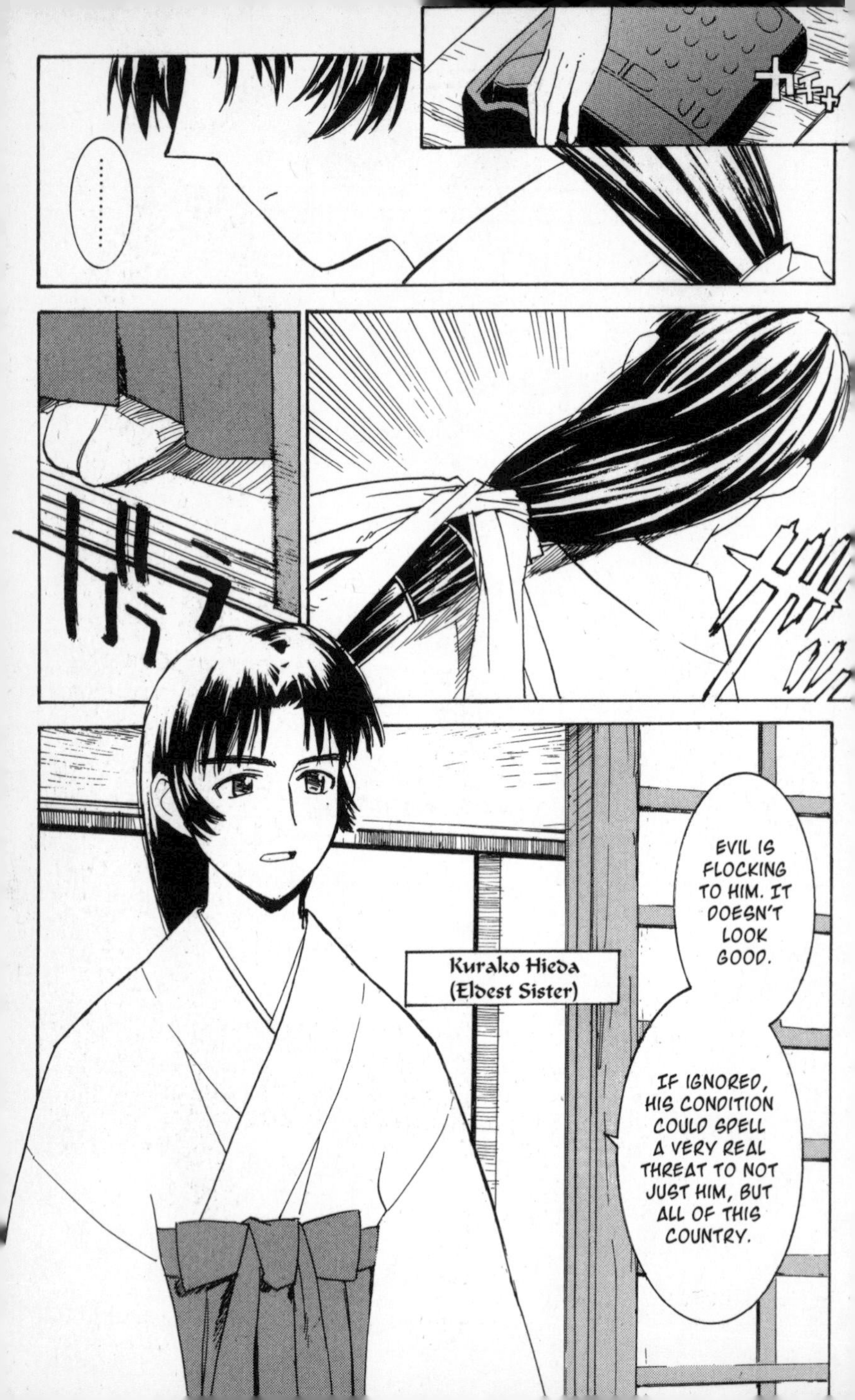
……
Kurako Hieda (Eldest Sister)
EVIL IS FLOCKING TO HIM. IT DOESN'T LOOK GOOD.
IF IGNORED, HIS CONDITION COULD SPELL A VERY REAL THREAT TO NOT JUST HIM, BUT ALL OF THIS COUNTRY.

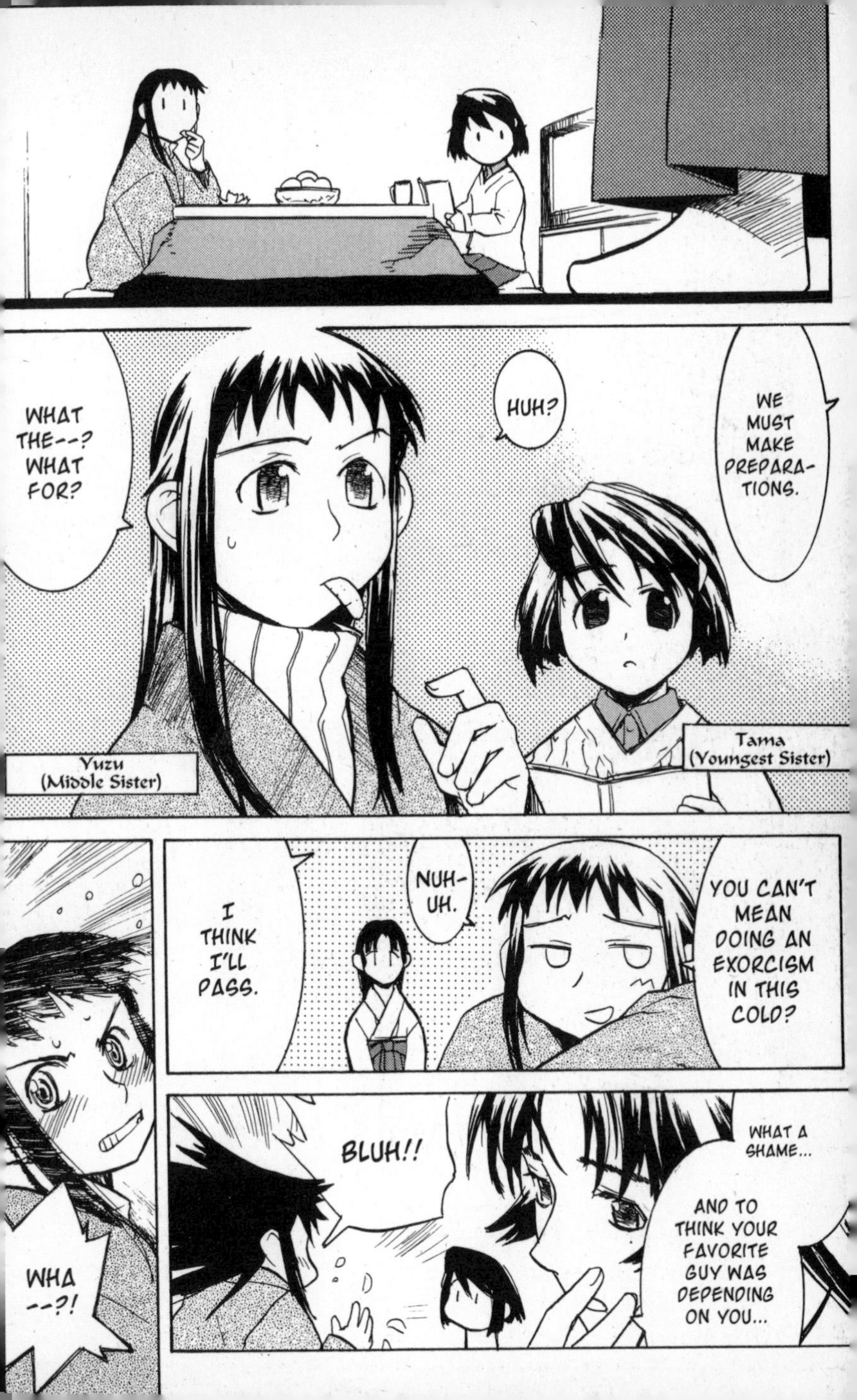
WE MUST MAKE PREPARATIONS.
HUH?
WHAT THE--? WHAT FOR?
Tama (Youngest Sister)
Yuzu (Middle Sister)
YOU CAN'T MEAN DOING AN EXORCISM IN THIS COLD?
NUH-UH.
I THINK I'LL PASS.
WHAT A SHAME...
AND TO THINK YOUR FAVORITE GUY WAS DEPENDING ON YOU...
BLUH!!
WHA--?!

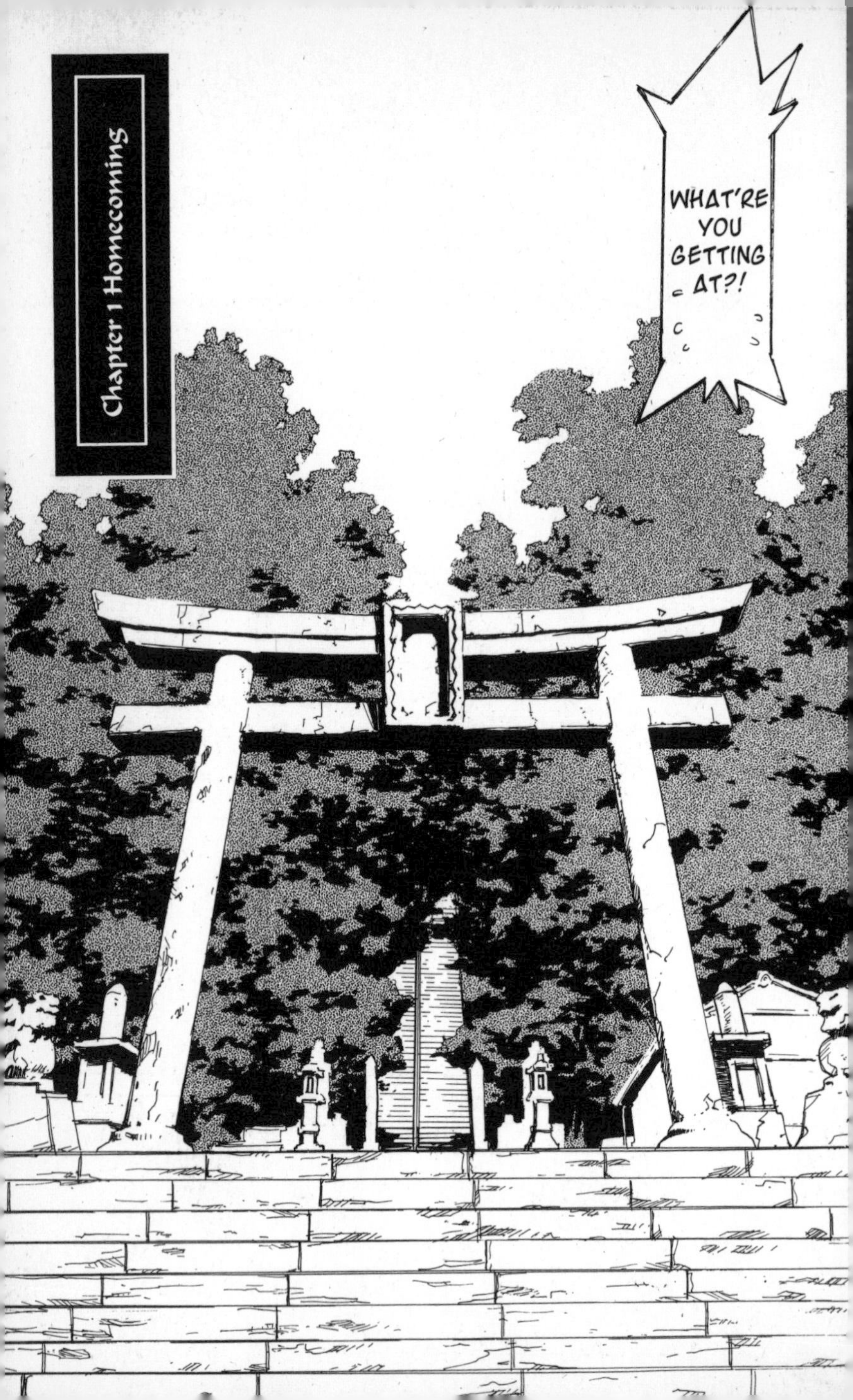
WHAT'RE YOU GETTING AT?!
Chapter 1 Homecoming

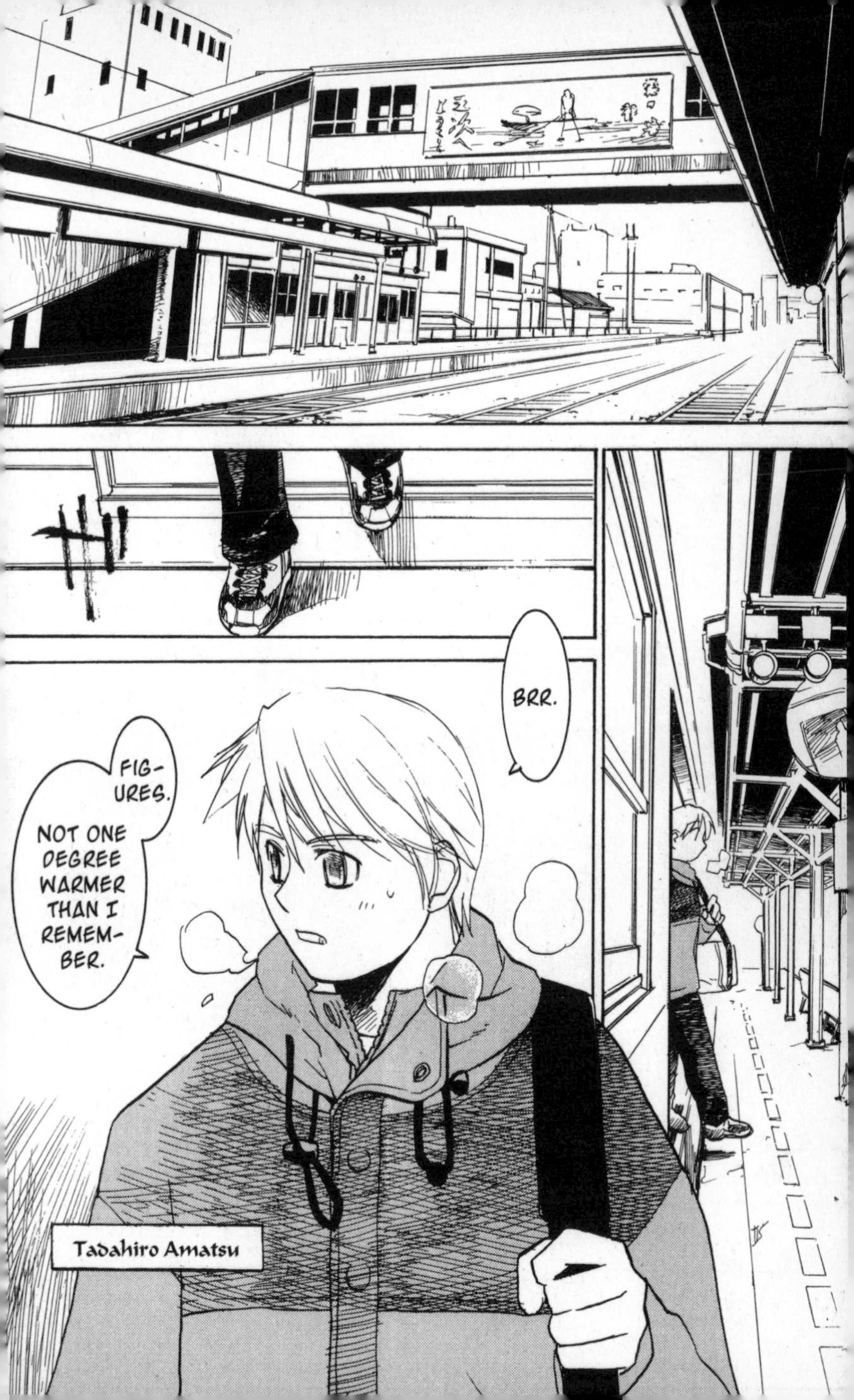
BRR.
FIG-URES.
NOT ONE DEGREE WARMER THAN I REMEMBER.
Tadahiro Amatsu

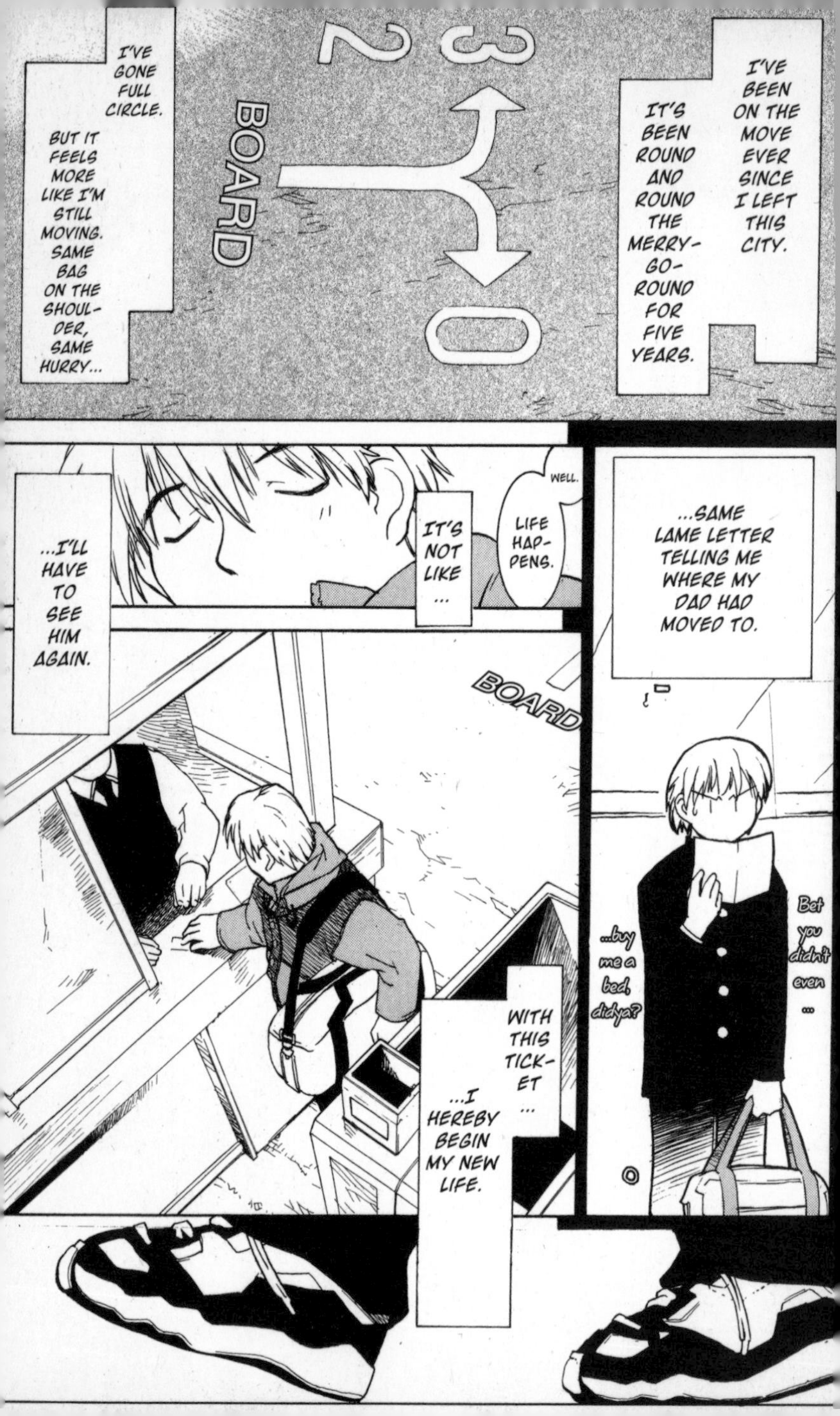
I'VE BEEN ON THE MOVE EVER SINCE I LEFT THIS CITY.
IT'S BEEN ROUND AND ROUND THE MERRY-GO-ROUND FOR FIVE YEARS.
3
2
0
BOARD
I'VE GONE FULL CIRCLE.
BUT IT FEELS MORE LIKE I'M STILL MOVING. SAME BAG ON THE SHOULDER, SAME HURRY...
...SAME LAME LETTER TELLING ME WHERE MY DAD HAD MOVED TO.
Bet you didn't even ...
...buy me a bed, didya?
WELL.
LIFE HAPPENS.
IT'S NOT LIKE ...
...I'LL HAVE TO SEE HIM AGAIN.
BOARD
WITH THIS TICKET ...
...I HEREBY BEGIN MY NEW LIFE.

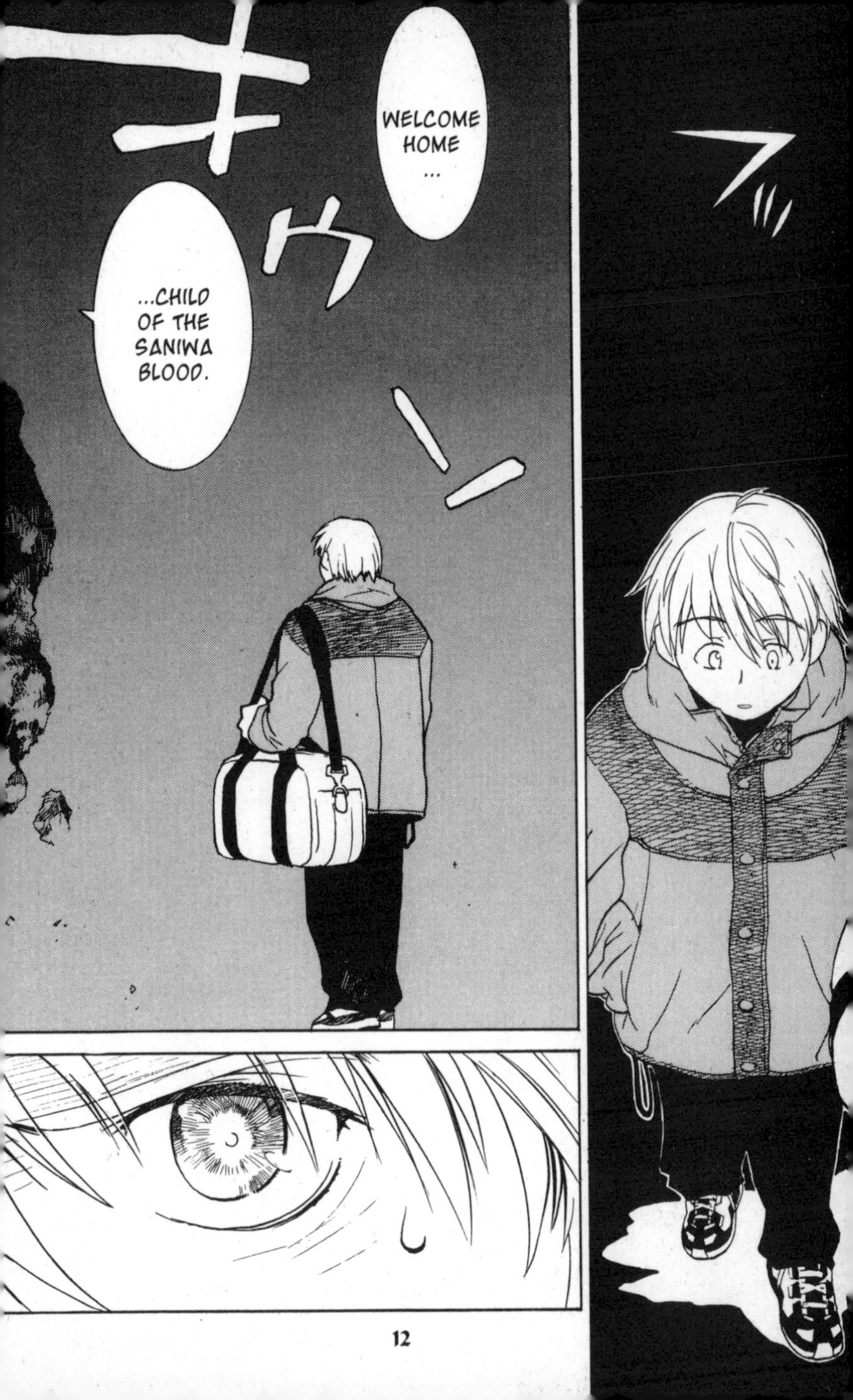
キウーー
WELCOME HOME ...
...CHILD OF THE SANIWA BLOOD.

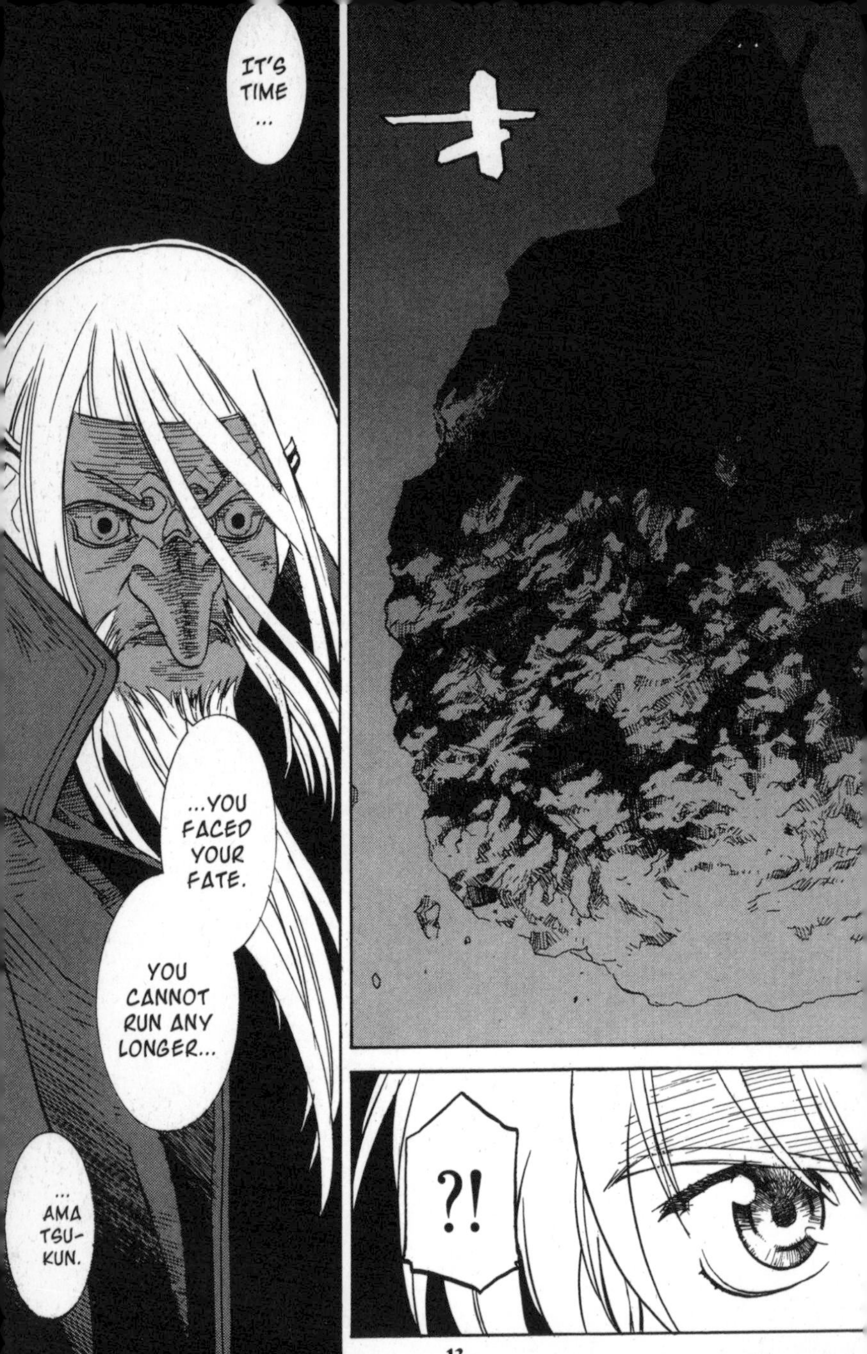
?!
IT'S TIME ...
...YOU FACED YOUR FATE.
YOU CANNOT RUN ANY LONGER...
... AMATSU-KUN.

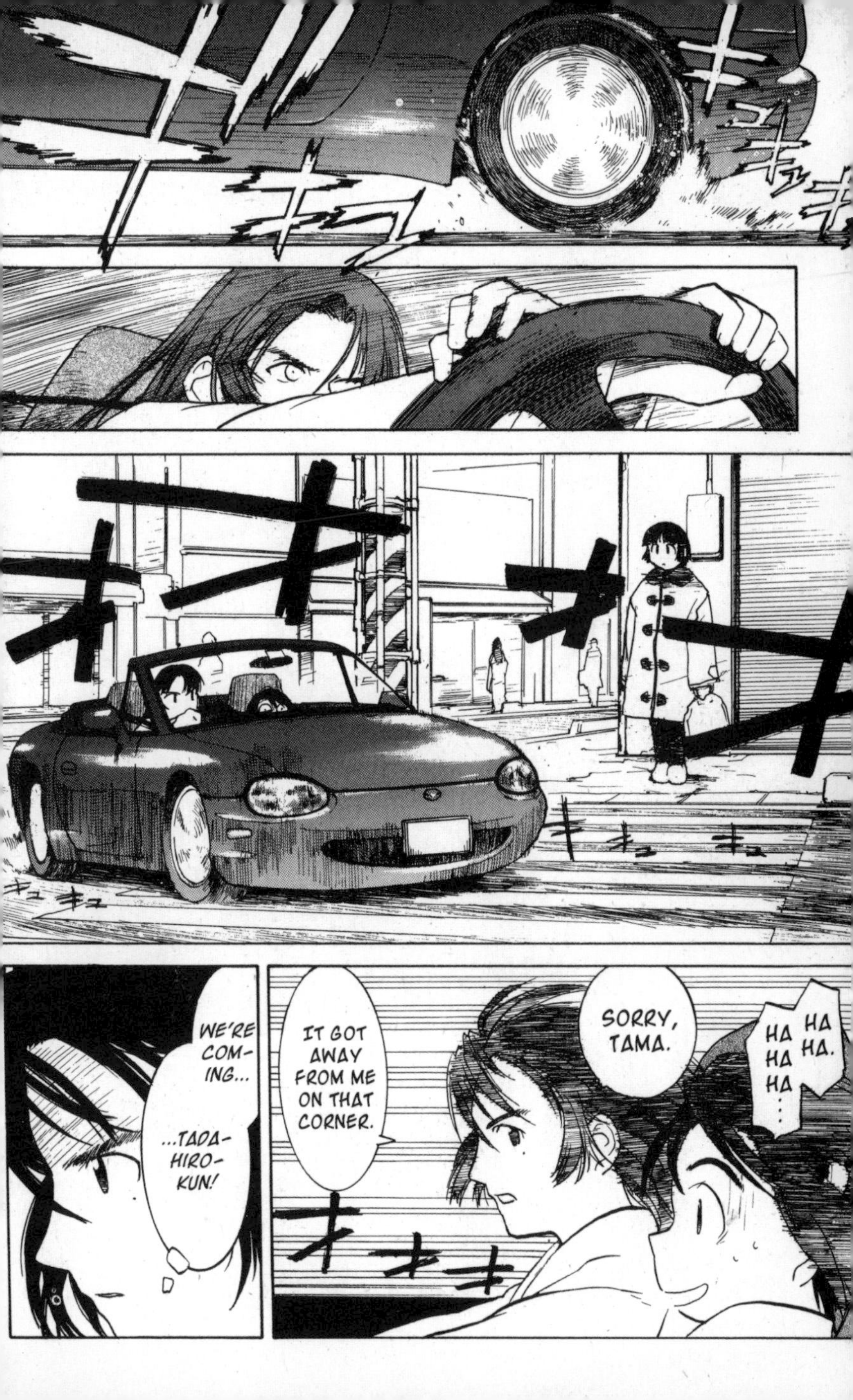
HA HA. HA HA HA...
SORRY, TAMA.
IT GOT AWAY FROM ME ON THAT CORNER.
WE'RE COMING...
...TADAHIRO-KUN!

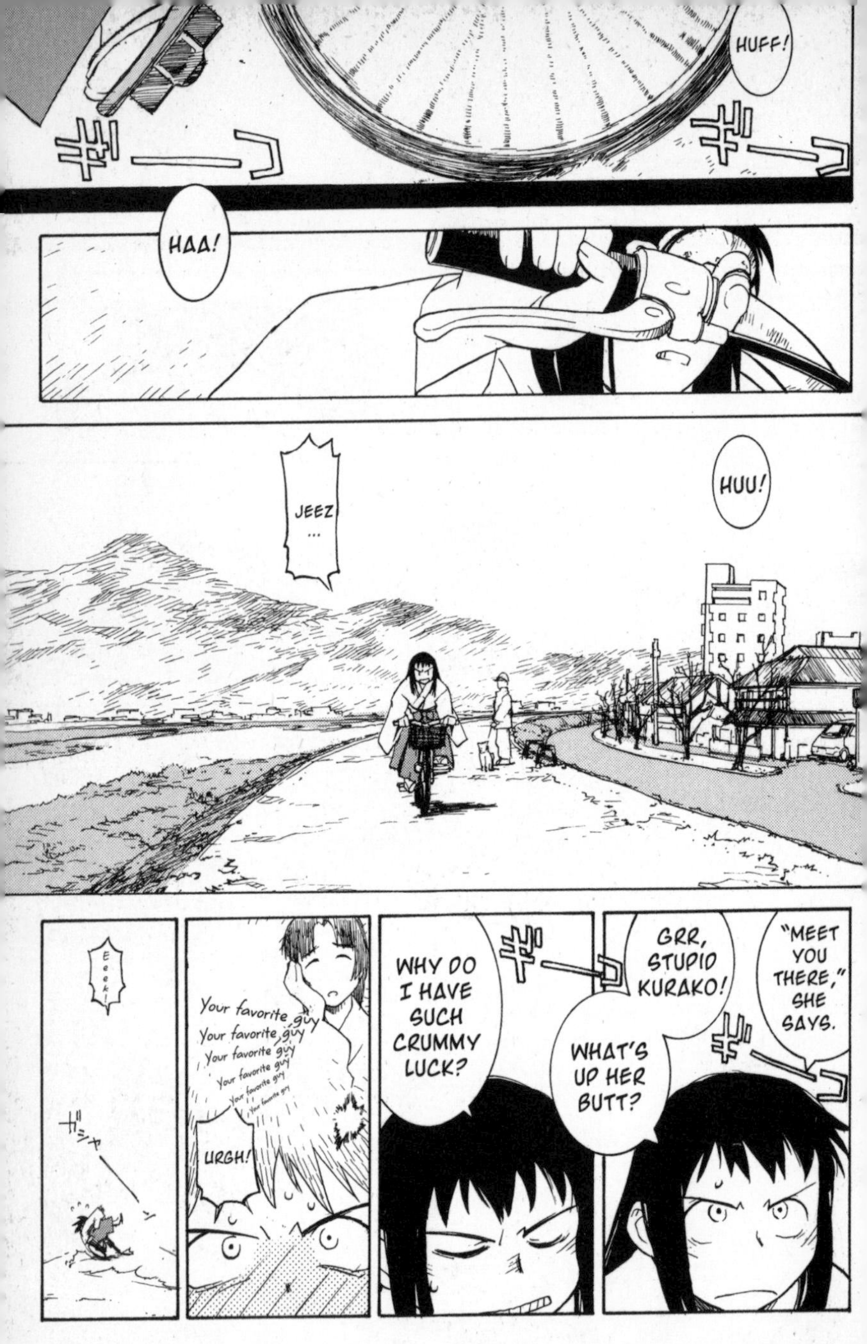
HUFF!
ギーコ
ギーコ
HAA!
HUU!
JEEZ ...
"MEET YOU THERE," SHE SAYS.
GRR, STUPID KURAKO!
WHAT'S UP HER BUTT?
WHY DO I HAVE SUCH CRUMMY LUCK?
Your favorite guy
Your favorite guy
Your favorite guy
Your favorite guy
Your favorite guy
Your favorite guy
URGH!
Eeek!

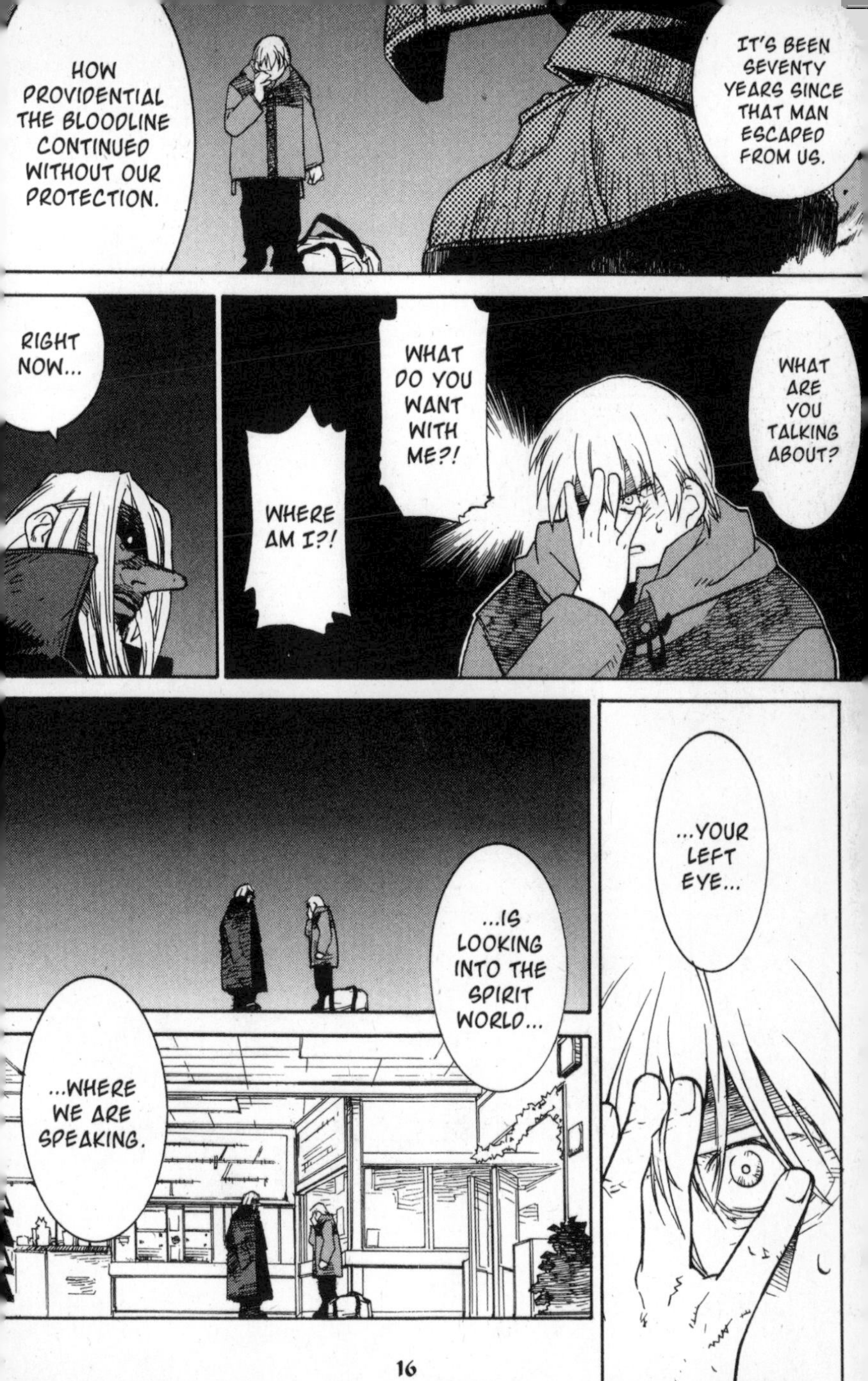
IT'S BEEN SEVENTY YEARS SINCE THAT MAN ESCAPED FROM US.
HOW PROVIDENTIAL THE BLOODLINE CONTINUED WITHOUT OUR PROTECTION.
WHAT ARE YOU TALKING ABOUT?
WHAT DO YOU WANT WITH ME?!
WHERE AM I?!
RIGHT NOW...
...YOUR LEFT EYE...
...IS LOOKING INTO THE SPIRIT WORLD...
...WHERE WE ARE SPEAKING.

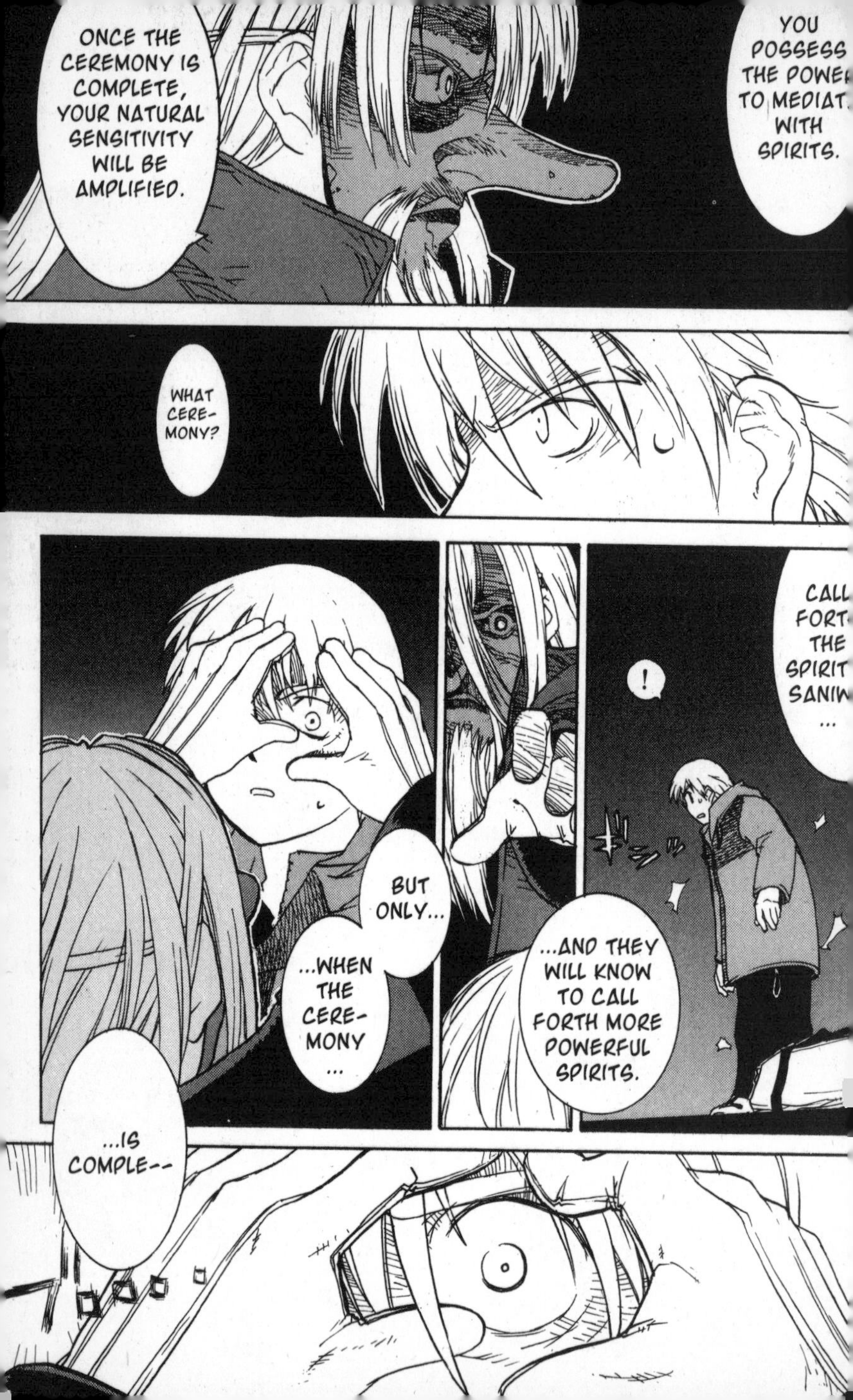
YOU POSSESS THE POWE TO MEDIAT WITH SPIRITS.
ONCE THE CEREMONY IS COMPLETE, YOUR NATURAL SENSITIVITY WILL BE AMPLIFIED.
WHAT CERE-MONY?
CALL FORT THE SPIRIT SANIW ...
!
...AND THEY WILL KNOW TO CALL FORTH MORE POWERFUL SPIRITS.
BUT ONLY...
...WHEN THE CERE-MONY ...
...IS COMPLE--

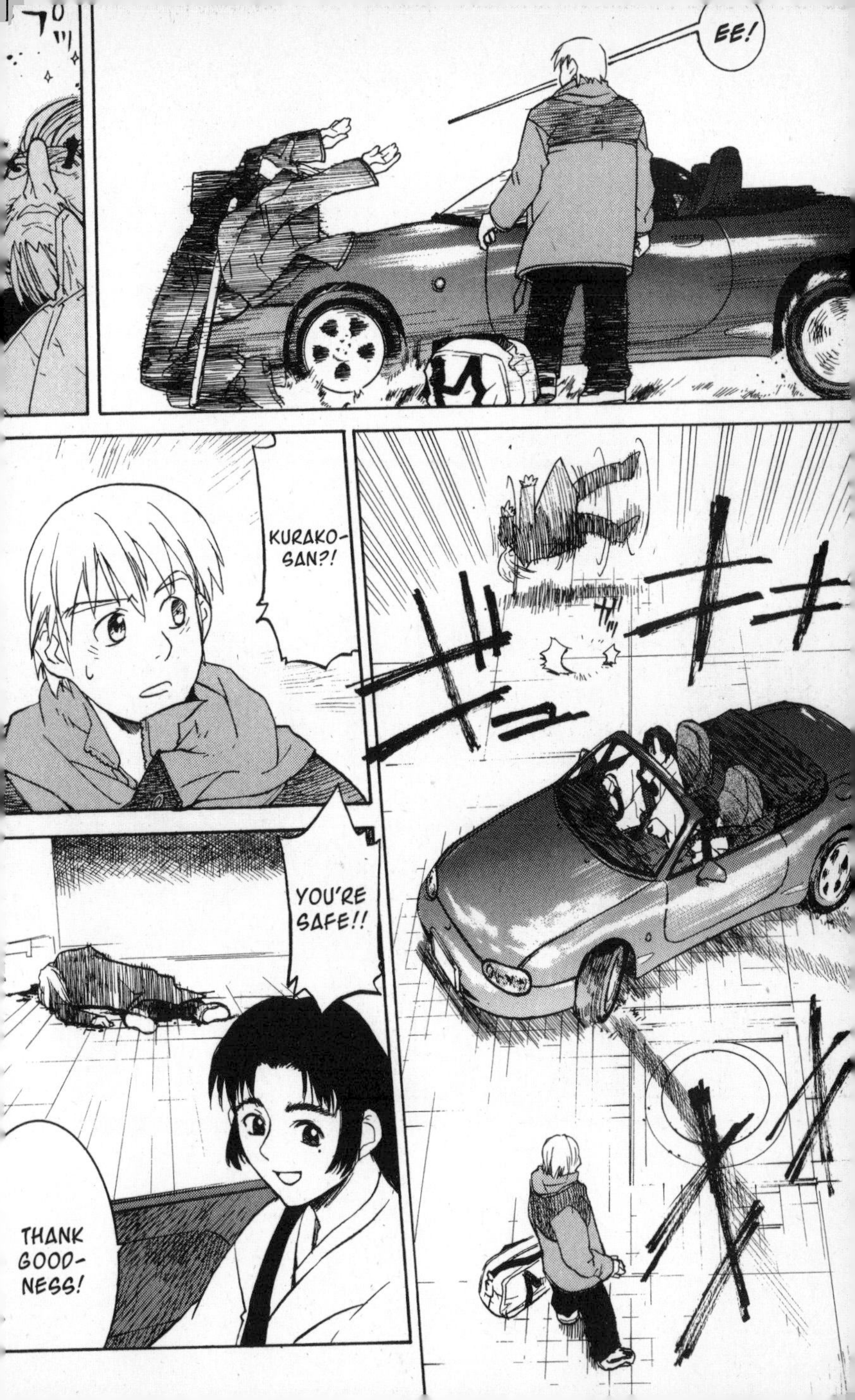

EE!
KURAKO-SAN?!
YOU'RE SAFE!!
THANK GOODNESS!

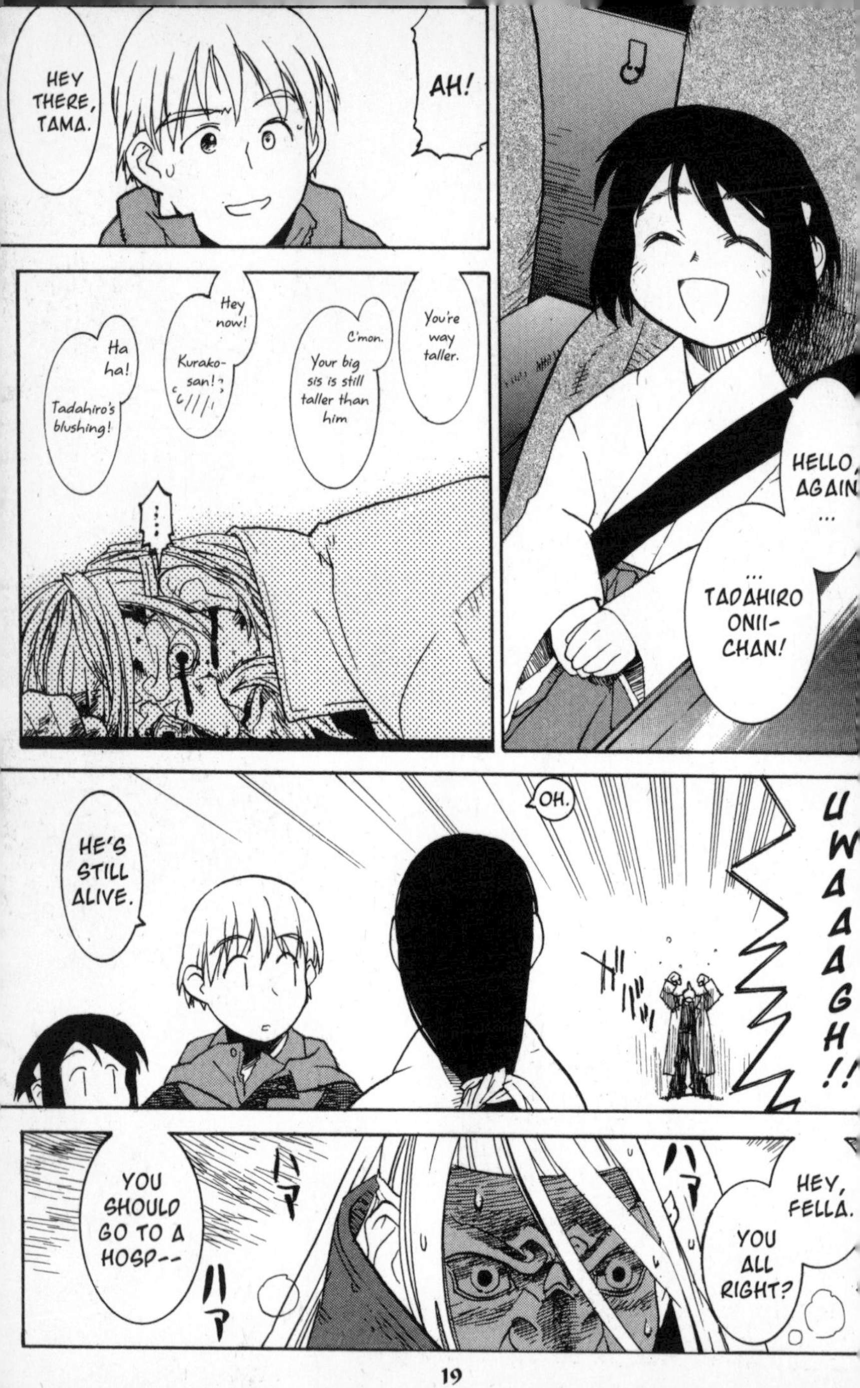
HELLO, AGAIN ...
... TADAHIRO ONII-CHAN!
AH!
HEY THERE, TAMA.
You're way taller.
C'mon. Your big sis is still taller than him
Hey now! Kurako-san!
Ha ha! Tadahiro's blushing!
...
UWAAAAAGH!!
OH.
HE'S STILL ALIVE.
HEY, FELLA. YOU ALL RIGHT?
YOU SHOULD GO TO A HOSP--

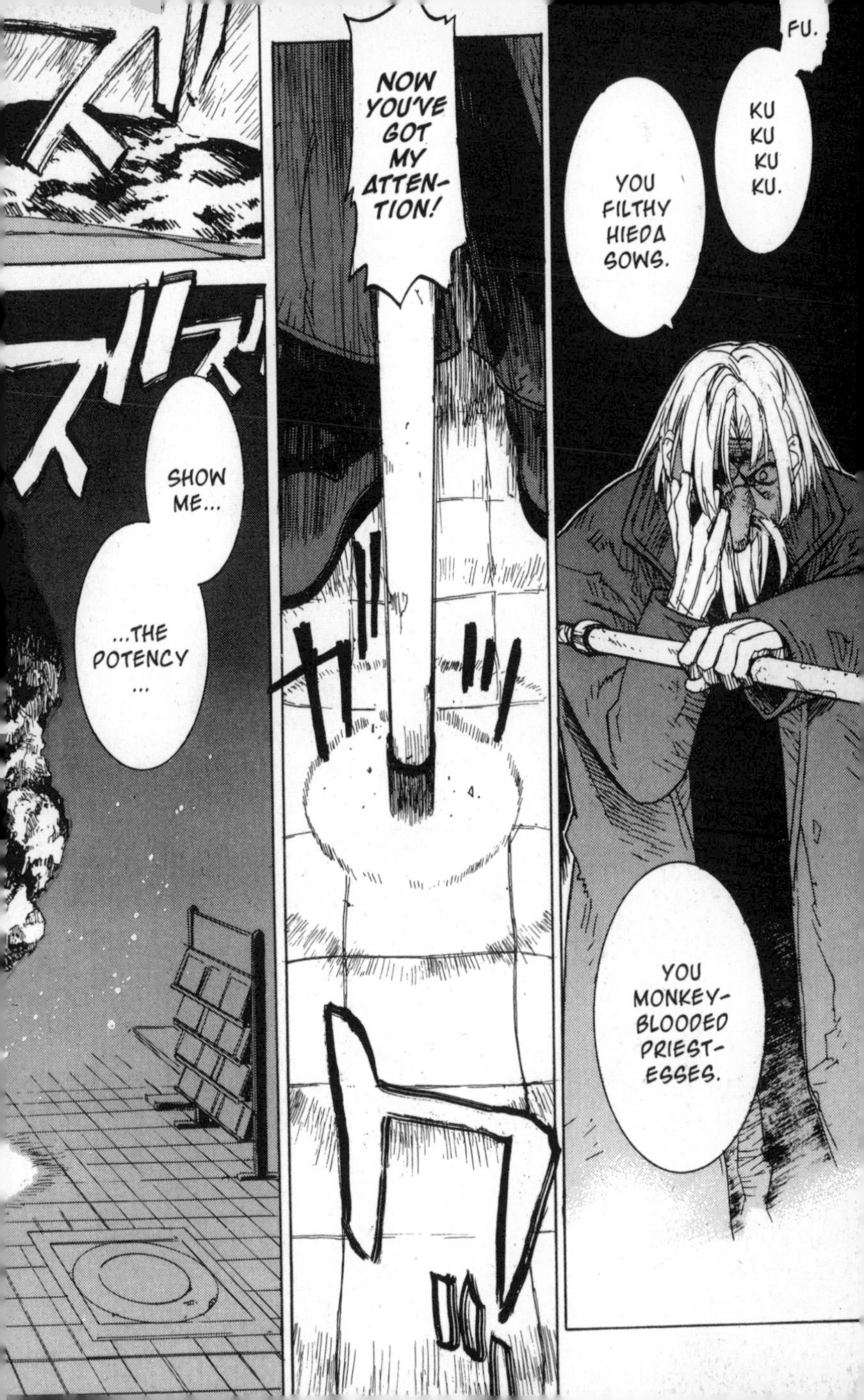
FU.
KU KU KU KU.
YOU FILTHY HIEDA SOWS.
YOU MONKEY-BLOODED PRIESTESSES.
NOW YOU'VE GOT MY ATTENTION!
SHOW ME...
...THE POTENCY ...

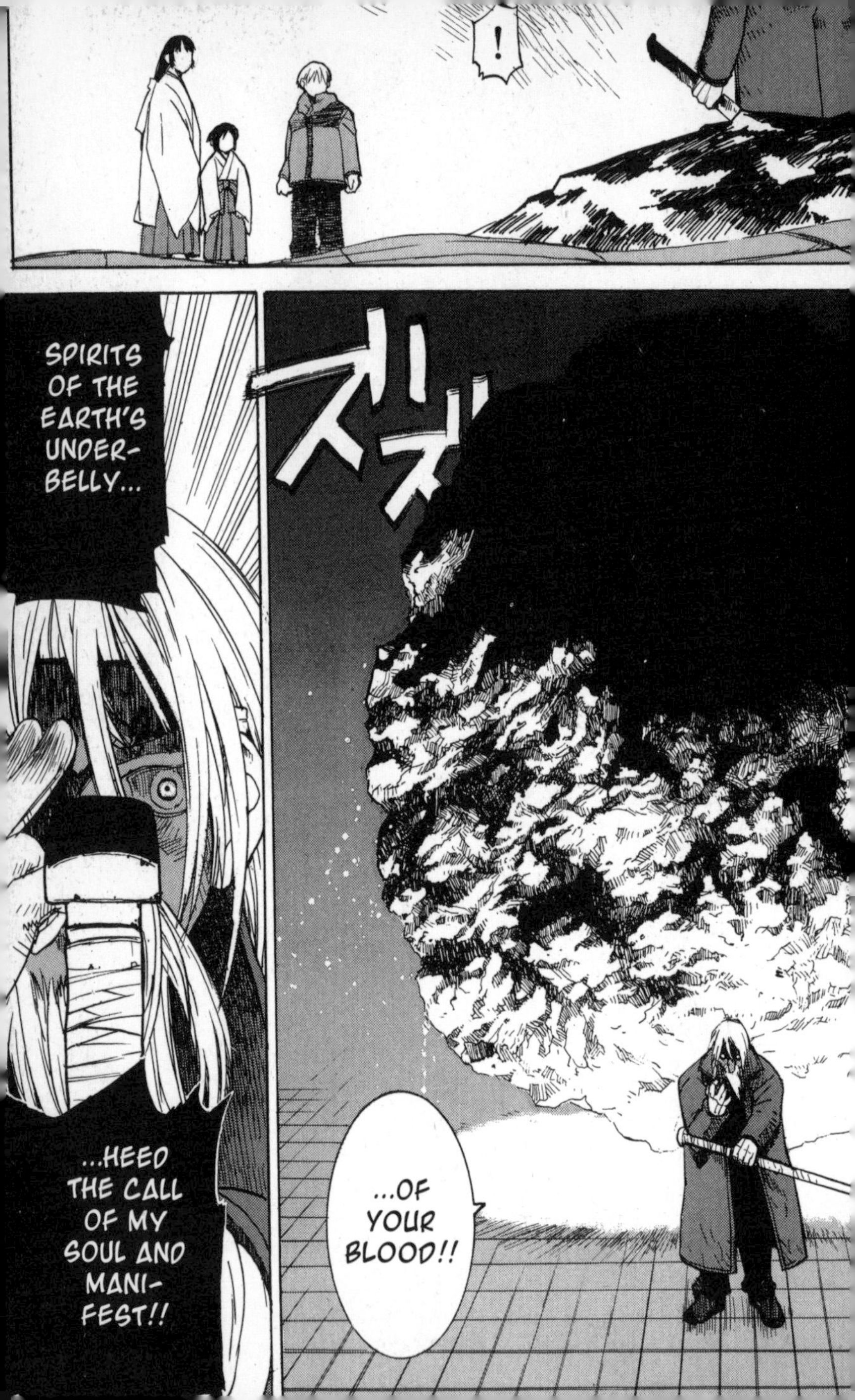
!
...OF YOUR BLOOD!!
SPIRITS OF THE EARTH'S UNDER-BELLY...
...HEED THE CALL OF MY SOUL AND MANI-FEST!!

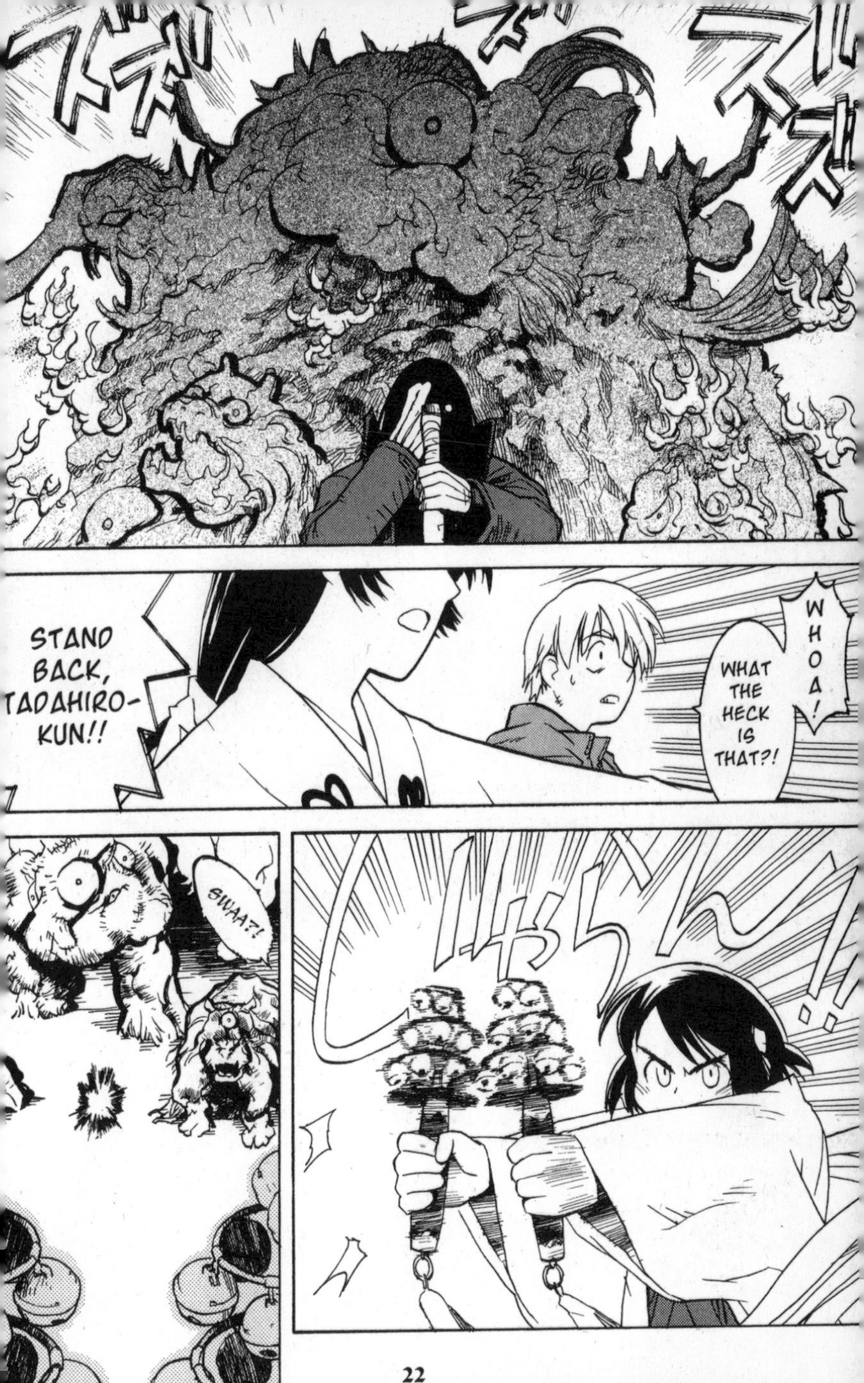
WHOA!
WHAT THE HECK IS THAT?!
STAND BACK, TADAHIRO-KUN!!
SWAA?!

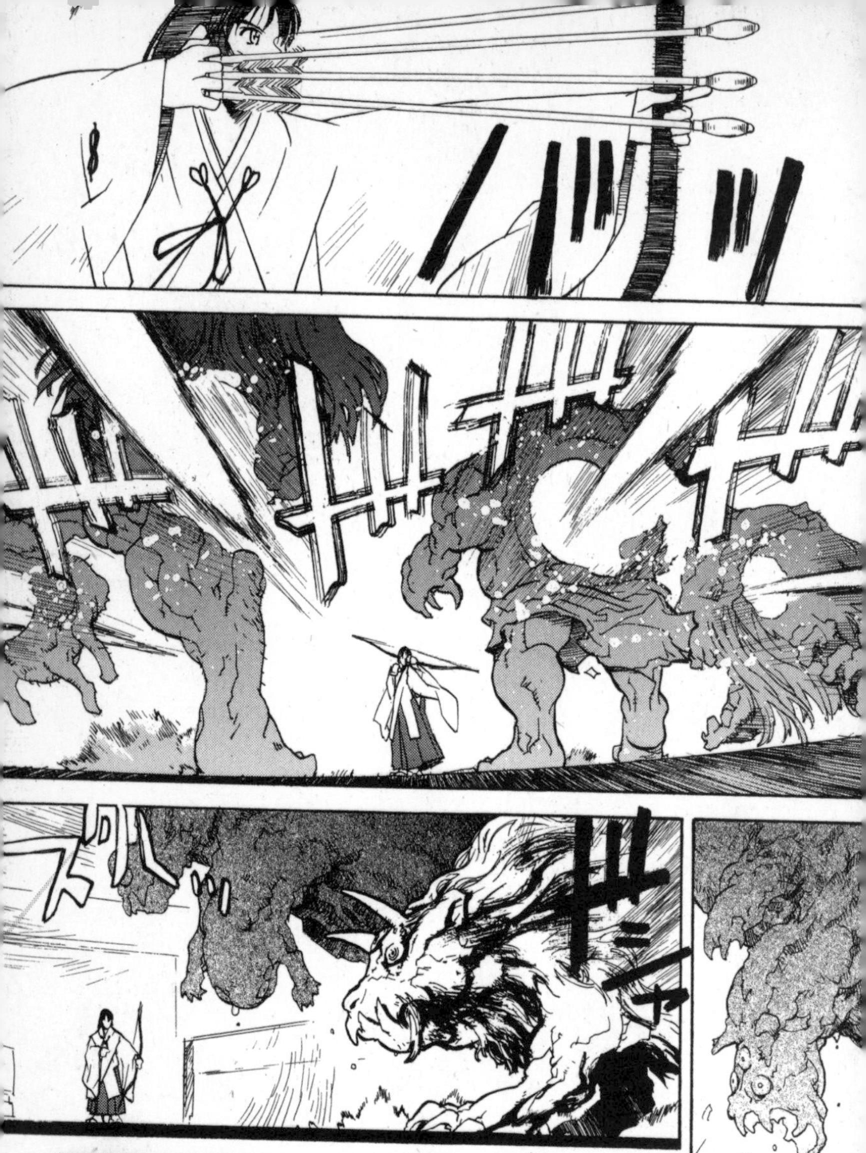
ズル
ズル
……!

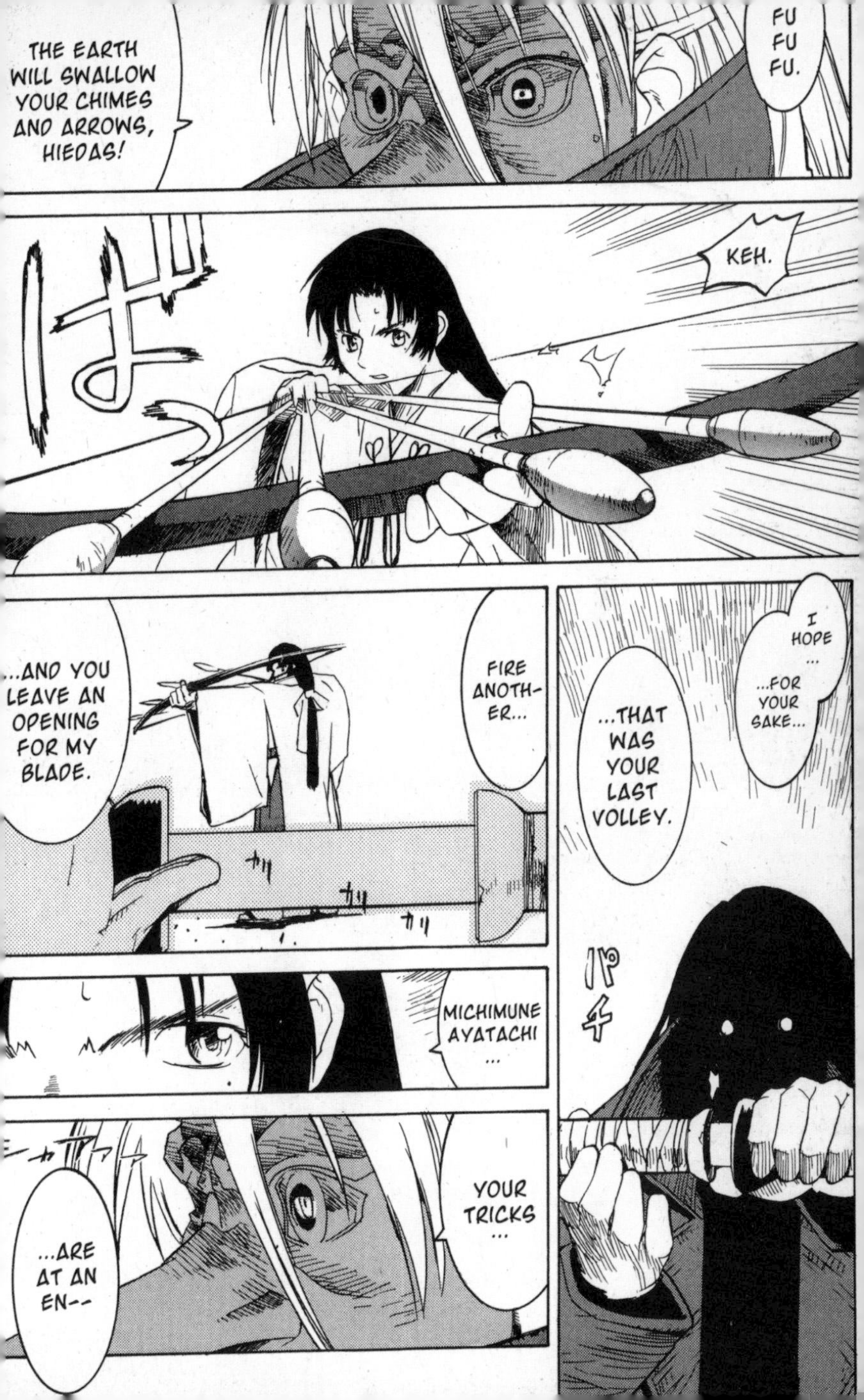
FU FU FU.
THE EARTH WILL SWALLOW YOUR CHIMES AND ARROWS, HIEDAS!
KEH.
I HOPE...
...FOR YOUR SAKE...
...THAT WAS YOUR LAST VOLLEY.
FIRE ANOTH-ER...
...AND YOU LEAVE AN OPENING FOR MY BLADE.
MICHIMUNE AYATACHI ...
YOUR TRICKS ...
...ARE AT AN EN--

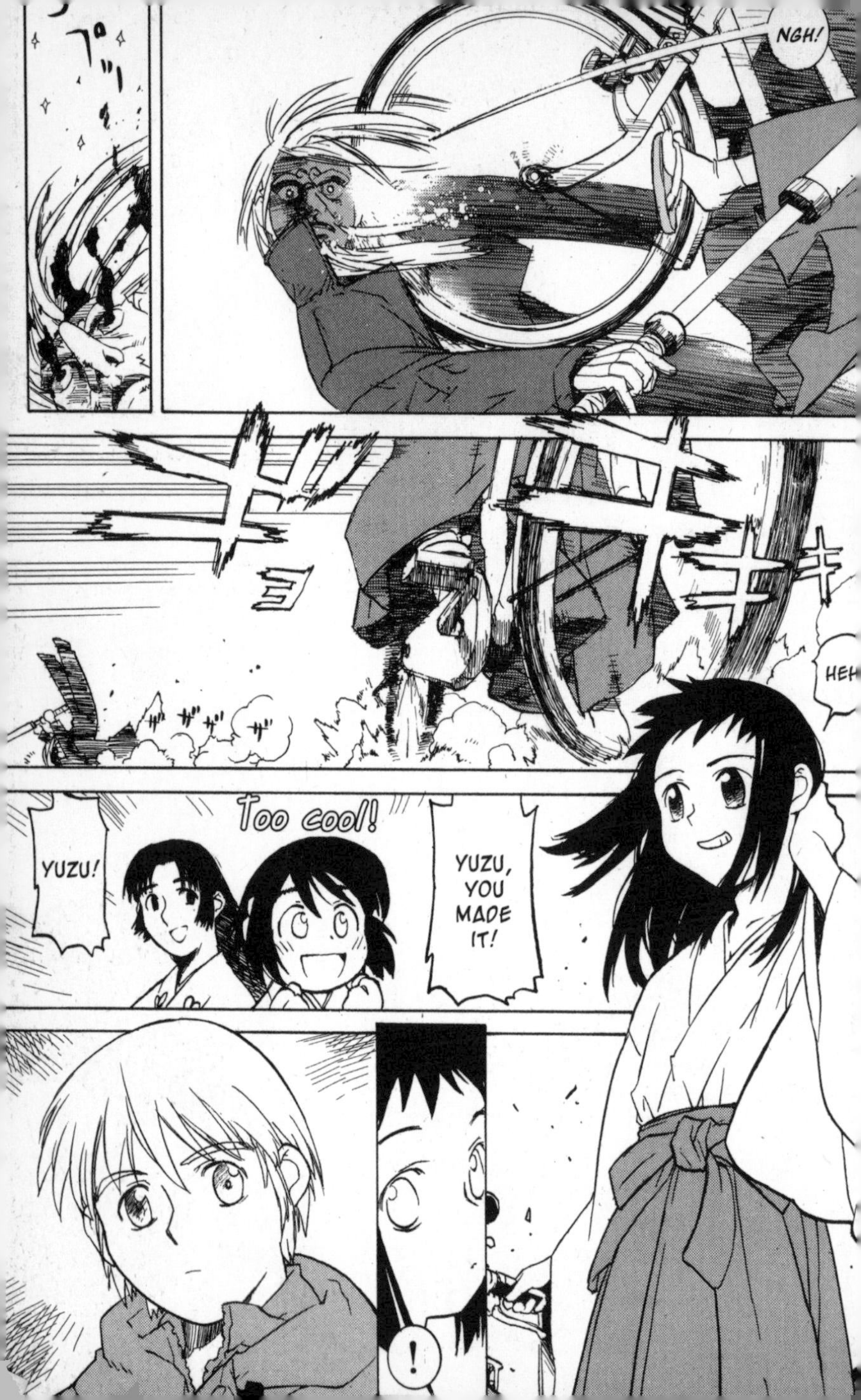
NGH!
HEH
YUZU, YOU MADE IT!
Too cool!
YUZU!
!

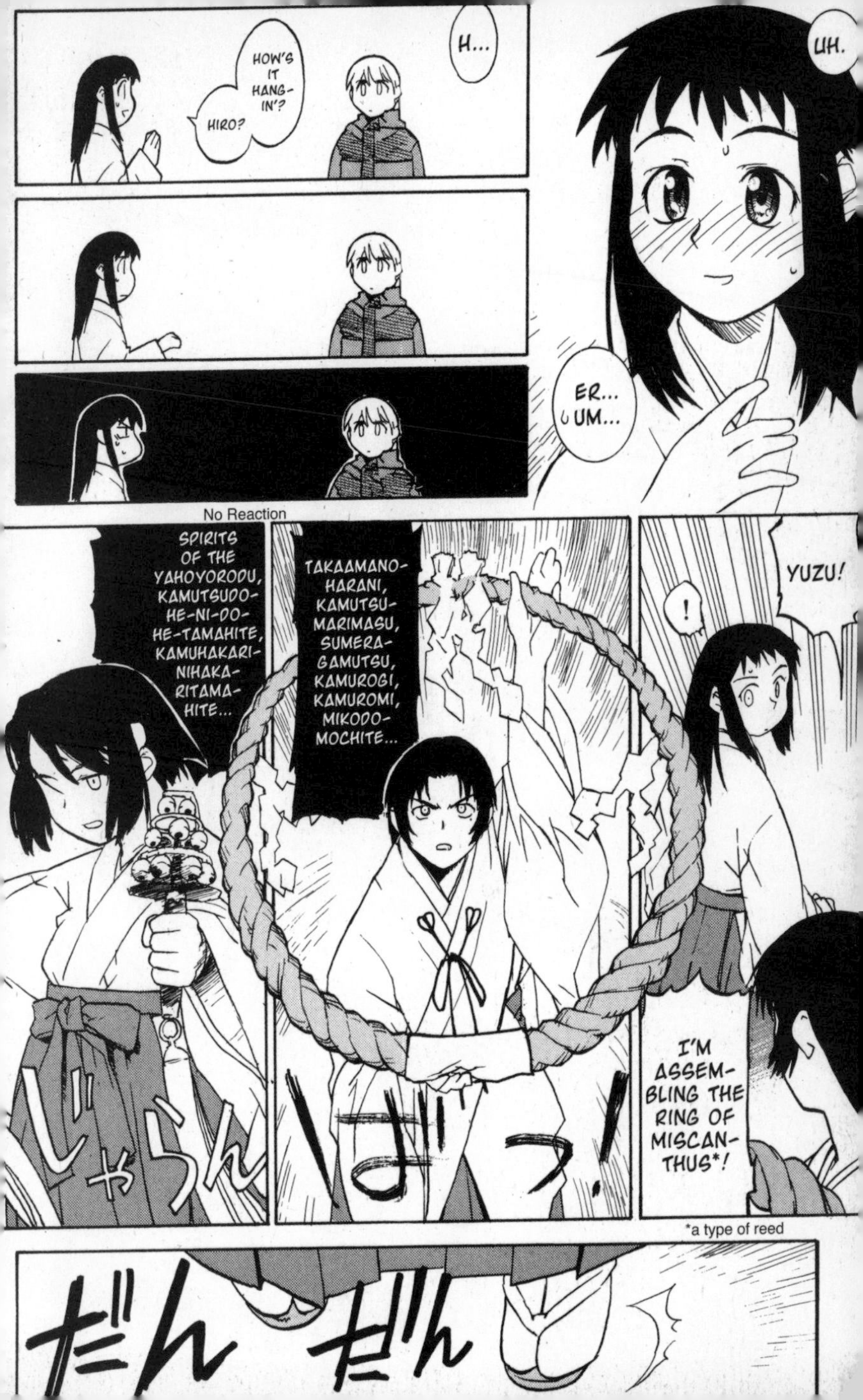
UH.
ER... UM...
H...
HOW'S IT HANGIN'?
HIRO?
YUZU!
!
I'M ASSEMBLING THE RING OF MISCANTHUS*!
TAKAAMANOHARANI, KAMUTSUMARIMASU, SUMERAGAMUTSU, KAMUROGI, KAMUROMI, MIKODOMOCHITE...
ばっ!
SPIRITS OF THE YAHOYORODU, KAMUTSUDOHE-NI-DOHE-TAMAHITE, KAMUHAKARINIHAKARITAMAHITE...
じゃらん
だん だん

No Reaction

*a type of reed

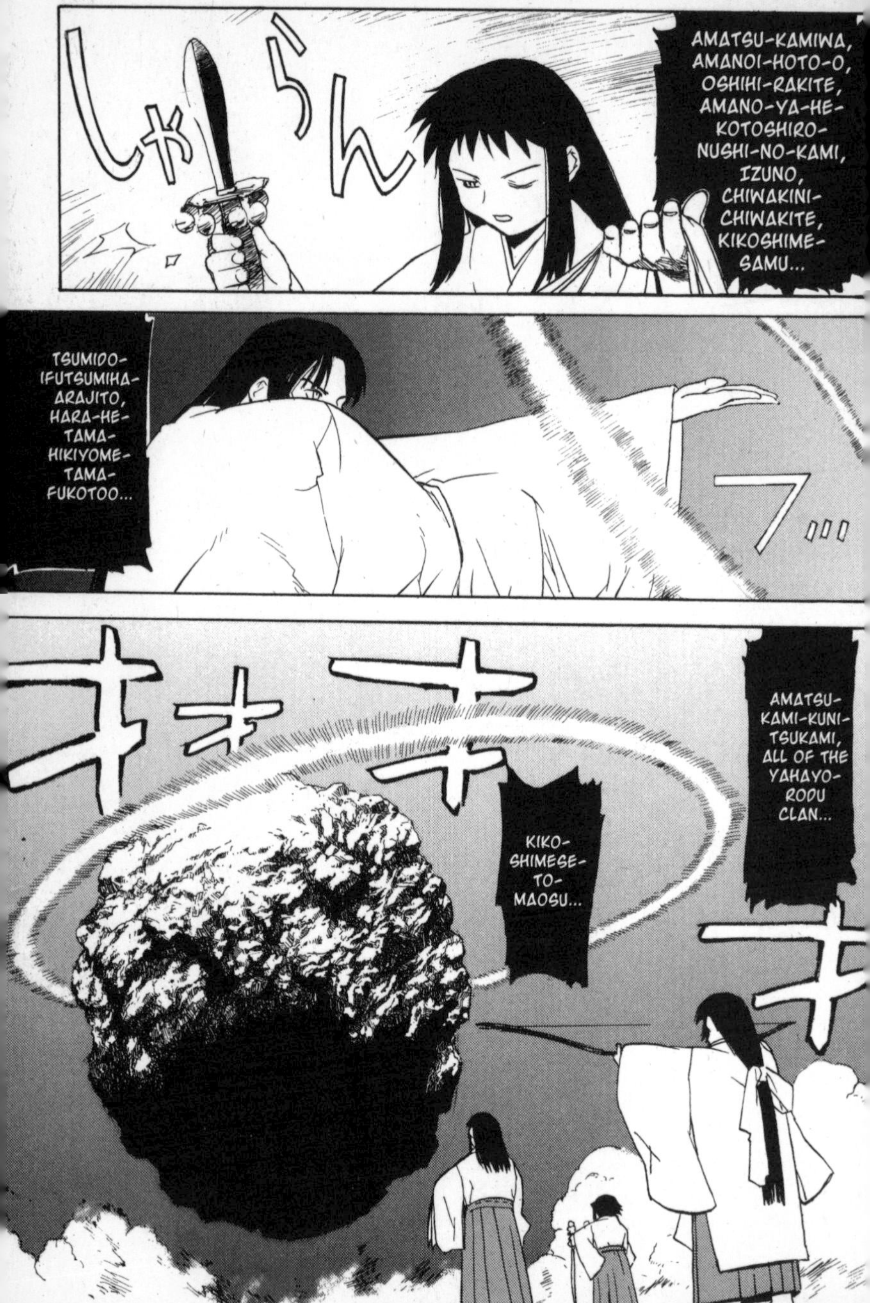
AMATSU-KAMIWA, AMANOI-HOTO-O, OSHIHI-RAKITE, AMANO-YA-HE-KOTOSHIRO-NUSHI-NO-KAMI, IZUNO, CHIWAKINI-CHIWAKITE, KIKOSHIME-SAMU...
しゃらん
フ...
TSUMIDO-IFUTSUMIHA-ARAJITO, HARA-HE-TAMA-HIKIYOME-TAMA-FUKOTOO...
AMATSU-KAMI-KUNI-TSUKAMI, ALL OF THE YAHAYO-RODU CLAN...
KIKO-SHIMESE-TO-MAOSU...

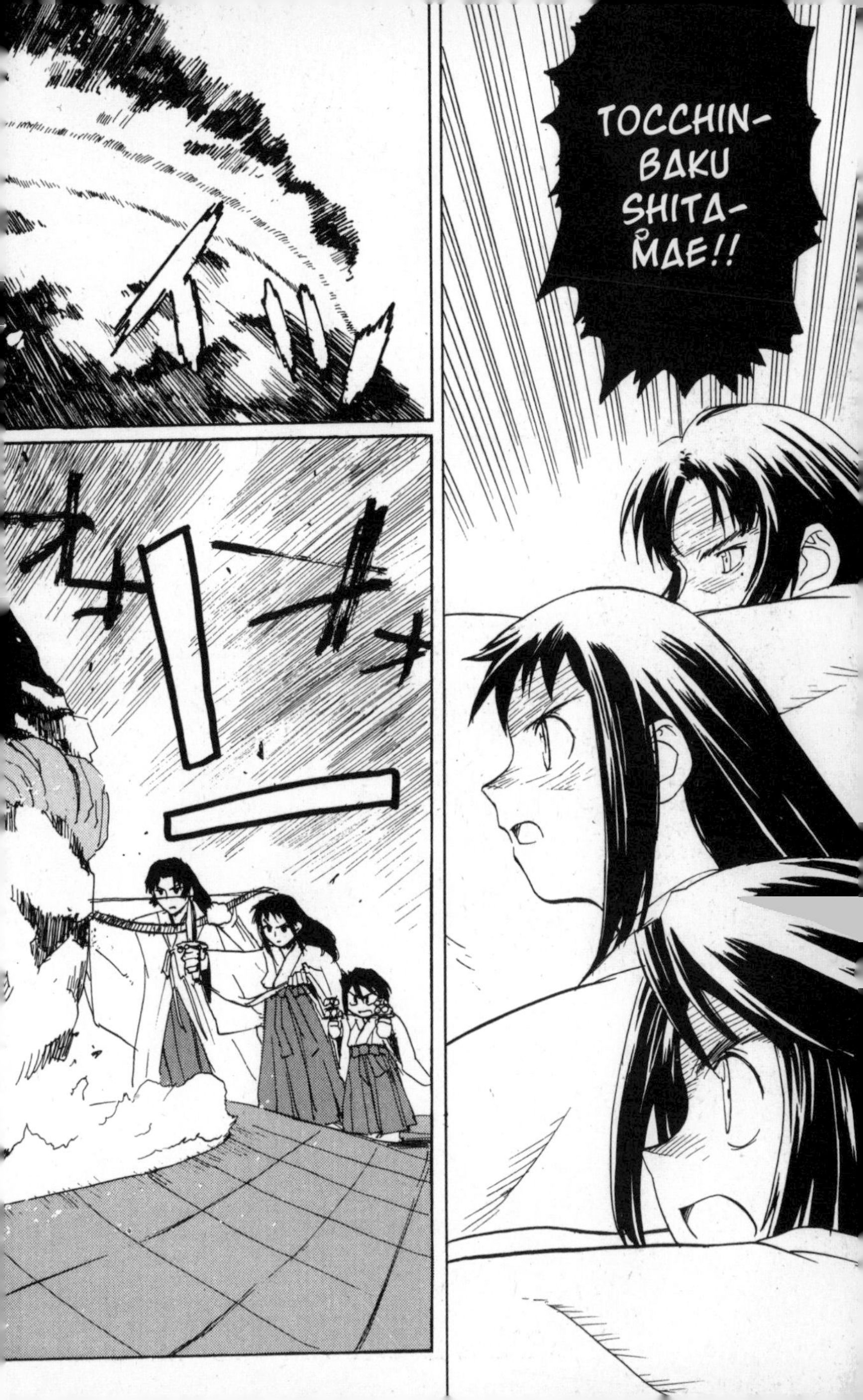
TOCCHIN-BAKU SHITA-MAE!!

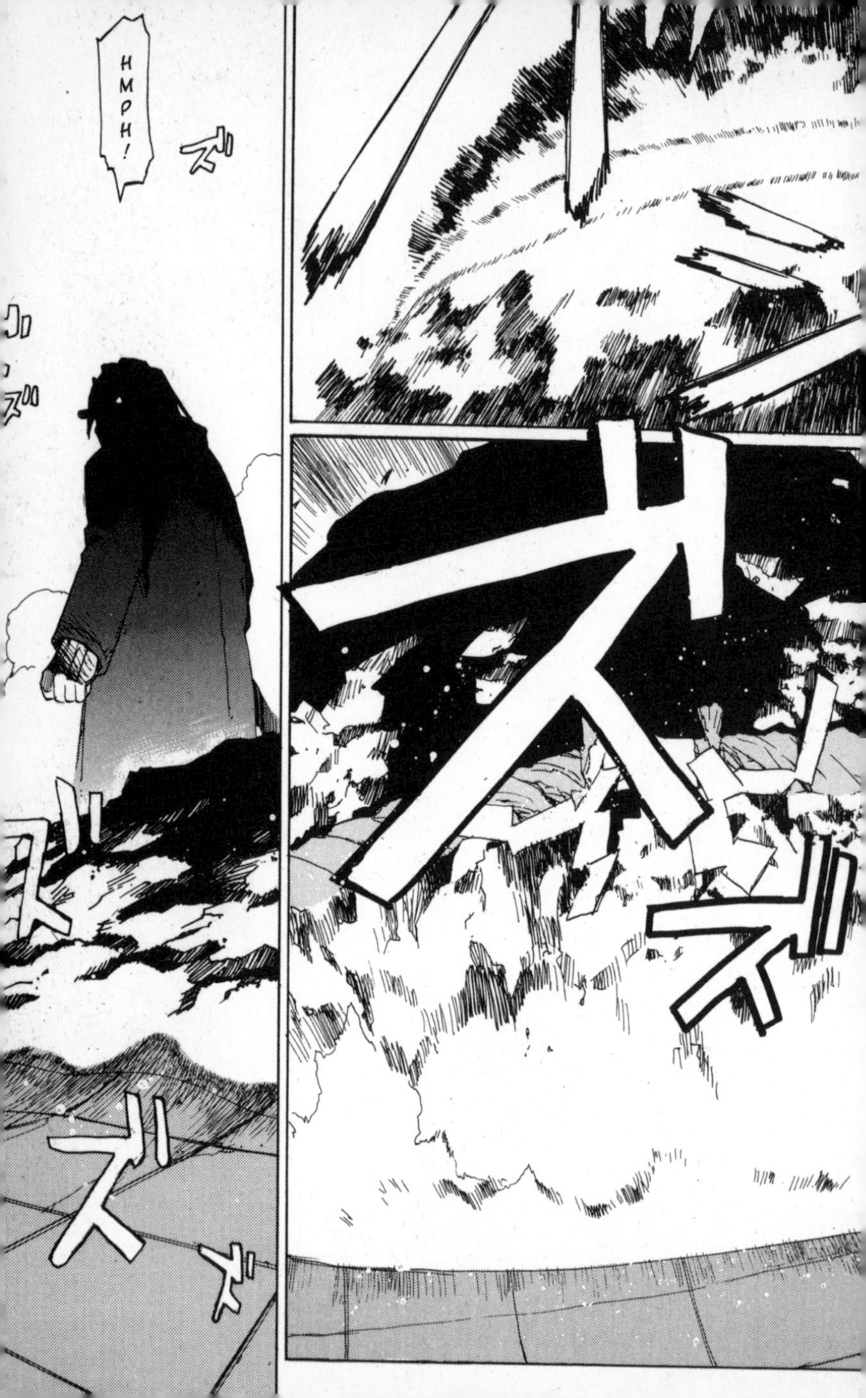
HMPH!

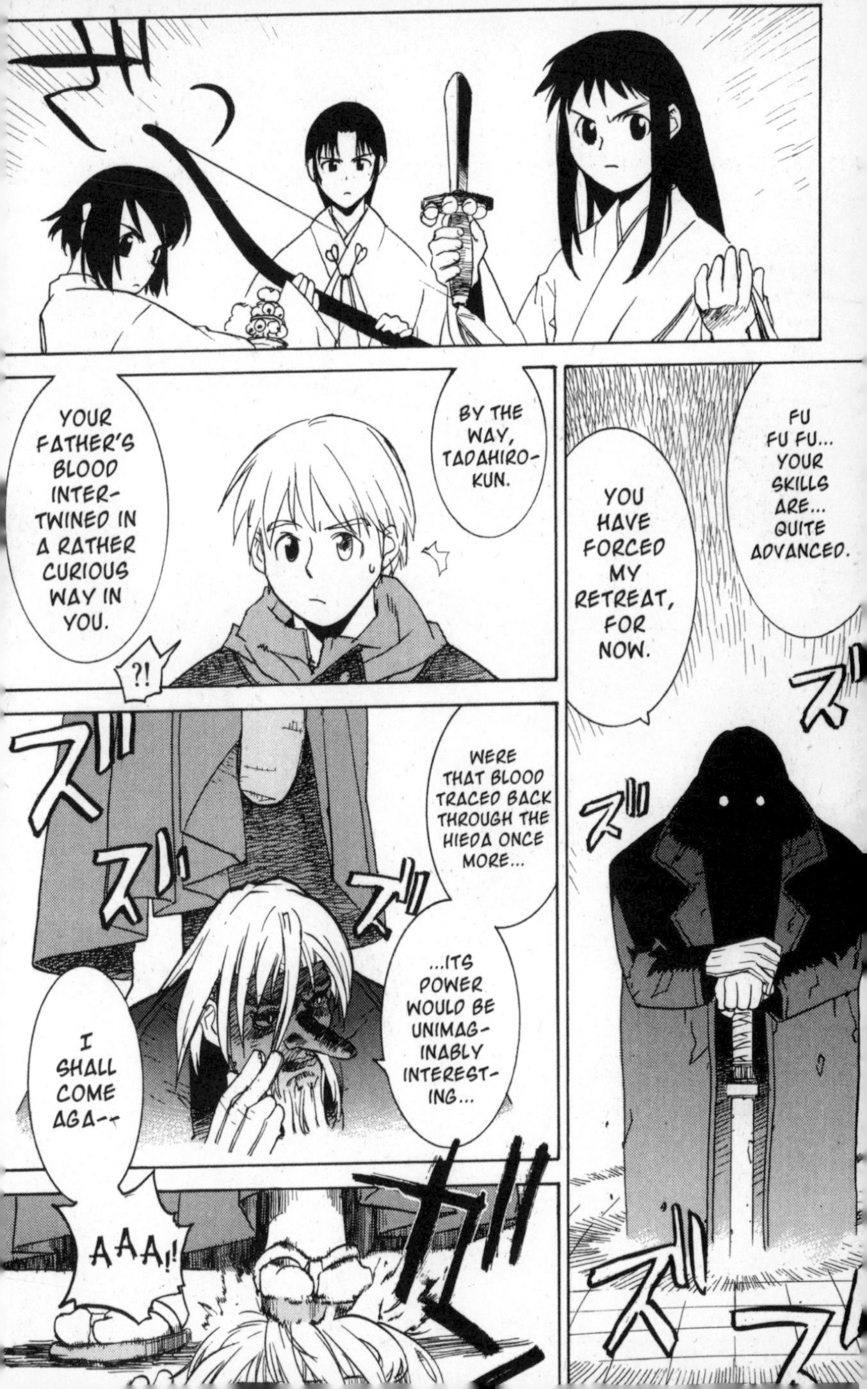
FU FU FU... YOUR SKILLS ARE... QUITE ADVANCED.
YOU HAVE FORCED MY RETREAT, FOR NOW.
BY THE WAY, TADAHIRO-KUN.
YOUR FATHER'S BLOOD INTER-TWINED IN A RATHER CURIOUS WAY IN YOU.
?!
WERE THAT BLOOD TRACED BACK THROUGH THE HIEDA ONCE MORE...
...ITS POWER WOULD BE UNIMAG-INABLY INTEREST-ING...
I SHALL COME AGA--
AAA!!

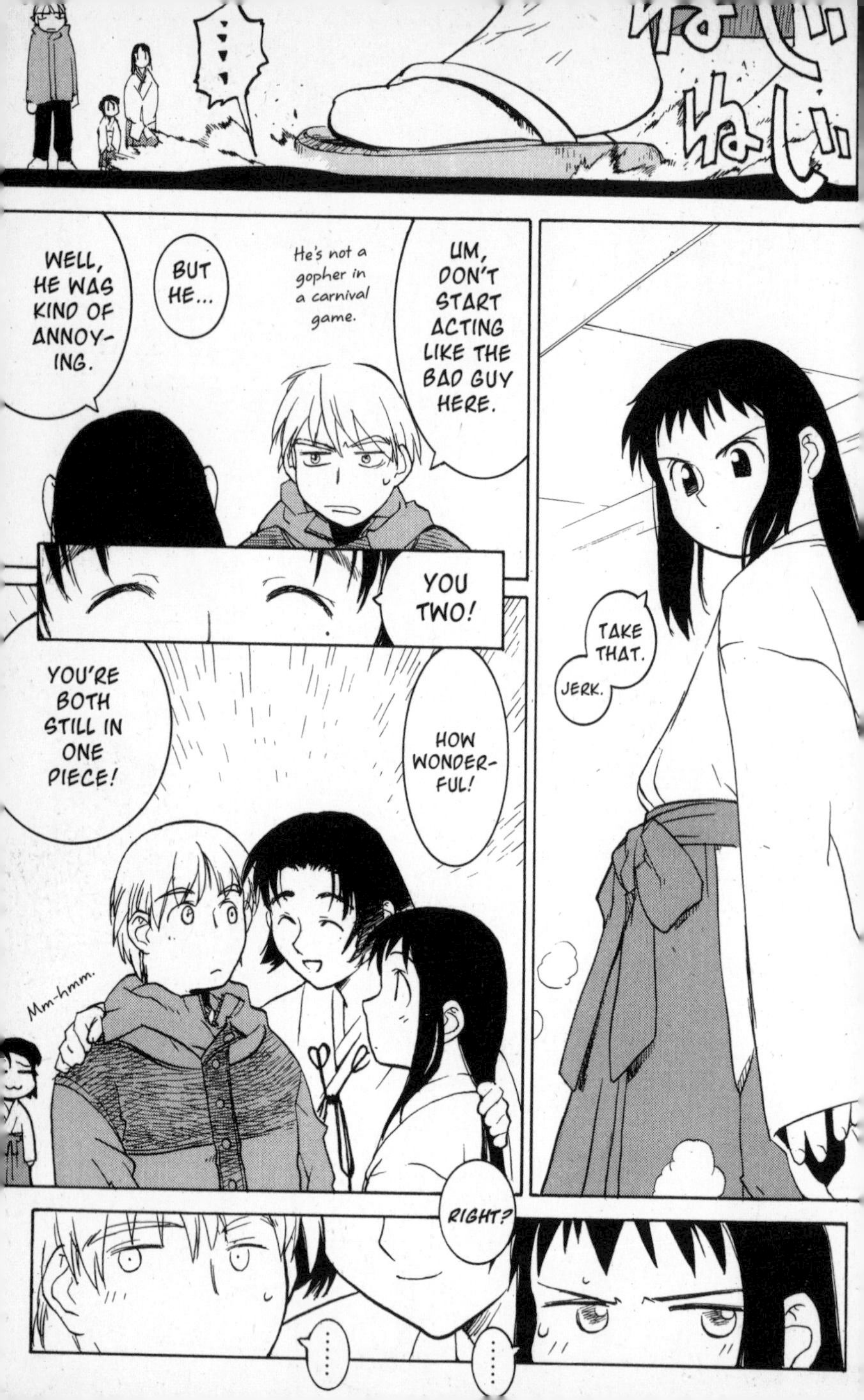
ねじ
ねじ
TAKE THAT.
JERK.
UM, DON'T START ACTING LIKE THE BAD GUY HERE.
He's not a gopher in a carnival game.
BUT HE...
WELL, HE WAS KIND OF ANNOYING.
YOU TWO!
HOW WONDERFUL!
YOU'RE BOTH STILL IN ONE PIECE!
Mm-hmm.
RIGHT?
......
......

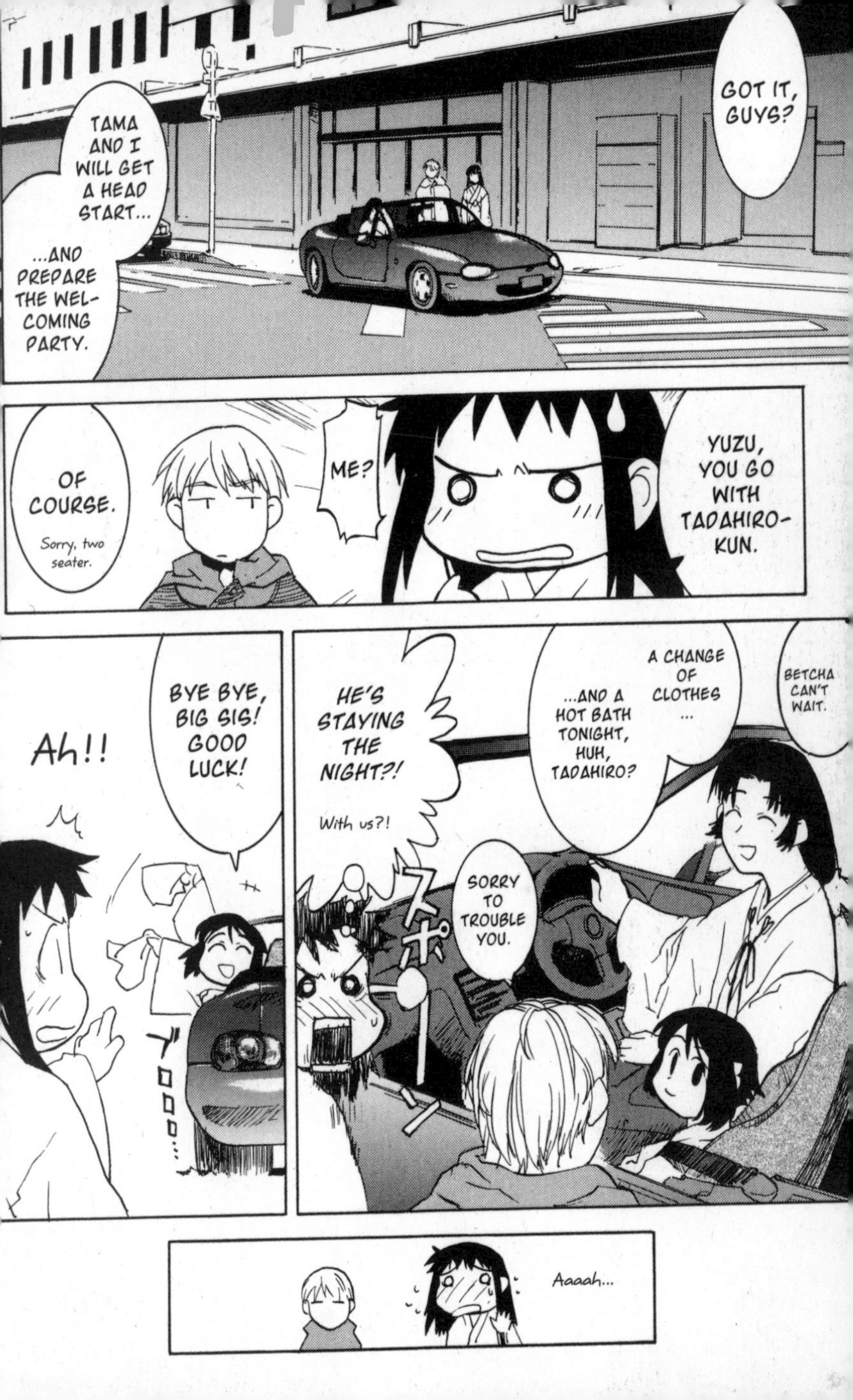
GOT IT, GUYS?
TAMA AND I WILL GET A HEAD START...
...AND PREPARE THE WEL-COMING PARTY.
YUZU, YOU GO WITH TADAHIRO-KUN.
ME?
OF COURSE.
Sorry, two seater.
BETCHA CAN'T WAIT.
A CHANGE OF CLOTHES ...
...AND A HOT BATH TONIGHT, HUH, TADAHIRO?
HE'S STAYING THE NIGHT?!
With us?!
SORRY TO TROUBLE YOU.
BYE BYE, BIG SIS! GOOD LUCK!
Ah!!
Aaaah...

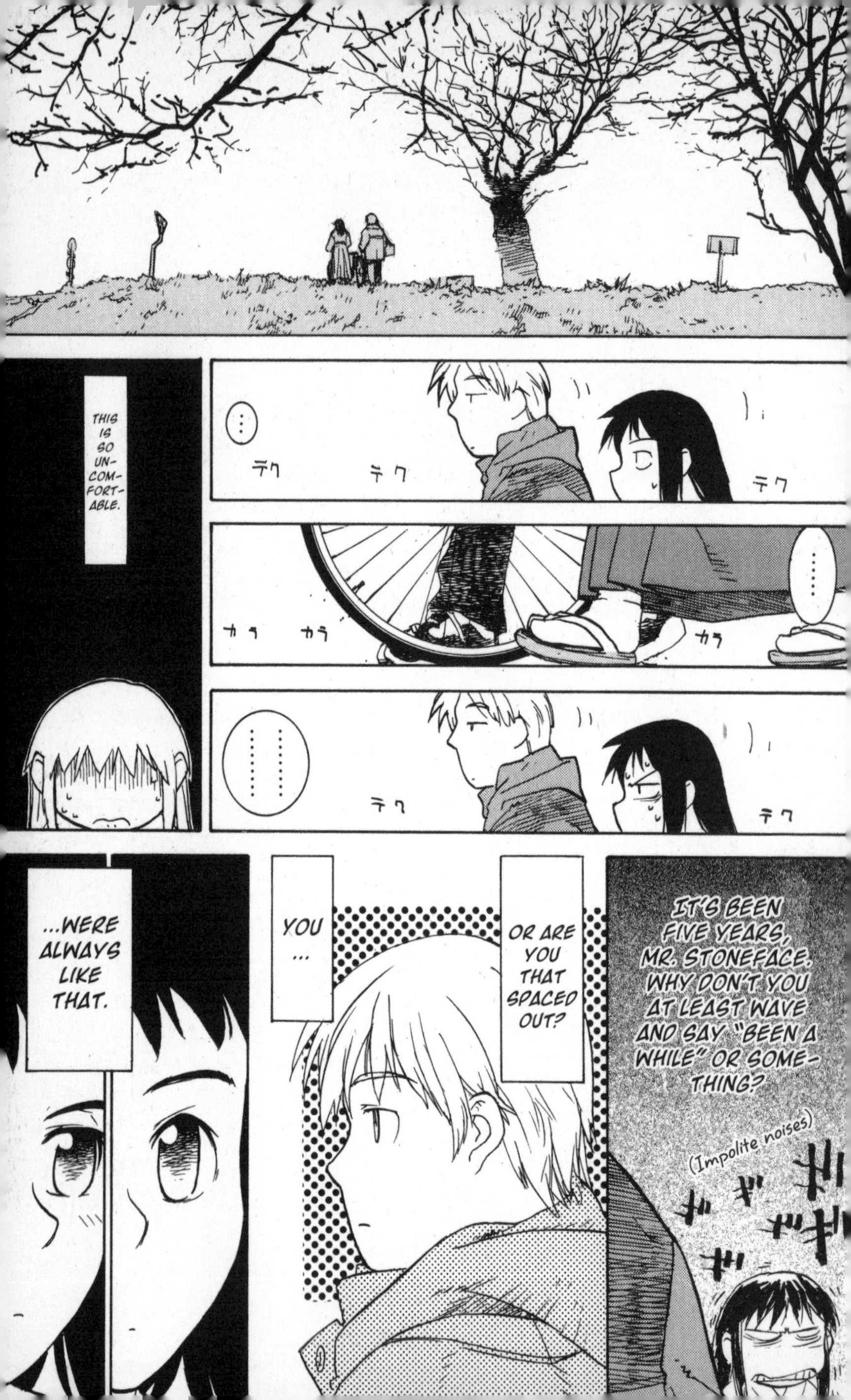

テク
テク
テク
…
……
カラ
カラ
カラ
テク
テク
……
THIS IS SO UN-COMFORT-ABLE.
IT'S BEEN FIVE YEARS, MR. STONEFACE. WHY DON'T YOU AT LEAST WAVE AND SAY "BEEN A WHILE" OR SOME-THING?
(Impolite noises)
ギリギリ
OR ARE YOU THAT SPACED OUT?
YOU ...
...WERE ALWAYS LIKE THAT.

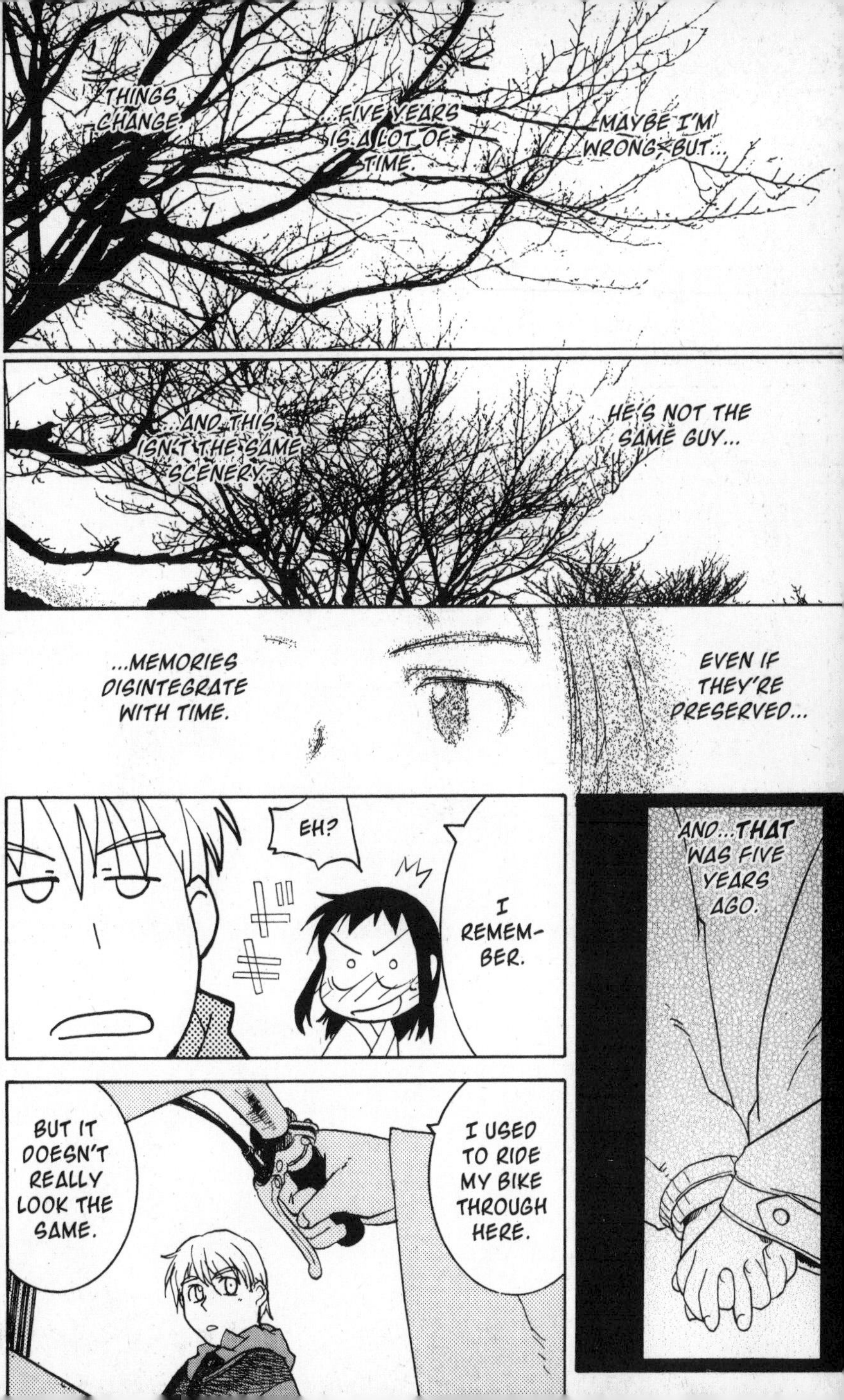
MAYBE I'M WRONG, BUT...
...FIVE YEARS IS A LOT OF TIME.
THINGS CHANGE.
HE'S NOT THE SAME GUY...
...AND THIS ISN'T THE SAME SCENERY.
EVEN IF THEY'RE PRESERVED...
...MEMORIES DISINTEGRATE WITH TIME.
AND...THAT WAS FIVE YEARS AGO.
I REMEMBER.
EH?
I USED TO RIDE MY BIKE THROUGH HERE.
BUT IT DOESN'T REALLY LOOK THE SAME.

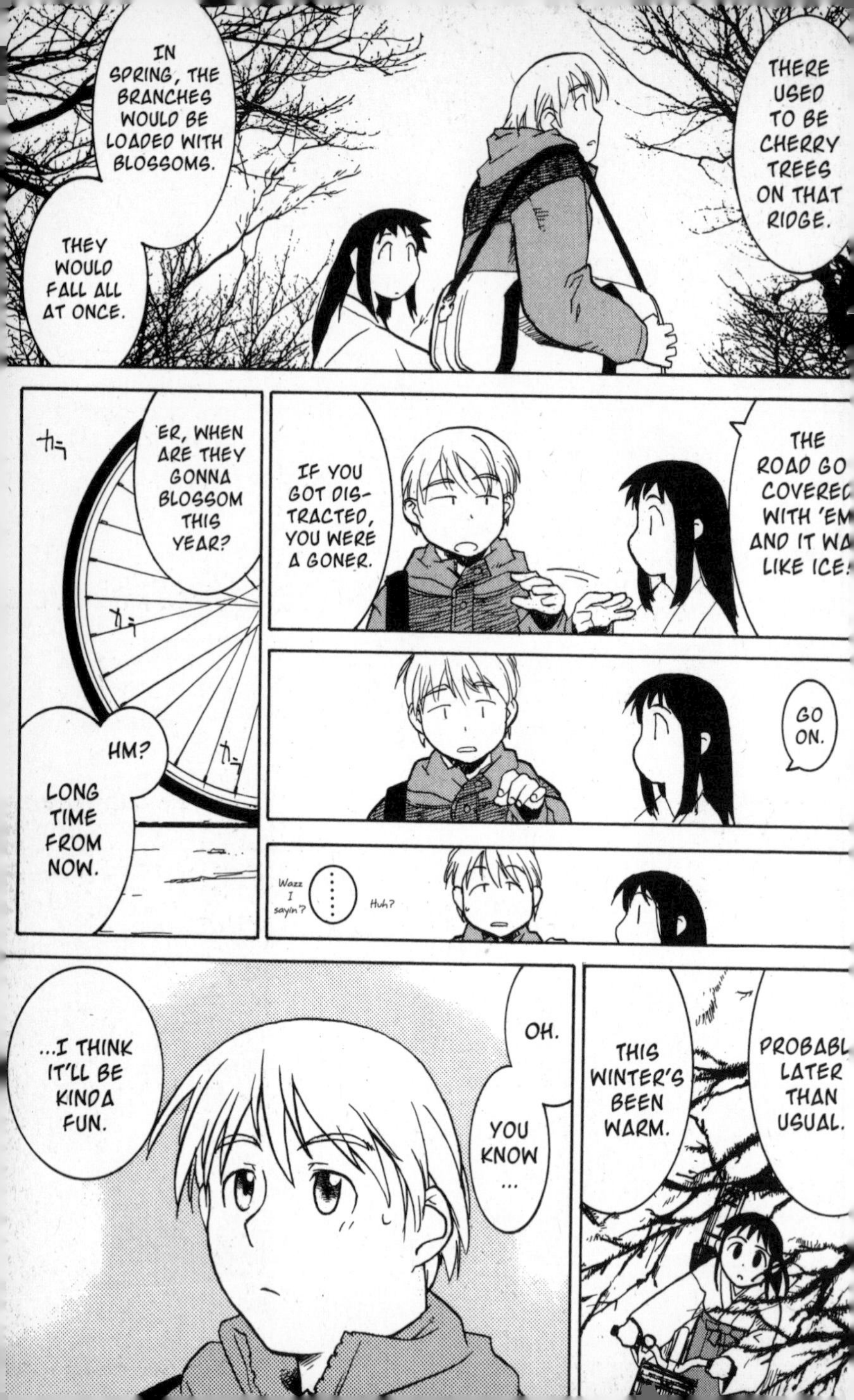
THERE USED TO BE CHERRY TREES ON THAT RIDGE.
IN SPRING, THE BRANCHES WOULD BE LOADED WITH BLOSSOMS.
THEY WOULD FALL ALL AT ONCE.
THE ROAD GO COVERED WITH 'EM AND IT WA LIKE ICE!
IF YOU GOT DIS-TRACTED, YOU WERE A GONER.
GO ON.
Huh?
...
Wazz I sayin'?
ER, WHEN ARE THEY GONNA BLOSSOM THIS YEAR?
HM?
LONG TIME FROM NOW.
PROBABL LATER THAN USUAL.
THIS WINTER'S BEEN WARM.
OH.
YOU KNOW ...
...I THINK IT'LL BE KINDA FUN.

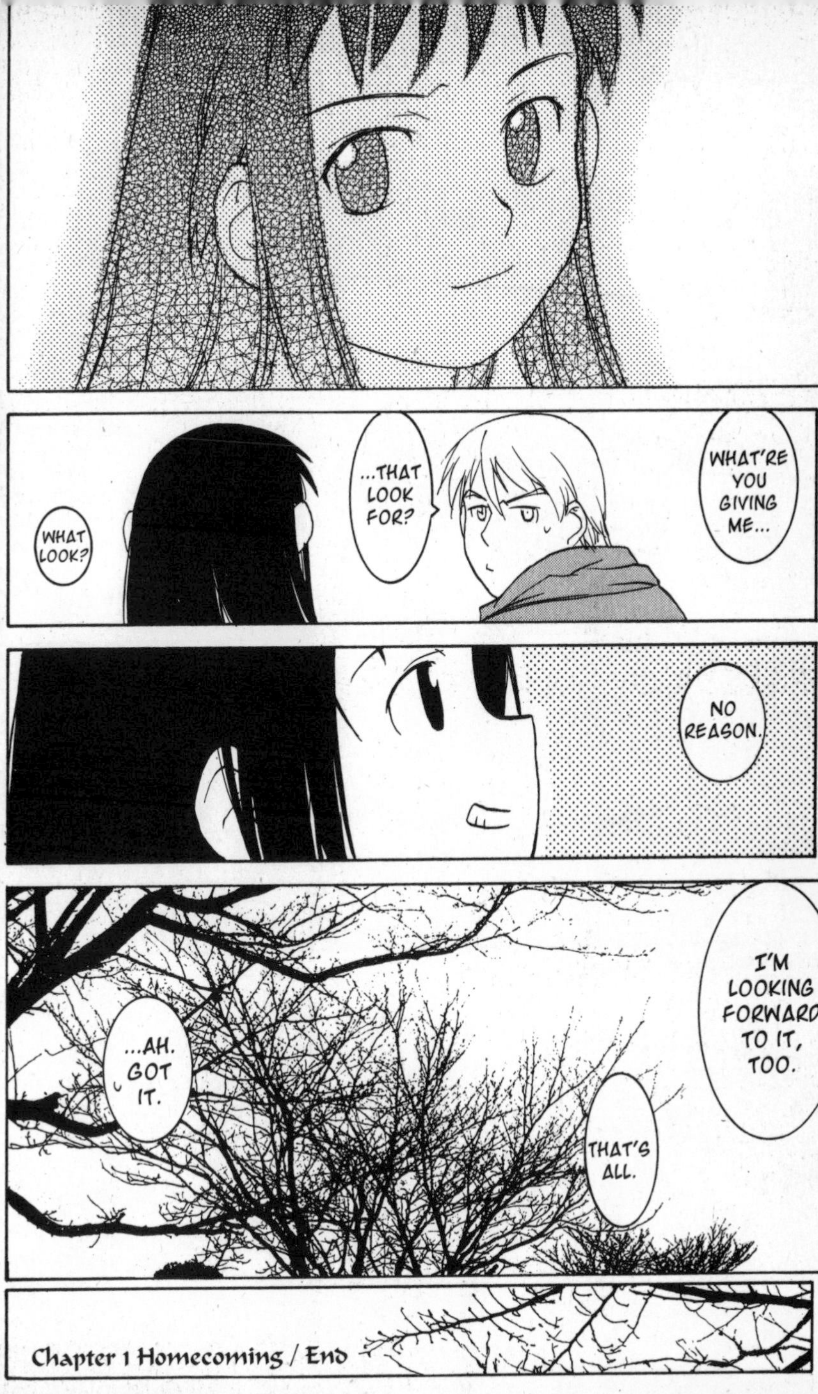
WHAT'RE YOU GIVING ME...
...THAT LOOK FOR?
WHAT LOOK?
NO REASON.
I'M LOOKING FORWARD TO IT, TOO.
THAT'S ALL.
...AH. GOT IT.
Chapter 1 Homecoming / End

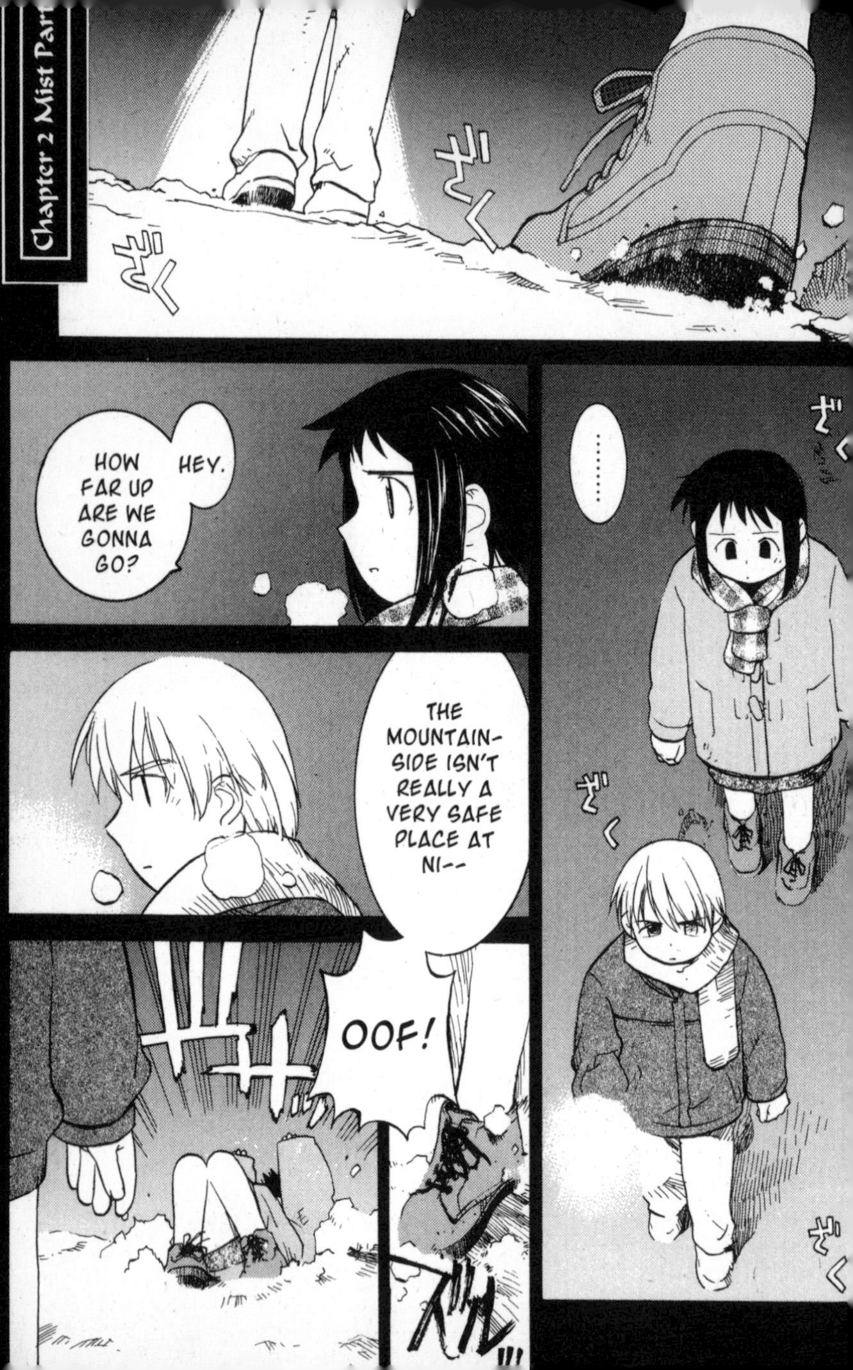
ざく
ざく
......
ざく
ざく
ざく
HEY.
HOW FAR UP ARE WE GONNA GO?
THE MOUNTAIN-SIDE ISN'T REALLY A VERY SAFE PLACE AT NI--
OOF!
ズル

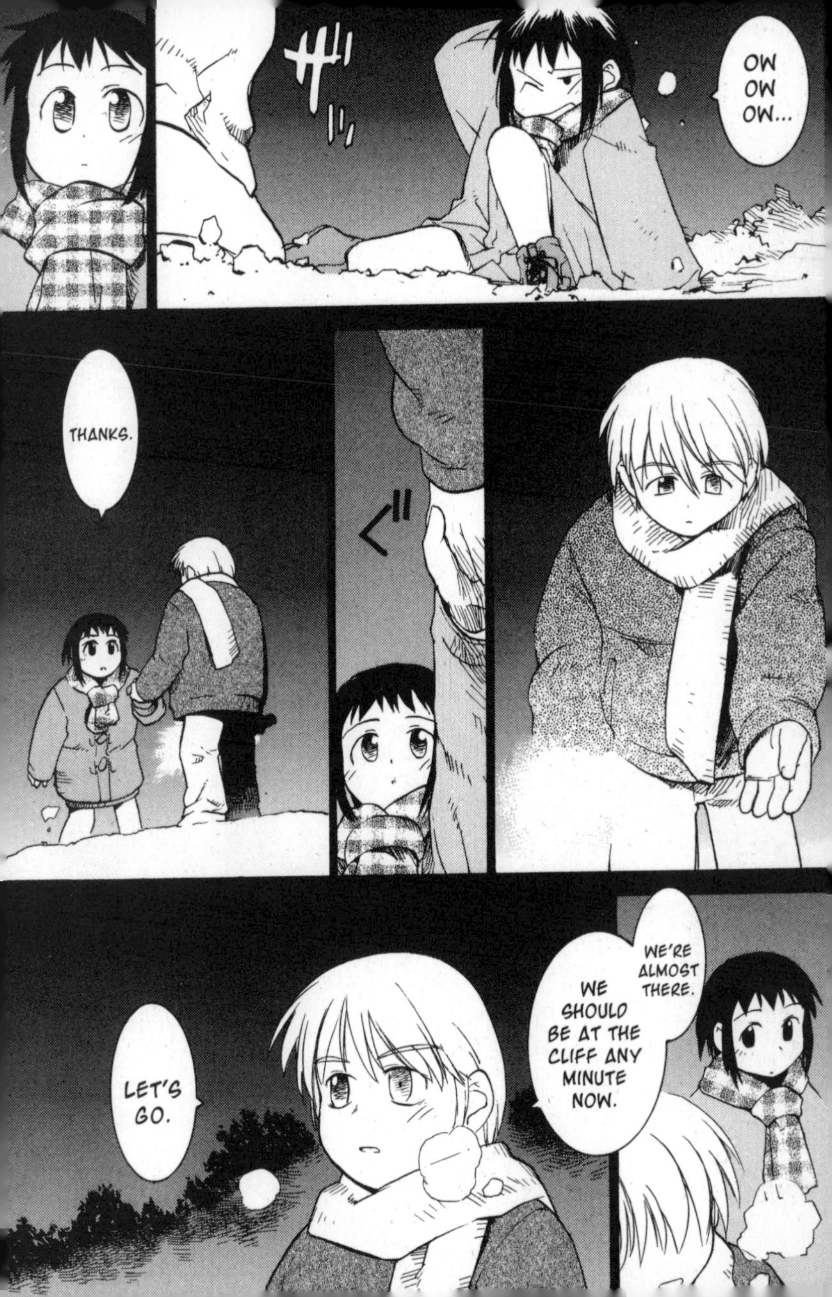
OW OW OW...
ぐ
THANKS.
WE'RE ALMOST THERE.
WE SHOULD BE AT THE CLIFF ANY MINUTE NOW.
LET'S GO.

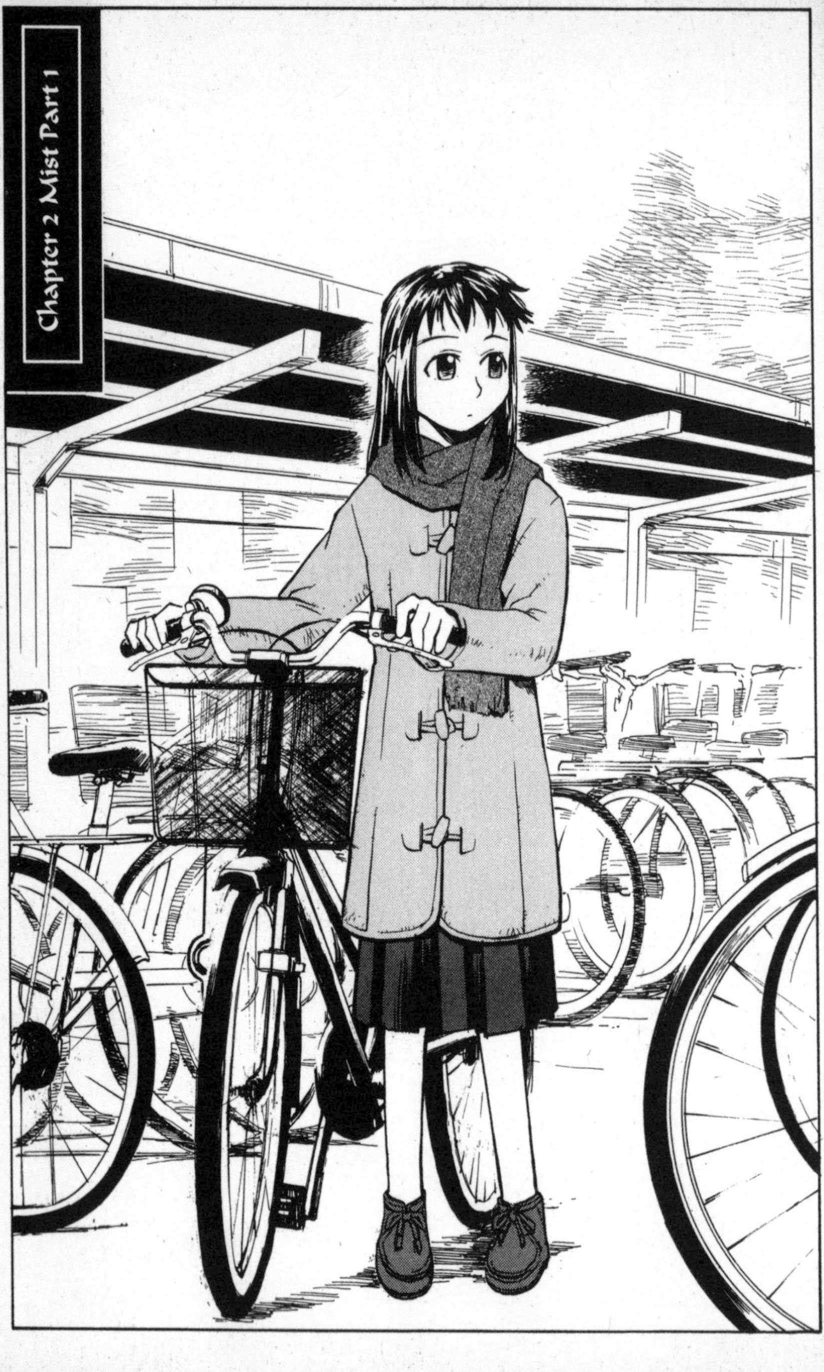
Chapter 2 Mist Part 1

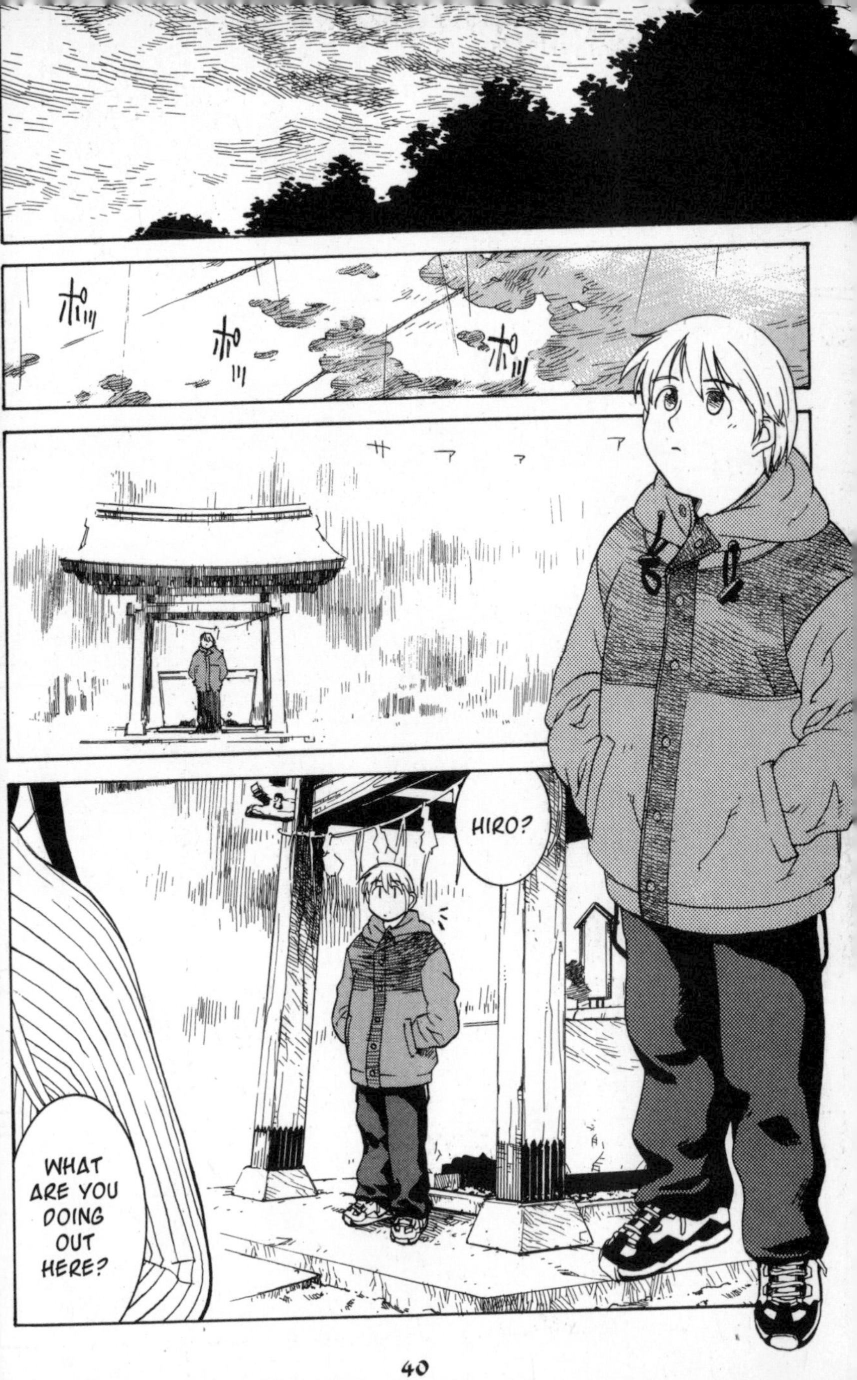
ポッ
ポッ
ポッ
サァァァ
HIRO?
WHAT ARE YOU DOING OUT HERE?

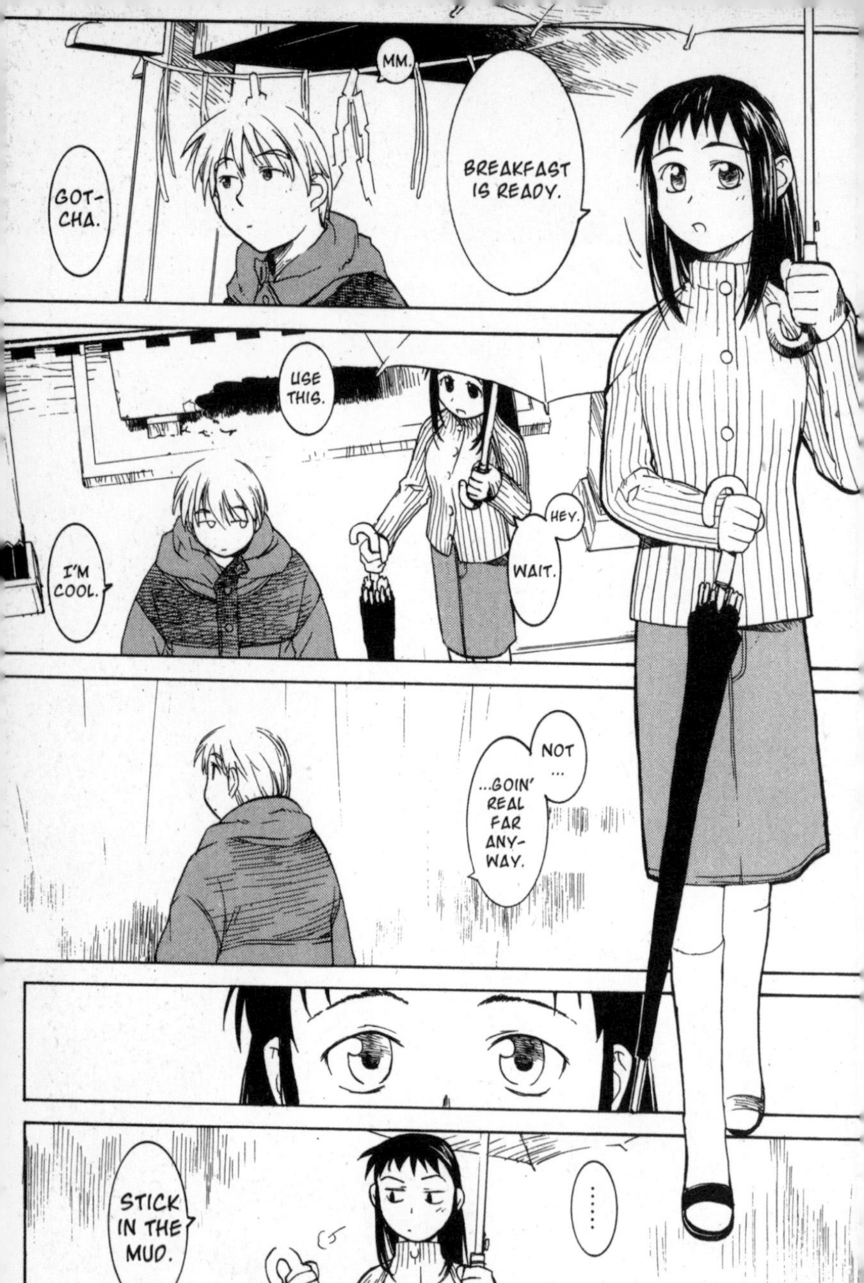
BREAKFAST IS READY.
MM.
GOT-CHA.
HEY.
WAIT.
USE THIS.
I'M COOL.
NOT ...
...GOIN' REAL FAR ANY-WAY.
......
STICK IN THE MUD.

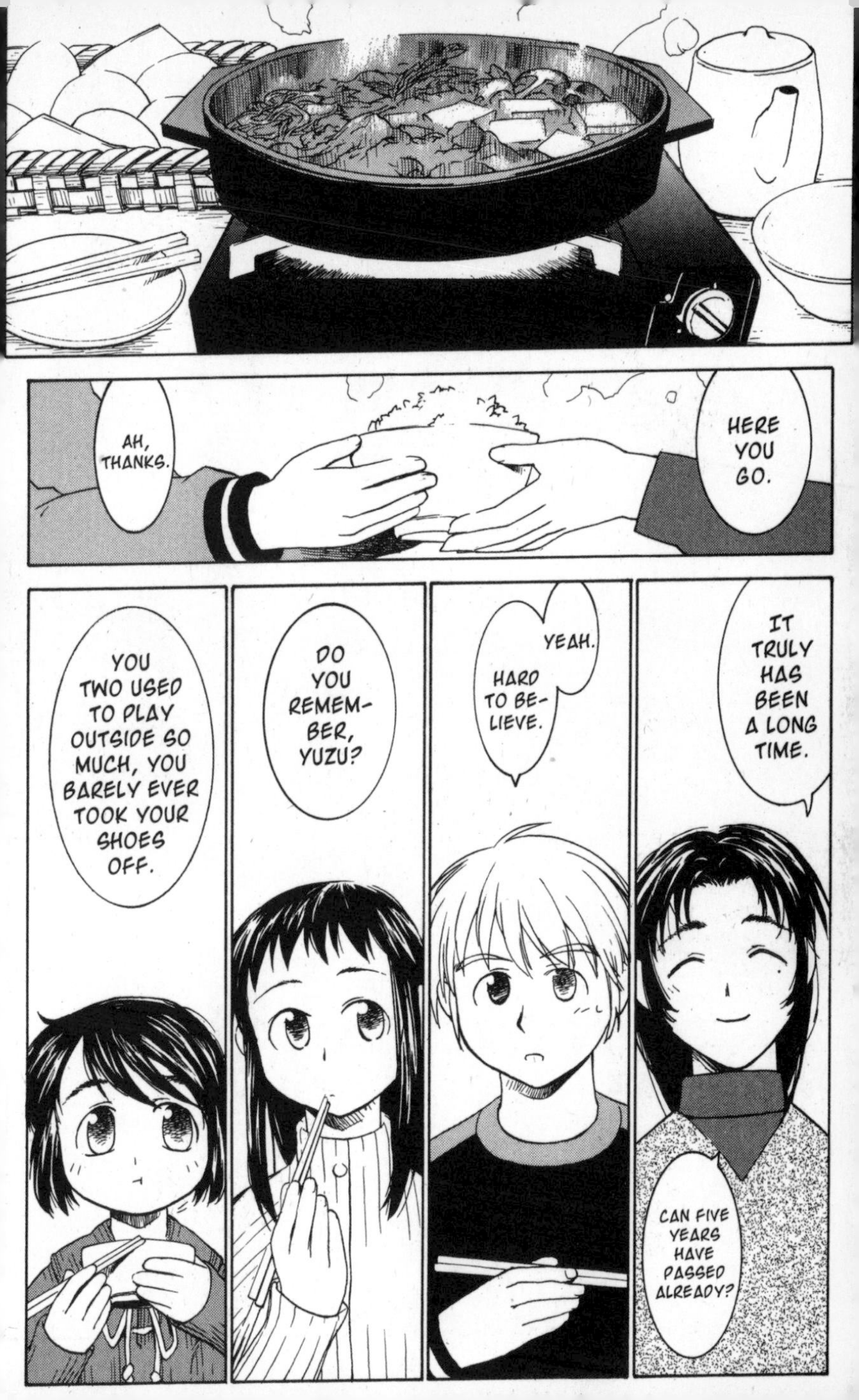
HERE YOU GO.
AH, THANKS.
IT TRULY HAS BEEN A LONG TIME.
CAN FIVE YEARS HAVE PASSED ALREADY?
YEAH.
HARD TO BELIEVE.
DO YOU REMEMBER, YUZU?
YOU TWO USED TO PLAY OUTSIDE SO MUCH, YOU BARELY EVER TOOK YOUR SHOES OFF.

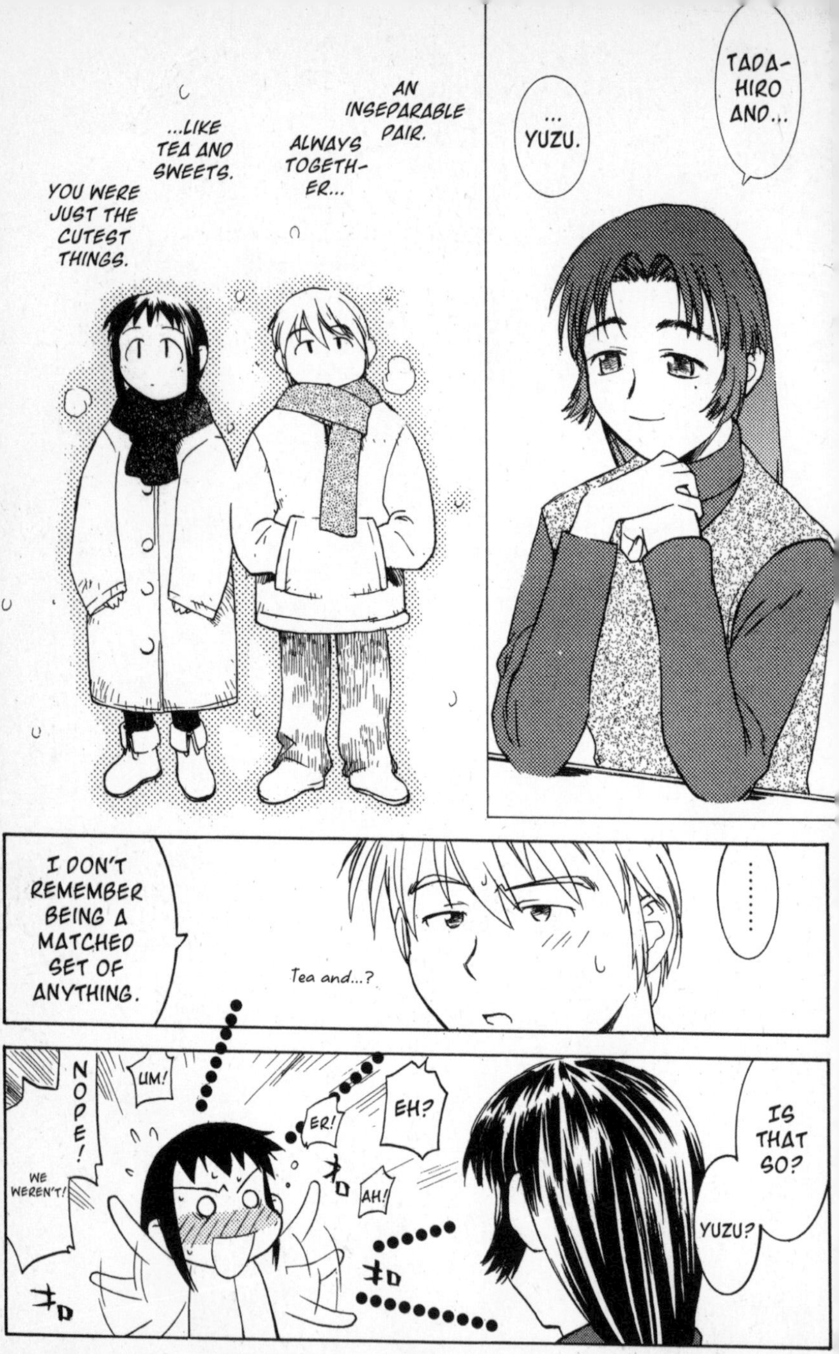
TADA-HIRO AND...
...YUZU.
AN INSEPARABLE PAIR.
ALWAYS TOGETH-ER...
...LIKE TEA AND SWEETS.
YOU WERE JUST THE CUTEST THINGS.
....
Tea and...?
I DON'T REMEMBER BEING A MATCHED SET OF ANYTHING.
IS THAT SO?
YUZU?
EH?
ER!
AH!
UM!
NOPE!
WE WEREN'T!

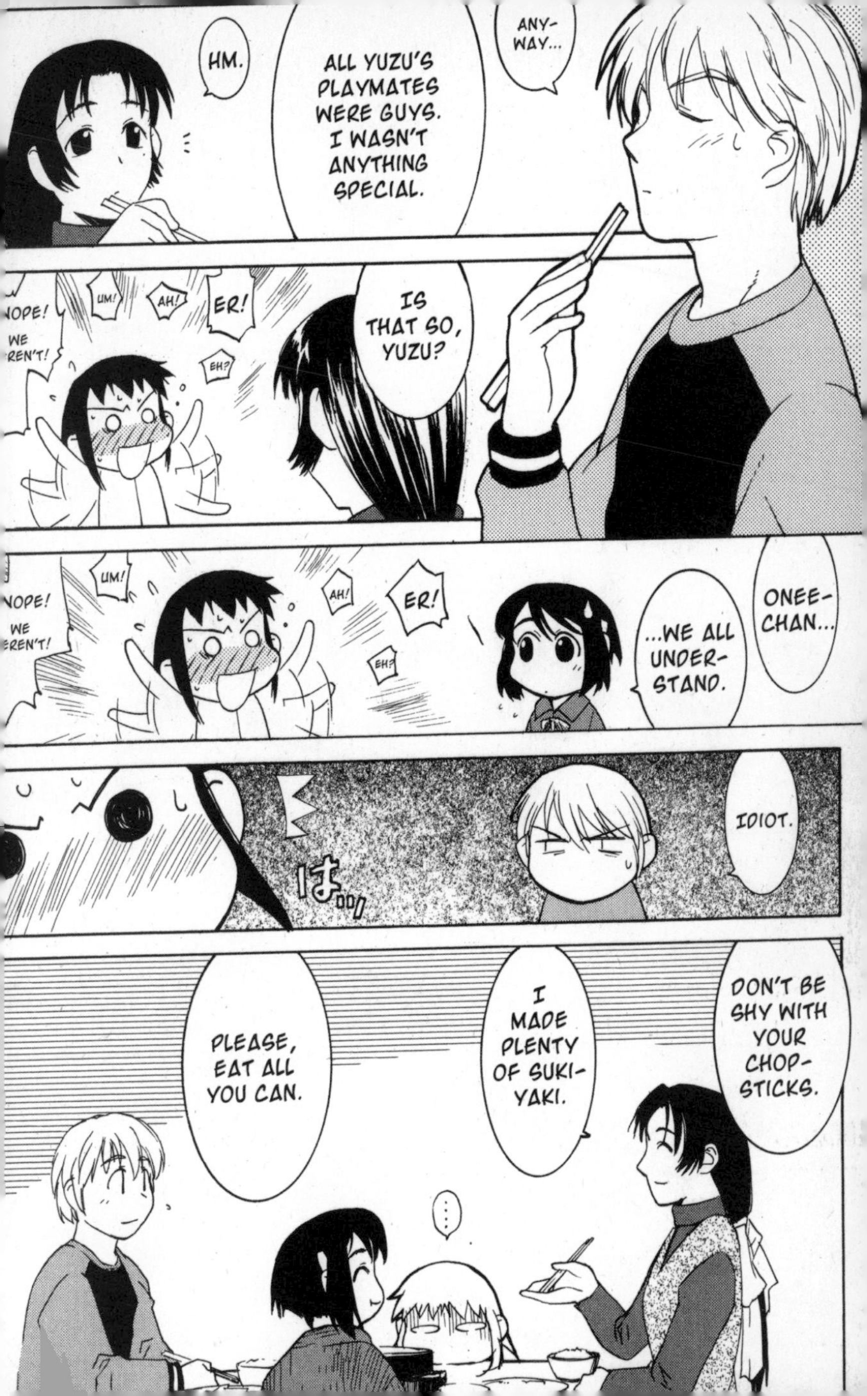
ANY-WAY...
ALL YUZU'S PLAYMATES WERE GUYS. I WASN'T ANYTHING SPECIAL.
HM.
IS THAT SO, YUZU?
ER!
AH!
UM!
EH?
NOPE! WE REN'T!
ONEE-CHAN...
...WE ALL UNDER-STAND.
ER!
AH!
EH?
UM!
NOPE! WE REN'T!
IDIOT.
は
DON'T BE SHY WITH YOUR CHOP-STICKS.
I MADE PLENTY OF SUKI-YAKI.
PLEASE, EAT ALL YOU CAN.
...

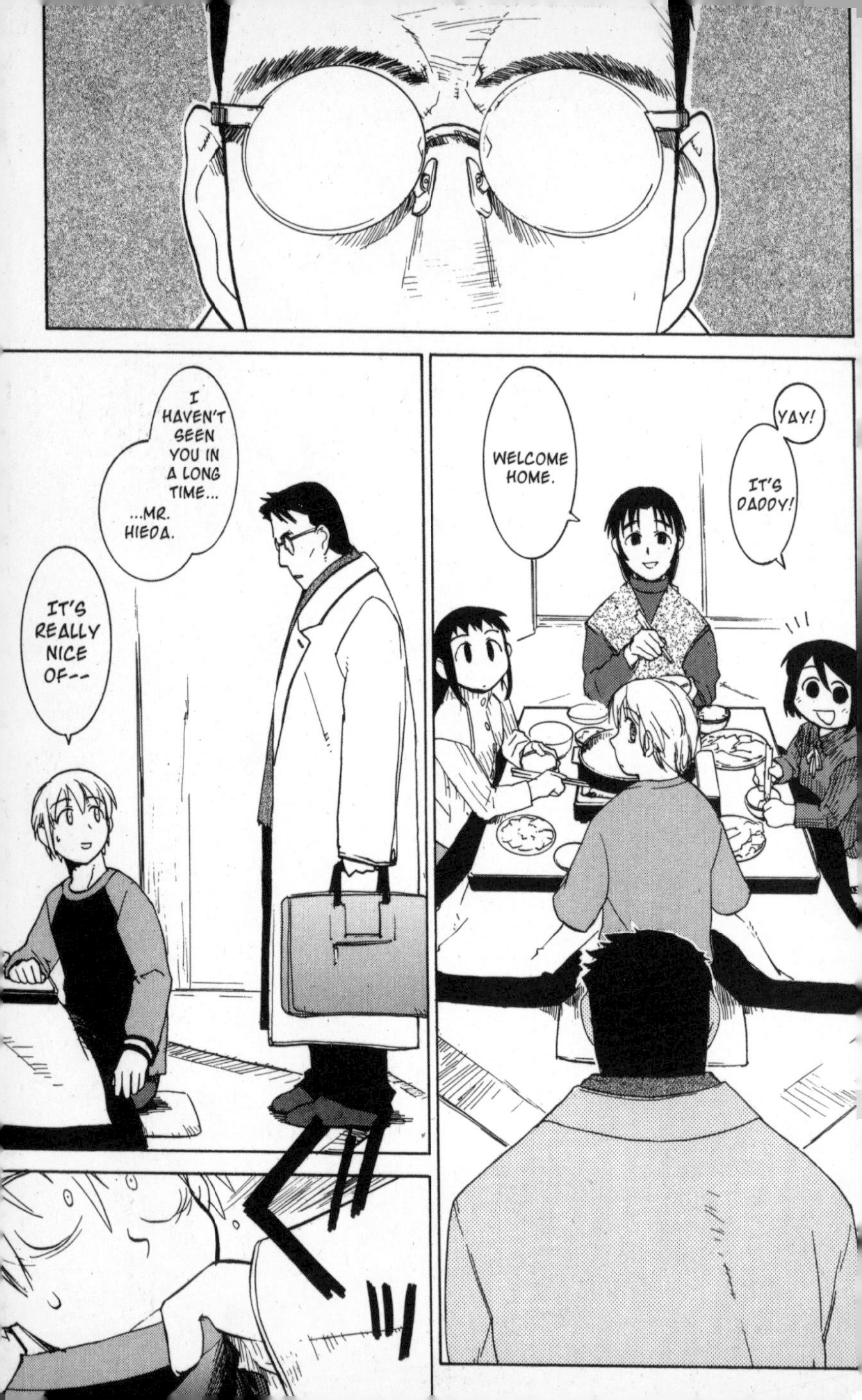
YAY!
IT'S DADDY!
WELCOME HOME.
I HAVEN'T SEEN YOU IN A LONG TIME... ...MR. HIEDA.
IT'S REALLY NICE OF--

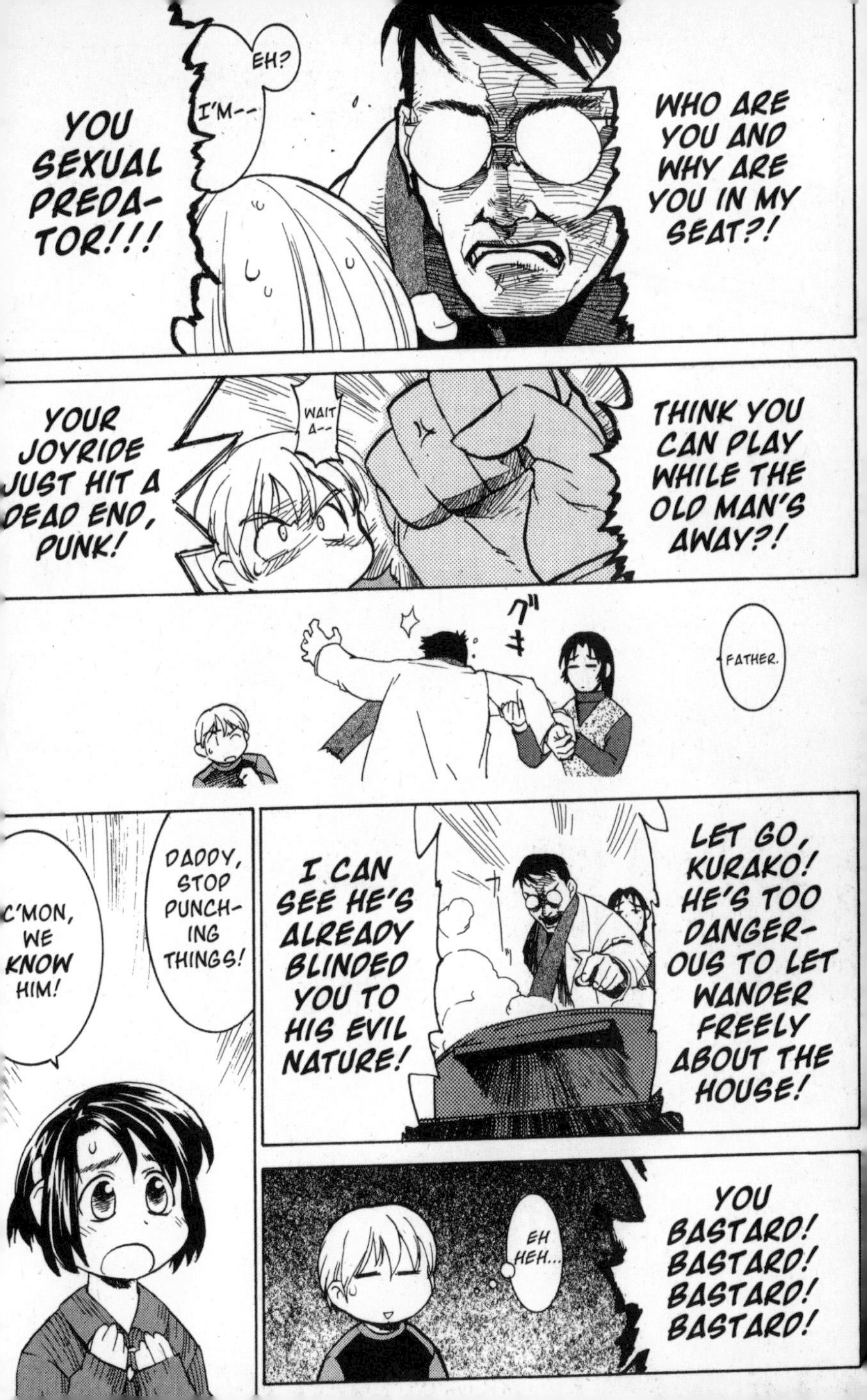
WHO ARE YOU AND WHY ARE YOU IN MY SEAT?!
EH?
I'M--
YOU SEXUAL PREDATOR!!!
THINK YOU CAN PLAY WHILE THE OLD MAN'S AWAY?!
WAIT A--
YOUR JOYRIDE JUST HIT A DEAD END, PUNK!
FATHER.
グキ
LET GO, KURAKO! HE'S TOO DANGEROUS TO LET WANDER FREELY ABOUT THE HOUSE!
I CAN SEE HE'S ALREADY BLINDED YOU TO HIS EVIL NATURE!
YOU BASTARD! BASTARD! BASTARD! BASTARD!
EH HEH...
DADDY, STOP PUNCHING THINGS!
C'MON, WE KNOW HIM!

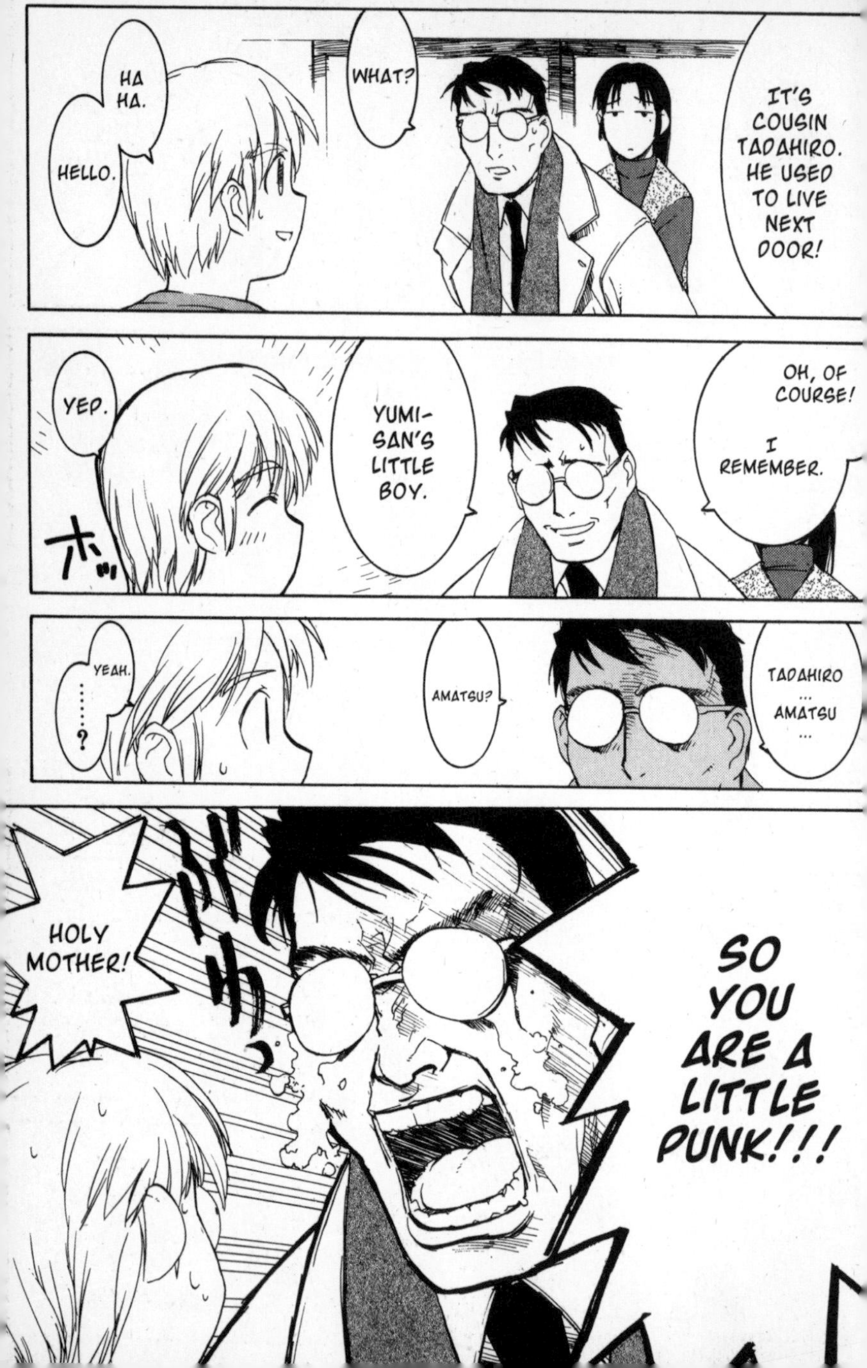
IT'S COUSIN TADAHIRO. HE USED TO LIVE NEXT DOOR!
WHAT?
HA HA.
HELLO.
OH, OF COURSE!
I REMEMBER.
YUMI-SAN'S LITTLE BOY.
YEP.
ホッ
TADAHIRO ... AMATSU ...
AMATSU?
YEAH.
......?
SO YOU ARE A LITTLE PUNK!!!
HOLY MOTHER!

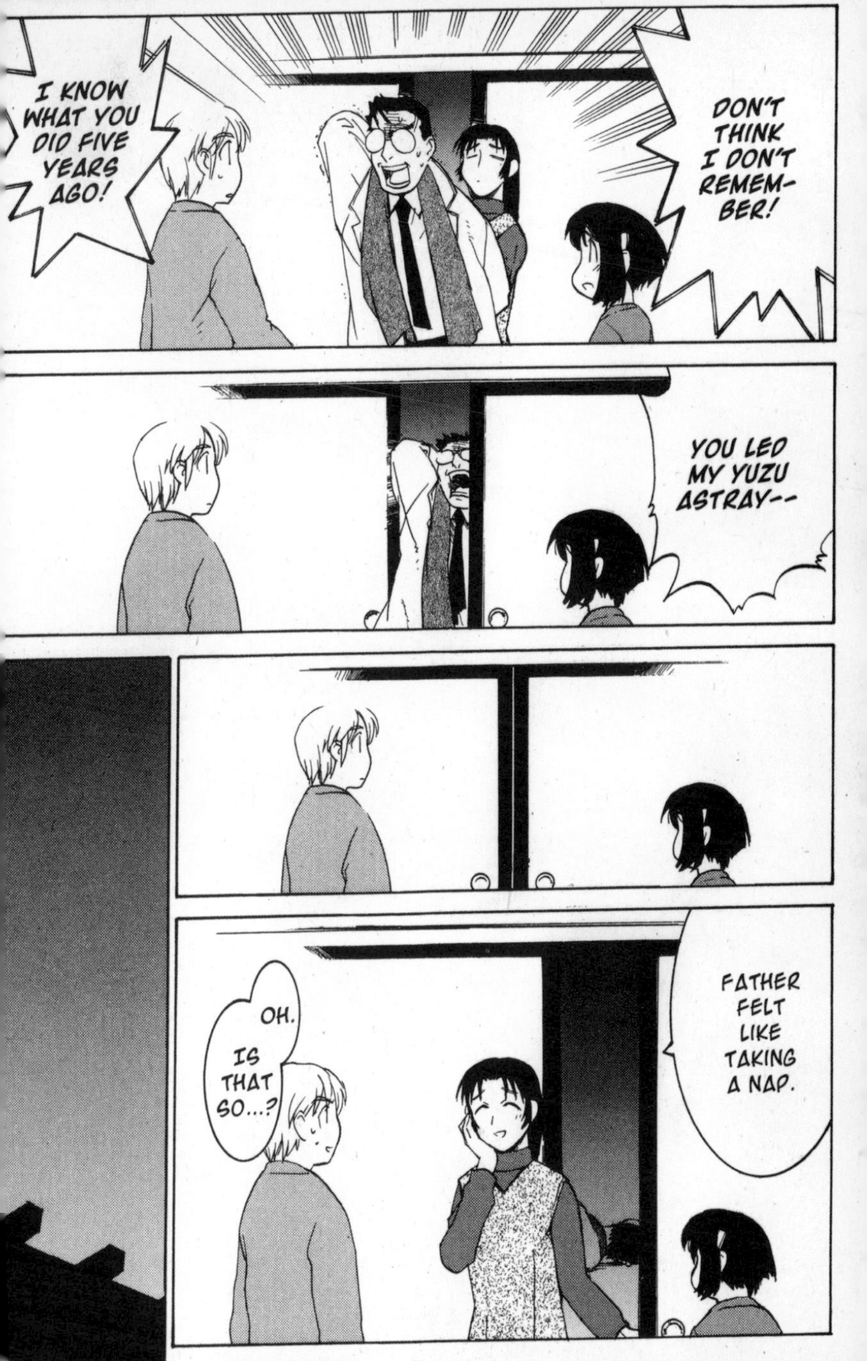
DON'T THINK I DON'T REMEMBER!
I KNOW WHAT YOU DID FIVE YEARS AGO!
YOU LED MY YUZU ASTRAY--
FATHER FELT LIKE TAKING A NAP.
OH.
IS THAT SO...?

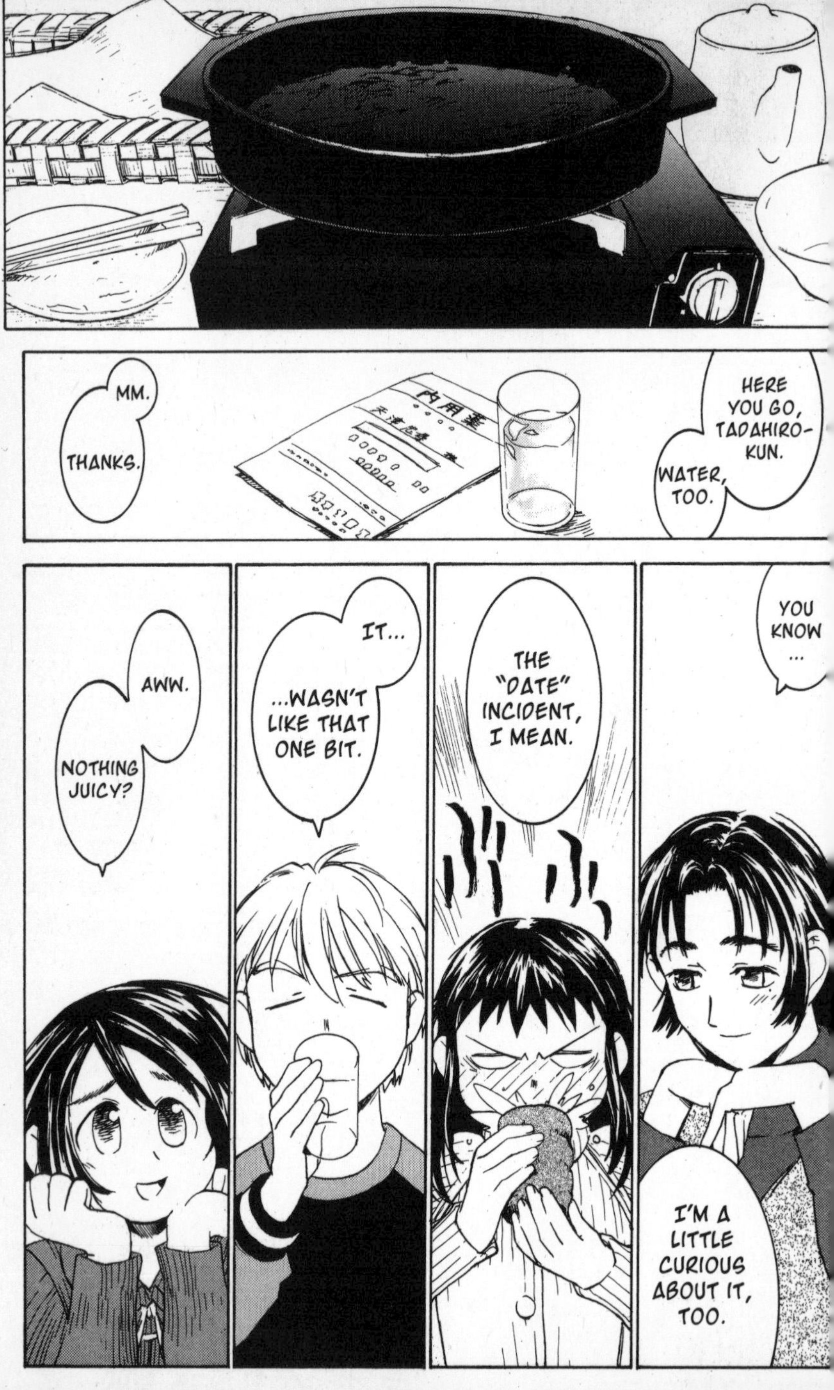
HERE YOU GO, TADAHIRO-KUN.
WATER, TOO.
MM.
THANKS.
YOU KNOW ...
I'M A LITTLE CURIOUS ABOUT IT, TOO.
THE "DATE" INCIDENT, I MEAN.
ぶふ
IT...
...WASN'T LIKE THAT ONE BIT.
AWW.
NOTHING JUICY?

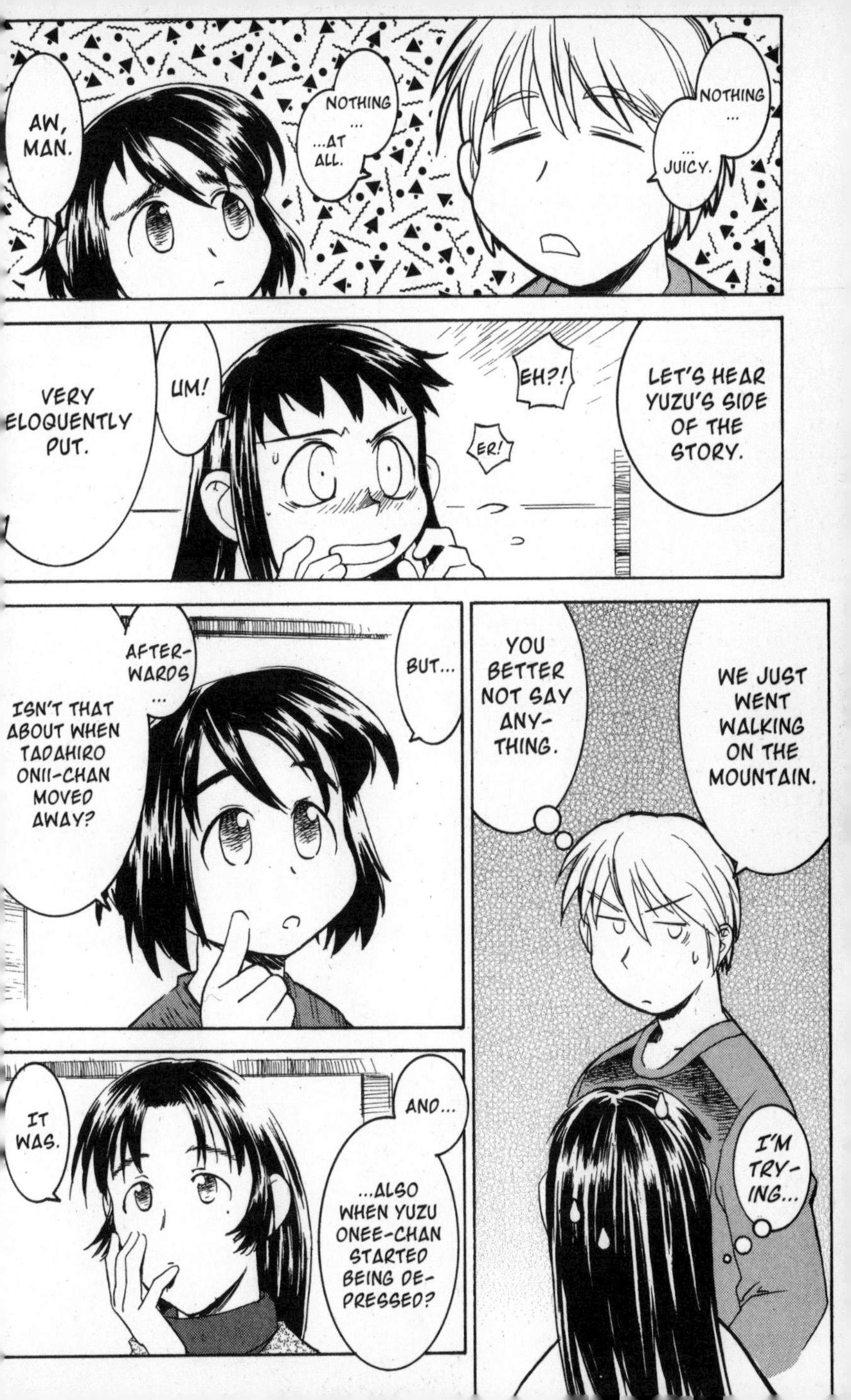
NOTHING ... ... JUICY.
NOTHING ... ...AT ALL.
AW, MAN.
LET'S HEAR YUZU'S SIDE OF THE STORY.
EH?!
ER!
UM!
VERY ELOQUENTLY PUT.
WE JUST WENT WALKING ON THE MOUNTAIN.
YOU BETTER NOT SAY ANY-THING.
I'M TRY-ING...
BUT...
AFTER-WARDS ...
ISN'T THAT ABOUT WHEN TADAHIRO ONII-CHAN MOVED AWAY?
AND...
...ALSO WHEN YUZU ONEE-CHAN STARTED BEING DE-PRESSED?
IT WAS.

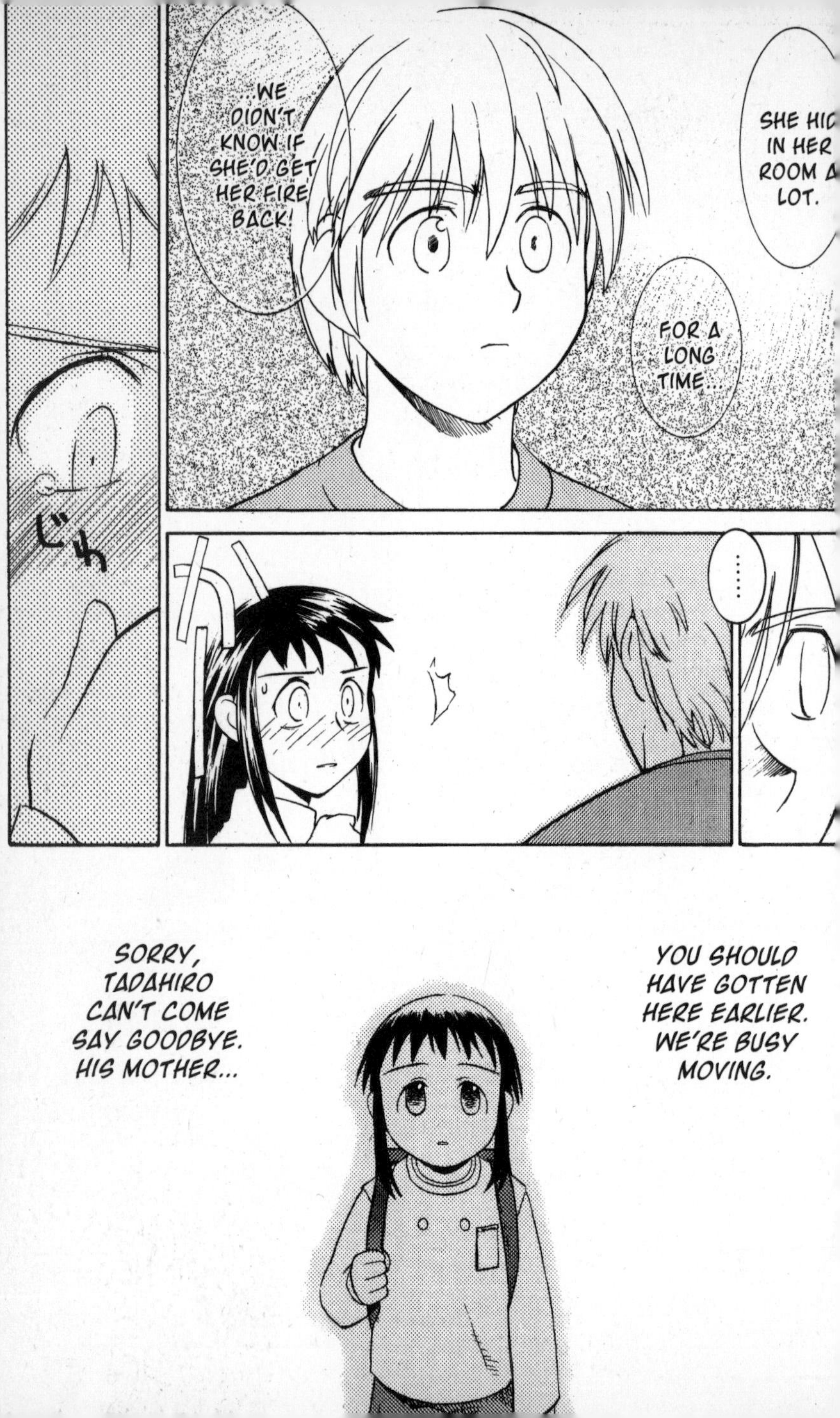
SHE HI IN HER ROOM A LOT.
FOR A LONG TIME...
...WE DIDN'T KNOW IF SHE'D GET HER FIRE BACK!
.....
じわ
YOU SHOULD HAVE GOTTEN HERE EARLIER. WE'RE BUSY MOVING.
SORRY, TADAHIRO CAN'T COME SAY GOODBYE. HIS MOTHER...

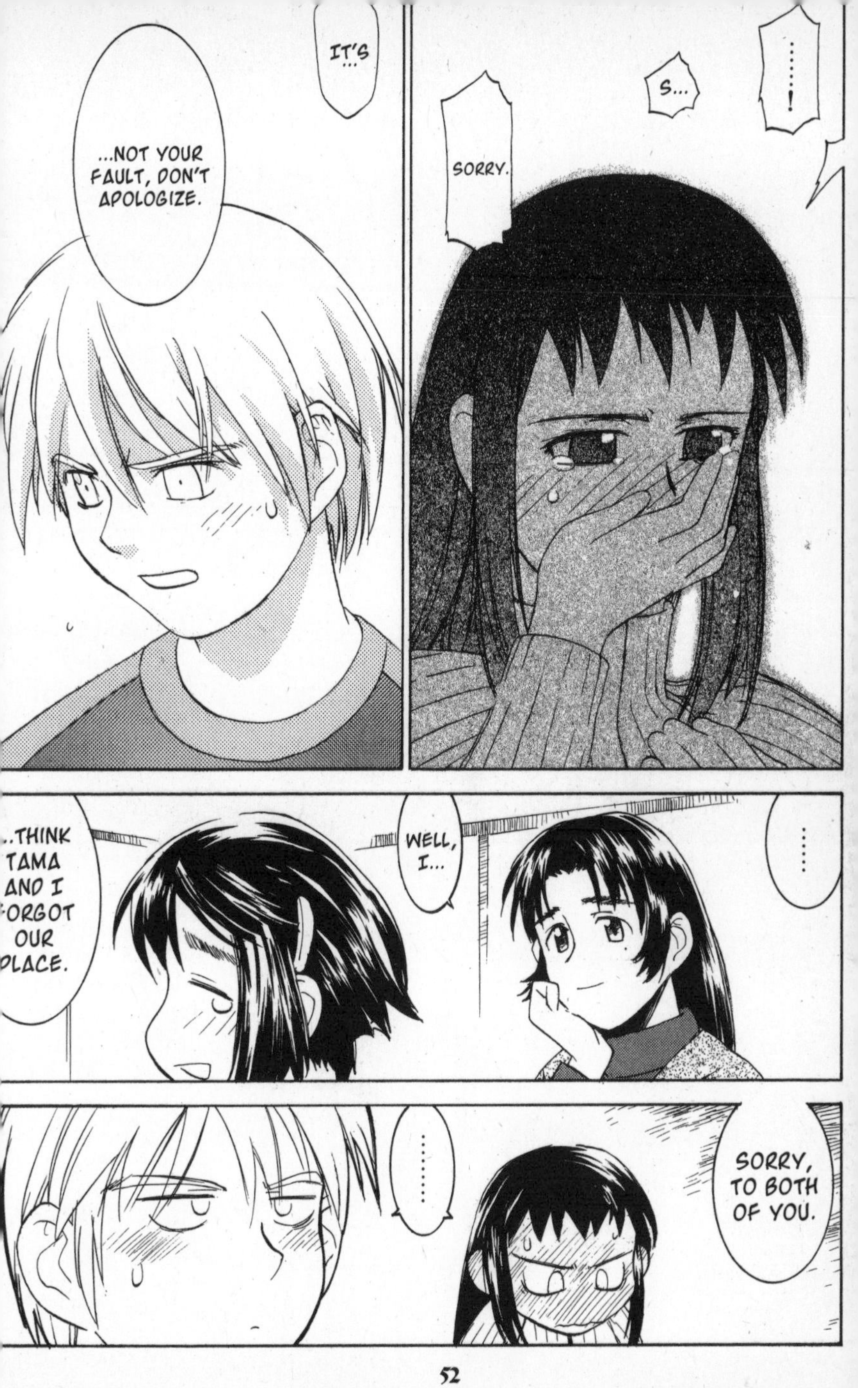
......!
S...
SORRY.
IT'S...
...NOT YOUR FAULT, DON'T APOLOGIZE.
......
WELL, I...
..THINK TAMA AND I FORGOT OUR PLACE.
SORRY, TO BOTH OF YOU.
......

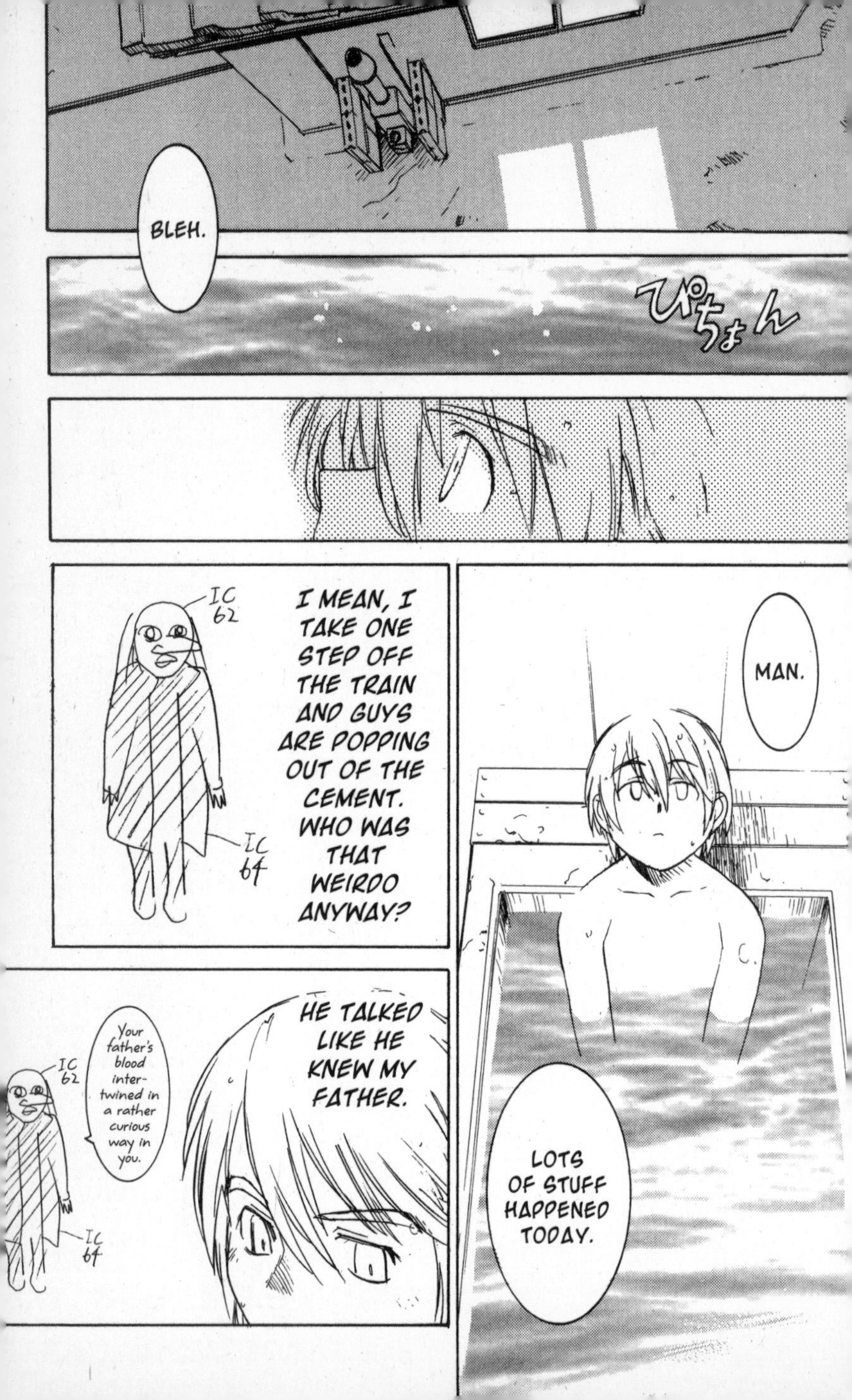
BLEH.
ぴちょん
MAN.
LOTS OF STUFF HAPPENED TODAY.
I MEAN, I TAKE ONE STEP OFF THE TRAIN AND GUYS ARE POPPING OUT OF THE CEMENT. WHO WAS THAT WEIRDO ANYWAY?
IC 62
IC 64
HE TALKED LIKE HE KNEW MY FATHER.
Your father's blood inter-twined in a rather curious way in you.
IC 62
IC 64

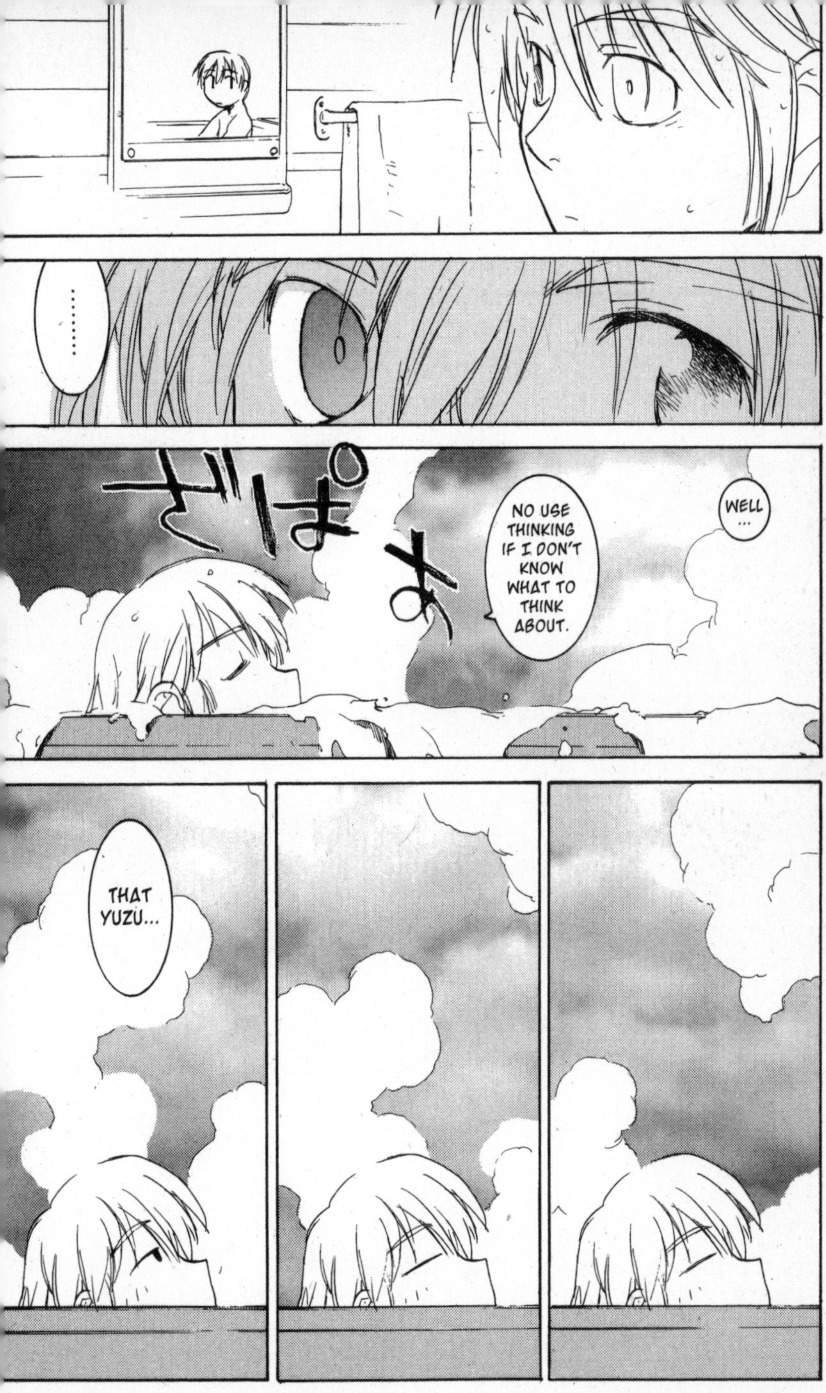
……
WELL ...
NO USE THINKING IF I DON'T KNOW WHAT TO THINK ABOUT.
THAT YUZU...

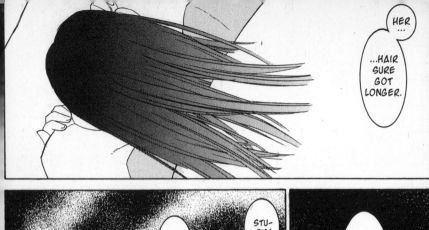

HER...

...HAIR SURE GOT LONGER.

STU-PID!

STU-PID!

STU-PID!

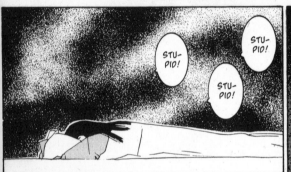

WHAT A STUPID...

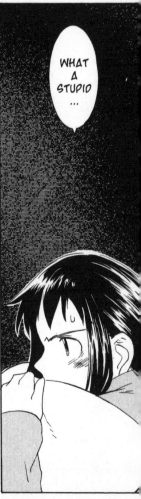

EMBARRASSING, EMBARRASSING, EMBARRASSING!!

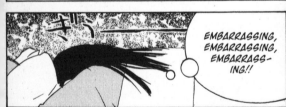

RRGH...

CAN'T I...

...DO TODAY OVER AGAIN?

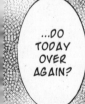

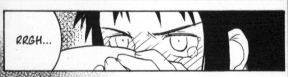

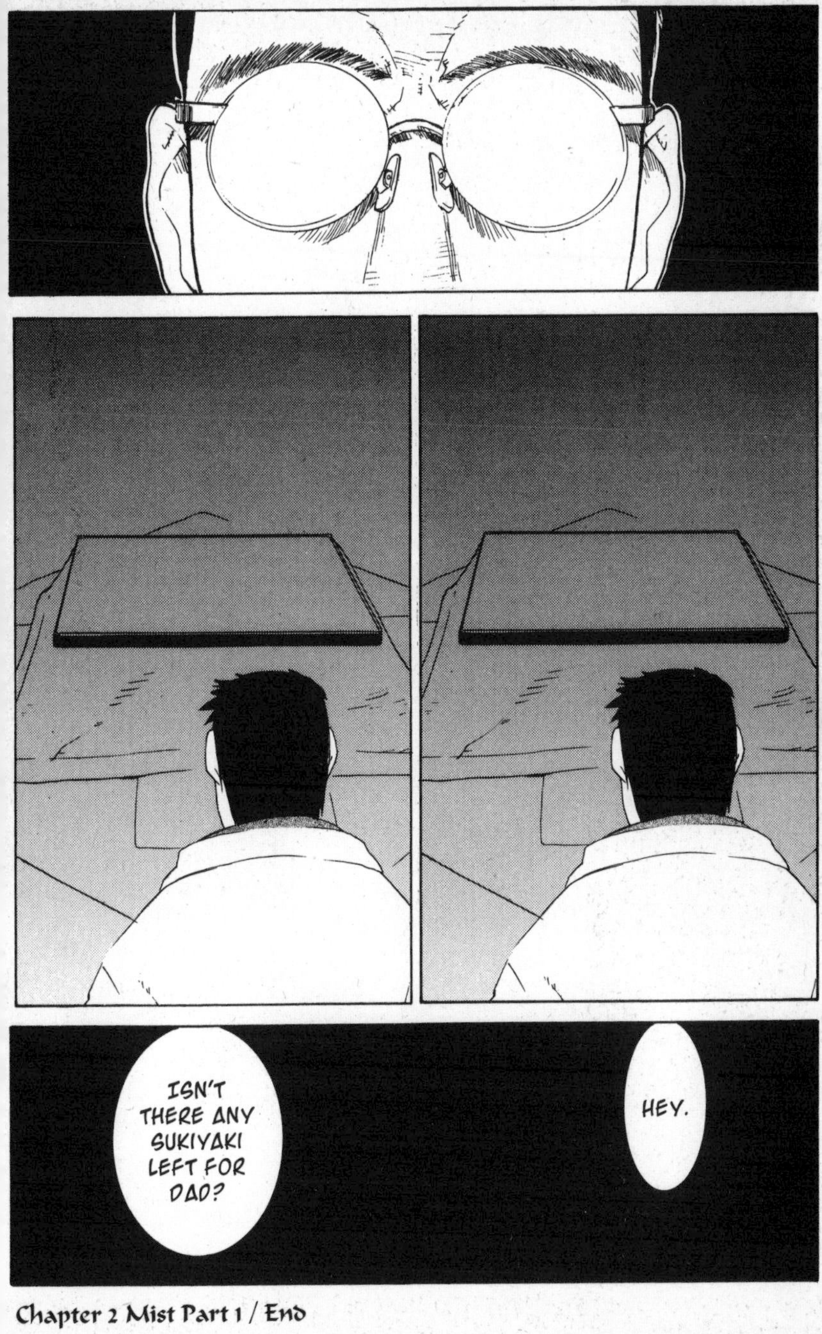
HEY.
ISN'T THERE ANY SUKIYAKI LEFT FOR DAD?

Chapter 2 Mist Part 1 / End

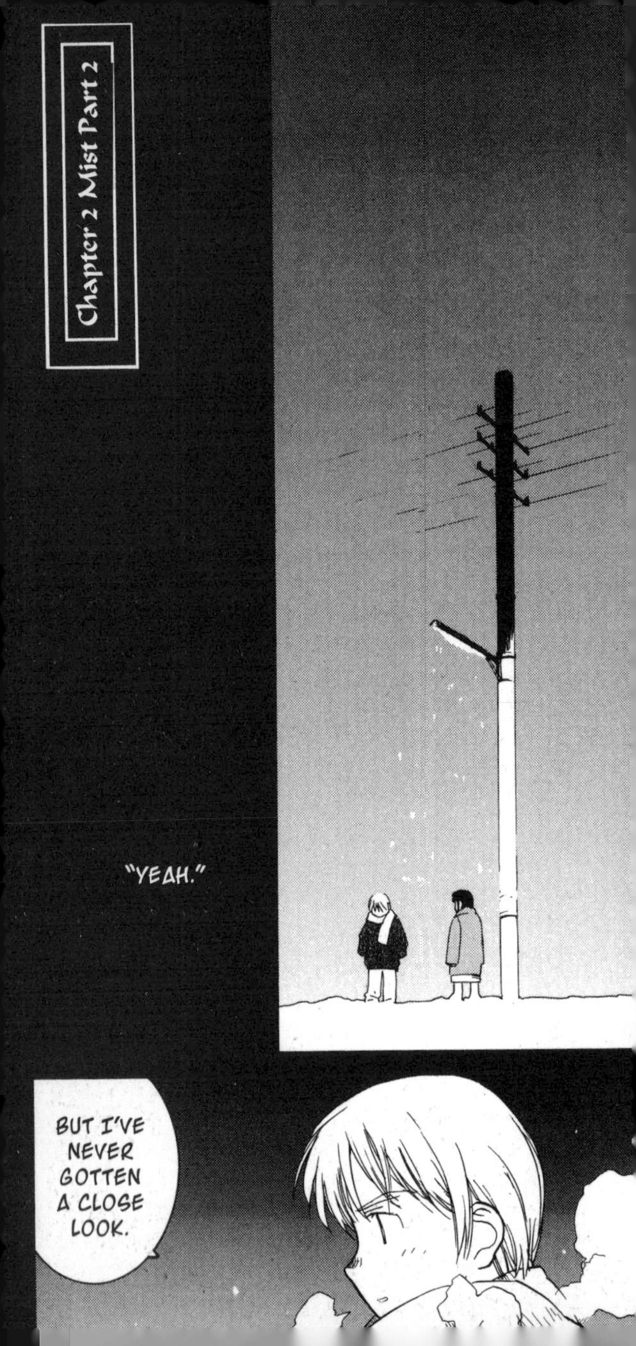
Chapter 2 Mist Part 2
"YEAH."
BUT I'VE NEVER GOTTEN A CLOSE LOOK.

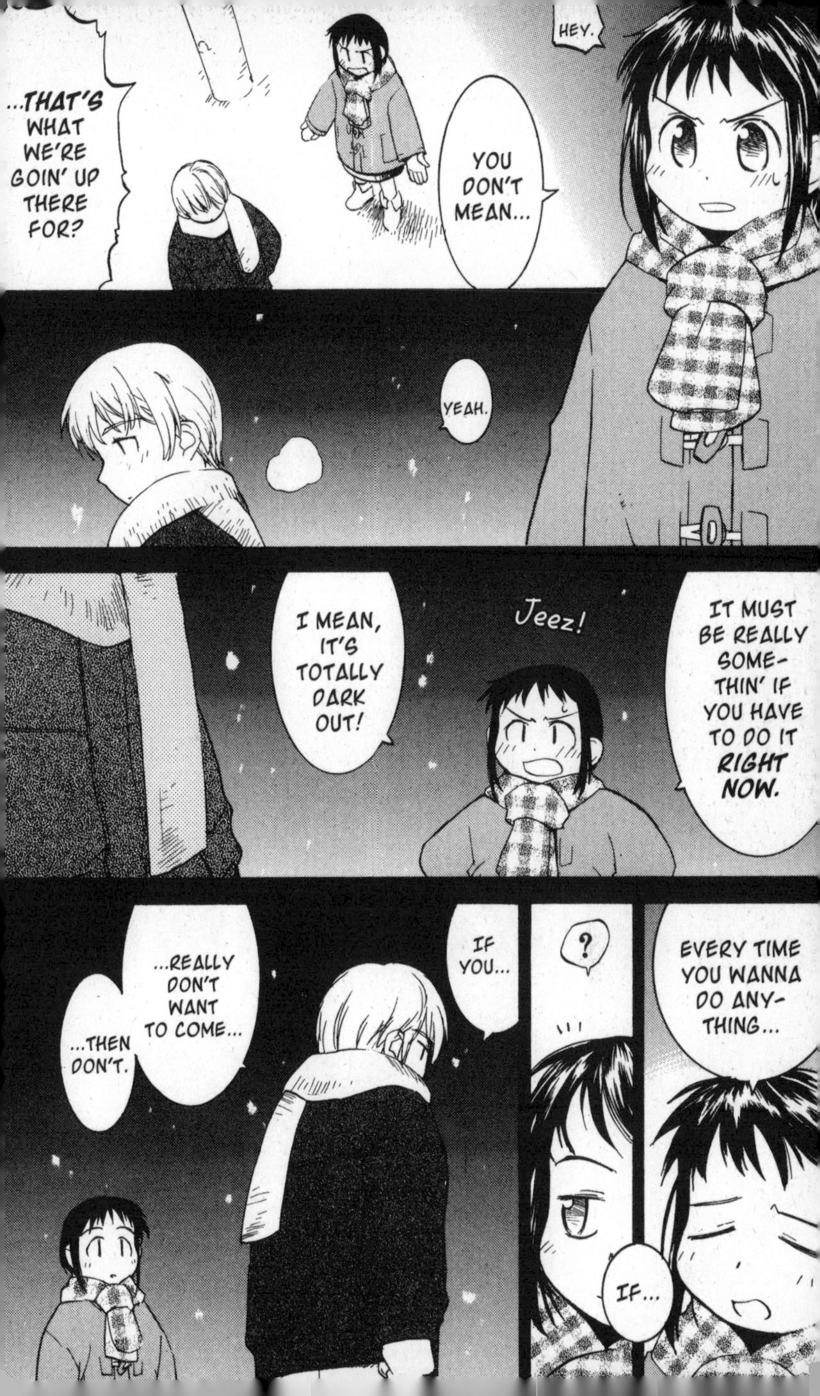
HEY.
YOU DON'T MEAN...
...THAT'S WHAT WE'RE GOIN' UP THERE FOR?
YEAH.
IT MUST BE REALLY SOME-THIN' IF YOU HAVE TO DO IT RIGHT NOW.
Jeez!
I MEAN, IT'S TOTALLY DARK OUT!
EVERY TIME YOU WANNA DO ANY-THING...
IF...
?
IF YOU...
...REALLY DON'T WANT TO COME...
...THEN DON'T.

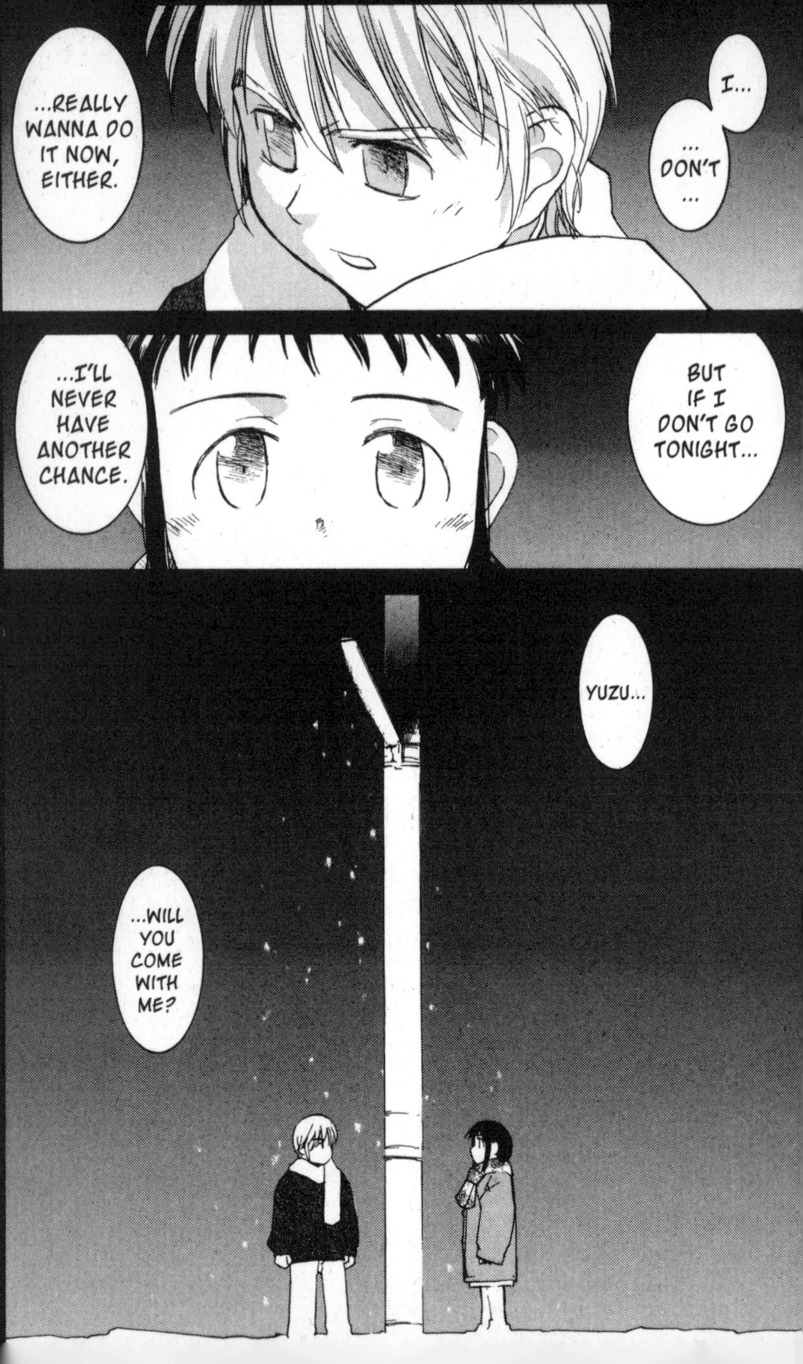
I...
... DON'T ...
...REALLY WANNA DO IT NOW, EITHER.
BUT IF I DON'T GO TONIGHT...
...I'LL NEVER HAVE ANOTHER CHANCE.
YUZU...
...WILL YOU COME WITH ME?

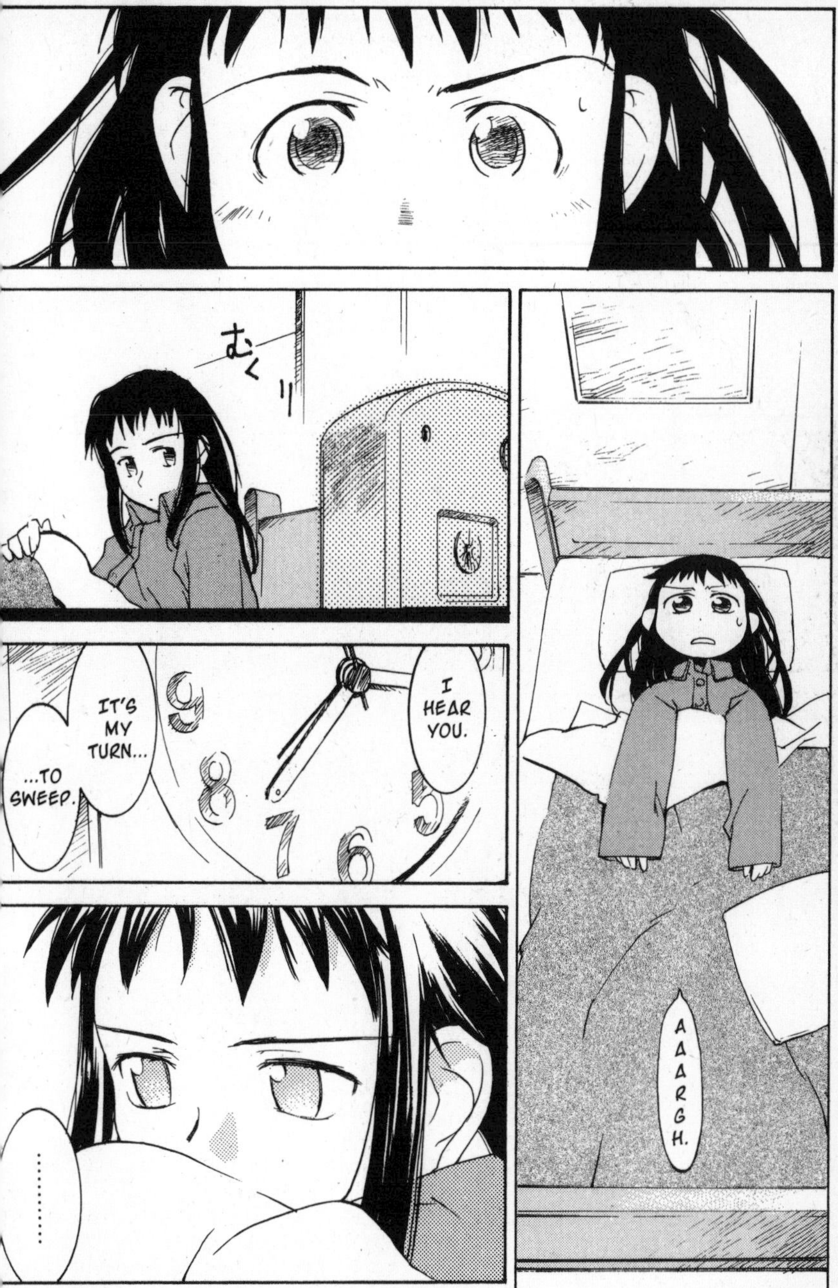
AAARGH.
むくり
I HEAR YOU.
IT'S MY TURN...
...TO SWEEP.
....

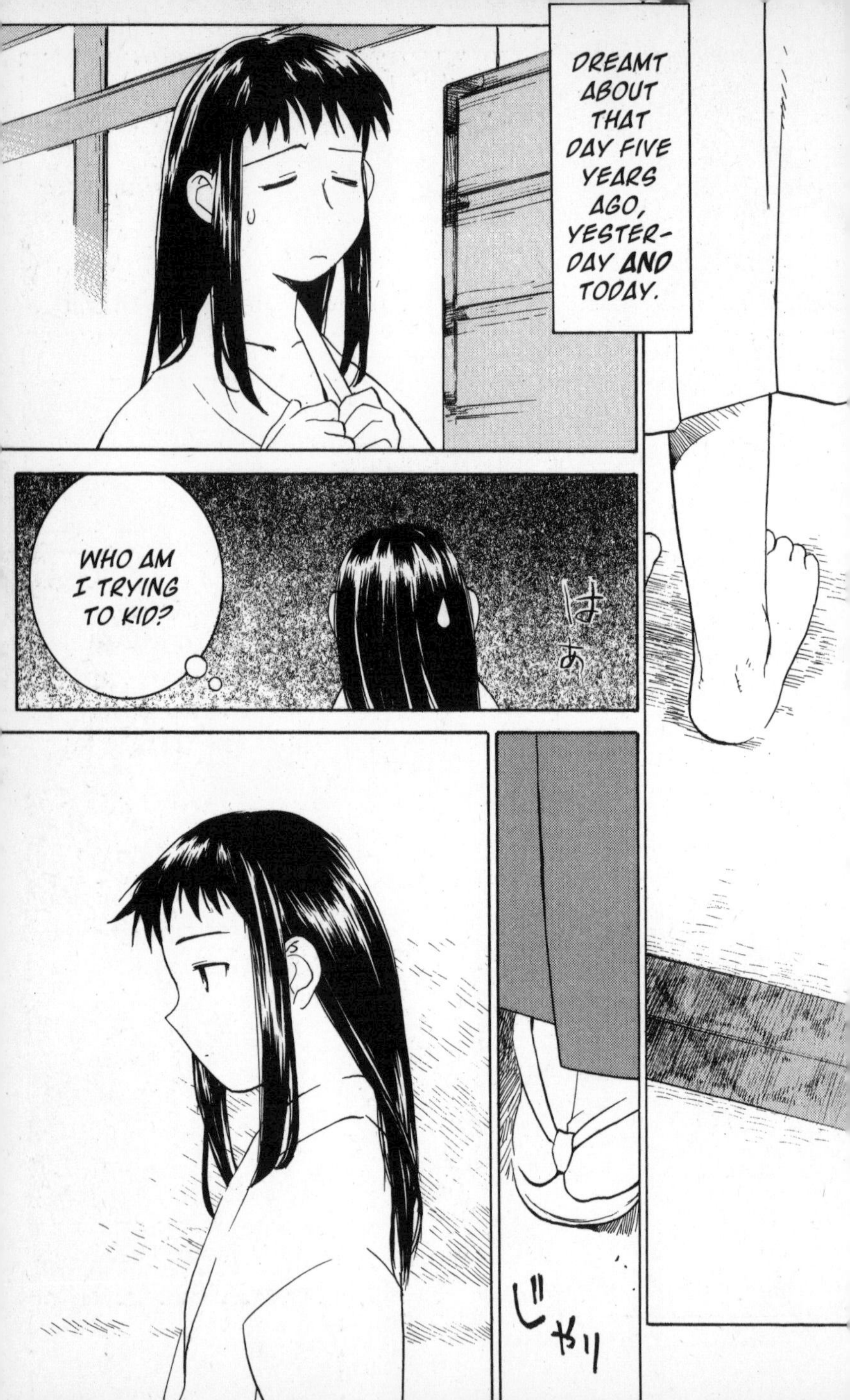
DREAMT ABOUT THAT DAY FIVE YEARS AGO, YESTER-DAY **AND** TODAY.
はぁ
WHO AM I TRYING TO KID?
じゃり

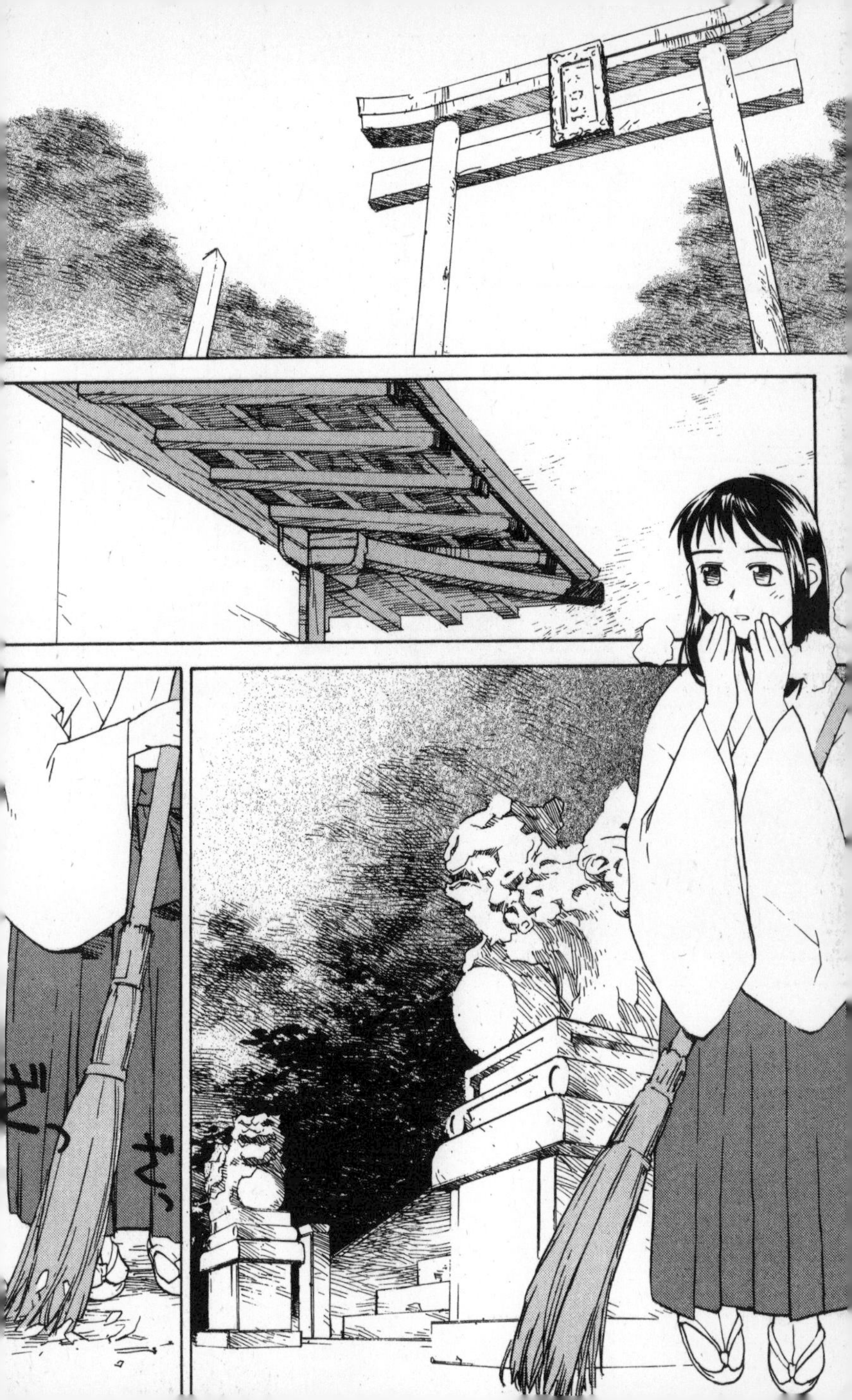
ざ、
ざっ

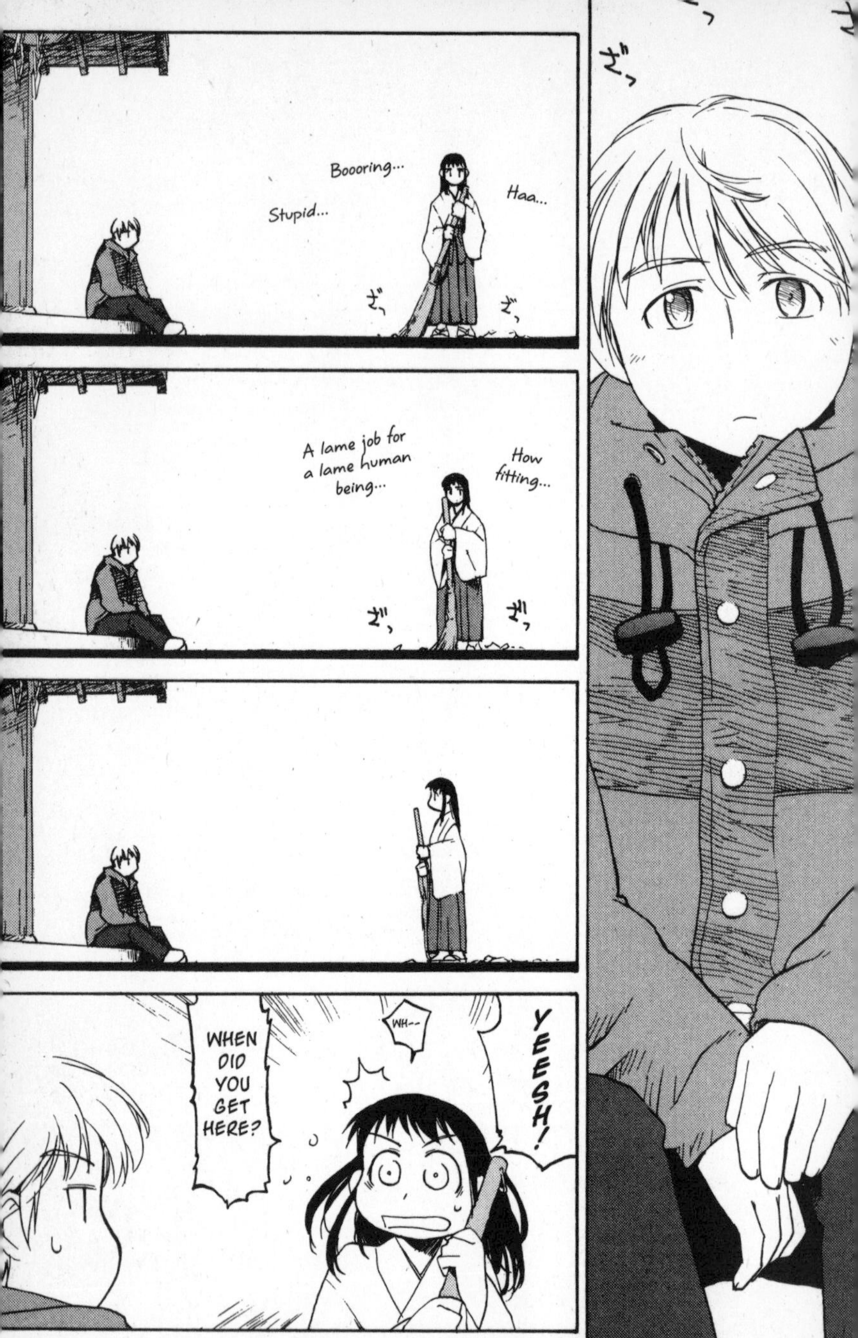
ざっ
Haa...
Boooring...
Stupid...
ざっ
ざっ
How fitting...
A lame job for a lame human being...
ざっ
ざっ
YEESH!
WH--
WHEN DID YOU GET HERE?

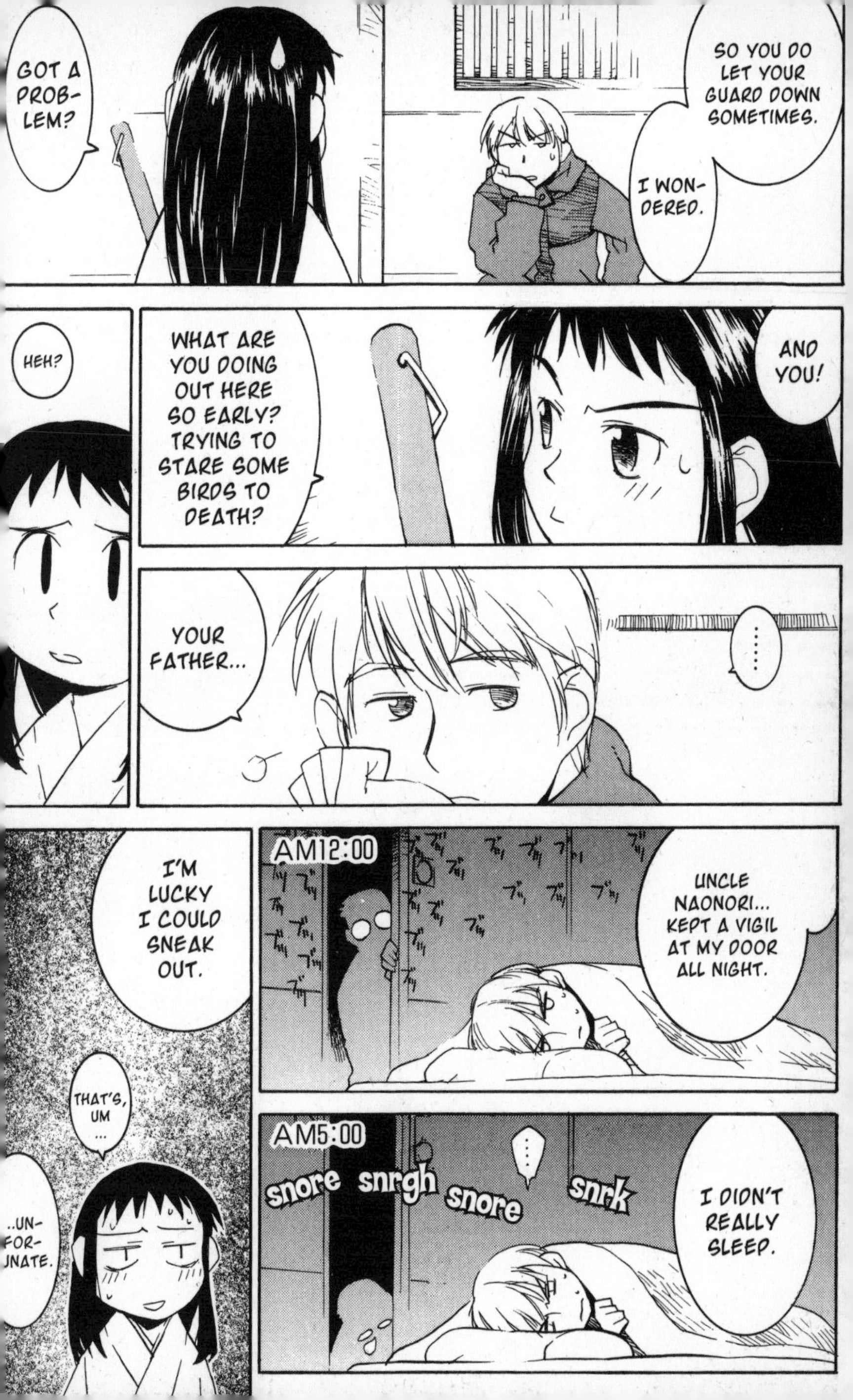
SO YOU DO LET YOUR GUARD DOWN SOMETIMES.
I WON-DERED.
GOT A PROB-LEM?
AND YOU!
WHAT ARE YOU DOING OUT HERE SO EARLY? TRYING TO STARE SOME BIRDS TO DEATH?
......
YOUR FATHER...
HEH?
AM12:00
UNCLE NAONORI... KEPT A VIGIL AT MY DOOR ALL NIGHT.
AM5:00
I DIDN'T REALLY SLEEP.
snrk
...
snore
snrgh
snore
I'M LUCKY I COULD SNEAK OUT.
THAT'S, UM ...
...UN-FOR-TUNATE.

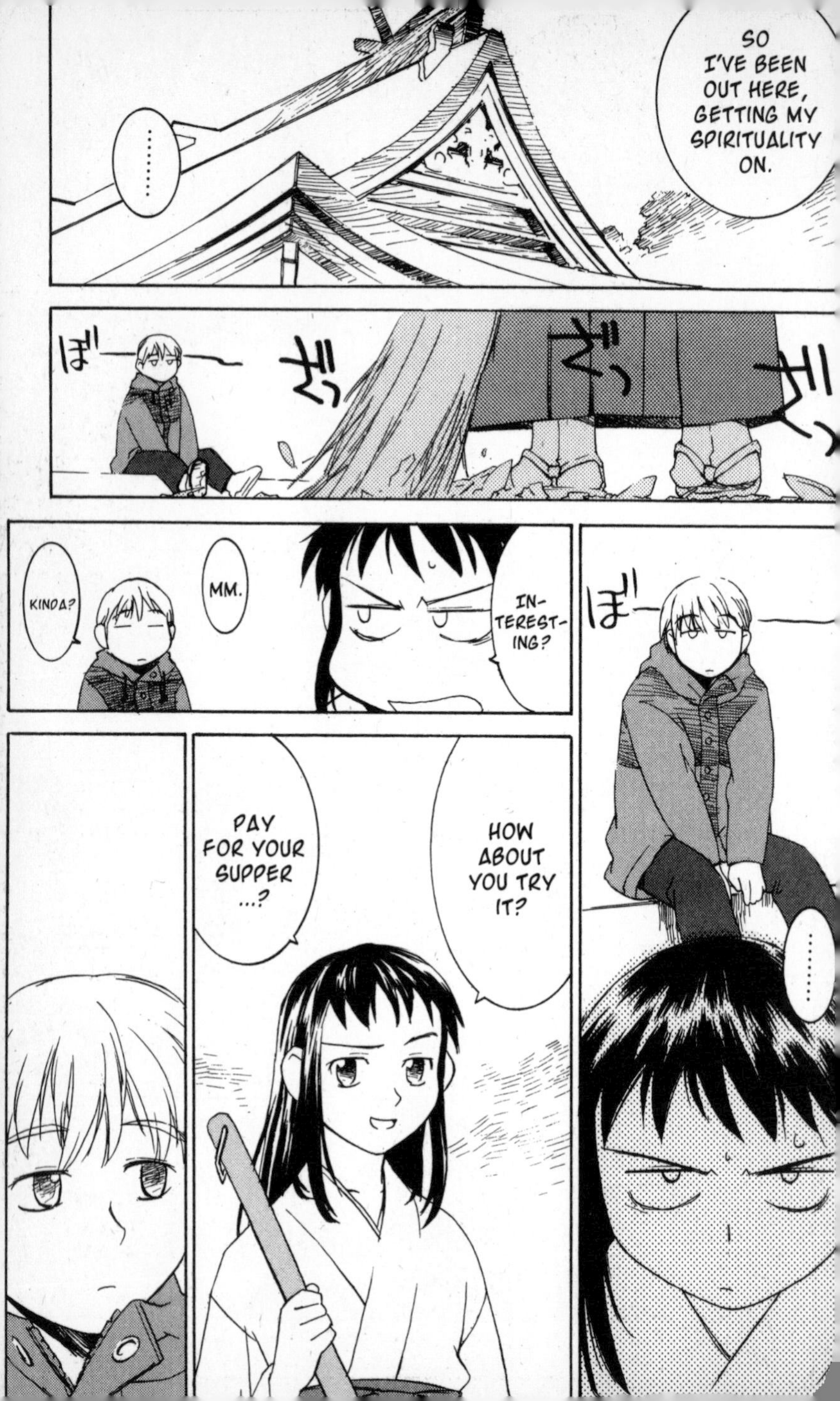
SO I'VE BEEN OUT HERE, GETTING MY SPIRITUALITY ON.
......
ざっ
ざっ
ざっ
ぼー
ぼー
......
IN-TERESTING?
MM.
KINDA?
HOW ABOUT YOU TRY IT?
PAY FOR YOUR SUPPER ...?

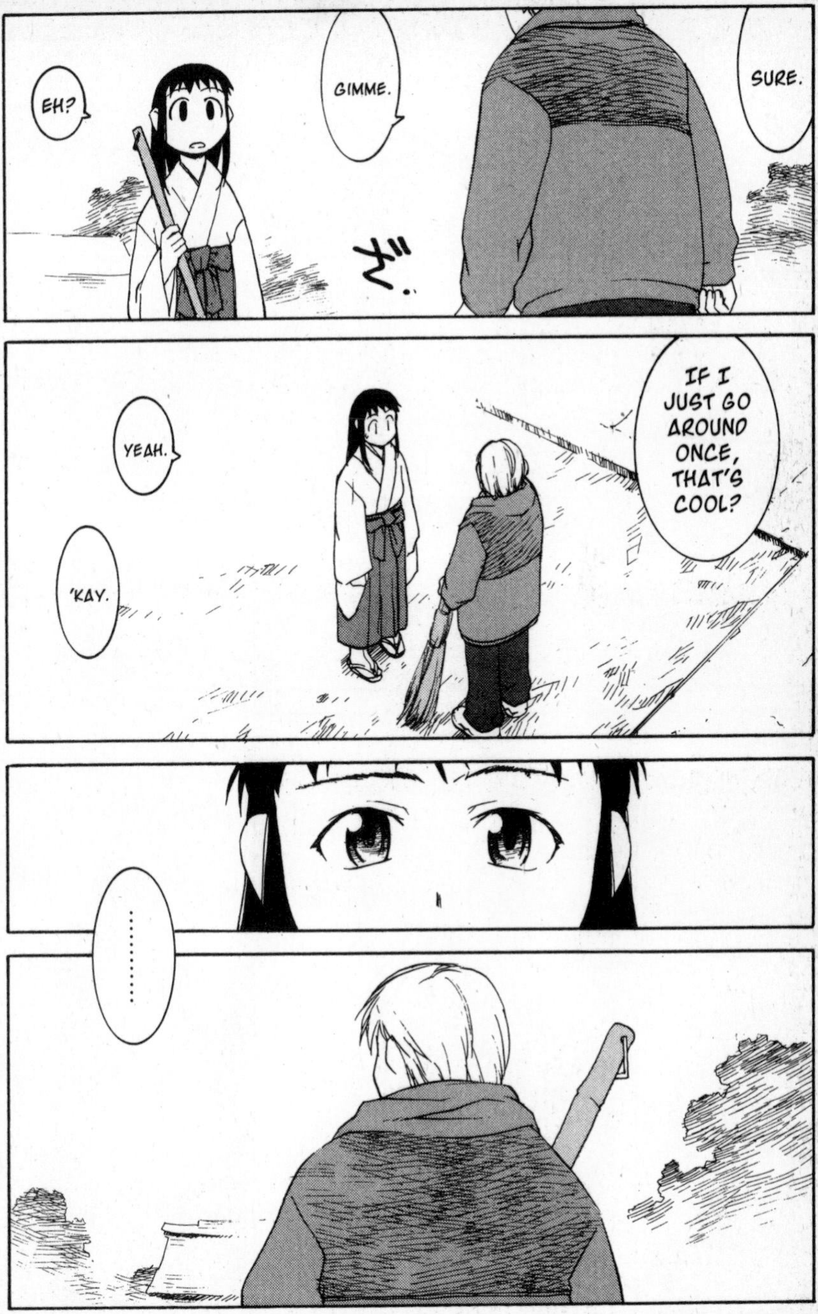
SURE.
GIMME.
ざ..
EH?
IF I JUST GO AROUND ONCE, THAT'S COOL?
YEAH.
'KAY.
……….

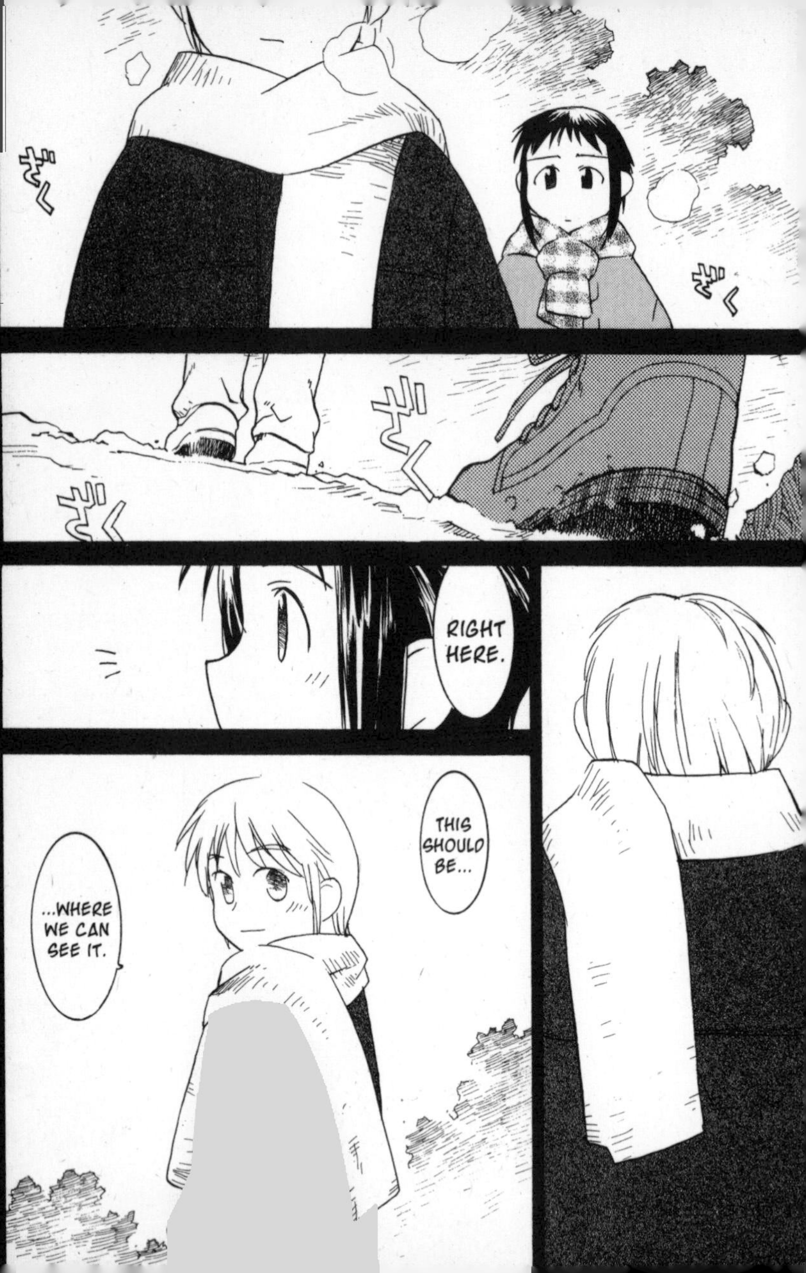
ざく
ざく
ざく
ざく
RIGHT HERE.
THIS SHOULD BE...
...WHERE WE CAN SEE IT.

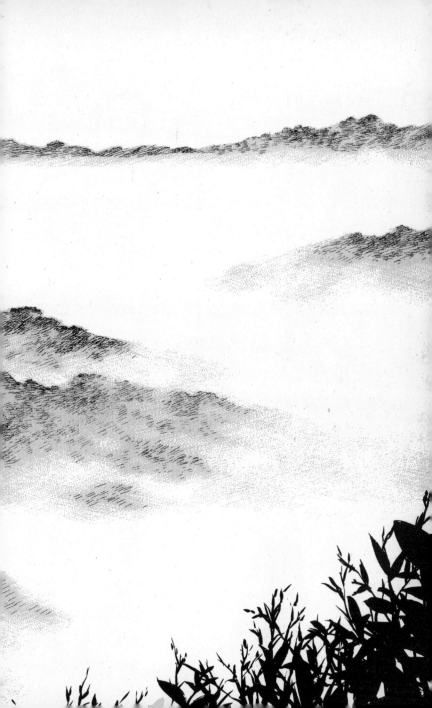

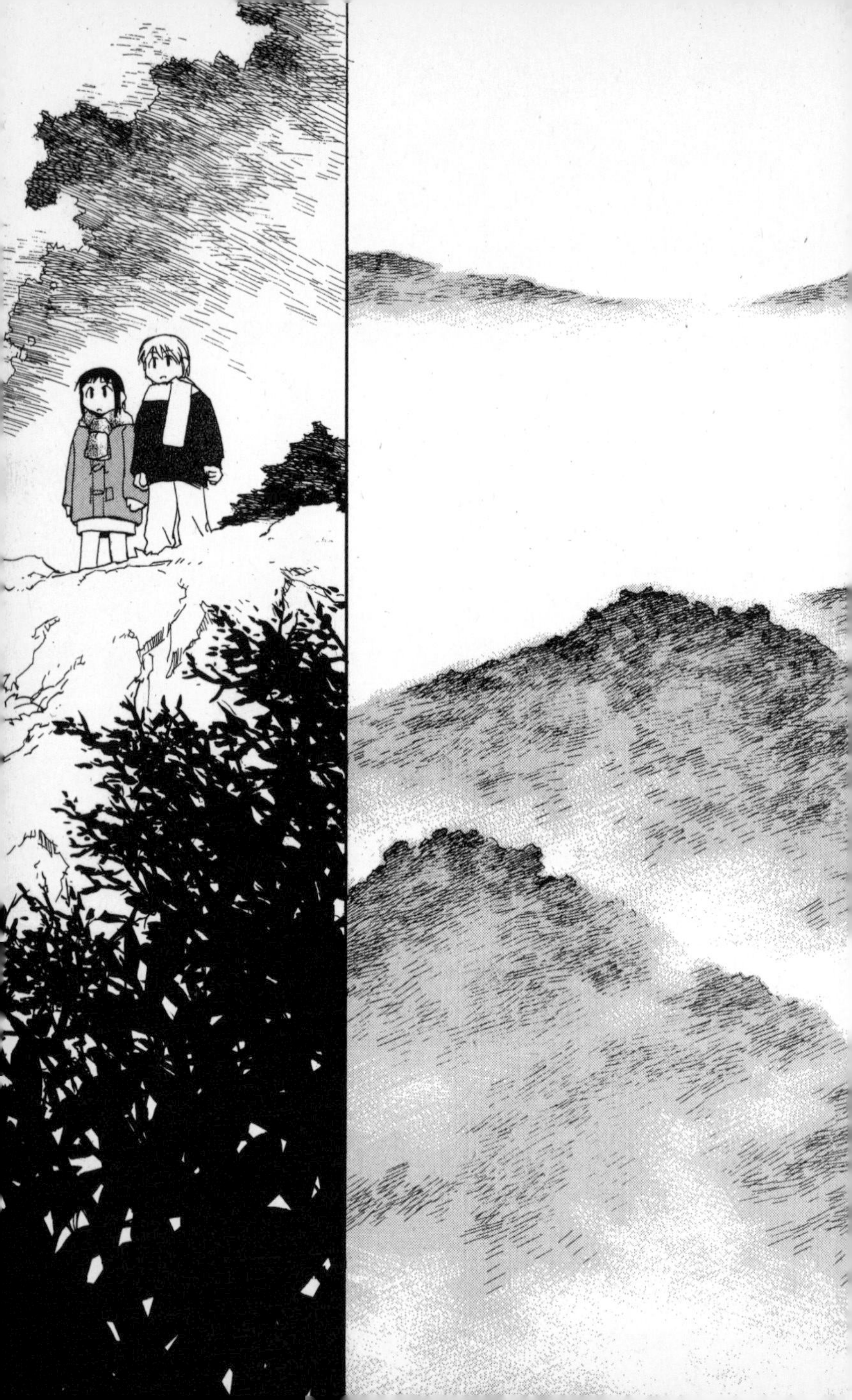

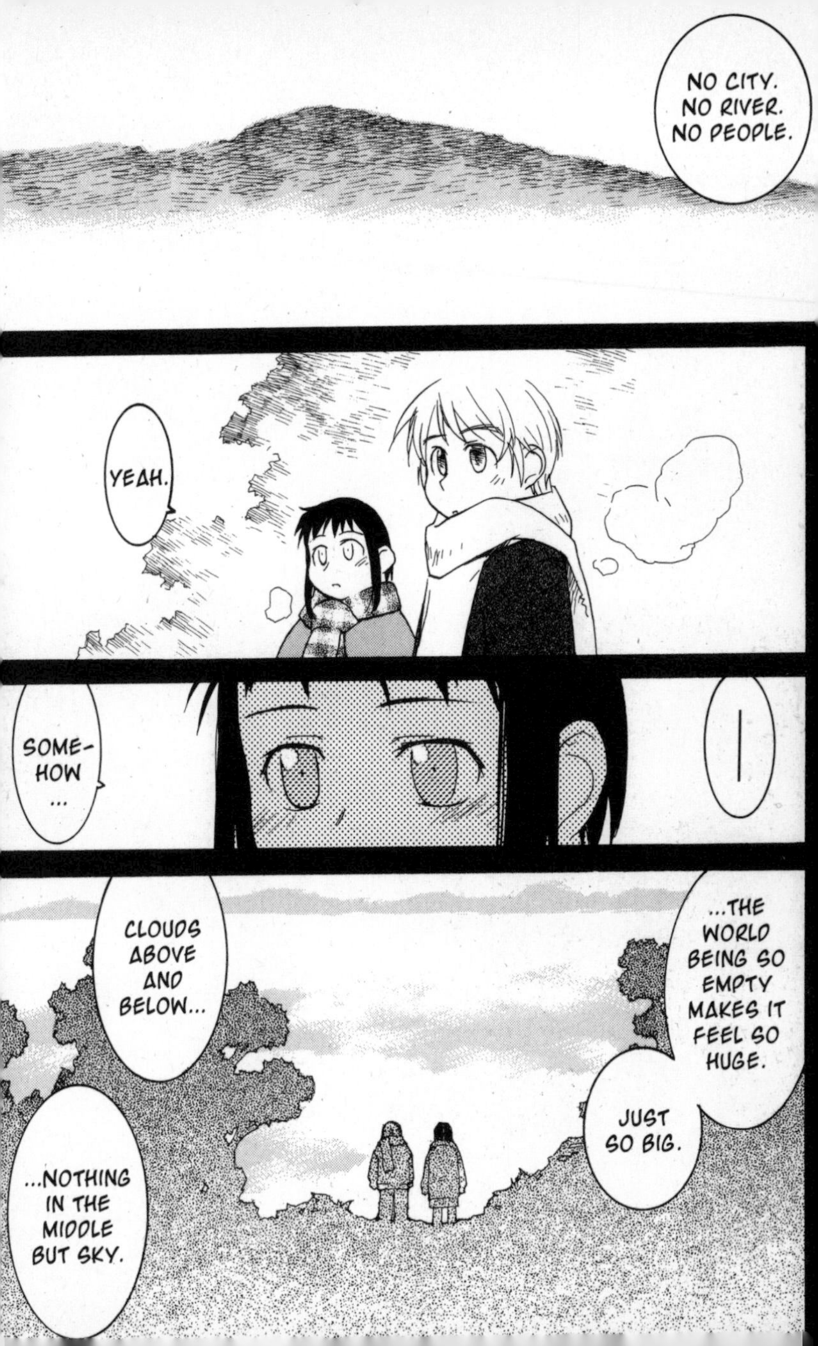
NO CITY. NO RIVER. NO PEOPLE.
YEAH.
I
SOME-HOW ...
...THE WORLD BEING SO EMPTY MAKES IT FEEL SO HUGE.
JUST SO BIG.
CLOUDS ABOVE AND BELOW...
...NOTHING IN THE MIDDLE BUT SKY.

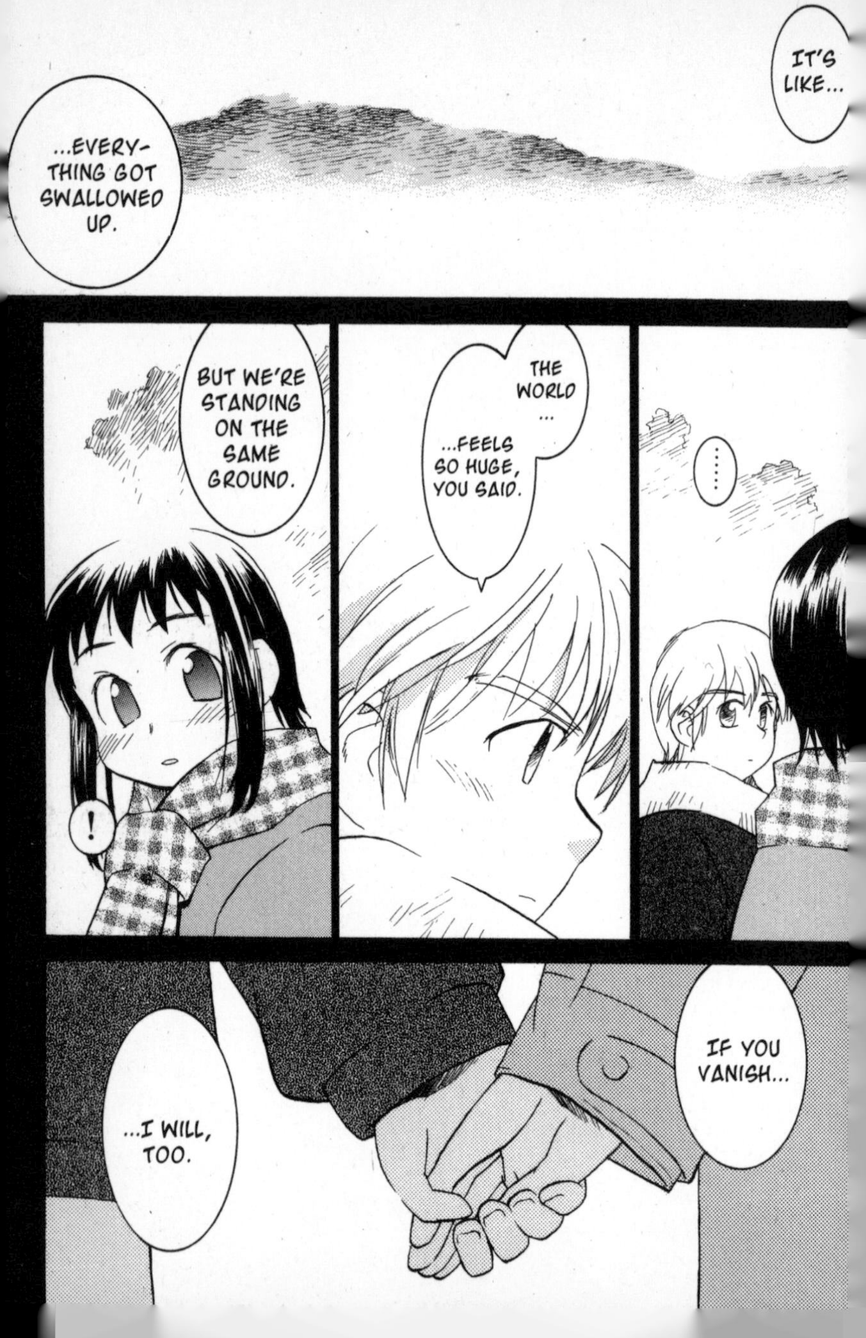
IT'S LIKE...
...EVERY-THING GOT SWALLOWED UP.
......
THE WORLD ...
...FEELS SO HUGE, YOU SAID.
BUT WE'RE STANDING ON THE SAME GROUND.
!
IF YOU VANISH...
...I WILL, TOO.

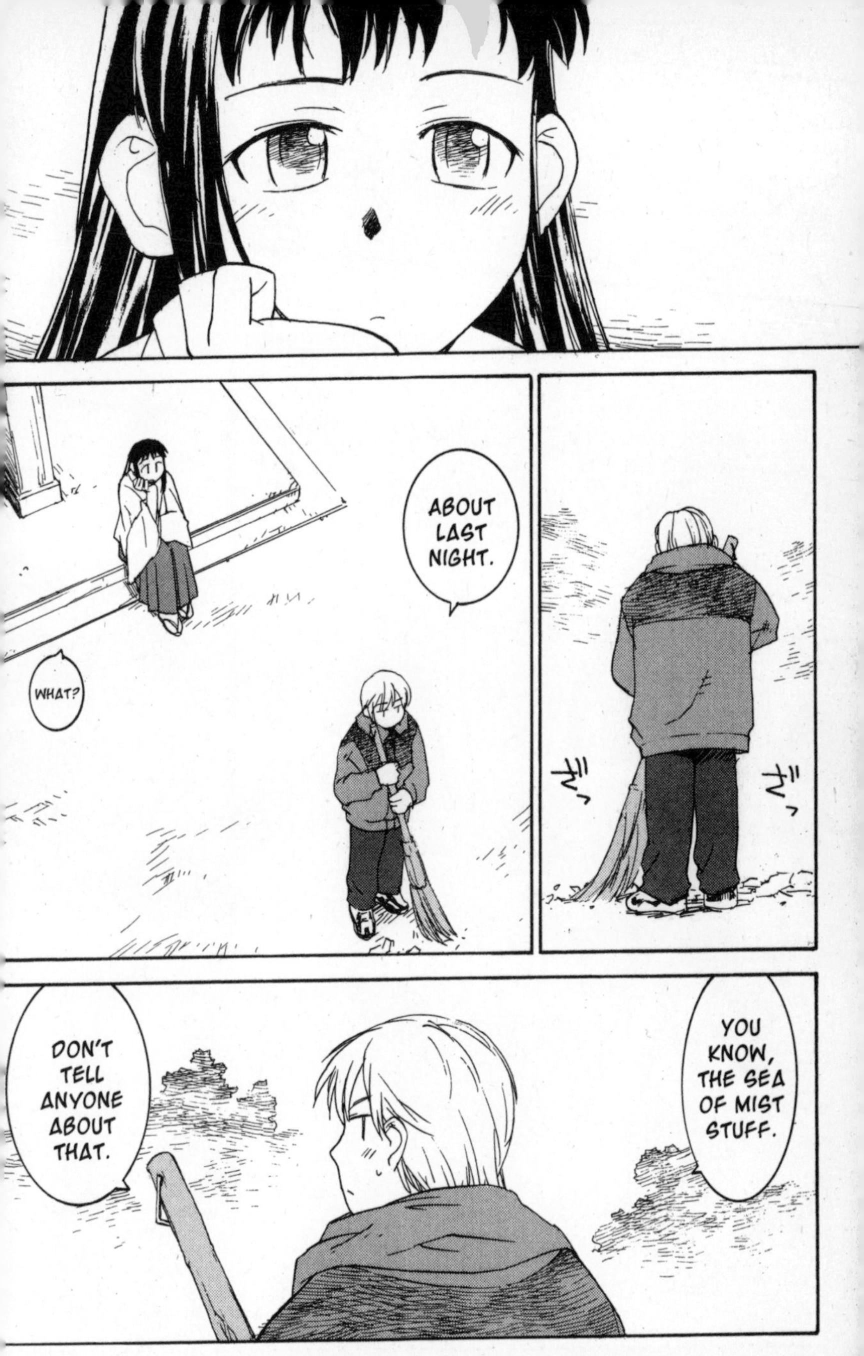
ABOUT LAST NIGHT.
WHAT?
YOU KNOW, THE SEA OF MIST STUFF.
DON'T TELL ANYONE ABOUT THAT.

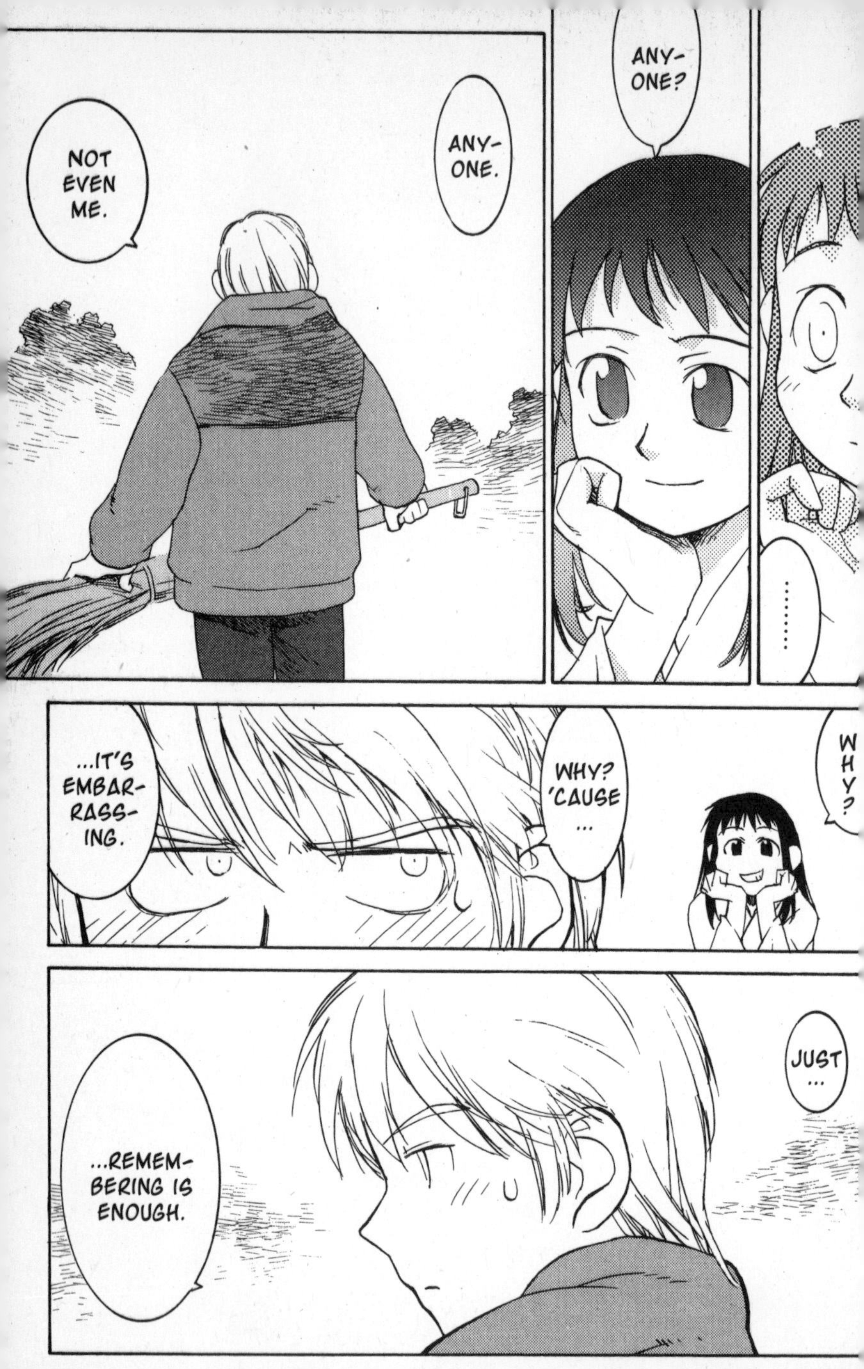
......
ANY-ONE?
ANY-ONE.
NOT EVEN ME.
WHY?
WHY? 'CAUSE ...
...IT'S EMBAR-RASS-ING.
JUST ...
...REMEM-BERING IS ENOUGH.

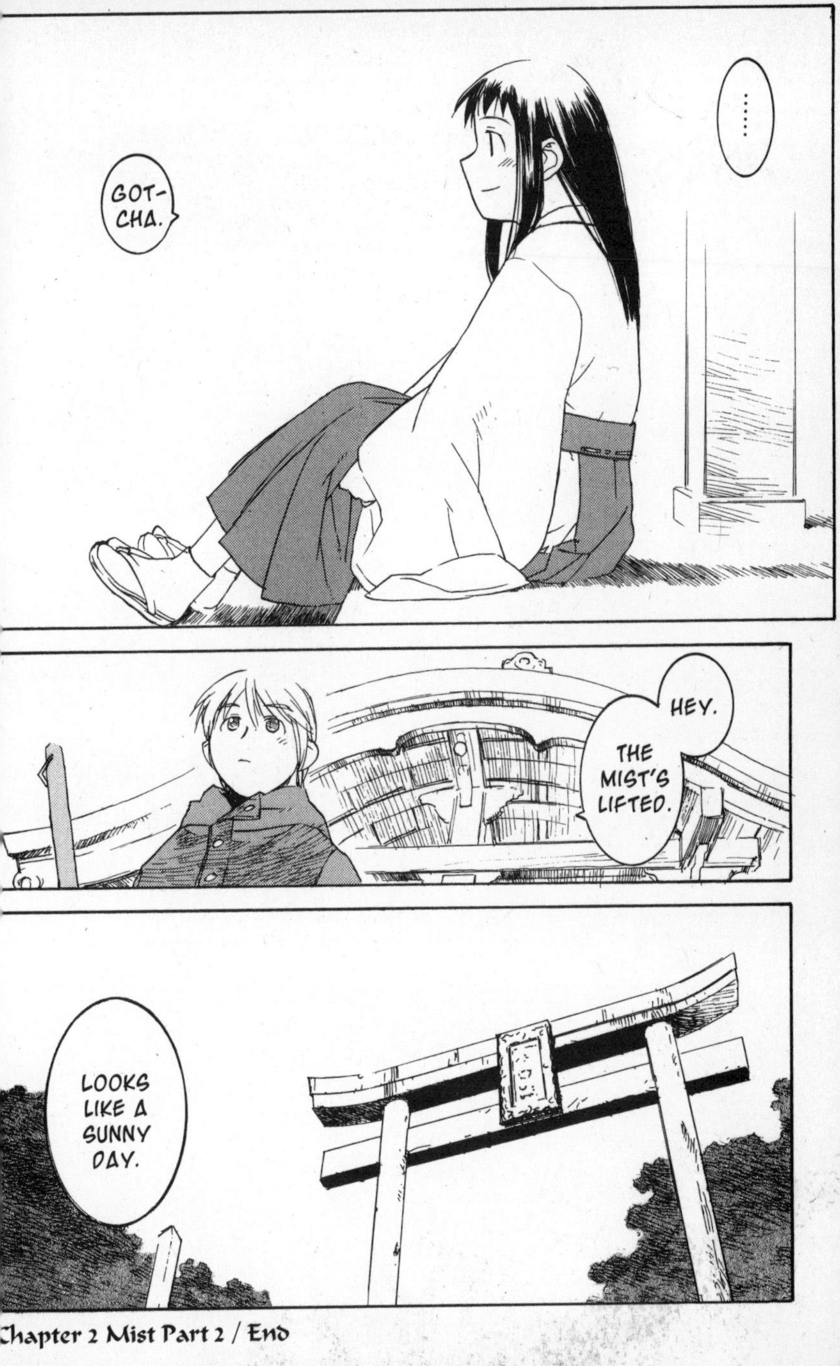
......
GOT-CHA.
HEY.
THE MIST'S LIFTED.
LOOKS LIKE A SUNNY DAY.

Chapter 2 Mist Part 2 / End

Shrine of the Morning Mist

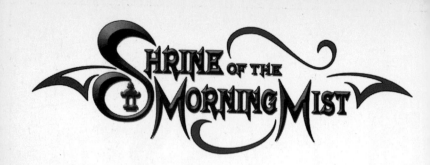

Chapter 3 Freeloader

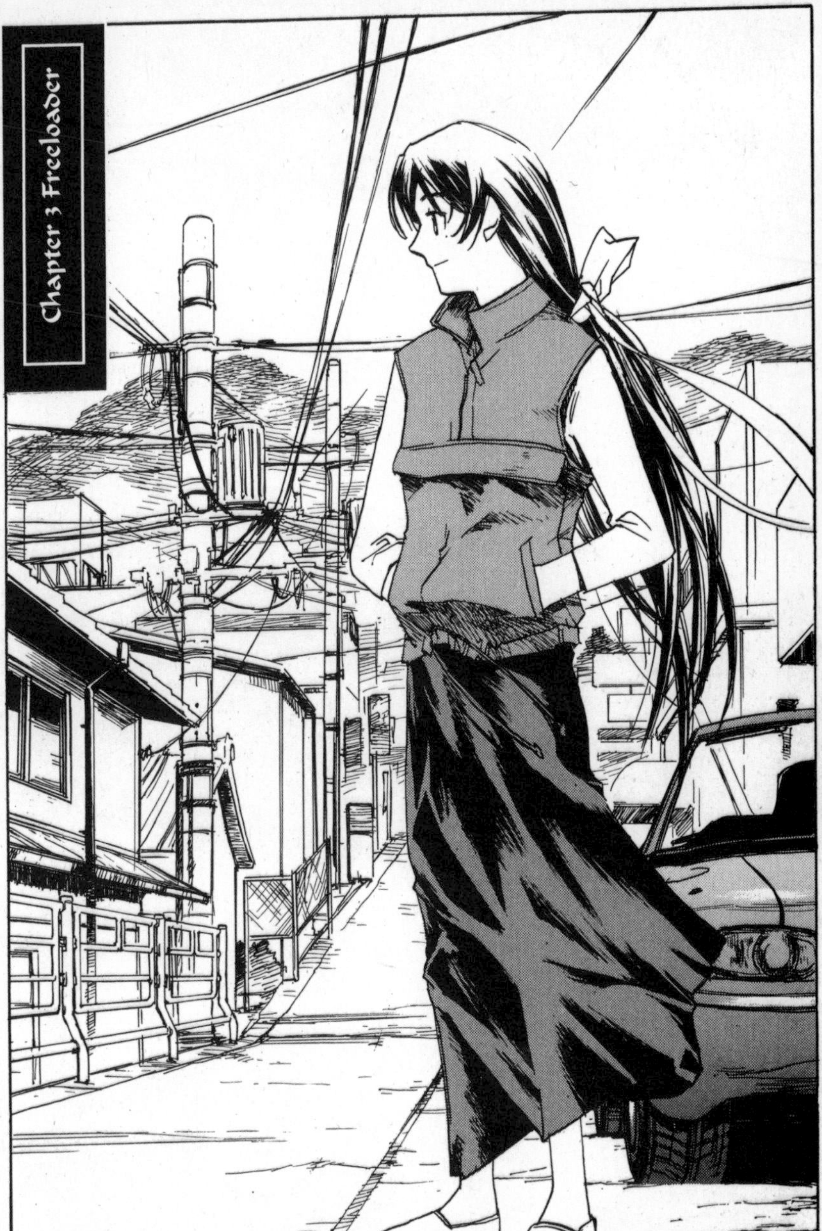

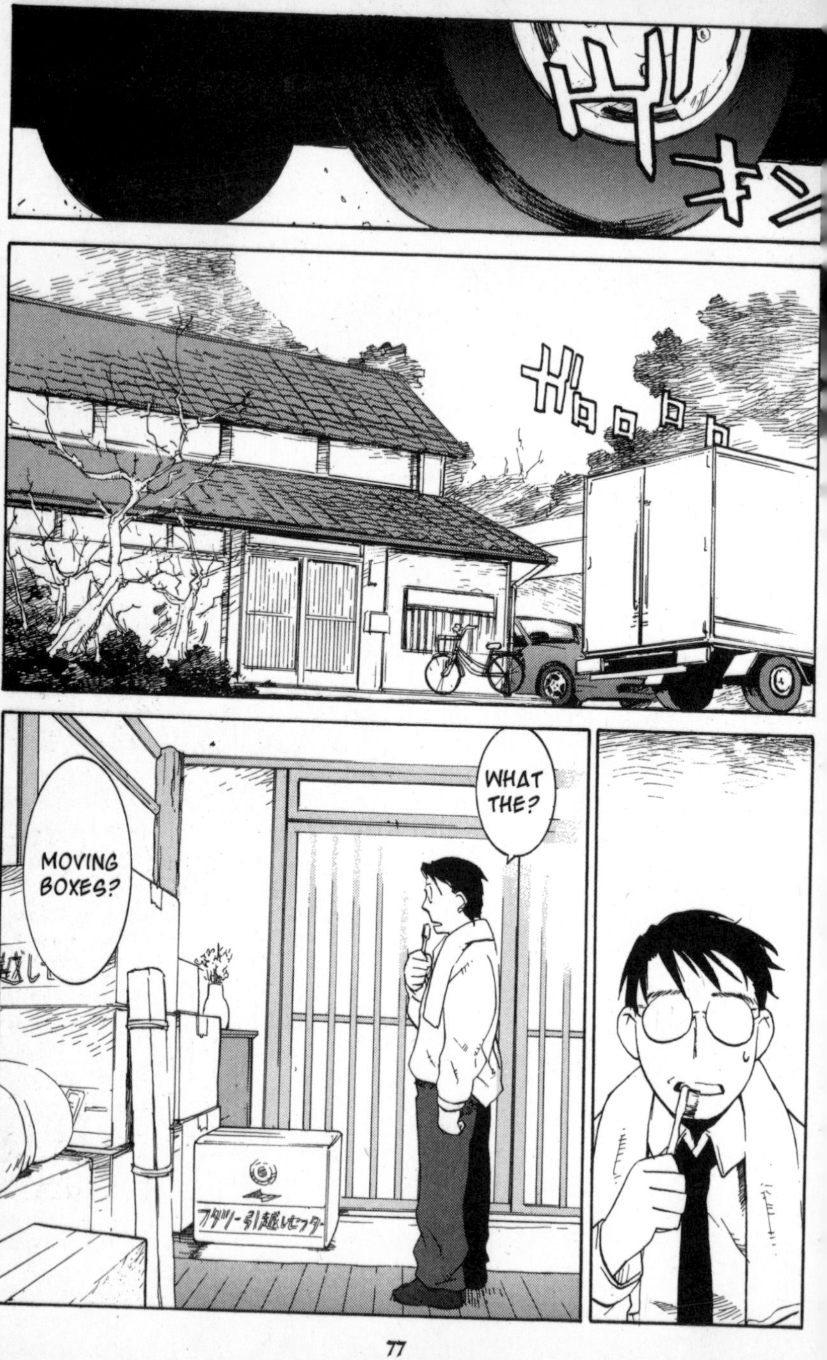
WHAT THE?
MOVING BOXES?
フタツー引越しセンター

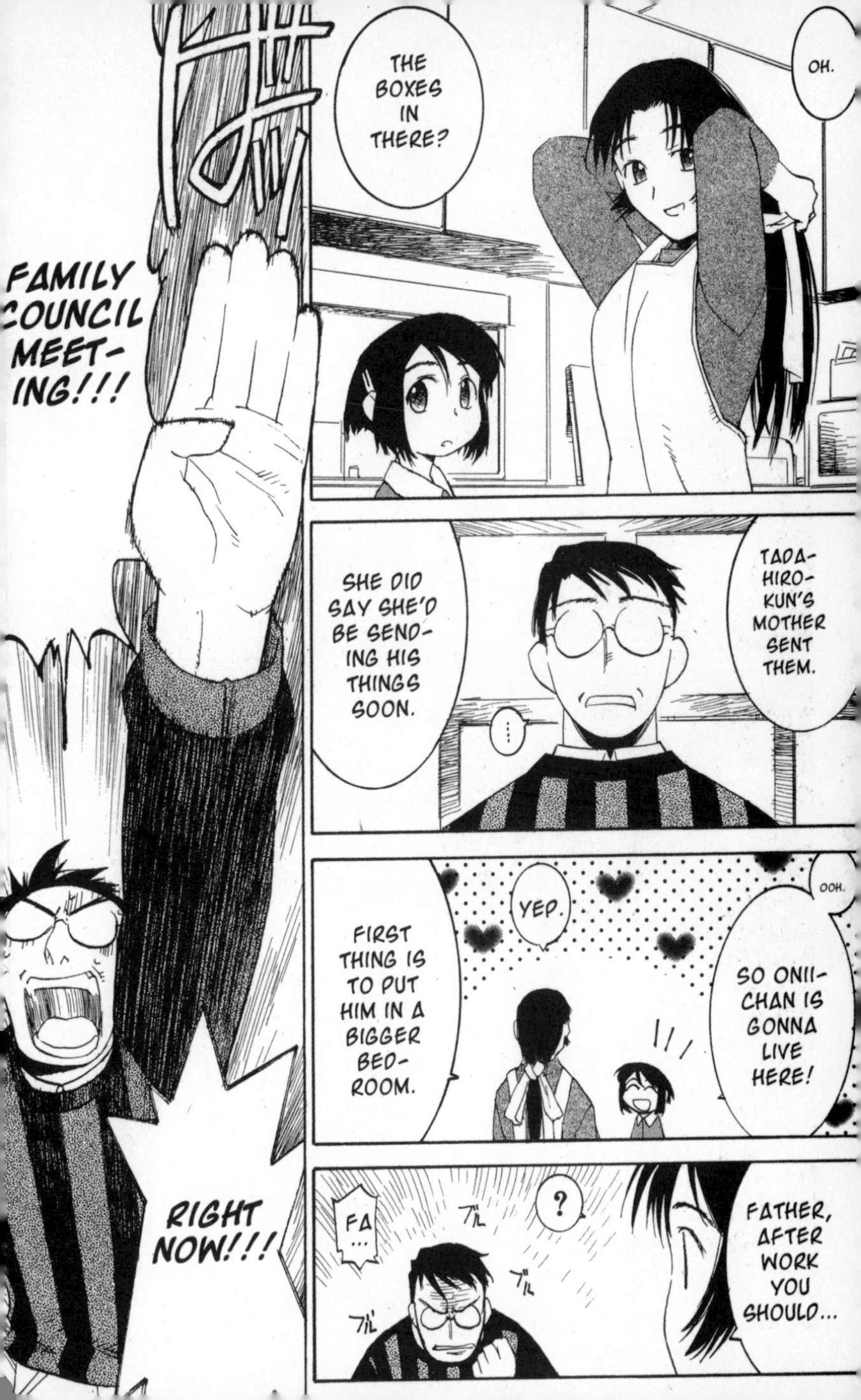
OH.
THE BOXES IN THERE?
TADA-HIRO-KUN'S MOTHER SENT THEM.
...
SHE DID SAY SHE'D BE SEND-ING HIS THINGS SOON.
OOH.
SO ONII-CHAN IS GONNA LIVE HERE!
YEP.
FIRST THING IS TO PUT HIM IN A BIGGER BED-ROOM.
FATHER, AFTER WORK YOU SHOULD...
?
ブル
ブル
ブル
FA...
FAMILY COUNCIL MEET-ING!!!
RIGHT NOW!!!

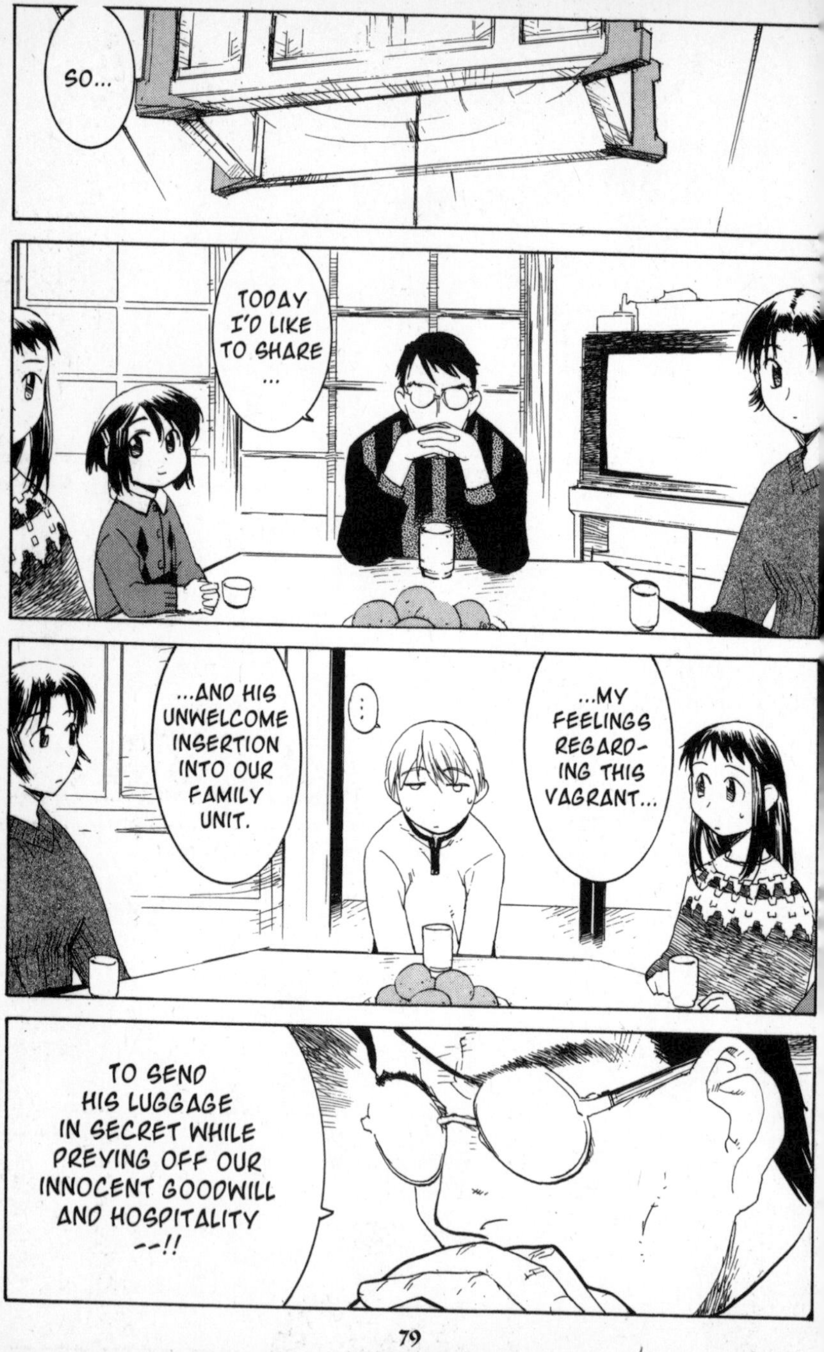
SO...
TODAY I'D LIKE TO SHARE ...
...MY FEELINGS REGARDING THIS VAGRANT...
...
...AND HIS UNWELCOME INSERTION INTO OUR FAMILY UNIT.
TO SEND HIS LUGGAGE IN SECRET WHILE PREYING OFF OUR INNOCENT GOODWILL AND HOSPITALITY --!!

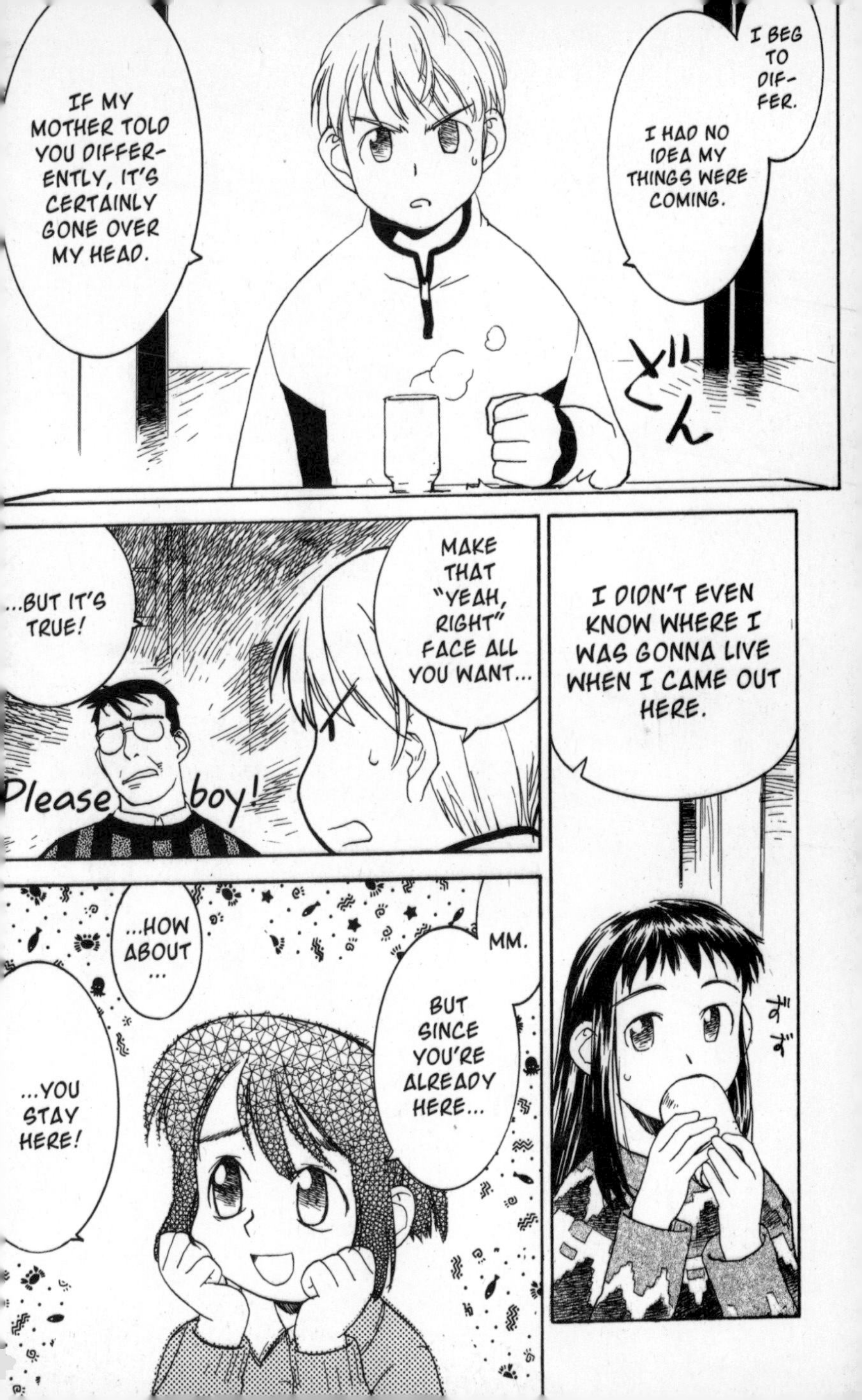
I BEG TO DIF-FER.
I HAD NO IDEA MY THINGS WERE COMING.
どん
IF MY MOTHER TOLD YOU DIFFER-ENTLY, IT'S CERTAINLY GONE OVER MY HEAD.
I DIDN'T EVEN KNOW WHERE I WAS GONNA LIVE WHEN I CAME OUT HERE.
MAKE THAT "YEAH, RIGHT" FACE ALL YOU WANT...
...BUT IT'S TRUE!
Please boy!
ずず
MM.
BUT SINCE YOU'RE ALREADY HERE...
...HOW ABOUT...
...YOU STAY HERE!

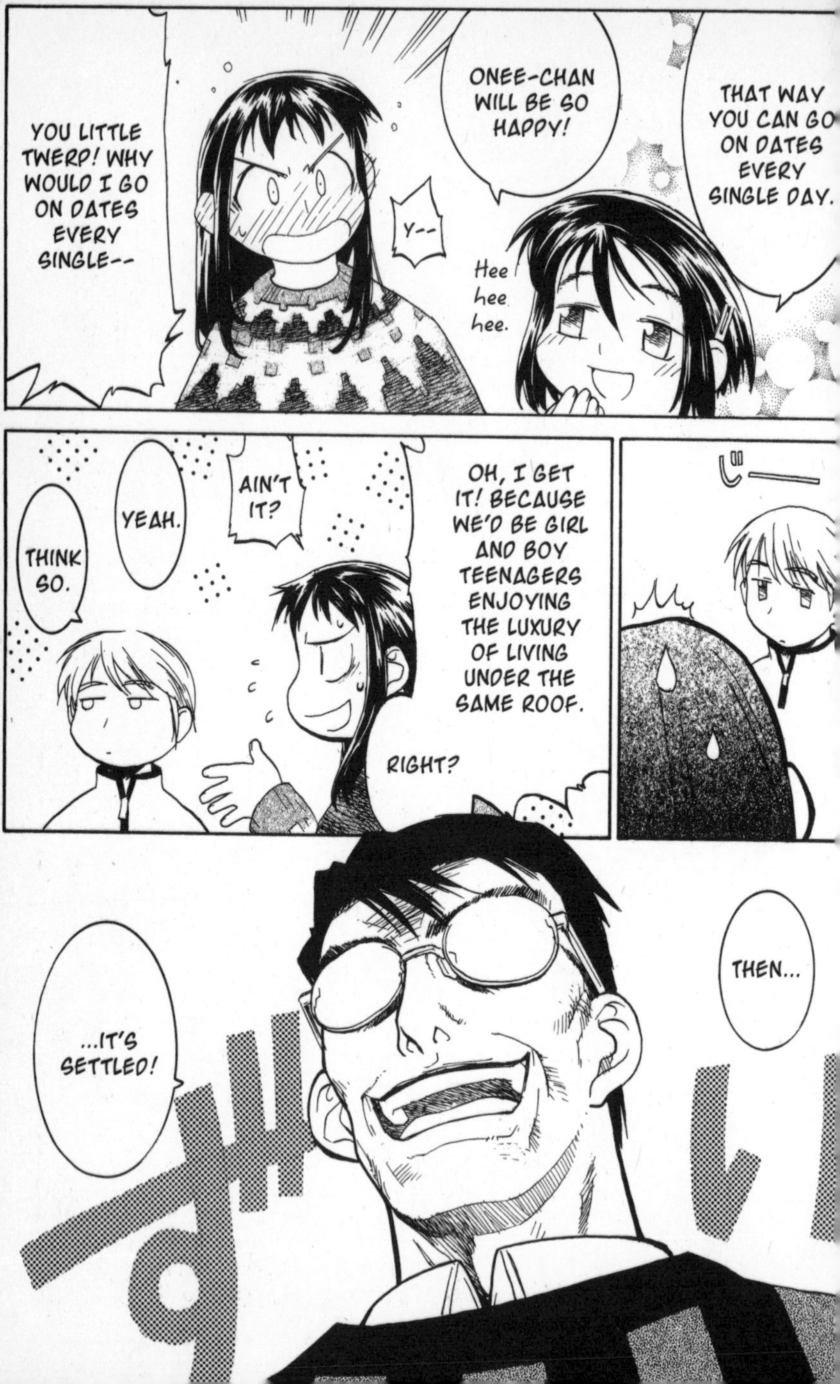
THAT WAY YOU CAN GO ON DATES EVERY SINGLE DAY.
ONEE-CHAN WILL BE SO HAPPY!
Hee hee hee.
Y--
YOU LITTLE TWERP! WHY WOULD I GO ON DATES EVERY SINGLE--
じー
OH, I GET IT! BECAUSE WE'D BE GIRL AND BOY TEENAGERS ENJOYING THE LUXURY OF LIVING UNDER THE SAME ROOF.
RIGHT?
AIN'T IT?
YEAH.
THINK SO.
THEN...
...IT'S SETTLED!

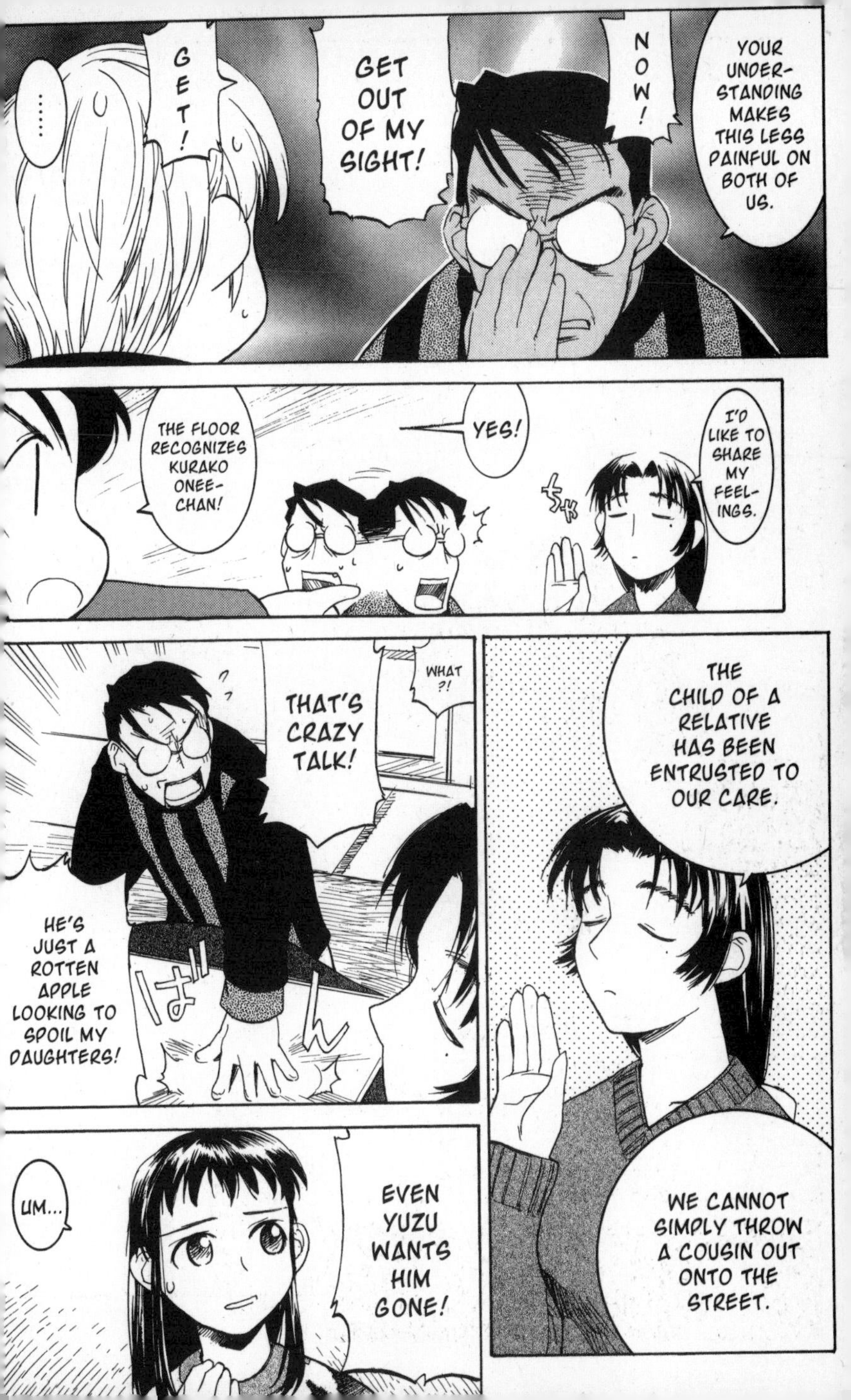
YOUR UNDER-STANDING MAKES THIS LESS PAINFUL ON BOTH OF US.
NOW!
GET OUT OF MY SIGHT!
GET!
......
I'D LIKE TO SHARE MY FEEL-INGS.
ちゃ
YES!
THE FLOOR RECOGNIZES KURAKO ONEE-CHAN!
THE CHILD OF A RELATIVE HAS BEEN ENTRUSTED TO OUR CARE.
WE CANNOT SIMPLY THROW A COUSIN OUT ONTO THE STREET.
WHAT?!
THAT'S CRAZY TALK!
HE'S JUST A ROTTEN APPLE LOOKING TO SPOIL MY DAUGHTERS!
ばん
EVEN YUZU WANTS HIM GONE!
UM...

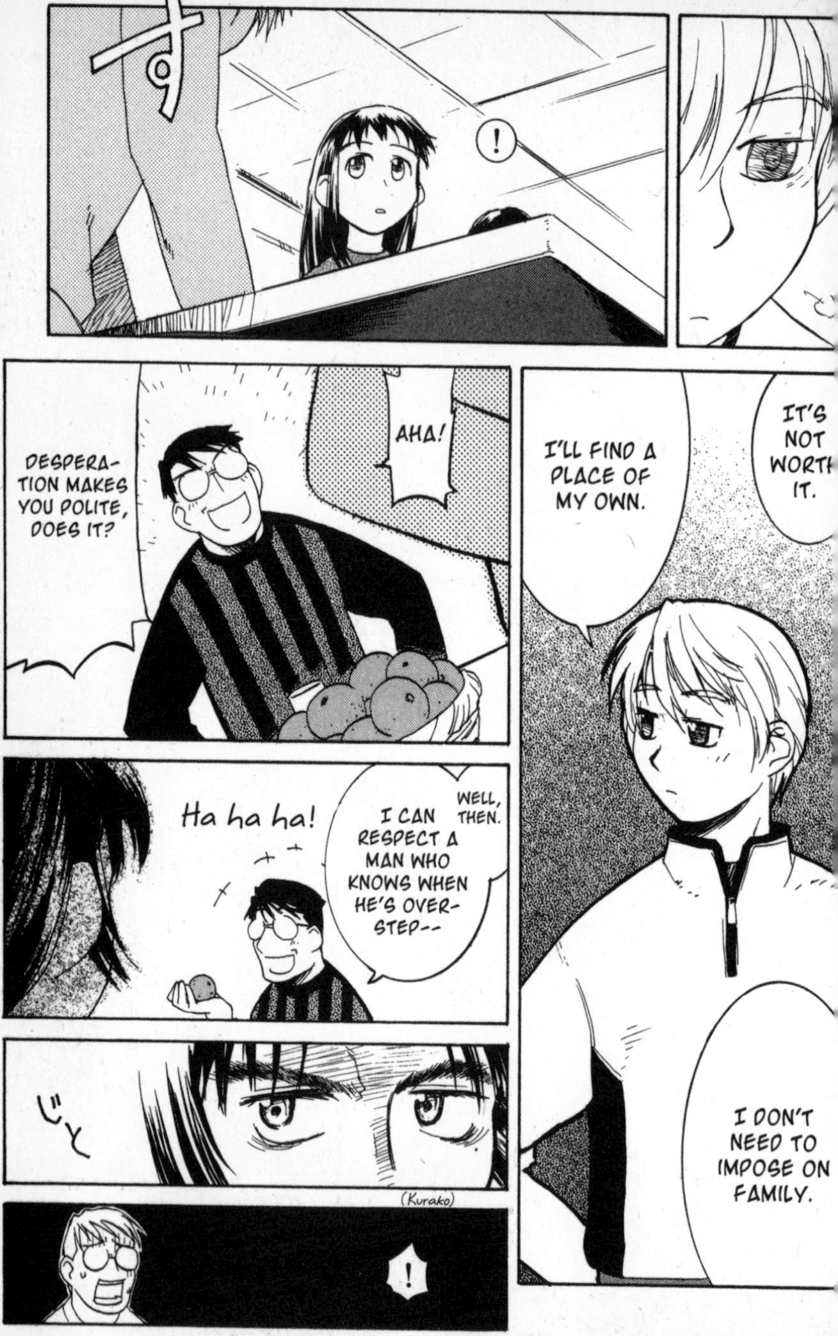
す
!
IT'S NOT WORTH IT.
I'LL FIND A PLACE OF MY OWN.
I DON'T NEED TO IMPOSE ON FAMILY.
AHA!
DESPERA-TION MAKES YOU POLITE, DOES IT?
WELL, THEN.
I CAN RESPECT A MAN WHO KNOWS WHEN HE'S OVER-STEP--
Ha ha ha!
じと
(Kurako)
!

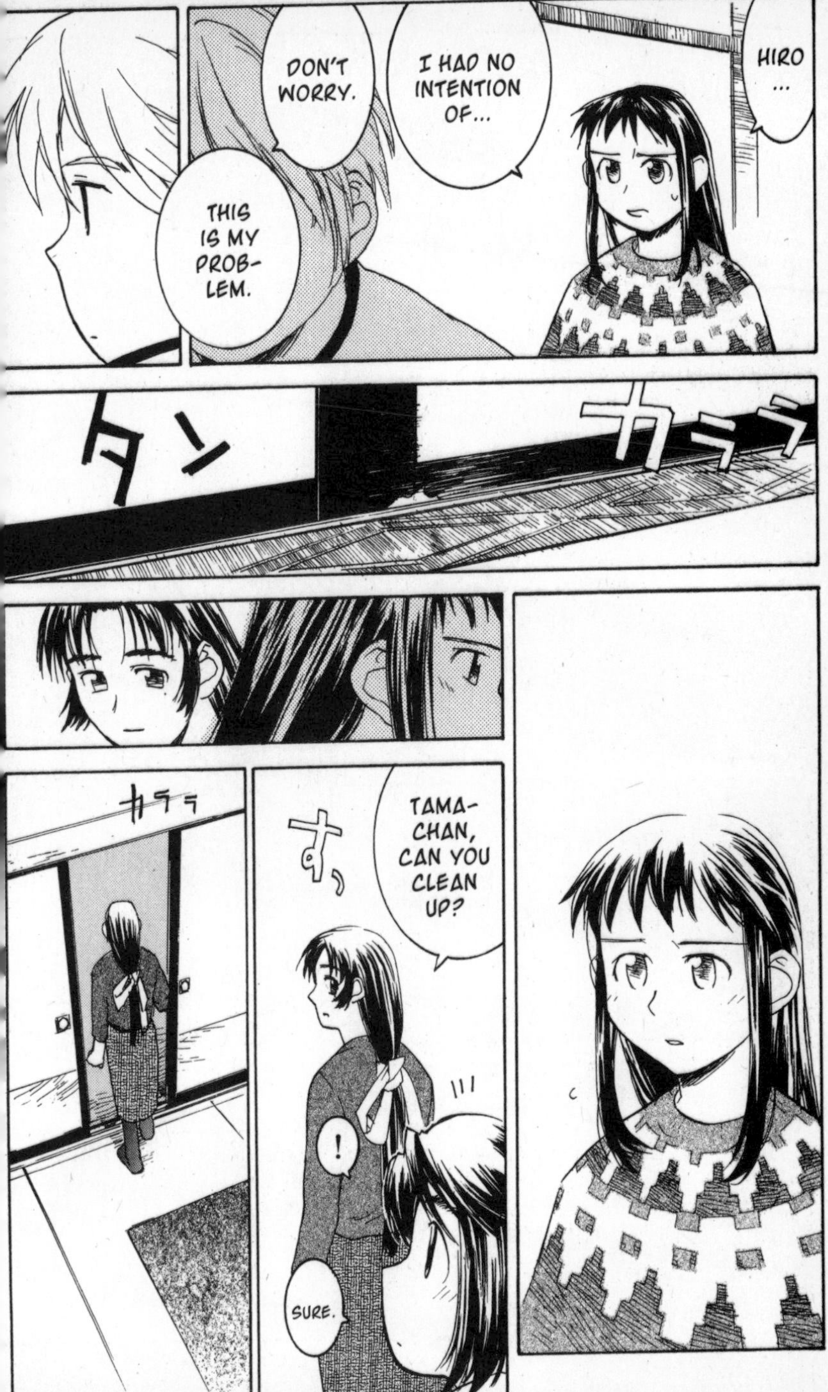
HIRO ...
I HAD NO INTENTION OF...
DON'T WORRY.
THIS IS MY PROB-LEM.
カララ
タン
TAMA-CHAN, CAN YOU CLEAN UP?
すっ
!
SURE.
カララ

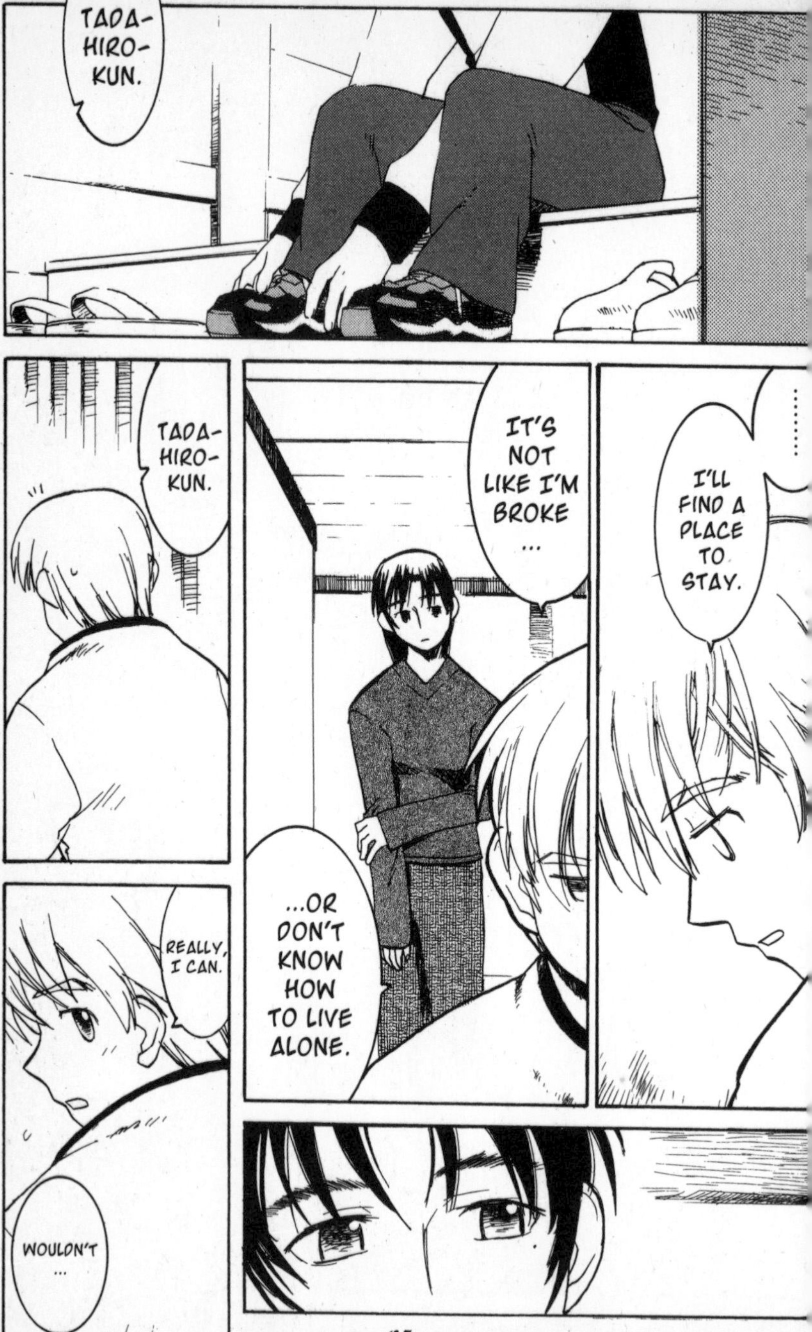
TADA-HIRO-KUN.
......
I'LL FIND A PLACE TO STAY.
IT'S NOT LIKE I'M BROKE ...
...OR DON'T KNOW HOW TO LIVE ALONE.
TADA-HIRO-KUN.
REALLY, I CAN.
WOULDN'T ...

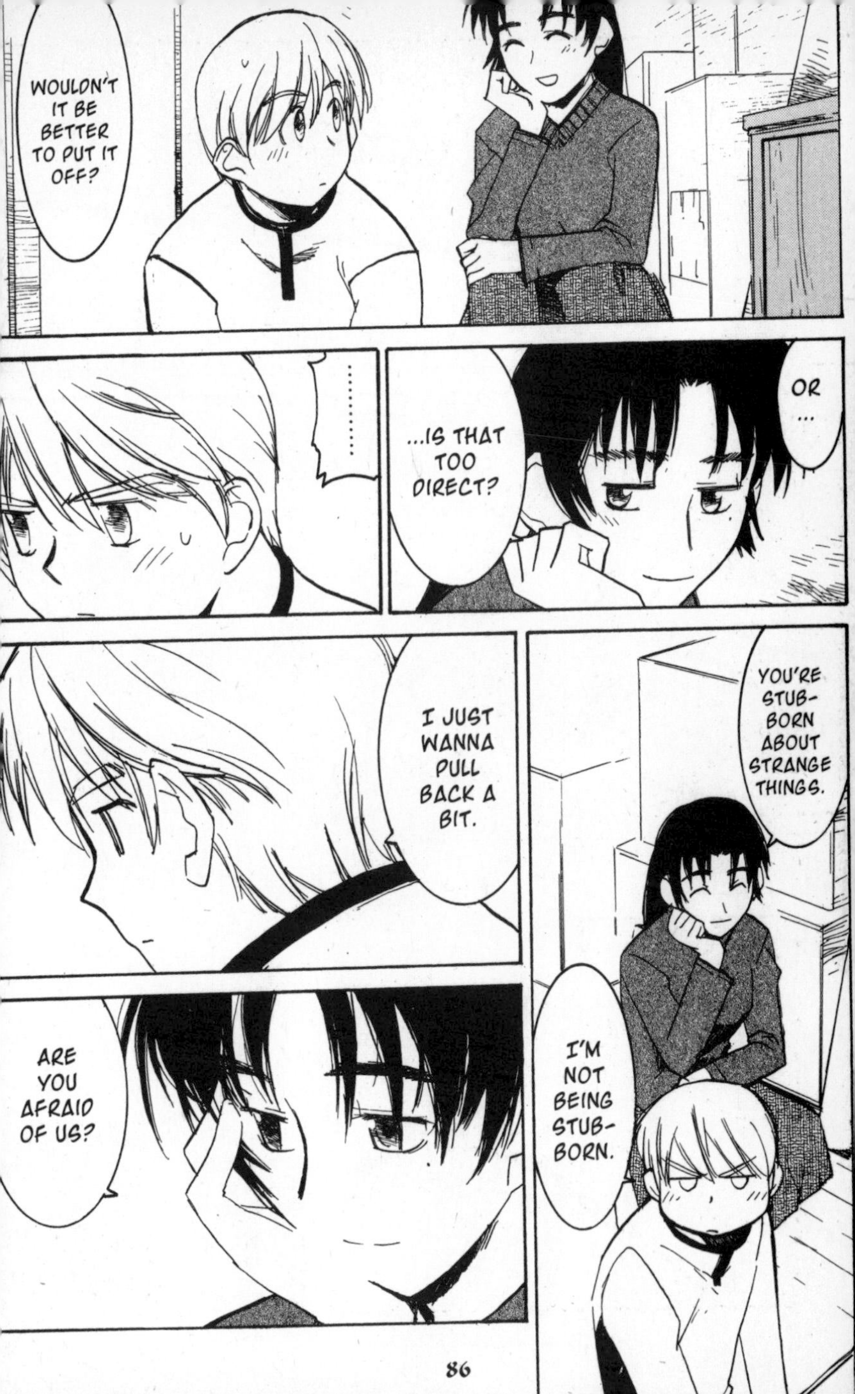
WOULDN'T IT BE BETTER TO PUT IT OFF?
OR ...
...IS THAT TOO DIRECT?
......
YOU'RE STUB-BORN ABOUT STRANGE THINGS.
I'M NOT BEING STUB-BORN.
I JUST WANNA PULL BACK A BIT.
ARE YOU AFRAID OF US?

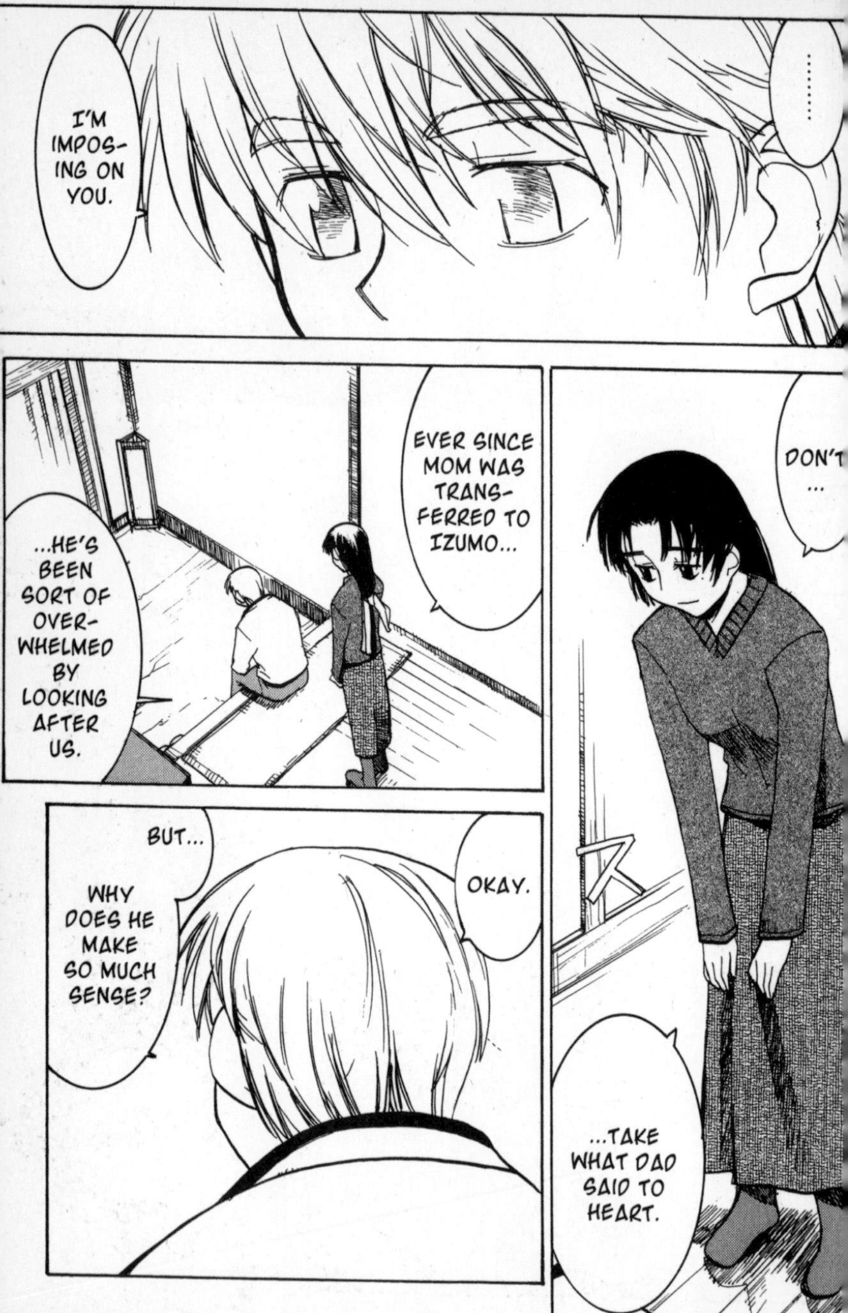
......
I'M IMPOSING ON YOU.
DON'T ...
...TAKE WHAT DAD SAID TO HEART.
EVER SINCE MOM WAS TRANSFERRED TO IZUMO...
...HE'S BEEN SORT OF OVERWHELMED BY LOOKING AFTER US.
OKAY.
BUT...
WHY DOES HE MAKE SO MUCH SENSE?

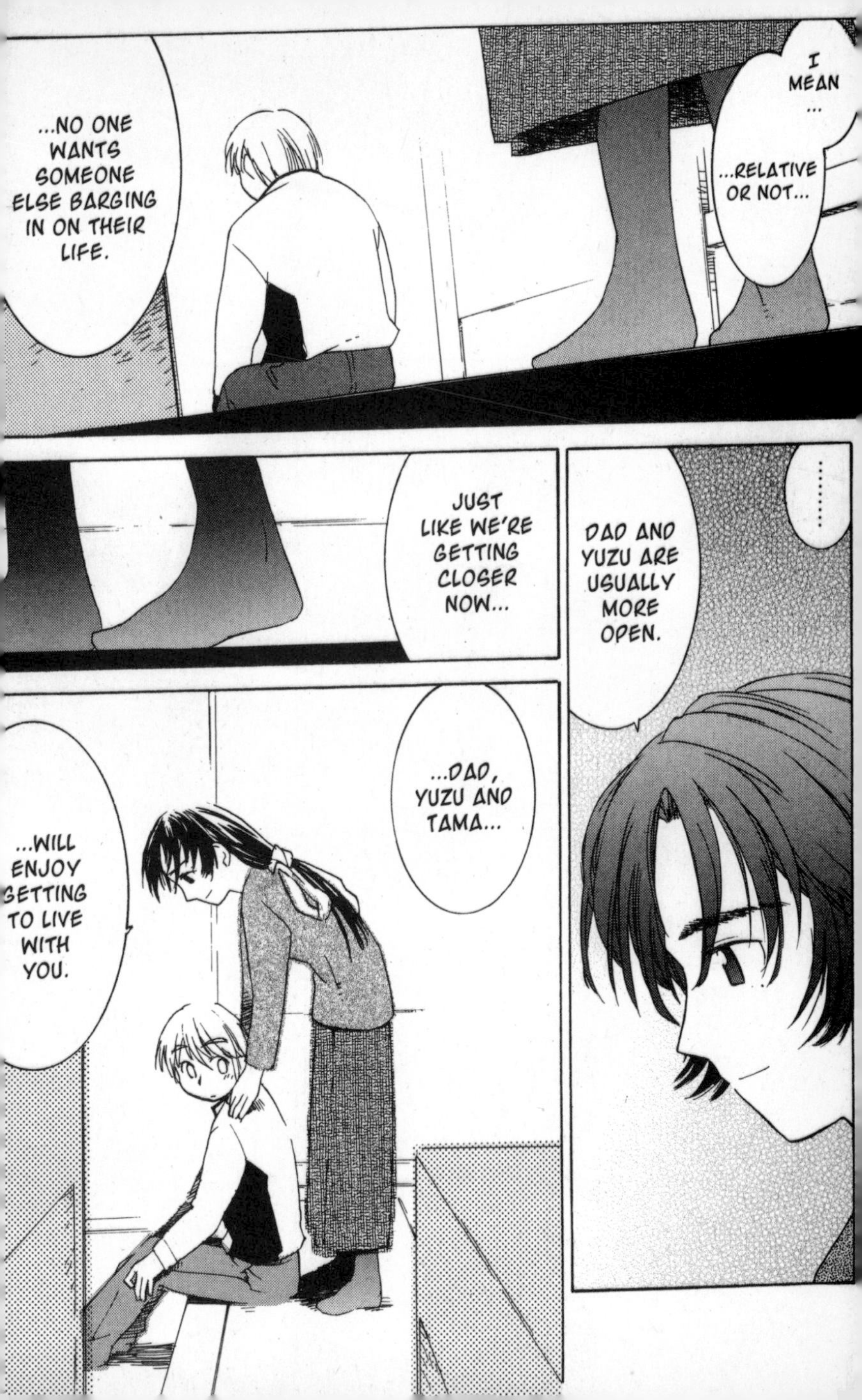
I MEAN ...
...RELATIVE OR NOT...
...NO ONE WANTS SOMEONE ELSE BARGING IN ON THEIR LIFE.
......
DAD AND YUZU ARE USUALLY MORE OPEN.
JUST LIKE WE'RE GETTING CLOSER NOW...
...DAD, YUZU AND TAMA...
...WILL ENJOY GETTING TO LIVE WITH YOU.

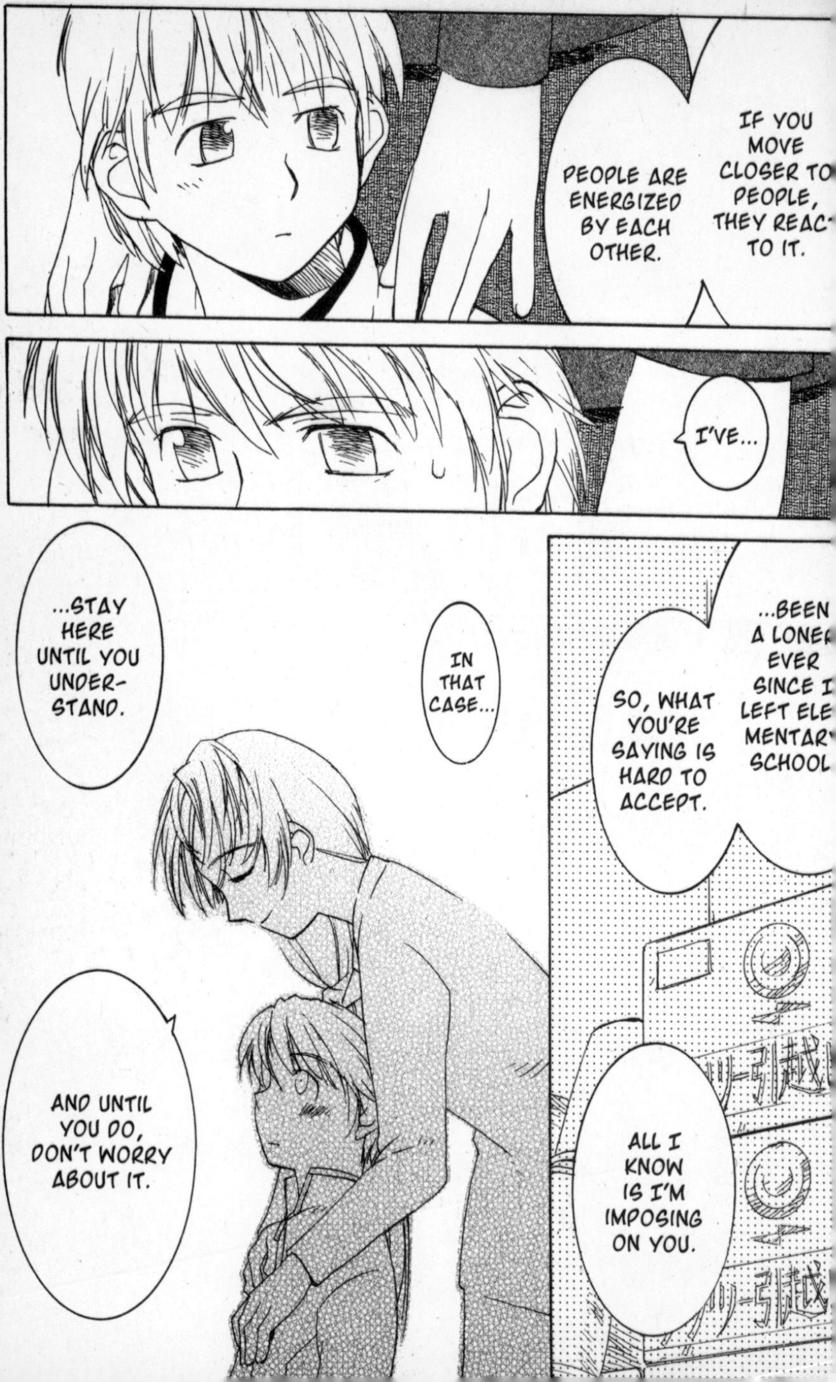
IF YOU MOVE CLOSER TO PEOPLE, THEY REACT TO IT.
PEOPLE ARE ENERGIZED BY EACH OTHER.
I'VE...
...BEEN A LONER EVER SINCE I LEFT ELEMENTARY SCHOOL
SO, WHAT YOU'RE SAYING IS HARD TO ACCEPT.
ALL I KNOW IS I'M IMPOSING ON YOU.
IN THAT CASE...
...STAY HERE UNTIL YOU UNDER-STAND.
AND UNTIL YOU DO, DON'T WORRY ABOUT IT.

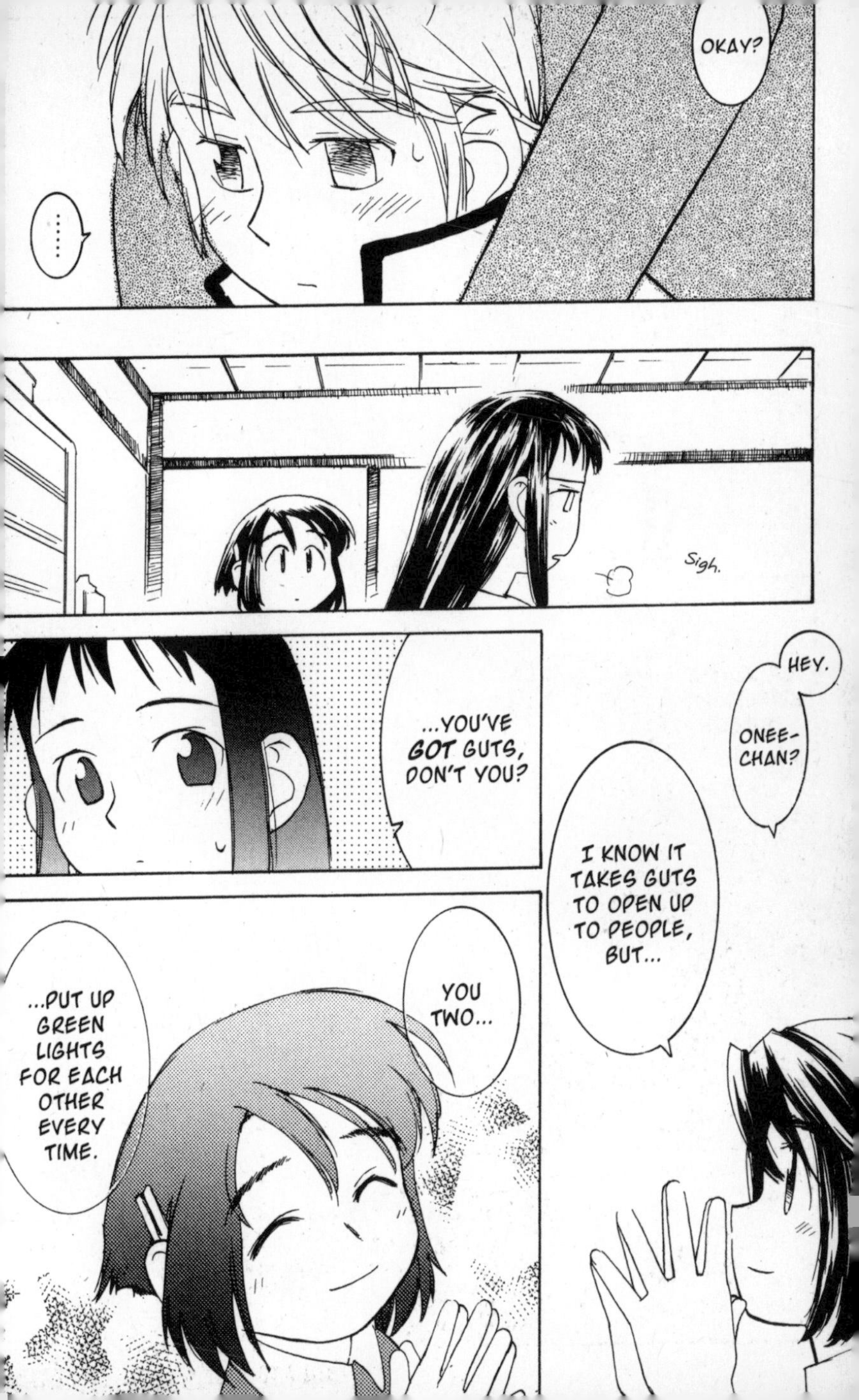
OKAY?
......
Sigh.
HEY.
ONEE-CHAN?
...YOU'VE GOT GUTS, DON'T YOU?
I KNOW IT TAKES GUTS TO OPEN UP TO PEOPLE, BUT...
YOU TWO...
...PUT UP GREEN LIGHTS FOR EACH OTHER EVERY TIME.

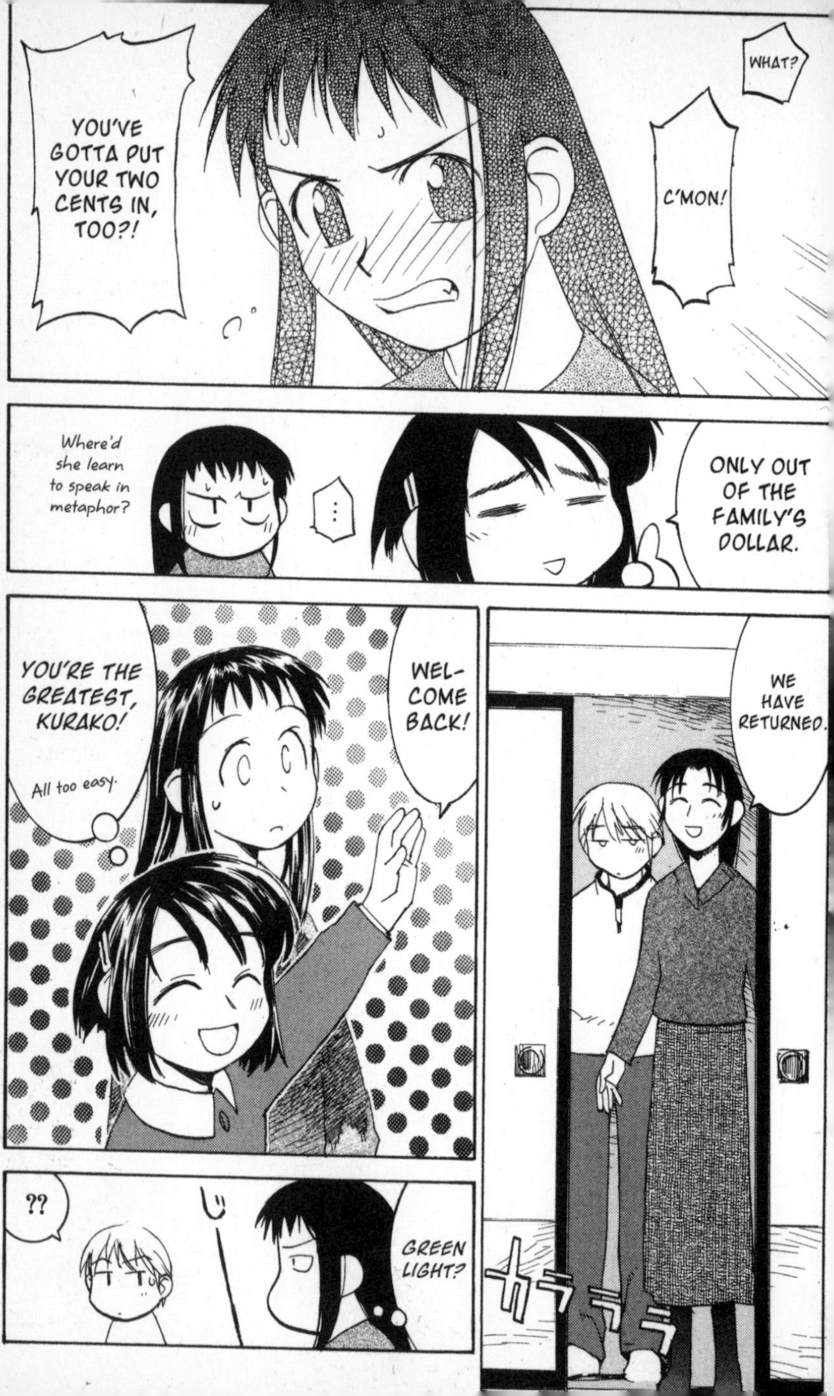
WHAT?
C'MON!
YOU'VE GOTTA PUT YOUR TWO CENTS IN, TOO?!
ONLY OUT OF THE FAMILY'S DOLLAR.
…
Where'd she learn to speak in metaphor?
WE HAVE RETURNED.
カラララ
WEL-COME BACK!
YOU'RE THE GREATEST, KURAKO!
All too easy.
GREEN LIGHT?
じ
??

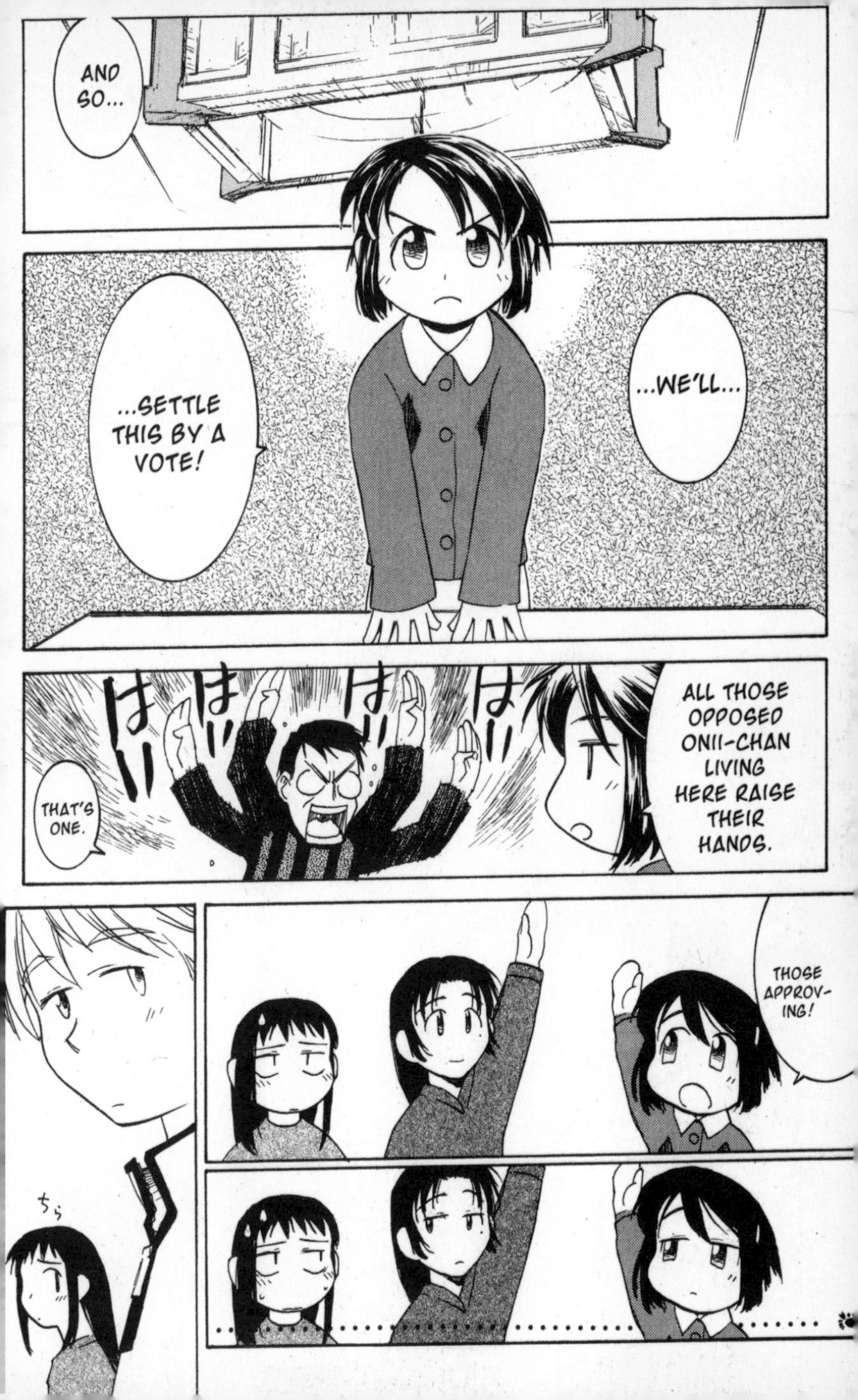
AND SO...
...WE'LL...
...SETTLE THIS BY A VOTE!
ALL THOSE OPPOSED ONII-CHAN LIVING HERE RAISE THEIR HANDS.
はい はい はい はい
THAT'S ONE.
THOSE APPROVING!
ちら

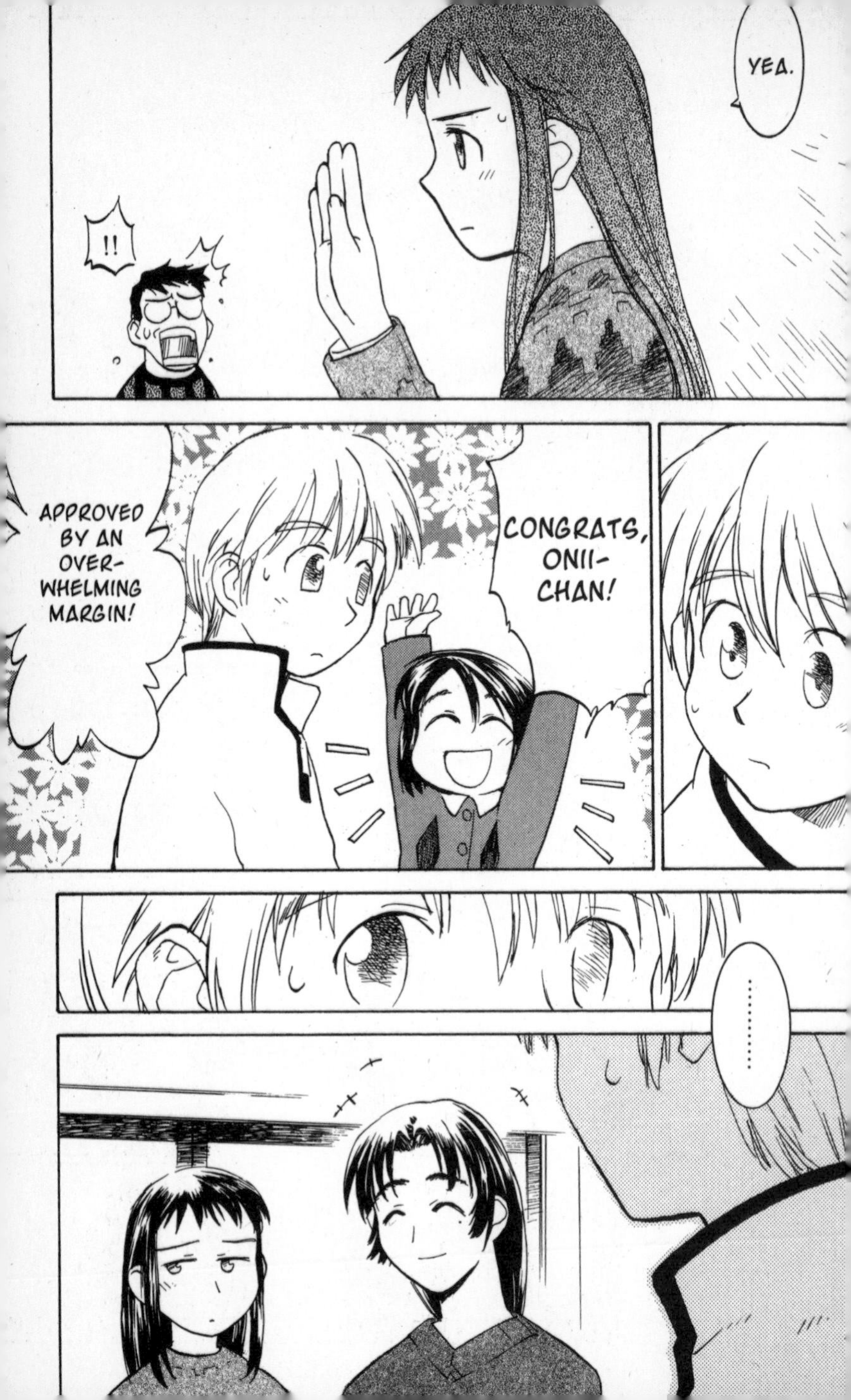
YEA.
!!
CONGRATS, ONII-CHAN!
APPROVED BY AN OVER-WHELMING MARGIN!
......

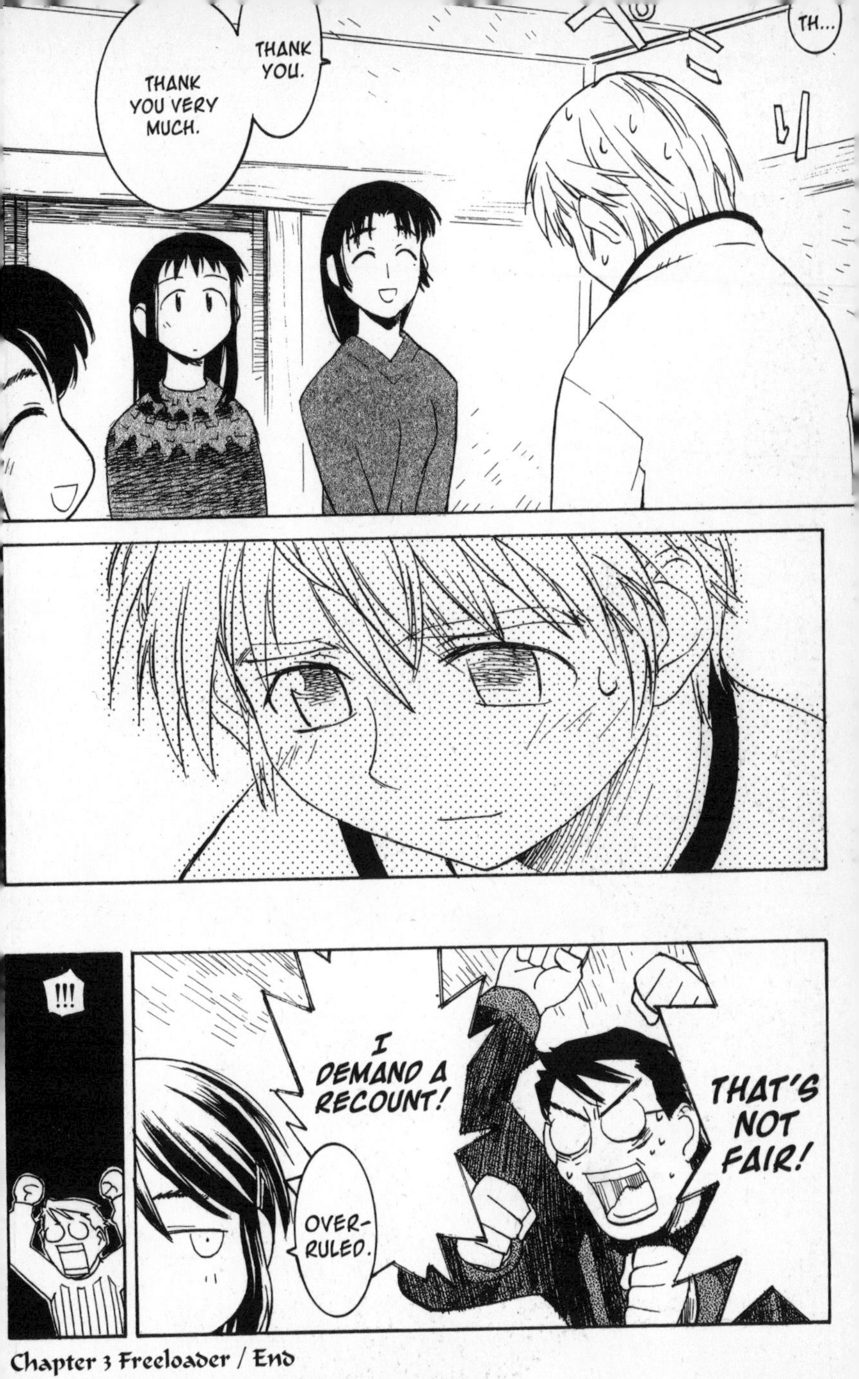
TH...
THANK YOU.
THANK YOU VERY MUCH.
THAT'S NOT FAIR!
I DEMAND A RECOUNT!
OVER-RULED.
!!!

Chapter 3 Freeloader / End

Chapter 4 Pre-Eminent Strangeness Part 1

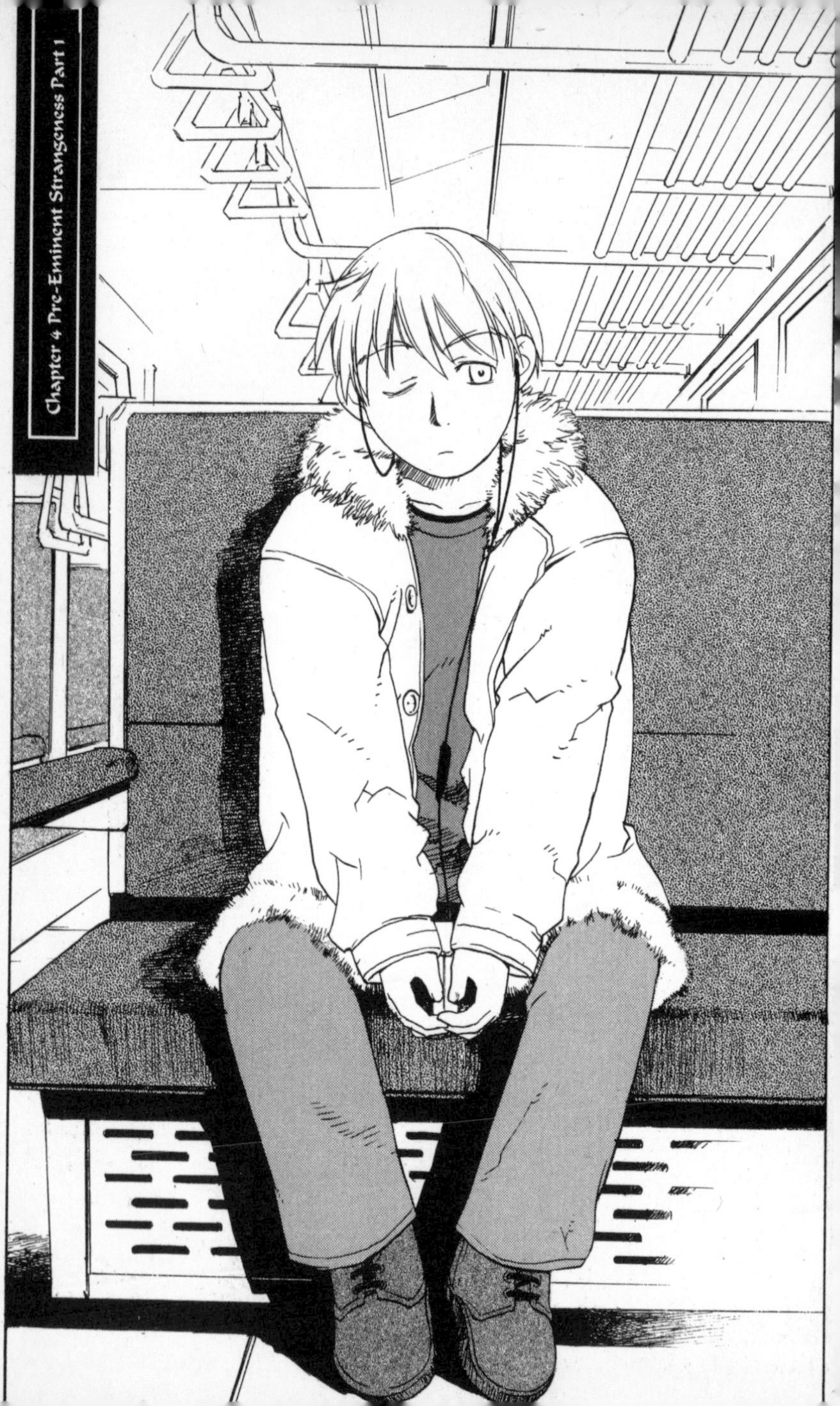

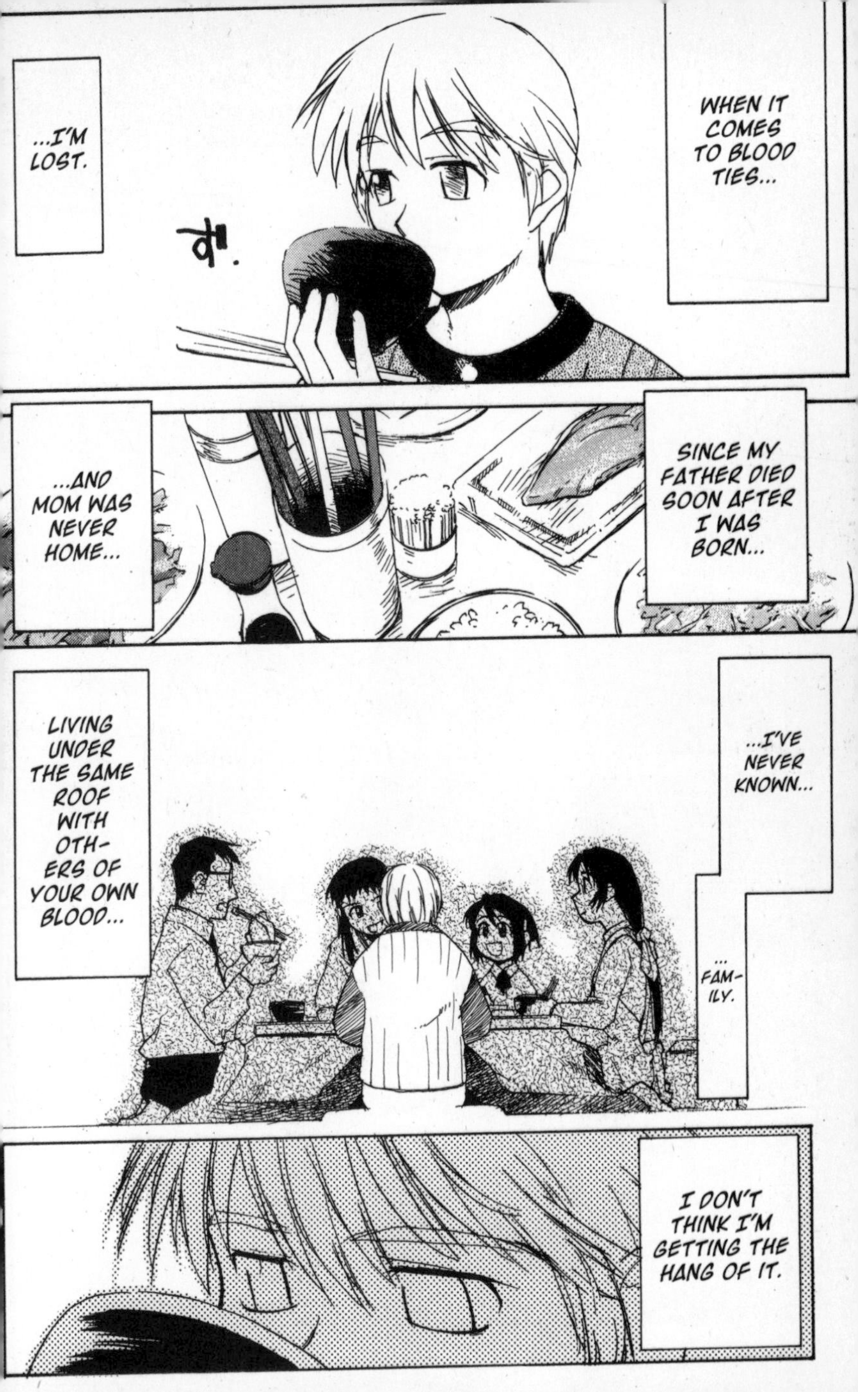
WHEN IT COMES TO BLOOD TIES...
...I'M LOST.
ず.
SINCE MY FATHER DIED SOON AFTER I WAS BORN...
...AND MOM WAS NEVER HOME...
...I'VE NEVER KNOWN...
... FAMILY.
LIVING UNDER THE SAME ROOF WITH OTHERS OF YOUR OWN BLOOD...
I DON'T THINK I'M GETTING THE HANG OF IT.

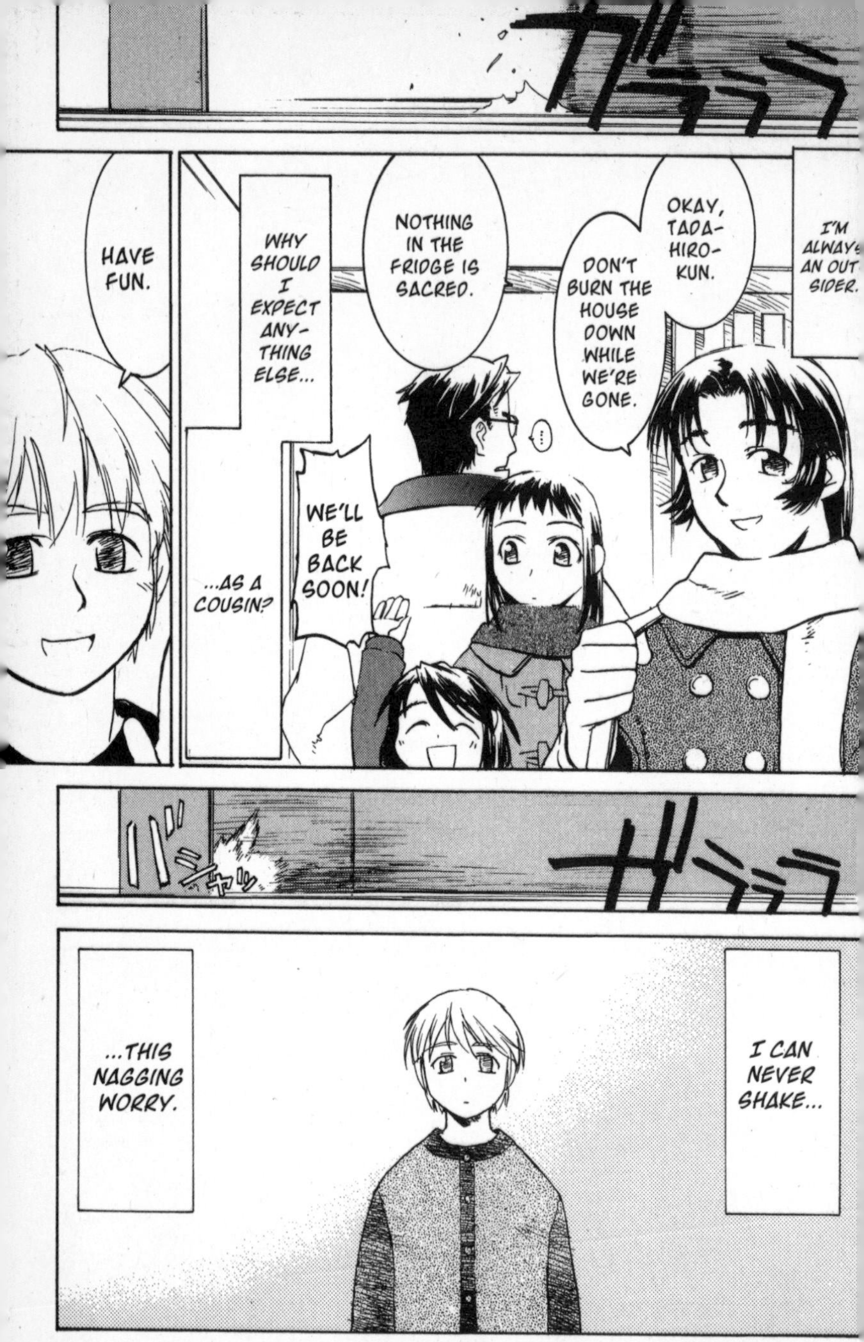
ガラララ
I'M ALWAYS AN OUTSIDER.
OKAY, TADA-HIRO-KUN.
DON'T BURN THE HOUSE DOWN WHILE WE'RE GONE.
NOTHING IN THE FRIDGE IS SACRED.
...
WE'LL BE BACK SOON!
WHY SHOULD I EXPECT ANYTHING ELSE...
...AS A COUSIN?
HAVE FUN.
ガラララ
バシャッ
I CAN NEVER SHAKE...
...THIS NAGGING WORRY.

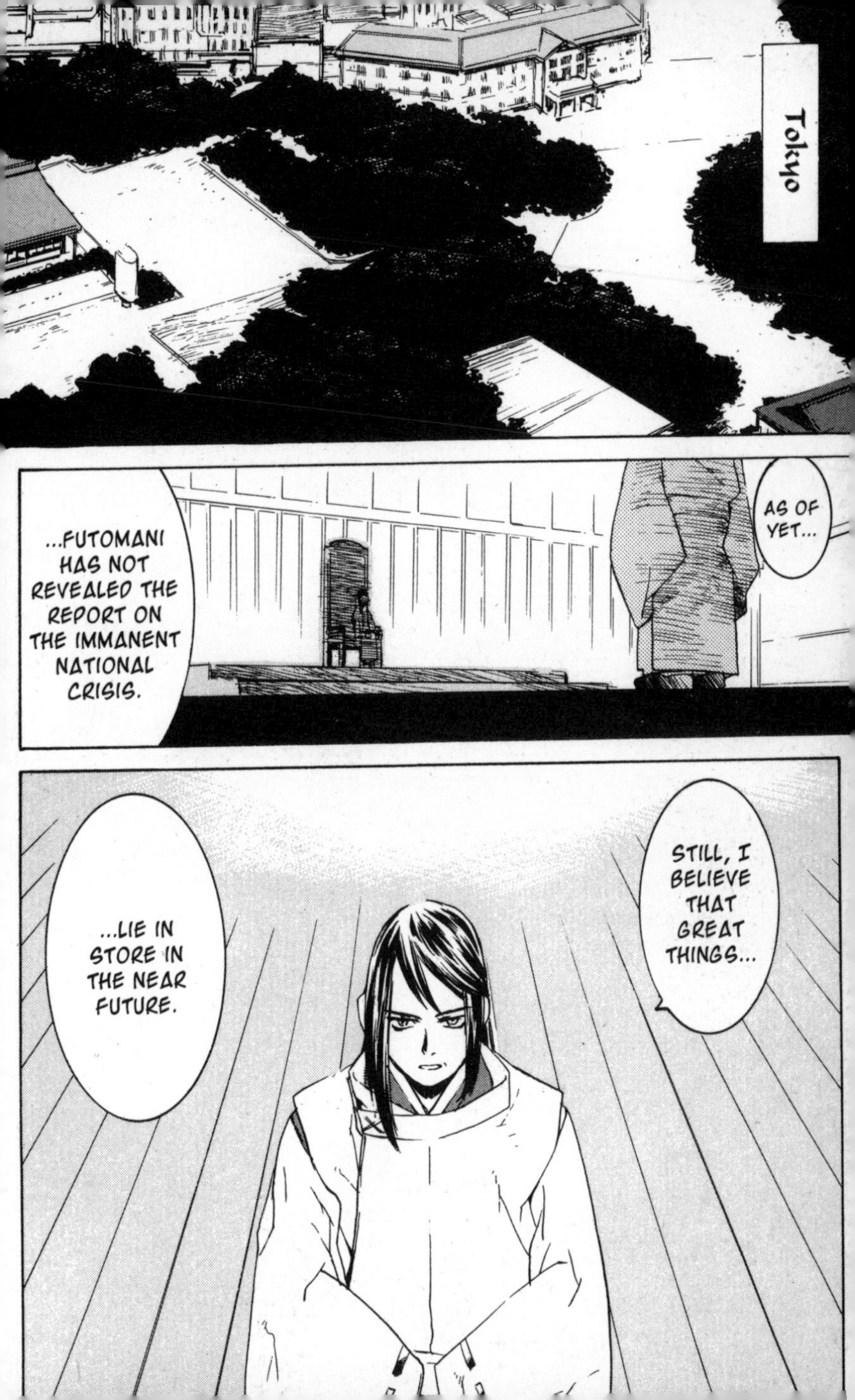
Tokyo
AS OF YET...
...FUTOMANI HAS NOT REVEALED THE REPORT ON THE IMMANENT NATIONAL CRISIS.
STILL, I BELIEVE THAT GREAT THINGS...
...LIE IN STORE IN THE NEAR FUTURE.

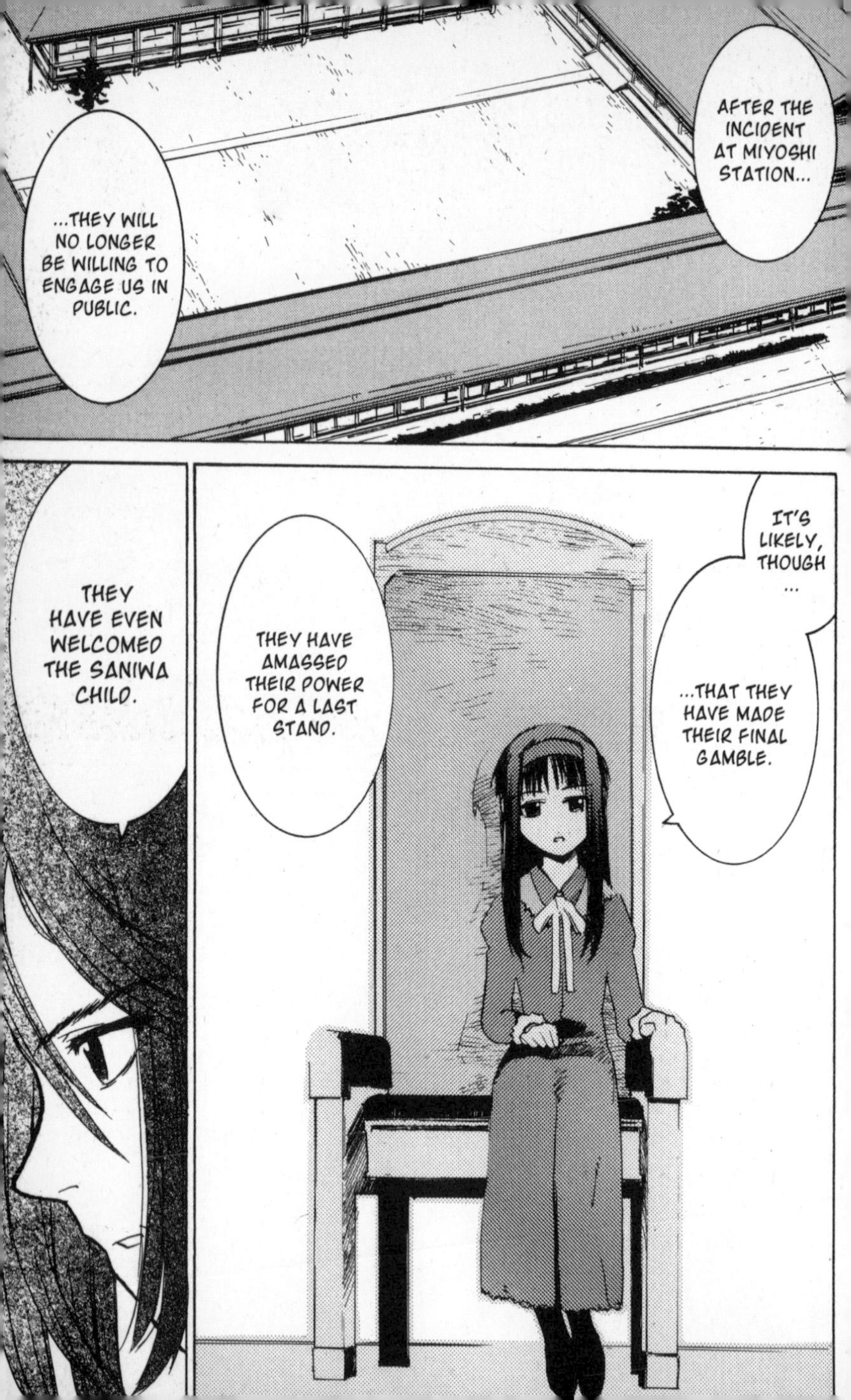
AFTER THE INCIDENT AT MIYOSHI STATION...
...THEY WILL NO LONGER BE WILLING TO ENGAGE US IN PUBLIC.
IT'S LIKELY, THOUGH ...
...THAT THEY HAVE MADE THEIR FINAL GAMBLE.
THEY HAVE AMASSED THEIR POWER FOR A LAST STAND.
THEY HAVE EVEN WELCOMED THE SANIWA CHILD.

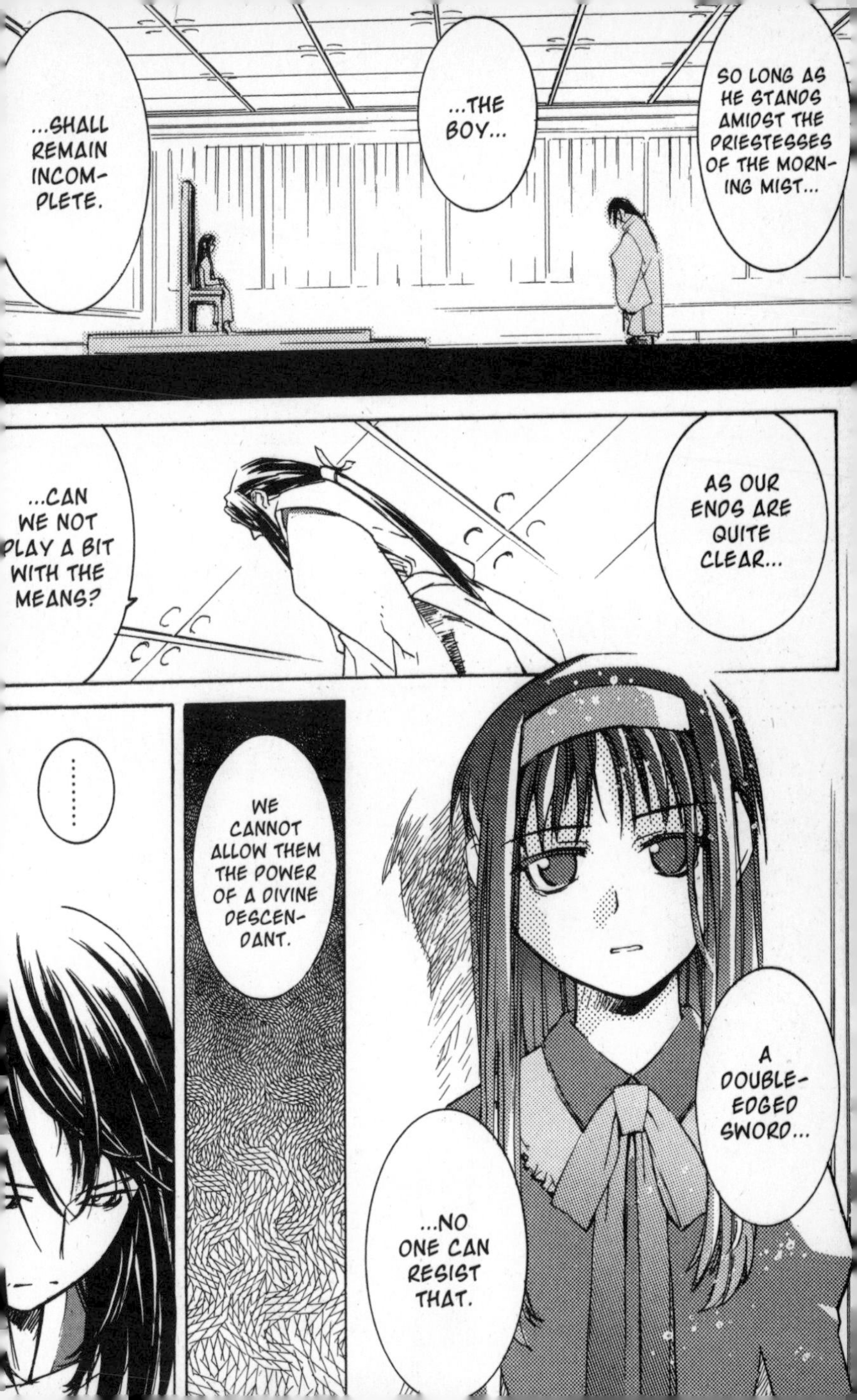
SO LONG AS HE STANDS AMIDST THE PRIESTESSES OF THE MORNING MIST...
...THE BOY...
...SHALL REMAIN INCOMPLETE.
AS OUR ENDS ARE QUITE CLEAR...
...CAN WE NOT PLAY A BIT WITH THE MEANS?
A DOUBLE-EDGED SWORD...
...NO ONE CAN RESIST THAT.
WE CANNOT ALLOW THEM THE POWER OF A DIVINE DESCENDANT.
......

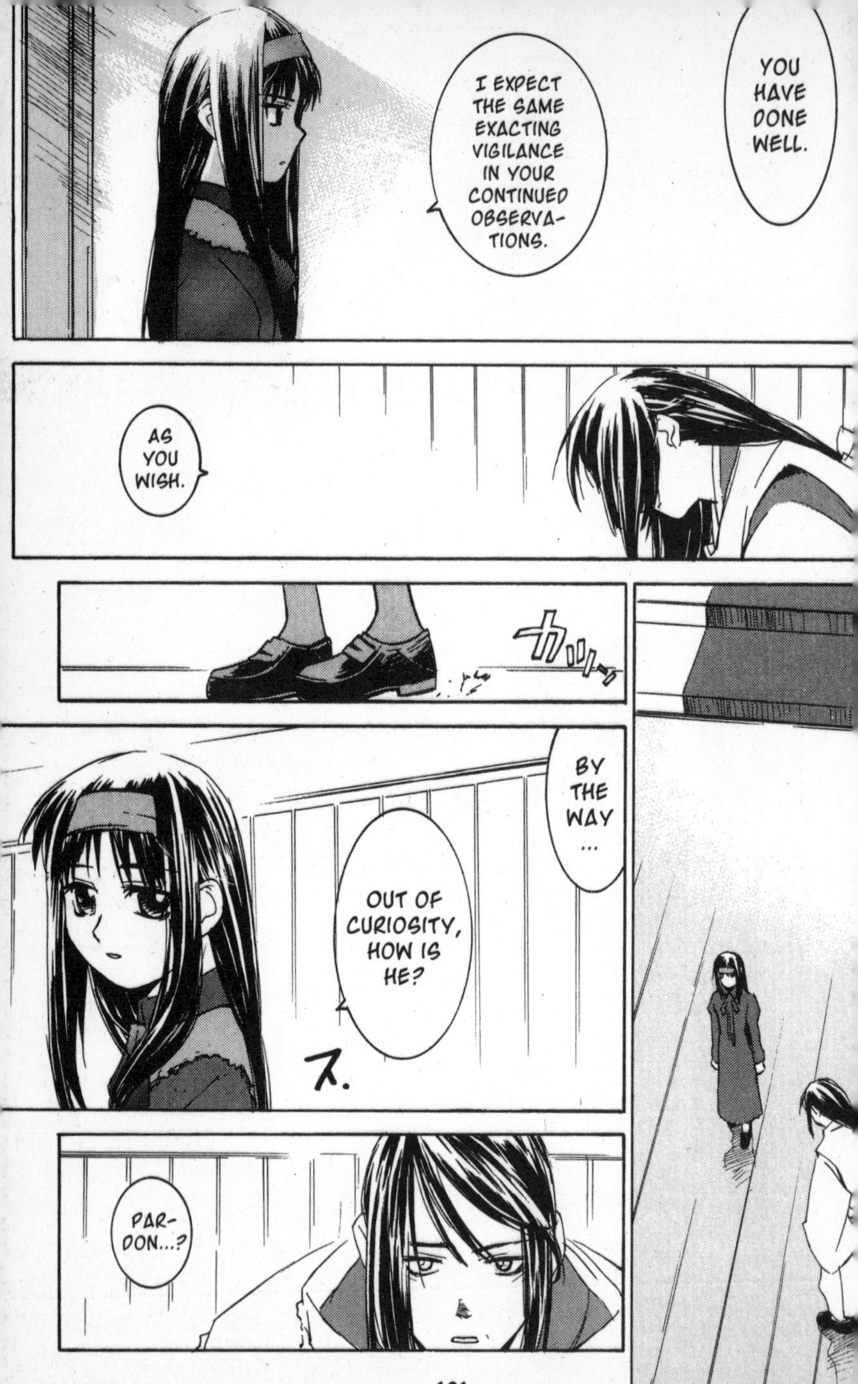
YOU HAVE DONE WELL.
I EXPECT THE SAME EXACTING VIGILANCE IN YOUR CONTINUED OBSERVATIONS.
AS YOU WISH.
BY THE WAY ...
OUT OF CURIOSITY, HOW IS HE?
ス.
PARDON...?

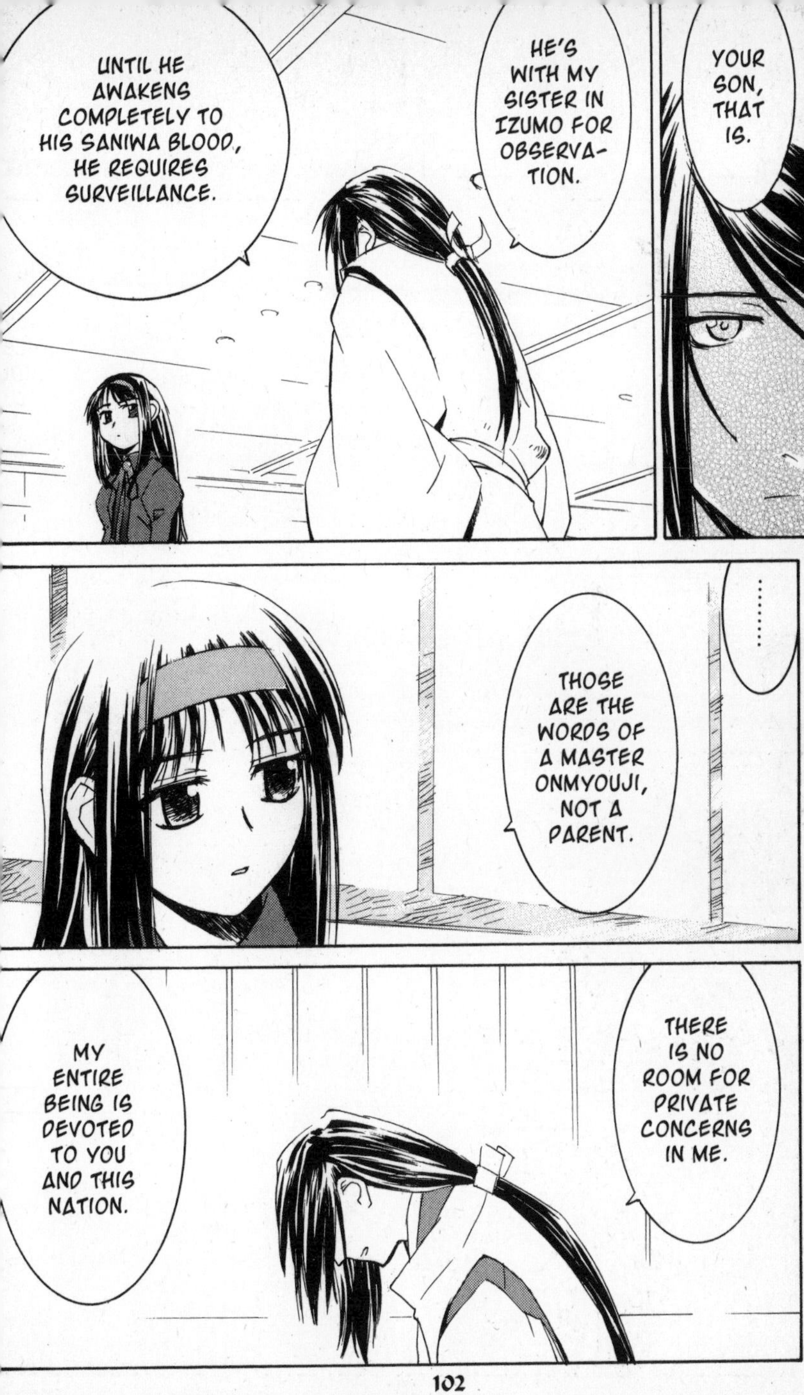
YOUR SON, THAT IS.
HE'S WITH MY SISTER IN IZUMO FOR OBSERVATION.
UNTIL HE AWAKENS COMPLETELY TO HIS SANIWA BLOOD, HE REQUIRES SURVEILLANCE.
......
THOSE ARE THE WORDS OF A MASTER ONMYOUJI, NOT A PARENT.
THERE IS NO ROOM FOR PRIVATE CONCERNS IN ME.
MY ENTIRE BEING IS DEVOTED TO YOU AND THIS NATION.

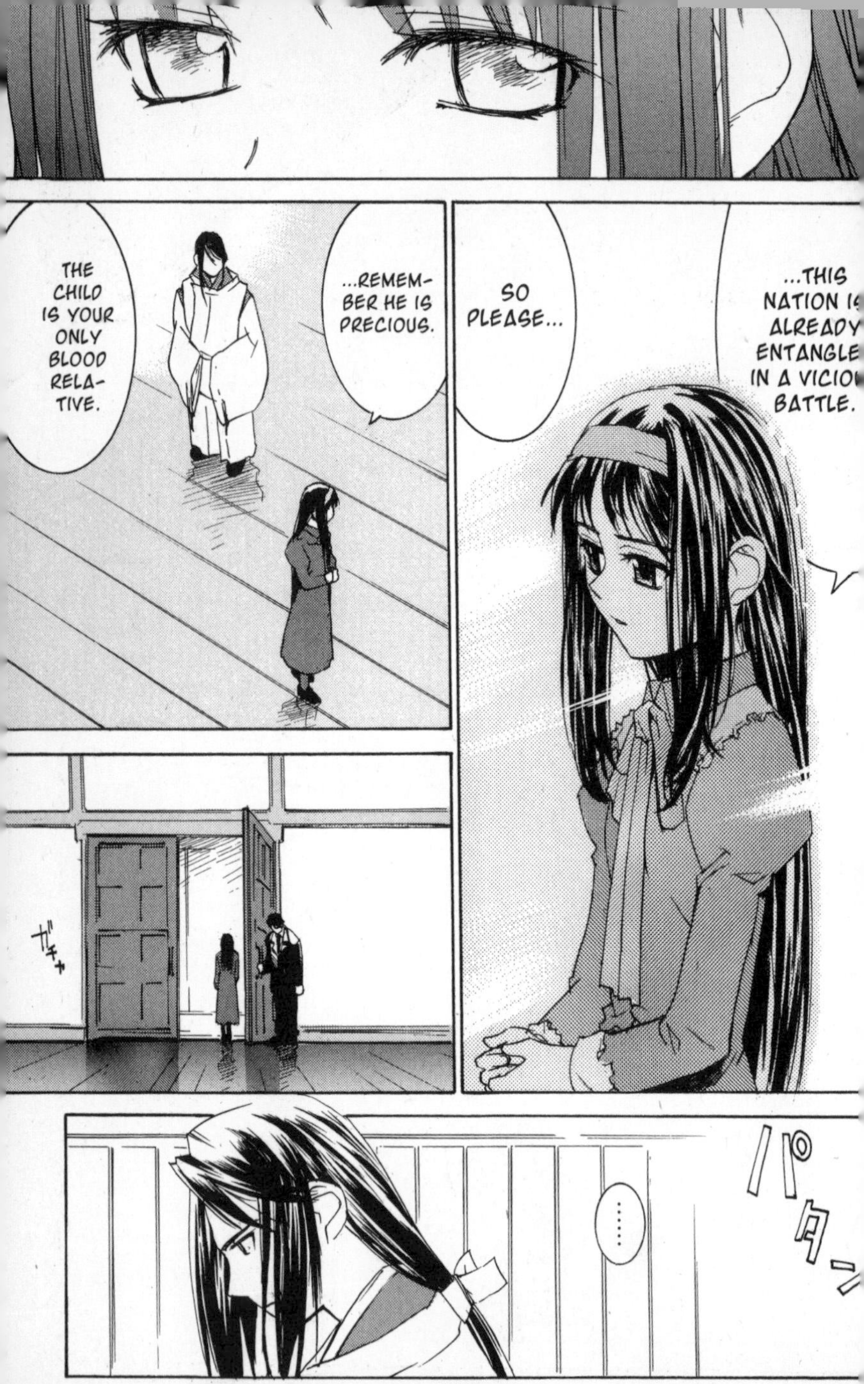

...THIS NATION I ALREADY ENTANGLE IN A VICIO BATTLE.
SO PLEASE...
...REMEM-BER HE IS PRECIOUS.
THE CHILD IS YOUR ONLY BLOOD RELA-TIVE.
ガチャ
パタン
......

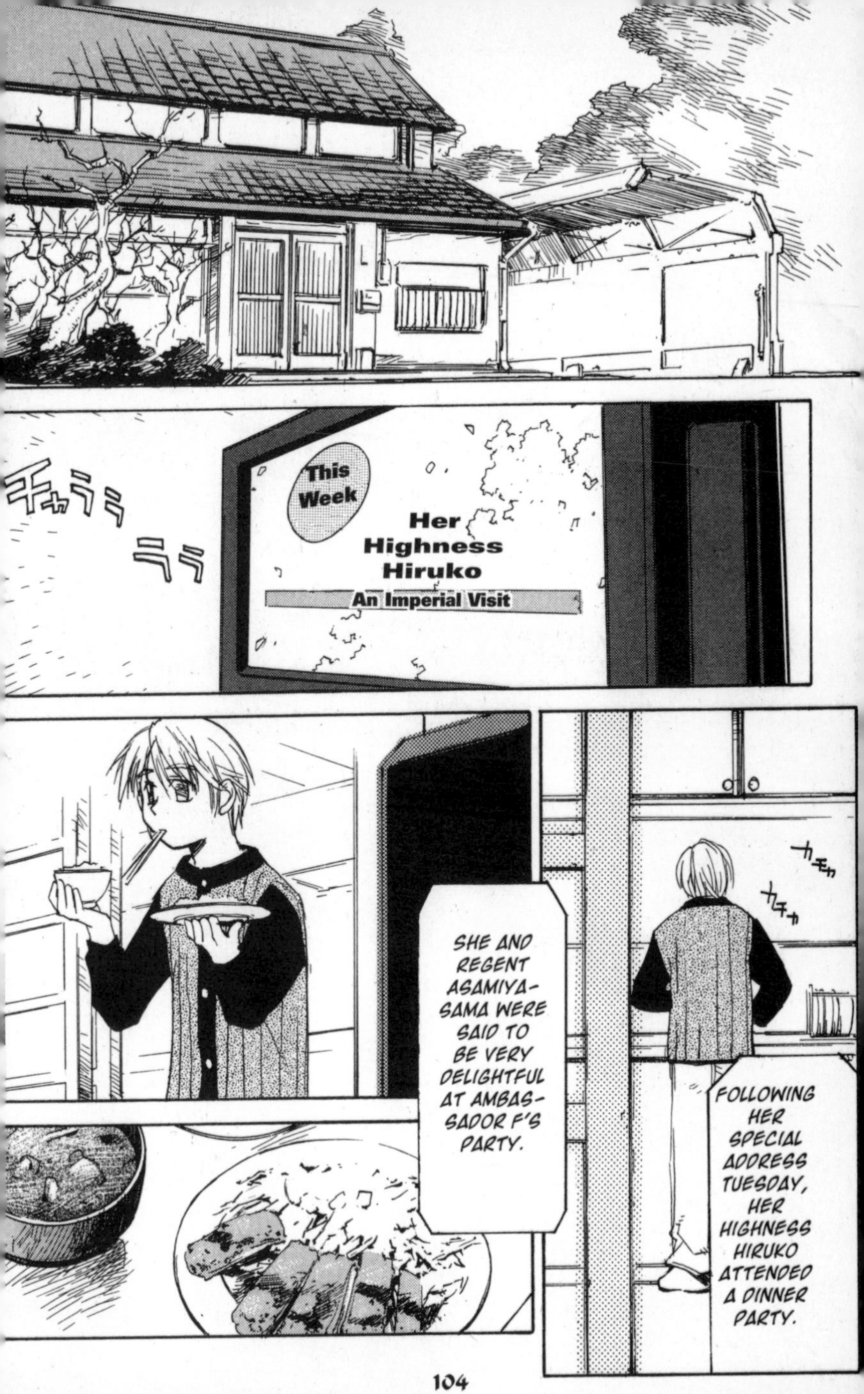
This Week
Her Highness Hiruko
An Imperial Visit
チャララ
ララ
カチャ
カチャ
FOLLOWING HER SPECIAL ADDRESS TUESDAY, HER HIGHNESS HIRUKO ATTENDED A DINNER PARTY.
SHE AND REGENT ASAMIYA-SAMA WERE SAID TO BE VERY DELIGHTFUL AT AMBASSADOR F'S PARTY.

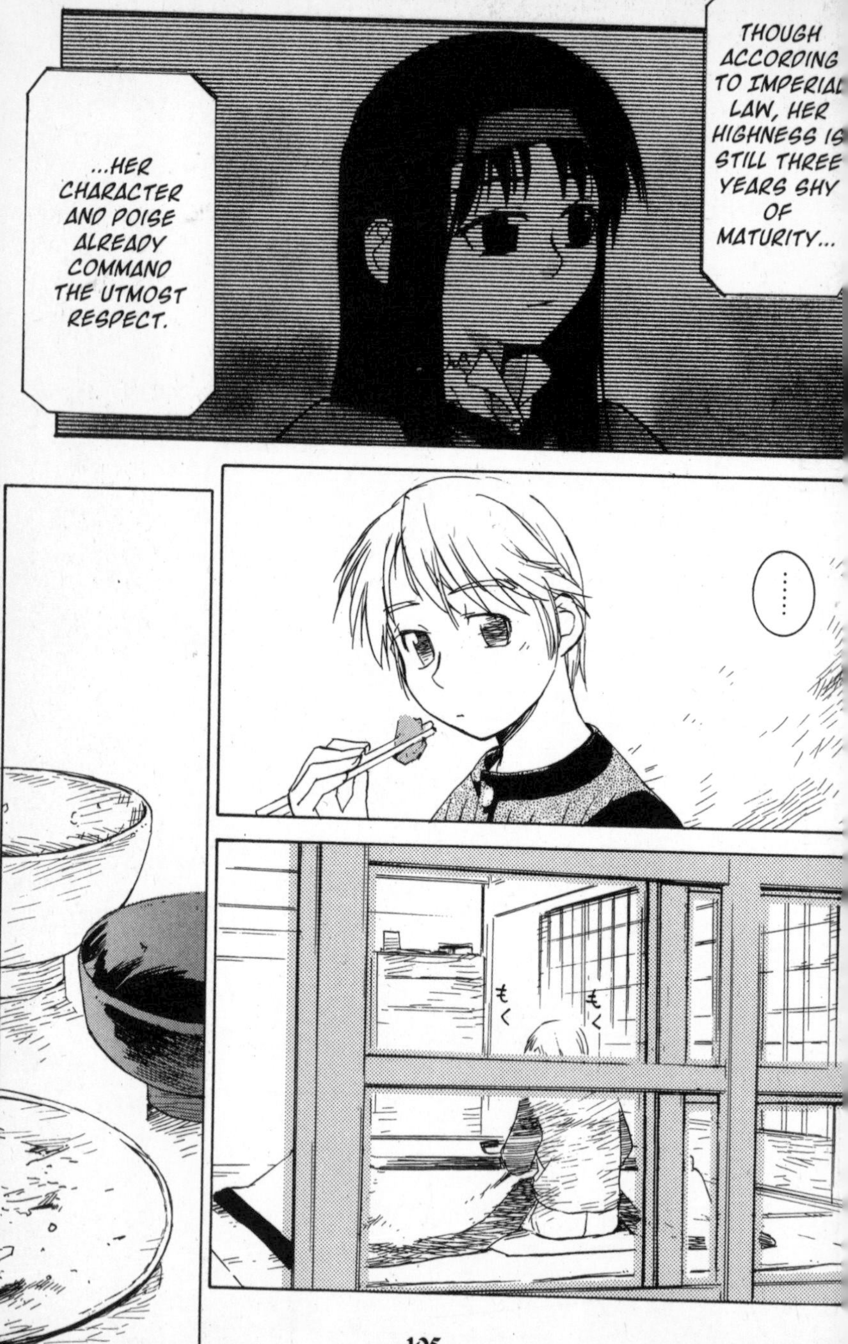
THOUGH ACCORDING TO IMPERIAL LAW, HER HIGHNESS IS STILL THREE YEARS SHY OF MATURITY...
...HER CHARACTER AND POISE ALREADY COMMAND THE UTMOST RESPECT.
......
もく
もく

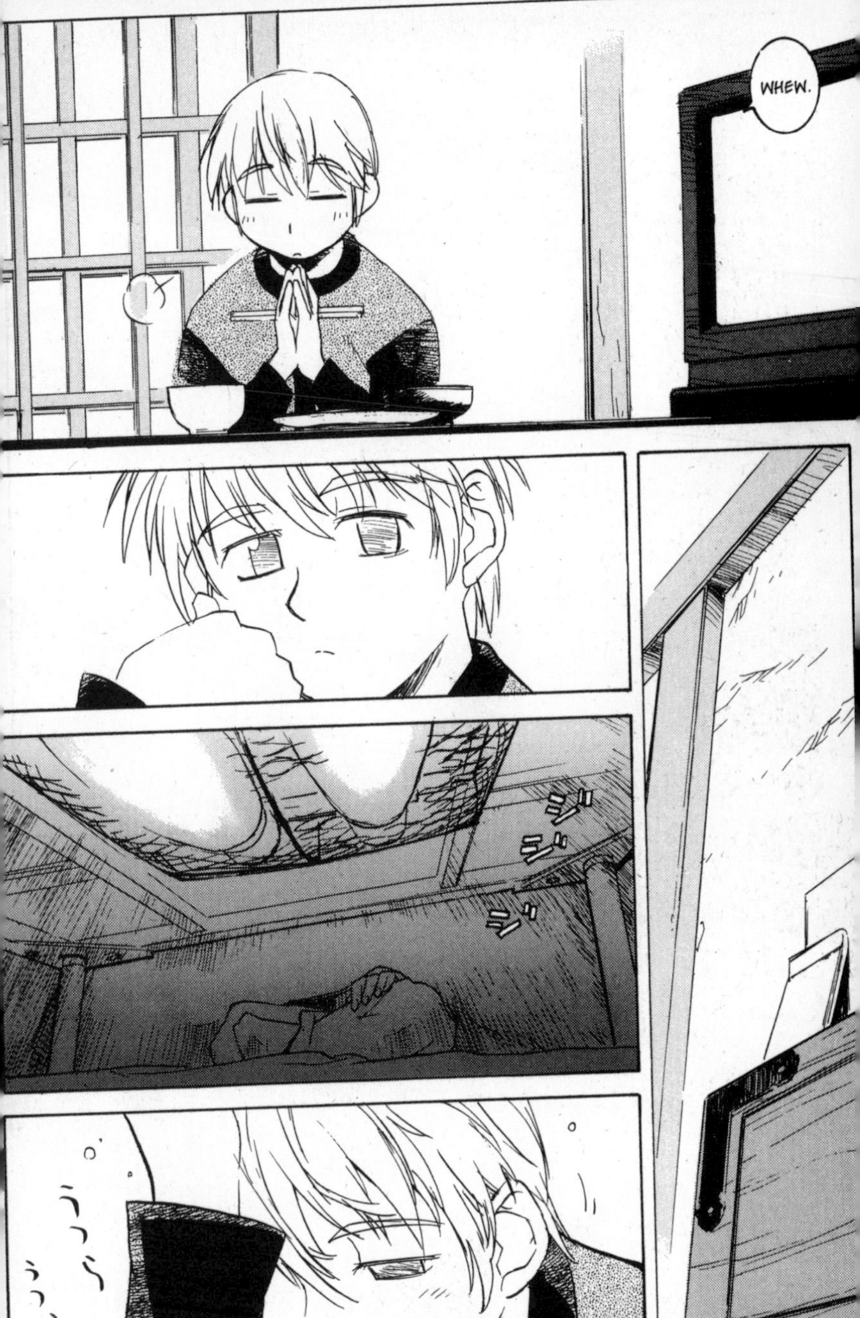
WHEW.

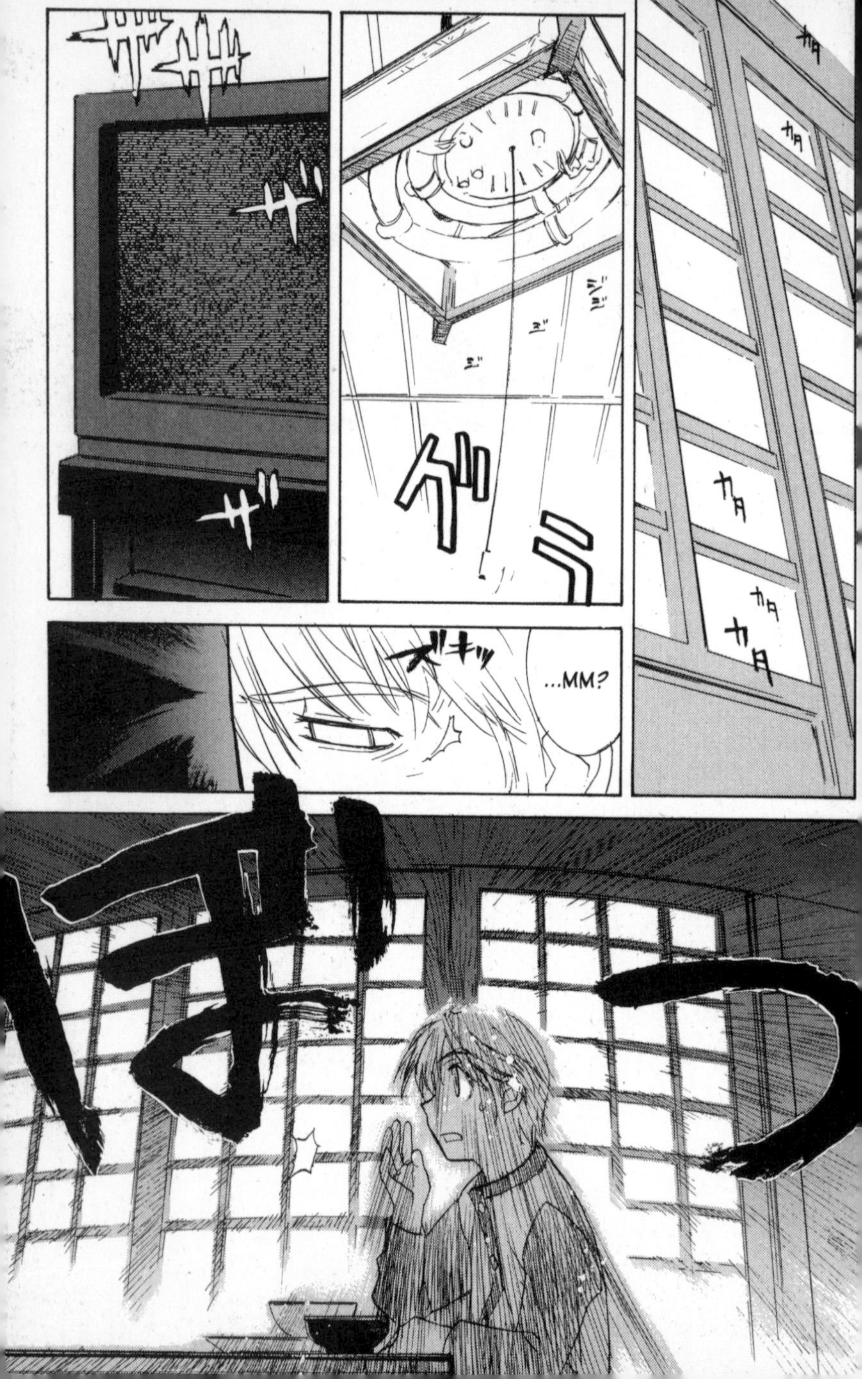
...MM?

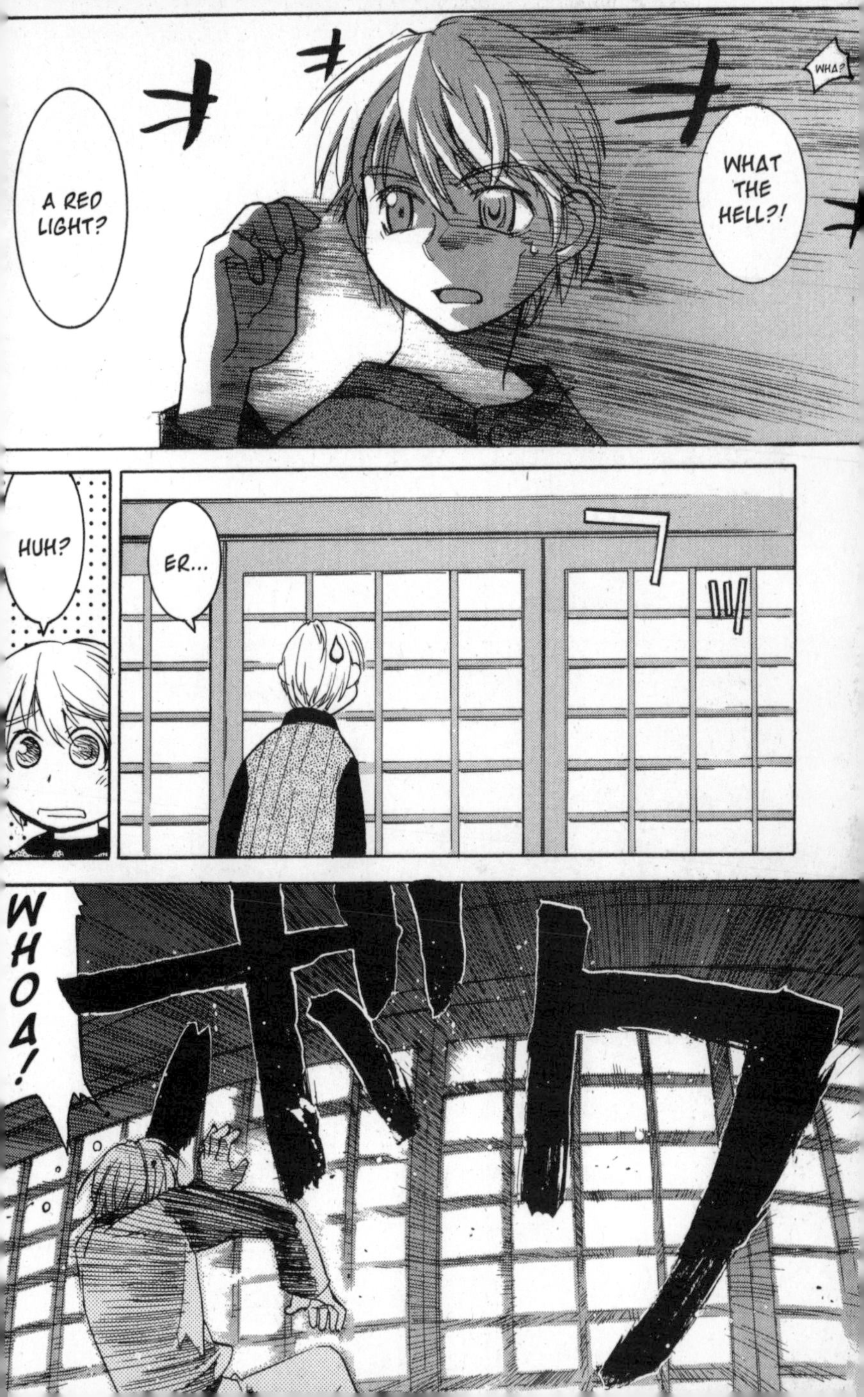
WHA?
WHAT THE HELL?!
A RED LIGHT?
ER...
HUH?
WHOA!

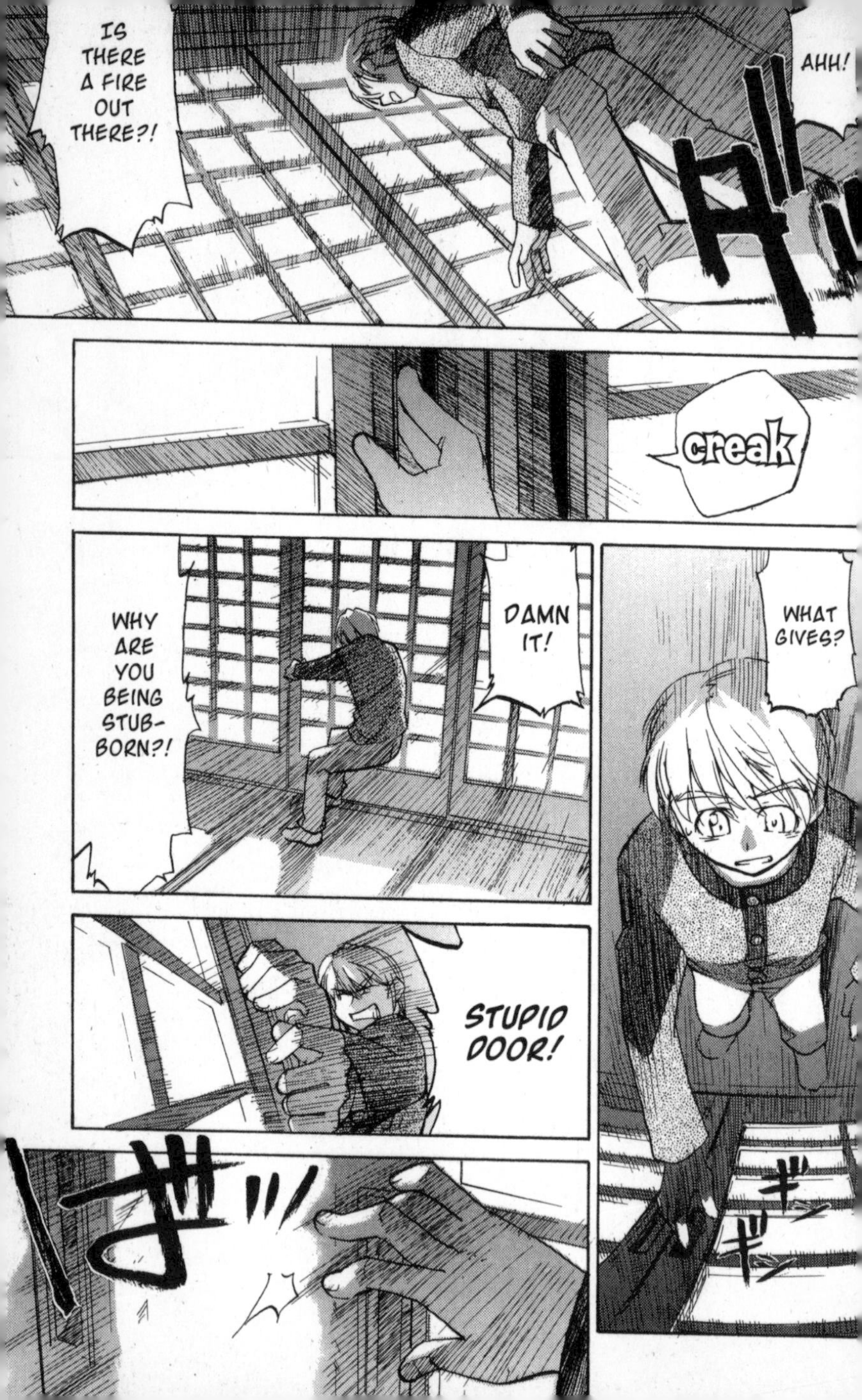
AHH!
IS THERE A FIRE OUT THERE?!
creak
WHAT GIVES?
ギ
ギ
DAMN IT!
WHY ARE YOU BEING STUB-BORN?!
STUPID DOOR!

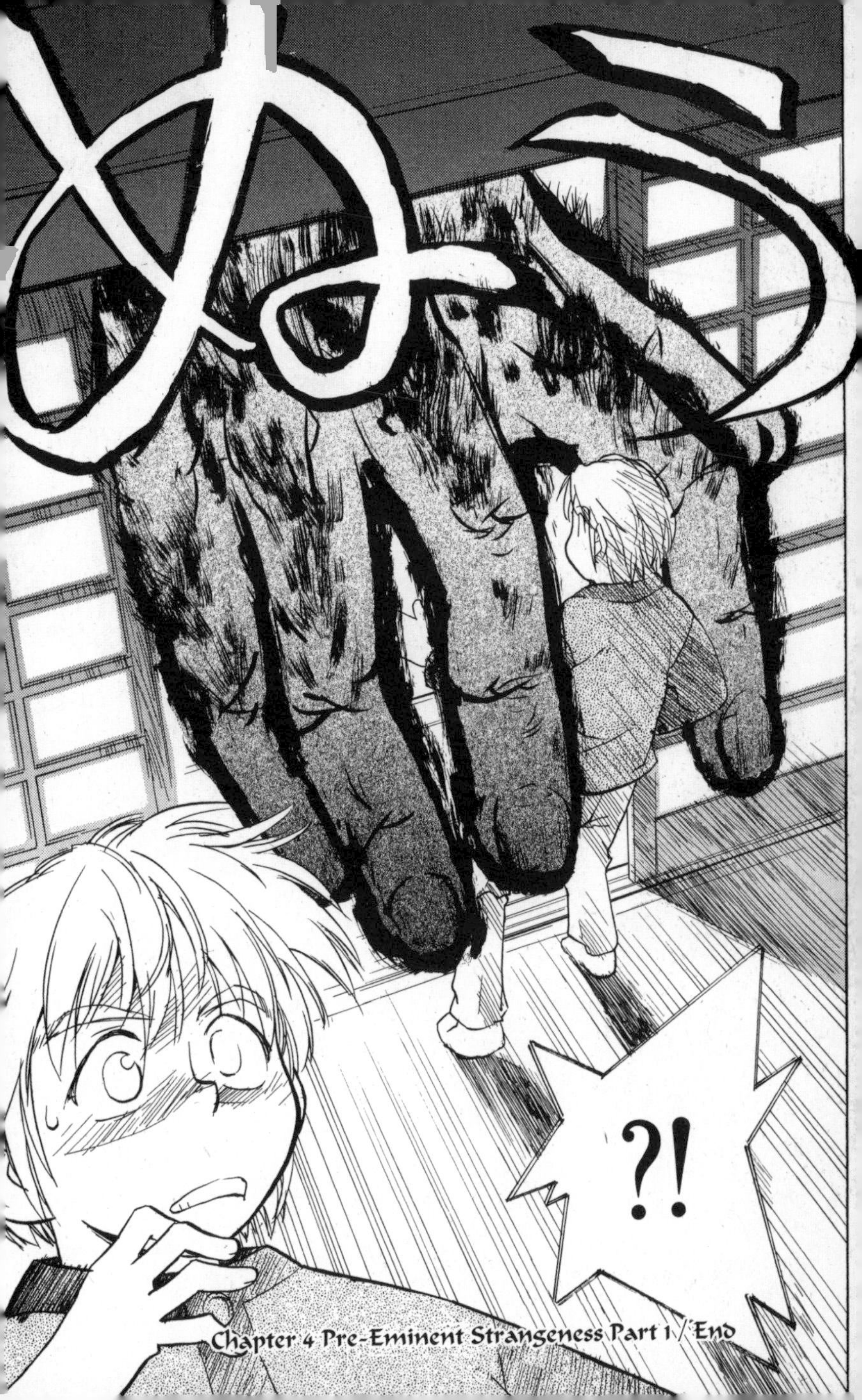
?!
Chapter 4 Pre-Eminent Strangeness Part 1 / End

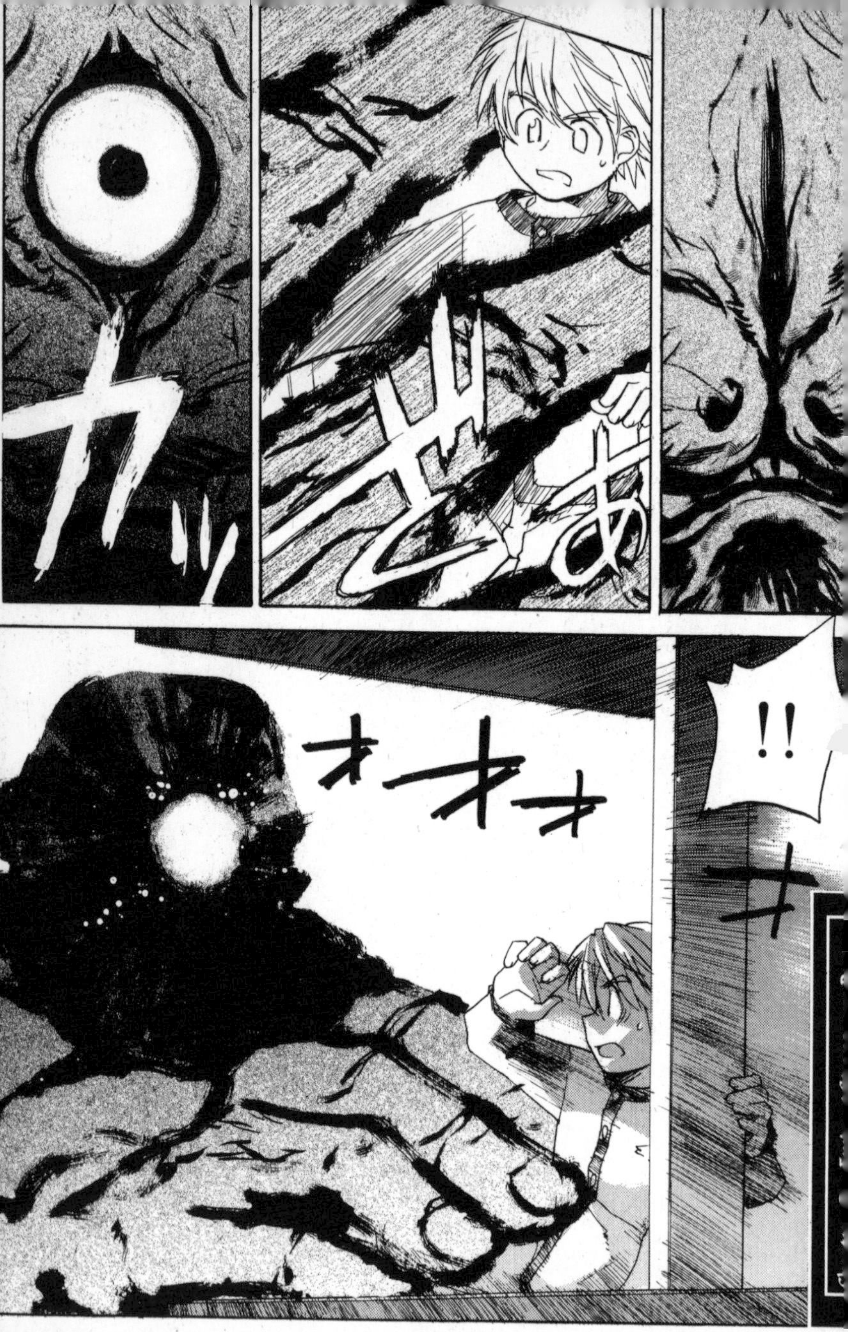
ぎゃあ
カッ
!!
オオォ
ォ

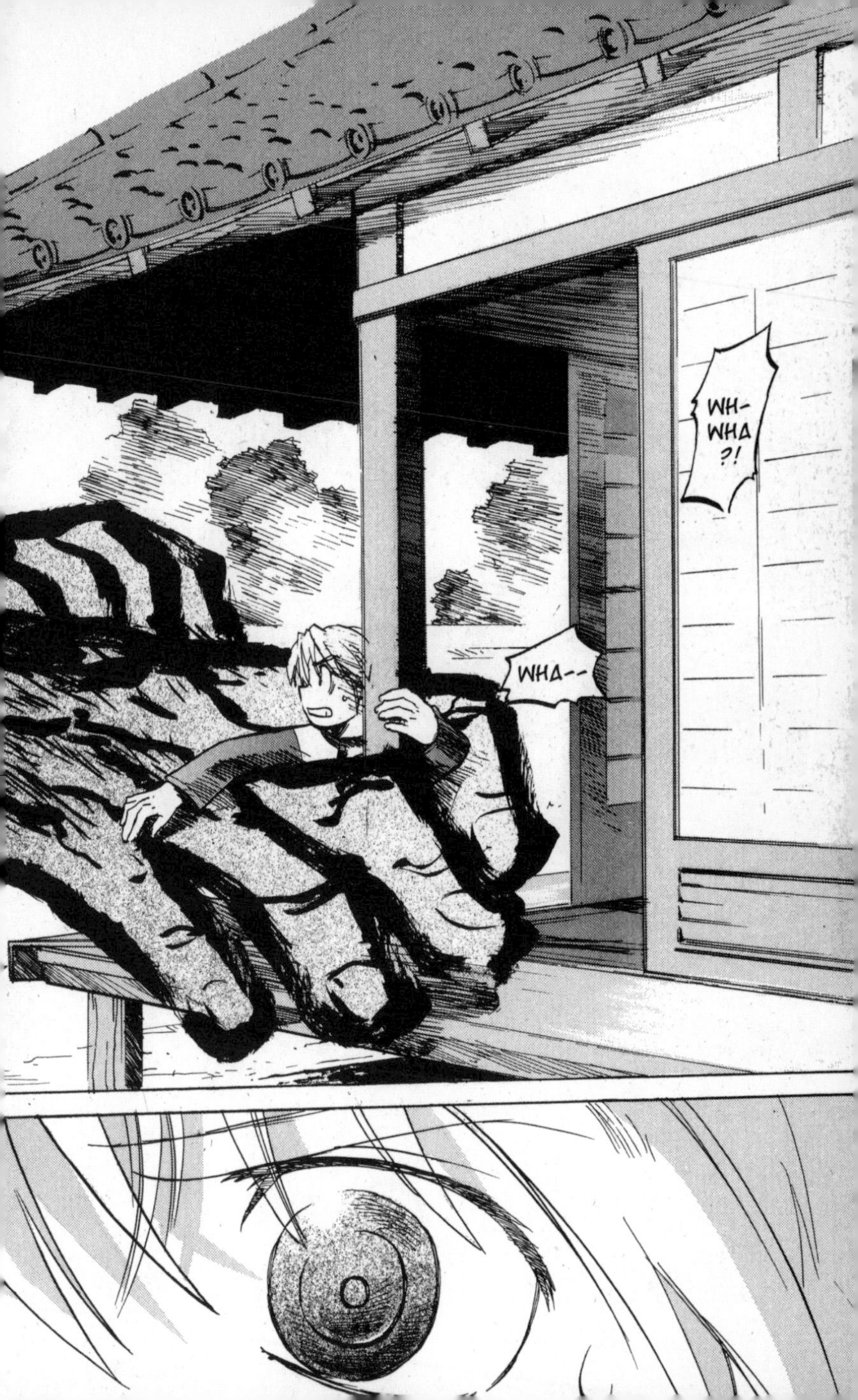
WH-WHA?!
WHA--

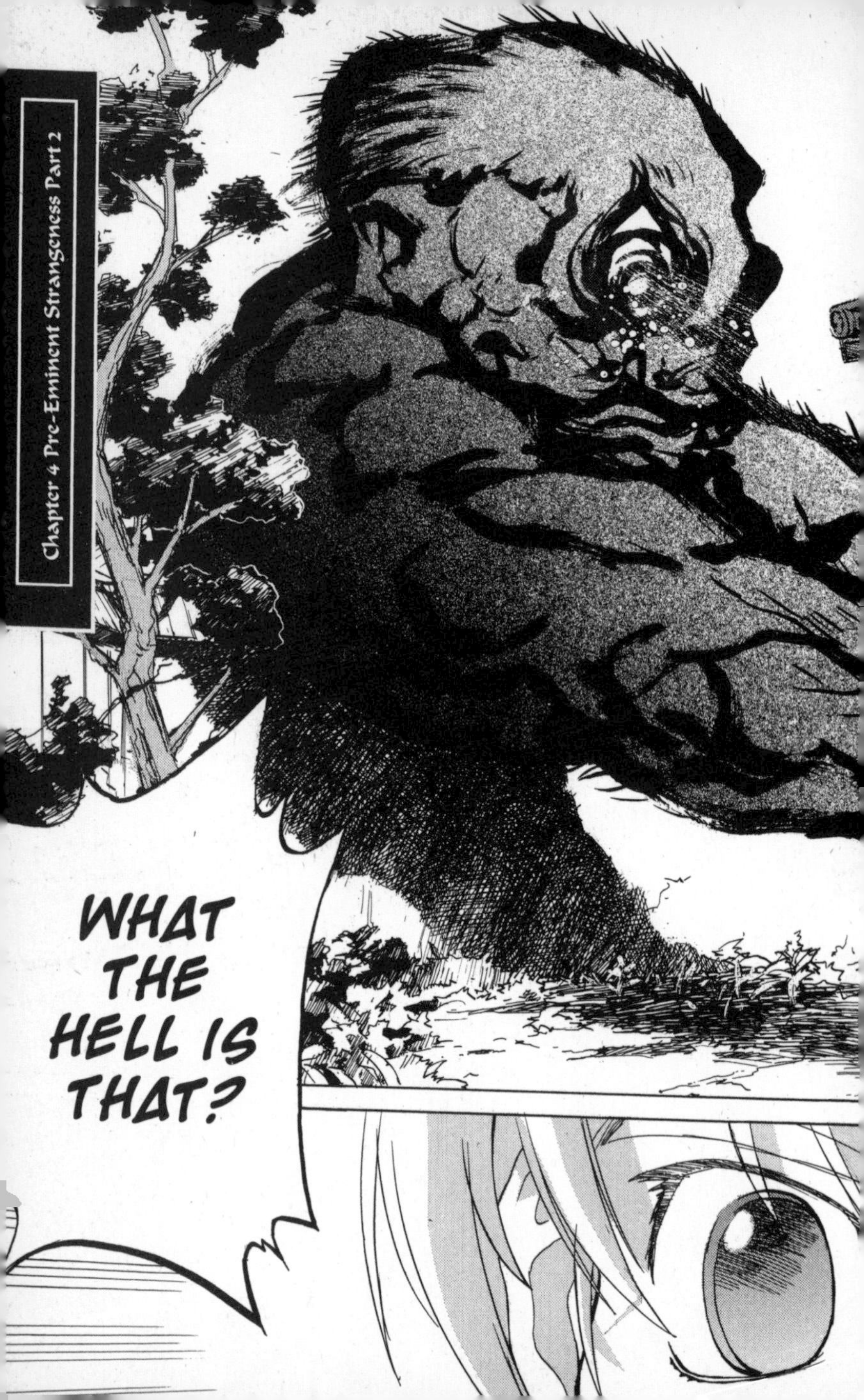
Chapter 4 Pre-Eminent Strangeness Part 2
WHAT THE HELL IS THAT?

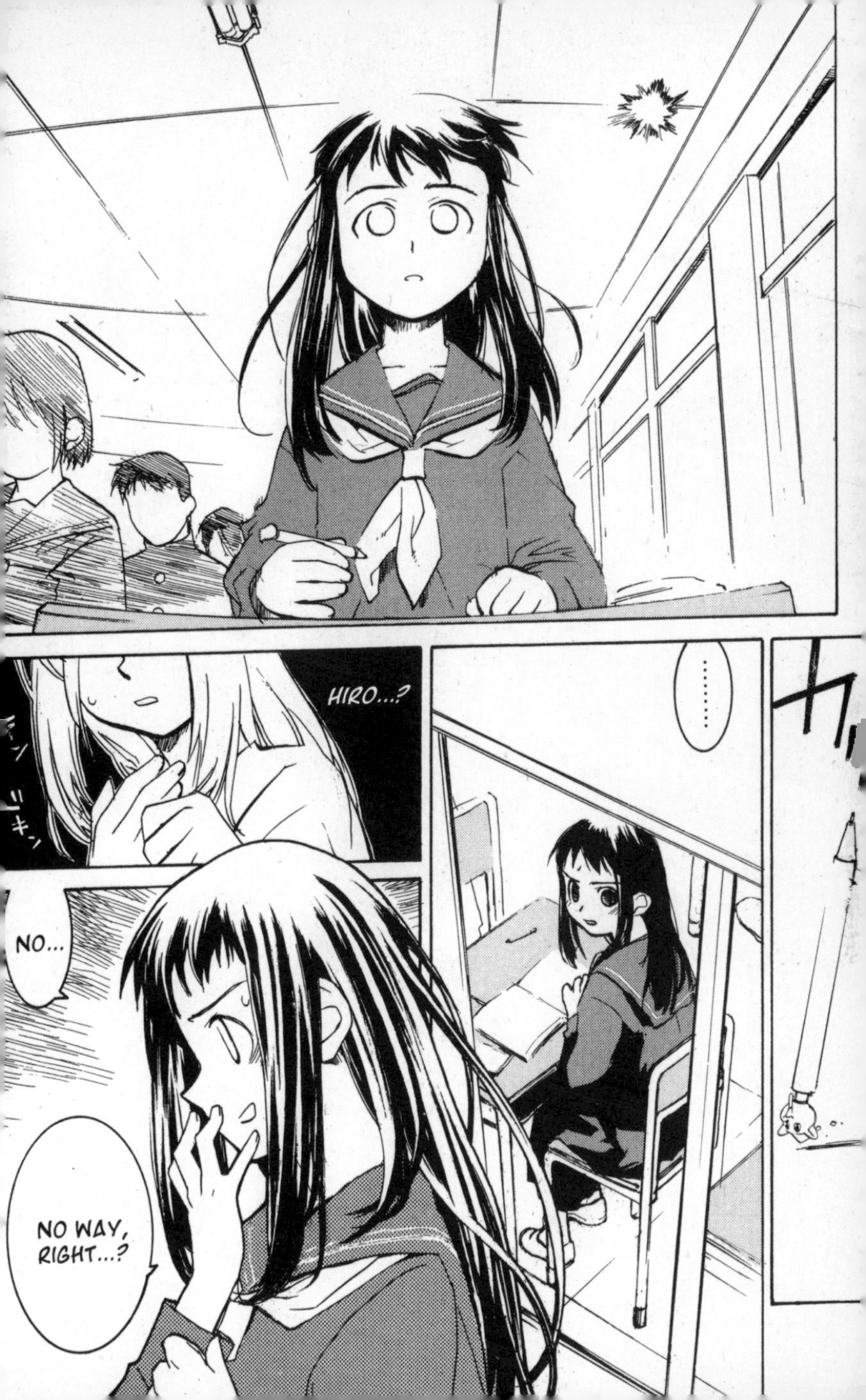
……
HIRO…?
NO…
NO WAY, RIGHT…?

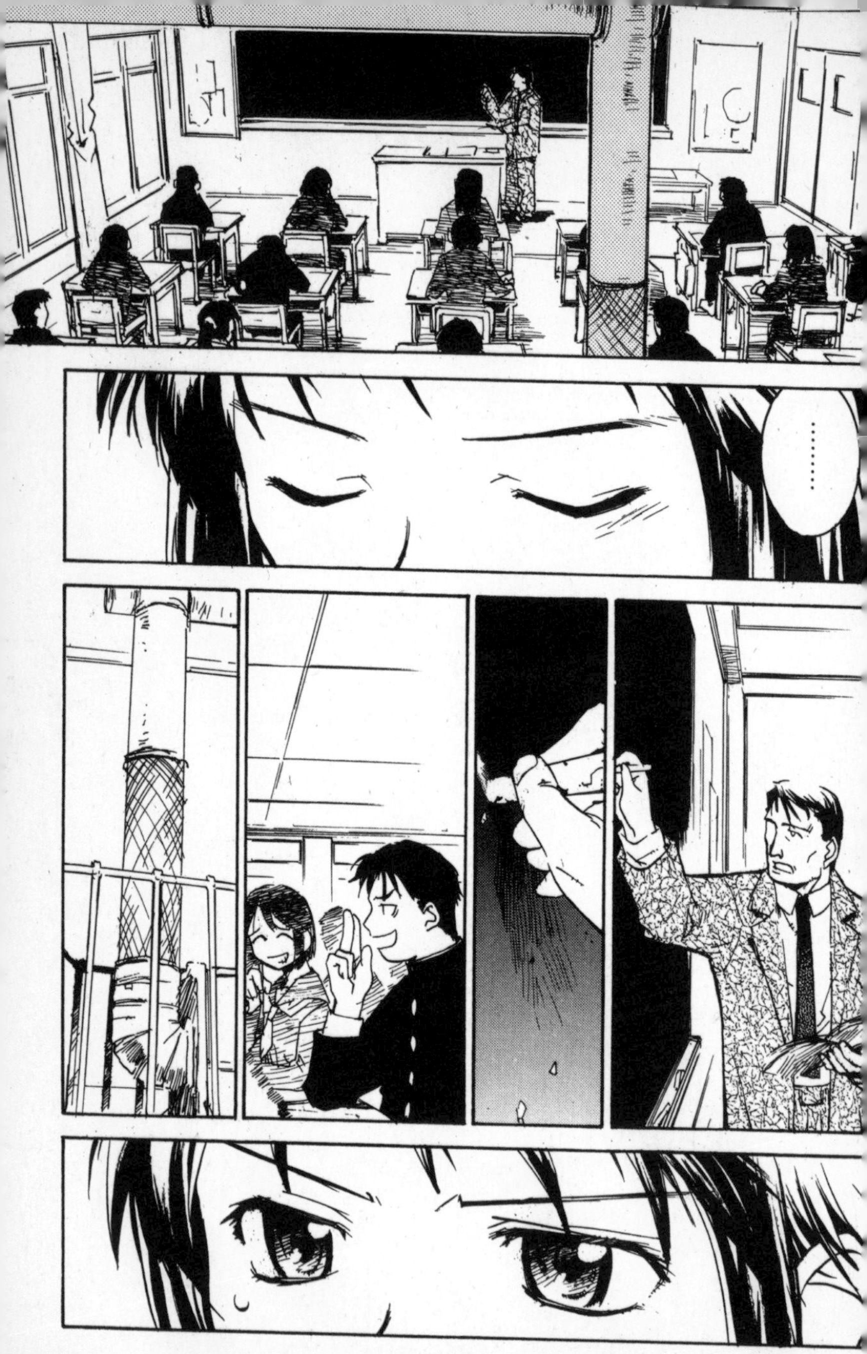
……

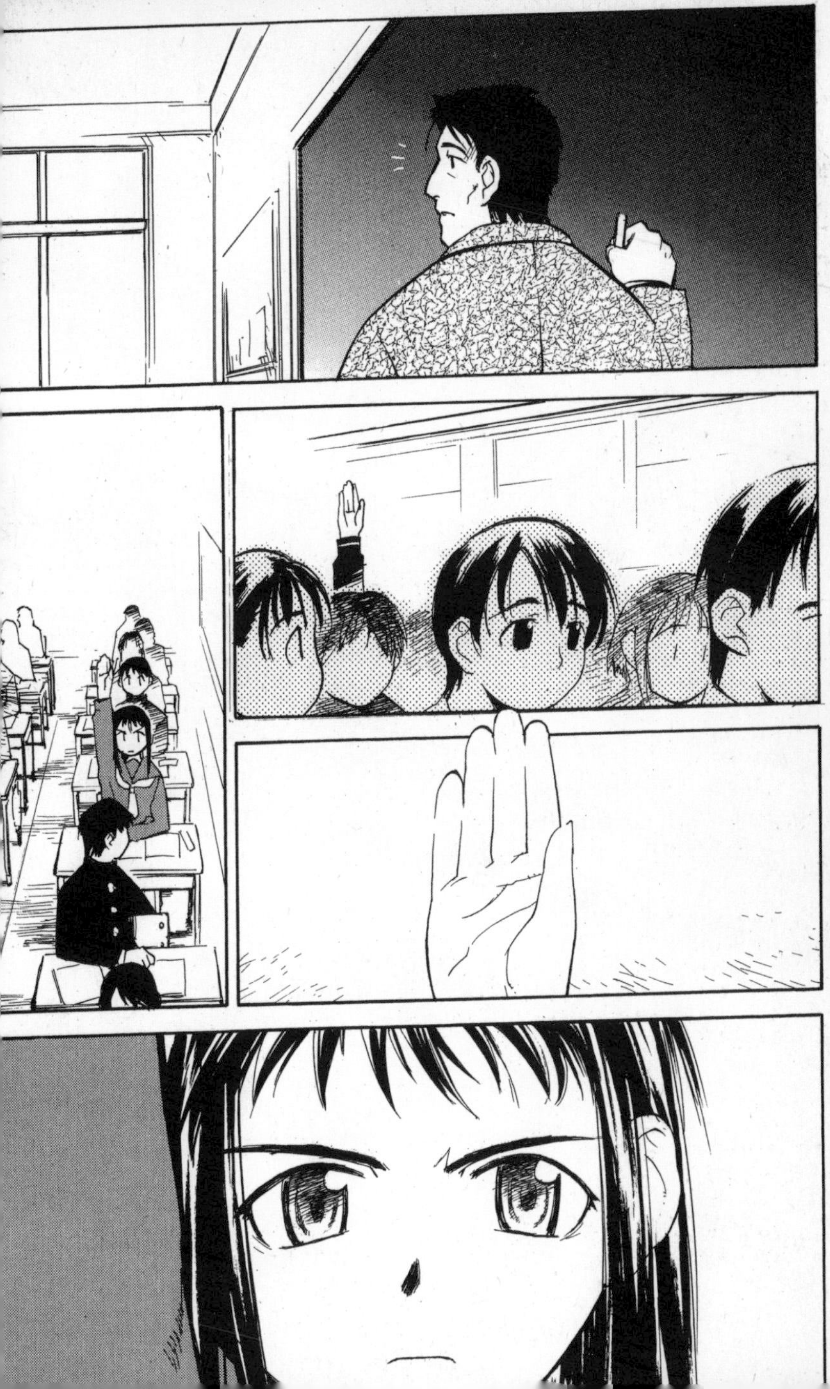

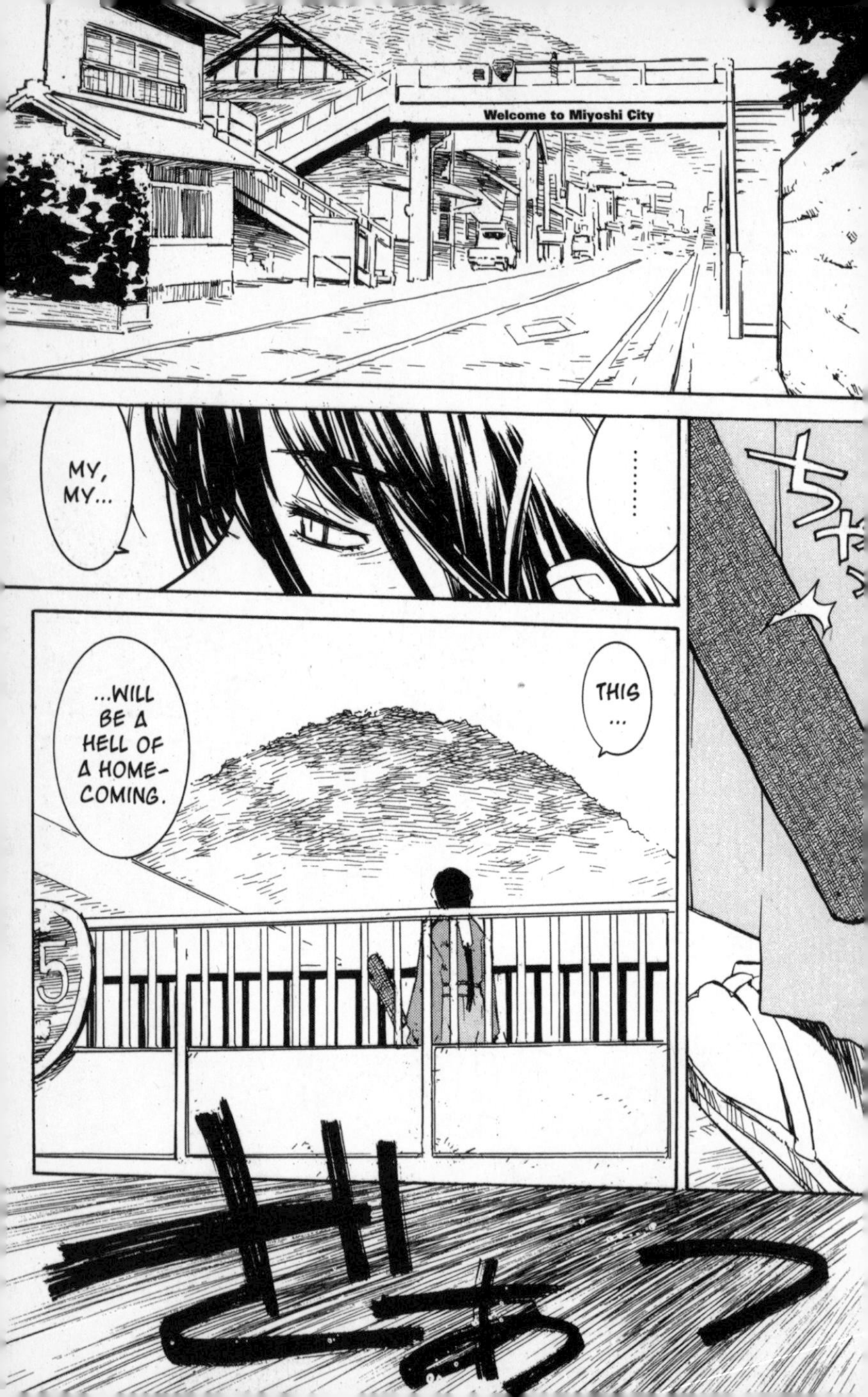
Welcome to Miyoshi City
......
MY, MY...
THIS...
...WILL BE A HELL OF A HOME-COMING.

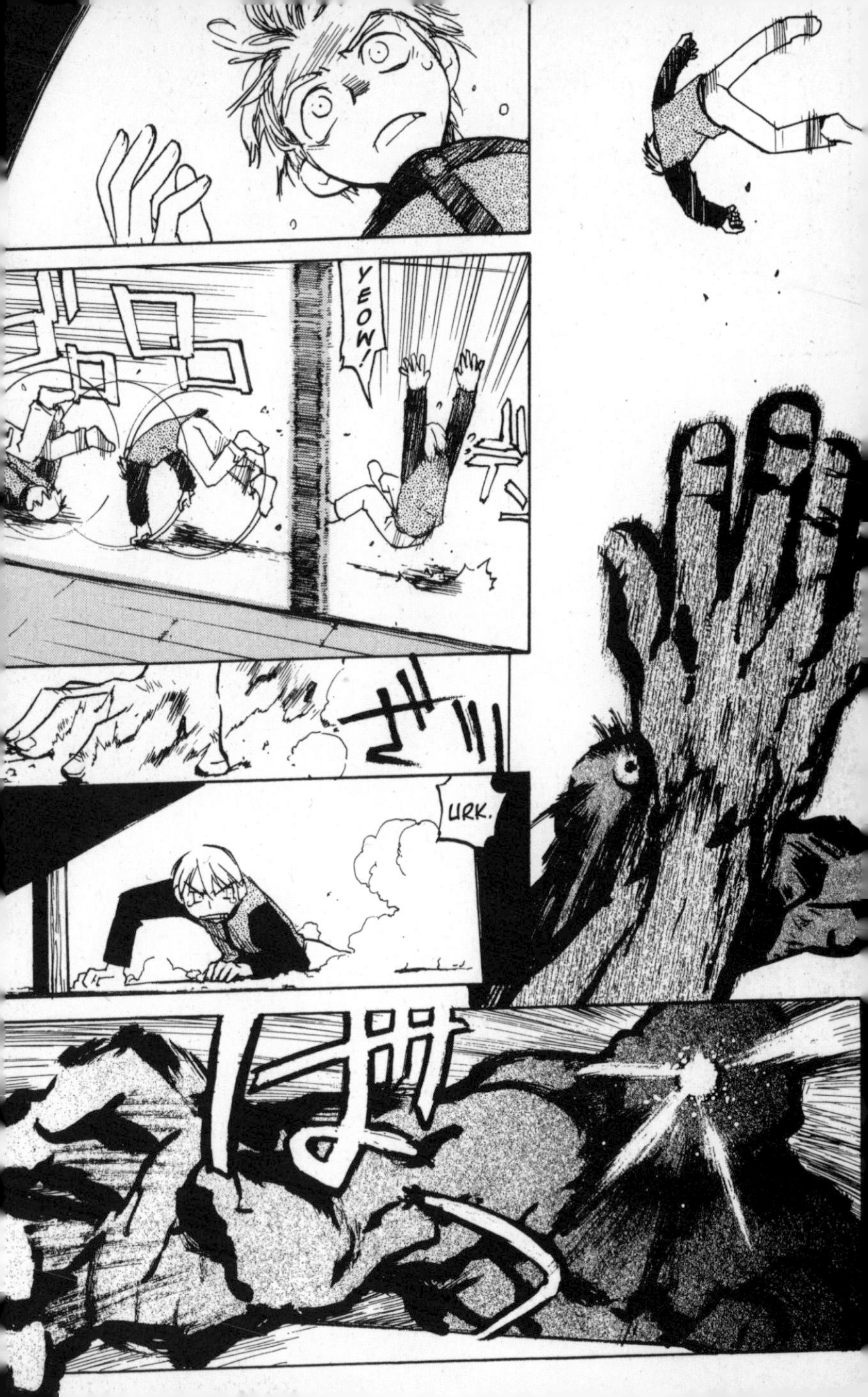
YEOW!
URK.

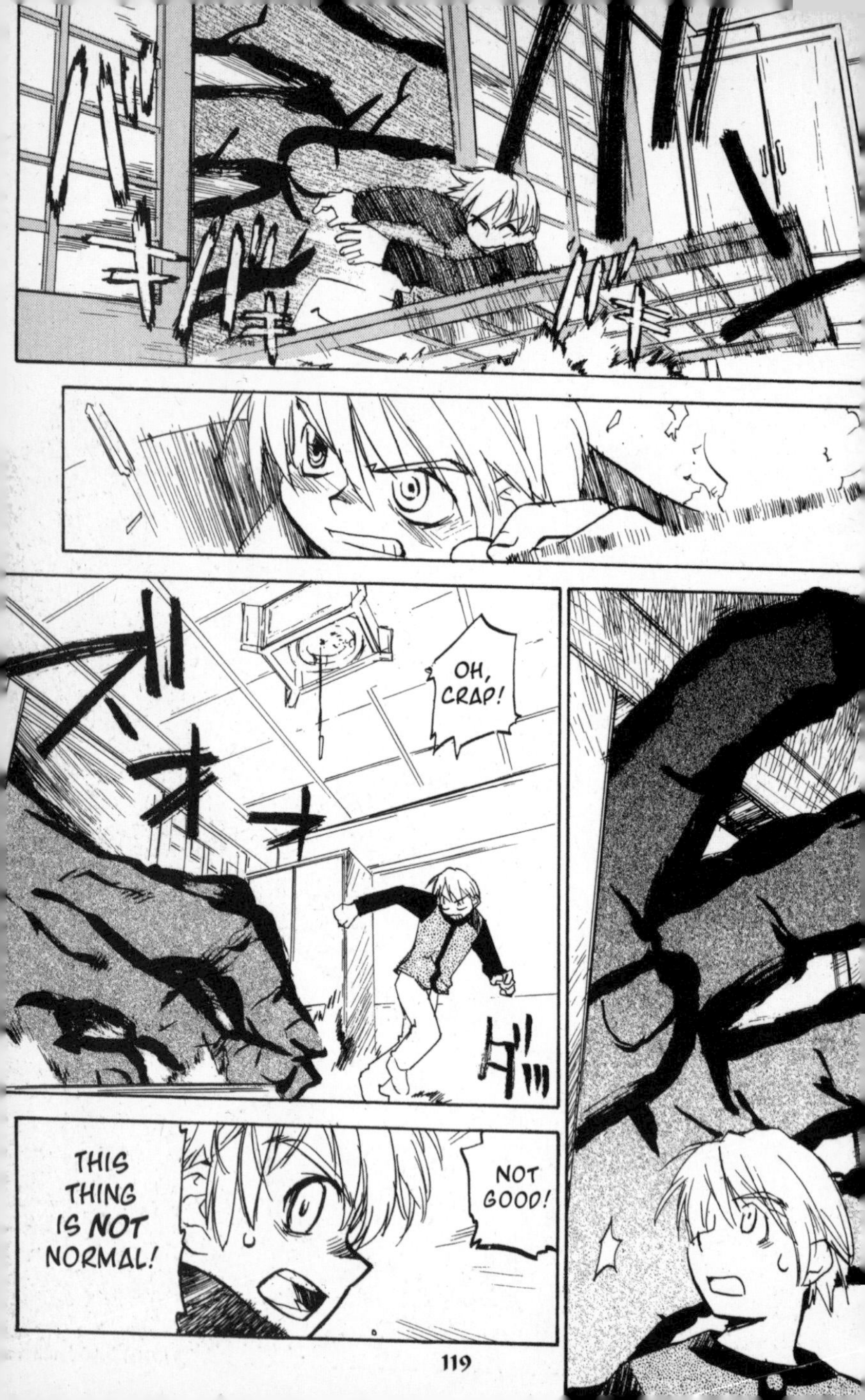
OH, CRAP!
NOT GOOD!
THIS THING IS NOT NORMAL!

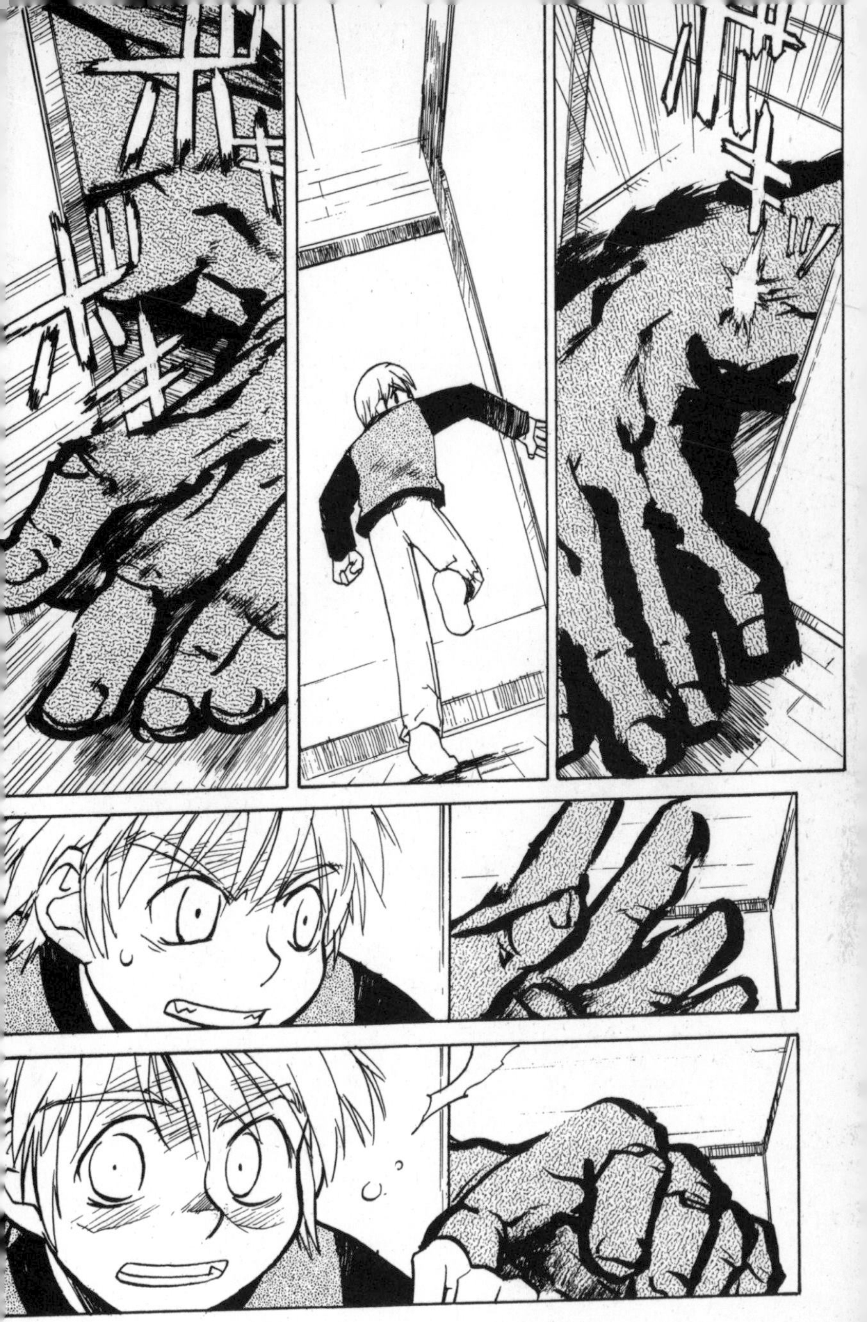

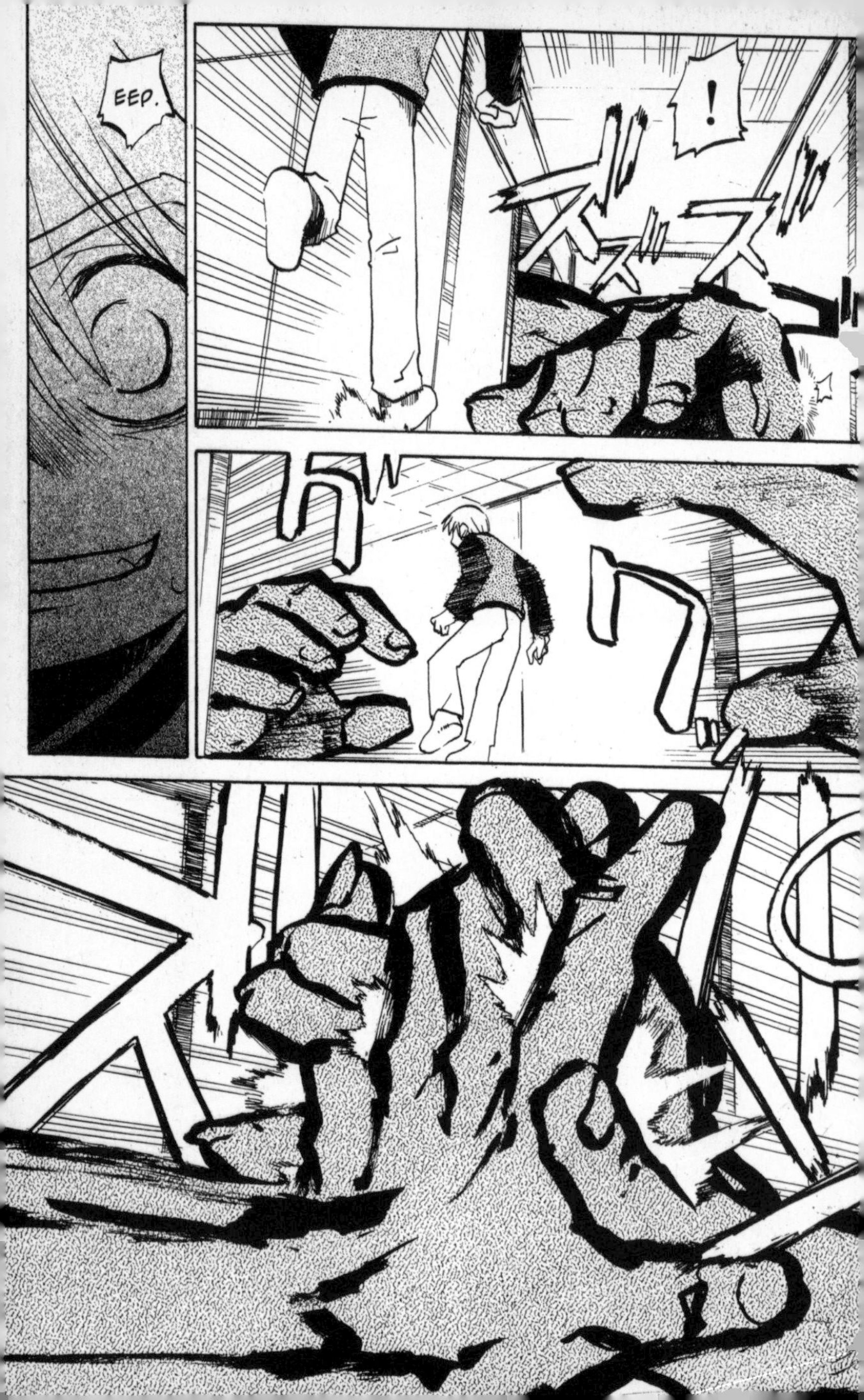
!
ズズズ
EEP.

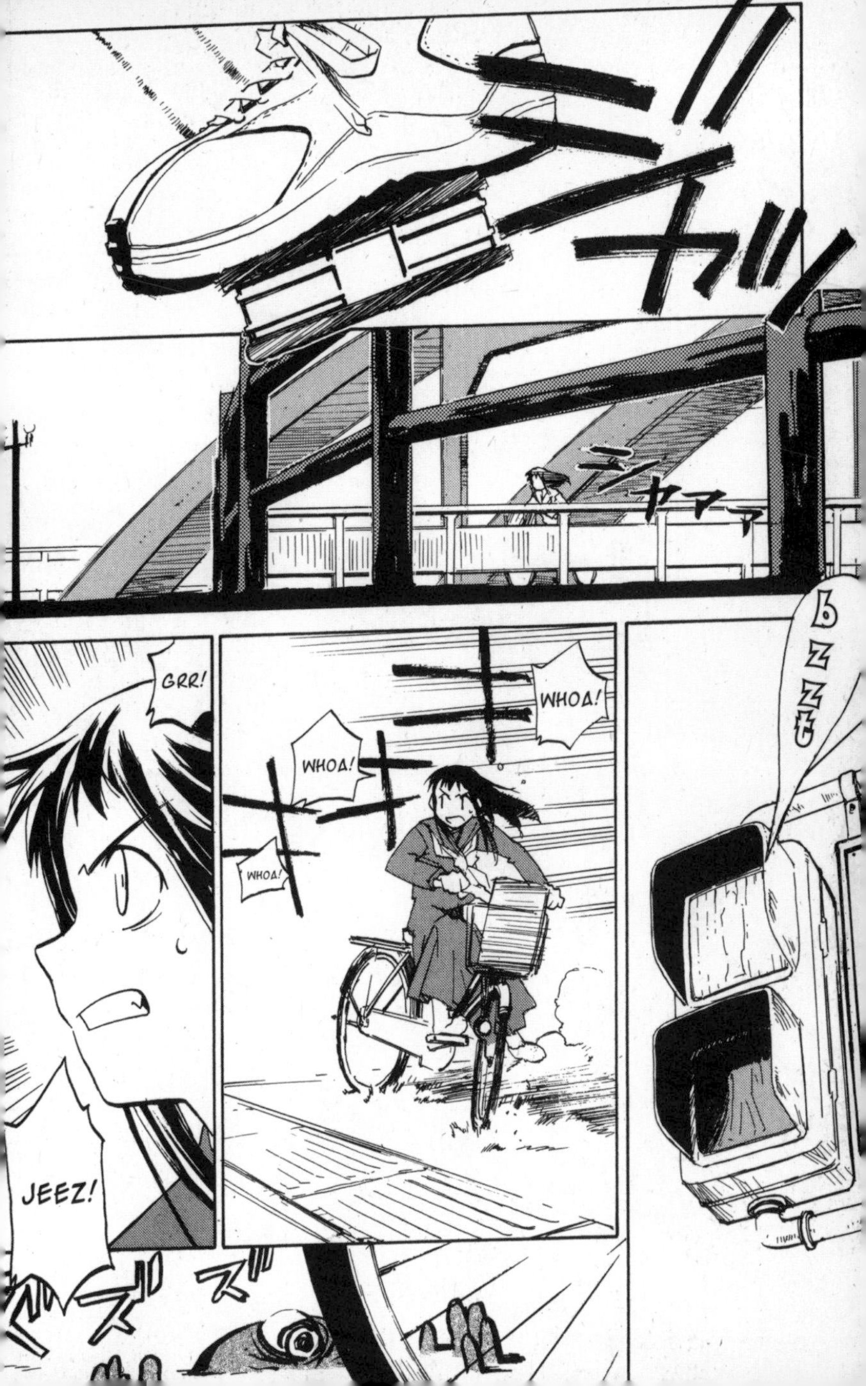
bzzt
WHOA!
WHOA!
WHOA!
GRR!
JEEZ!

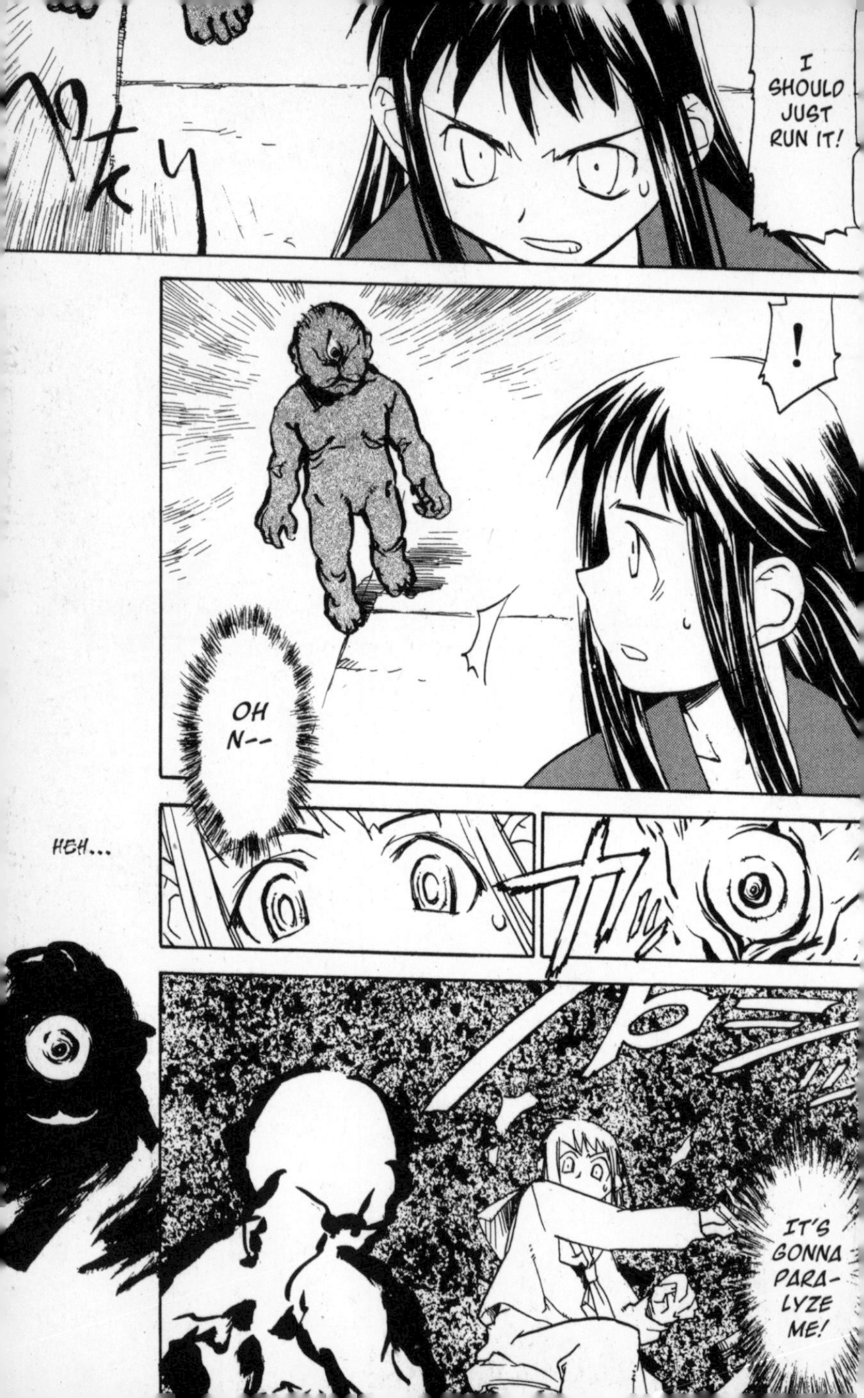
I SHOULD JUST RUN IT!
!
OH N--
HEH...
IT'S GONNA PARALYZE ME!

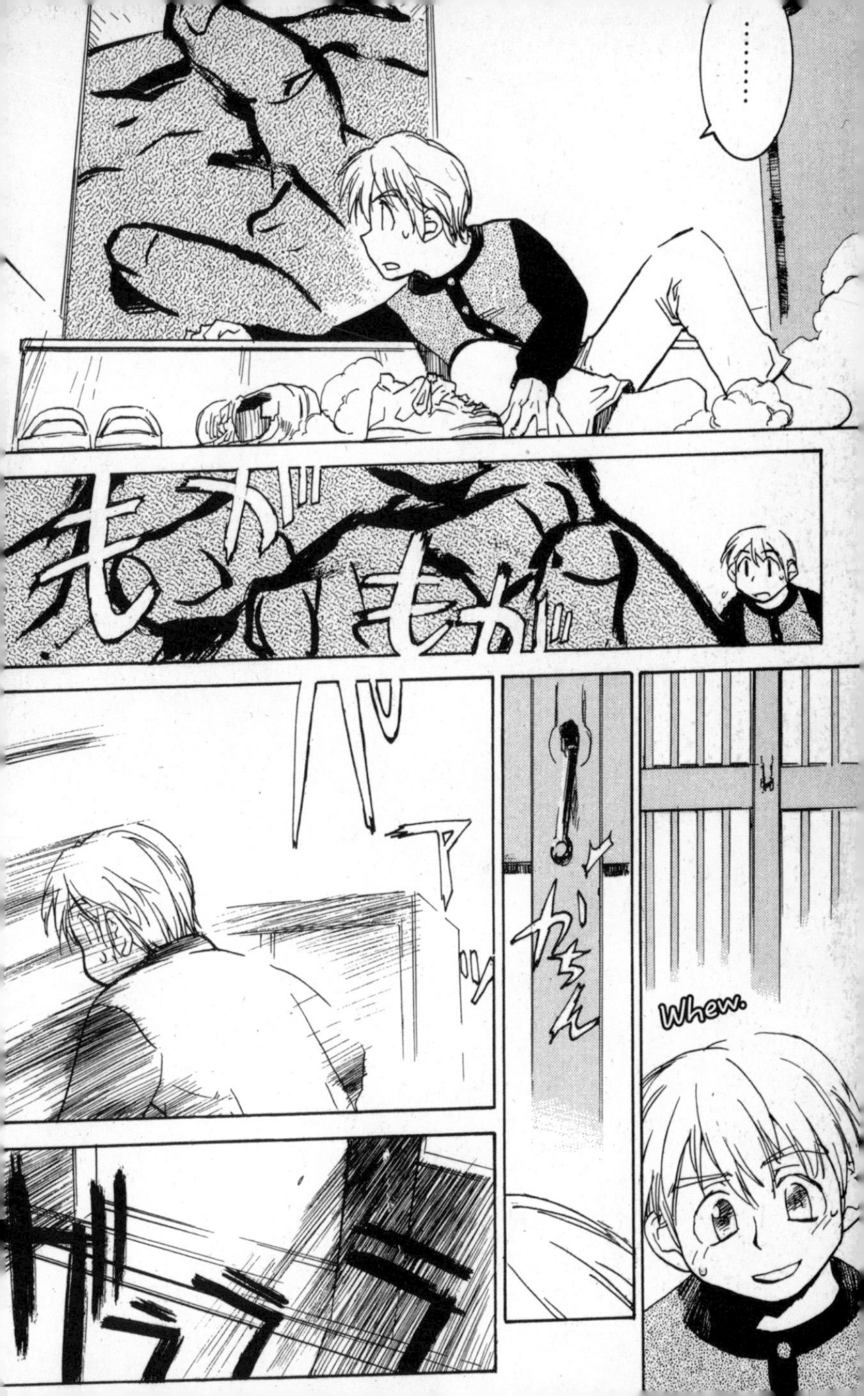
……
Whew.

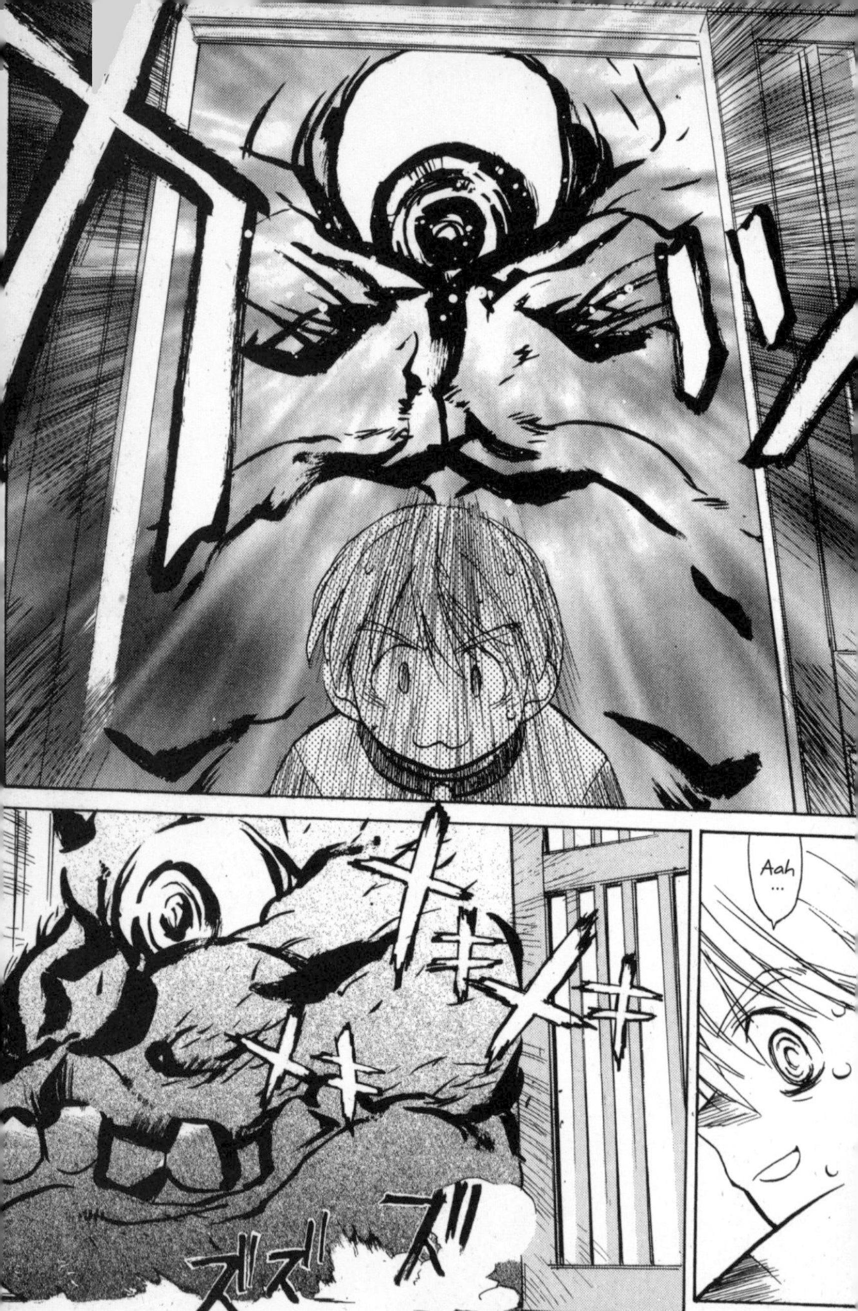
Aah …

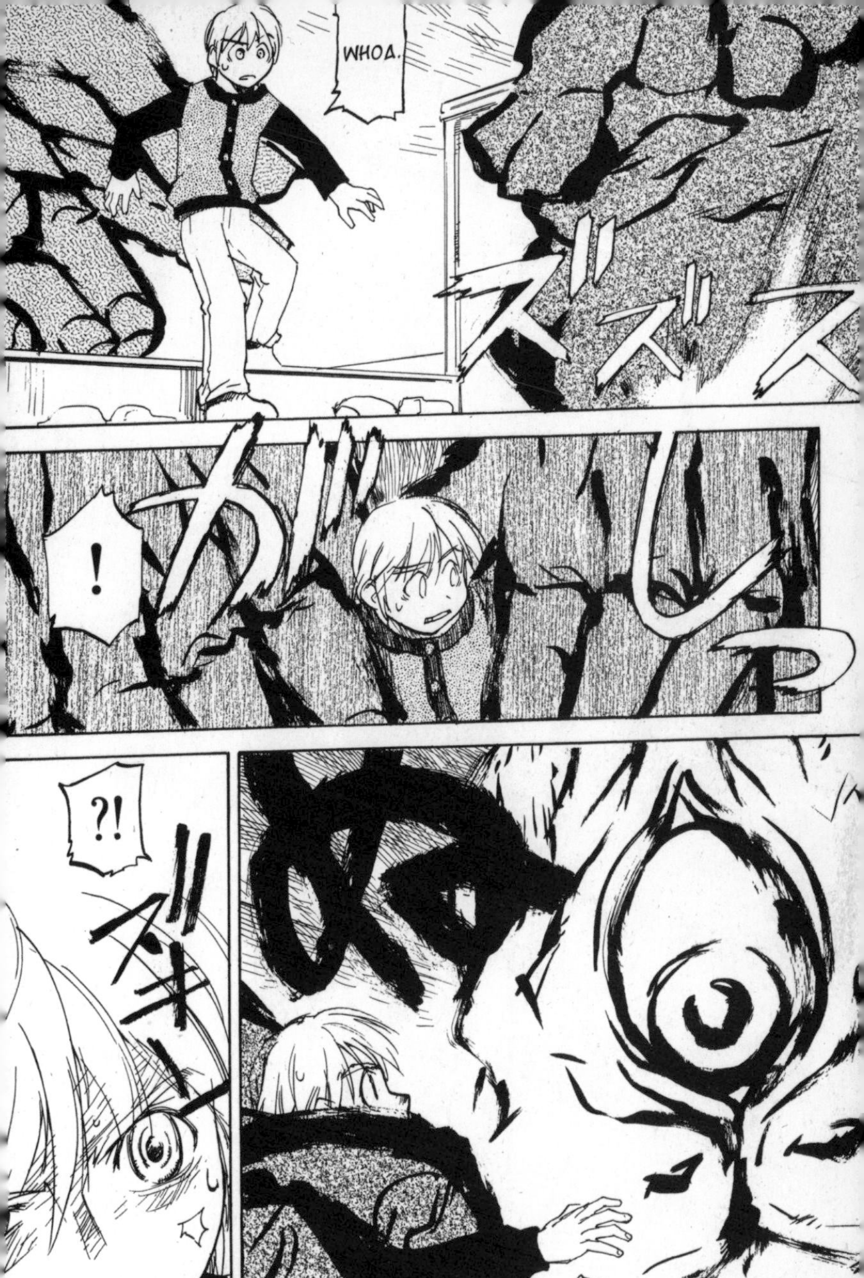
WHOA.
!
?!

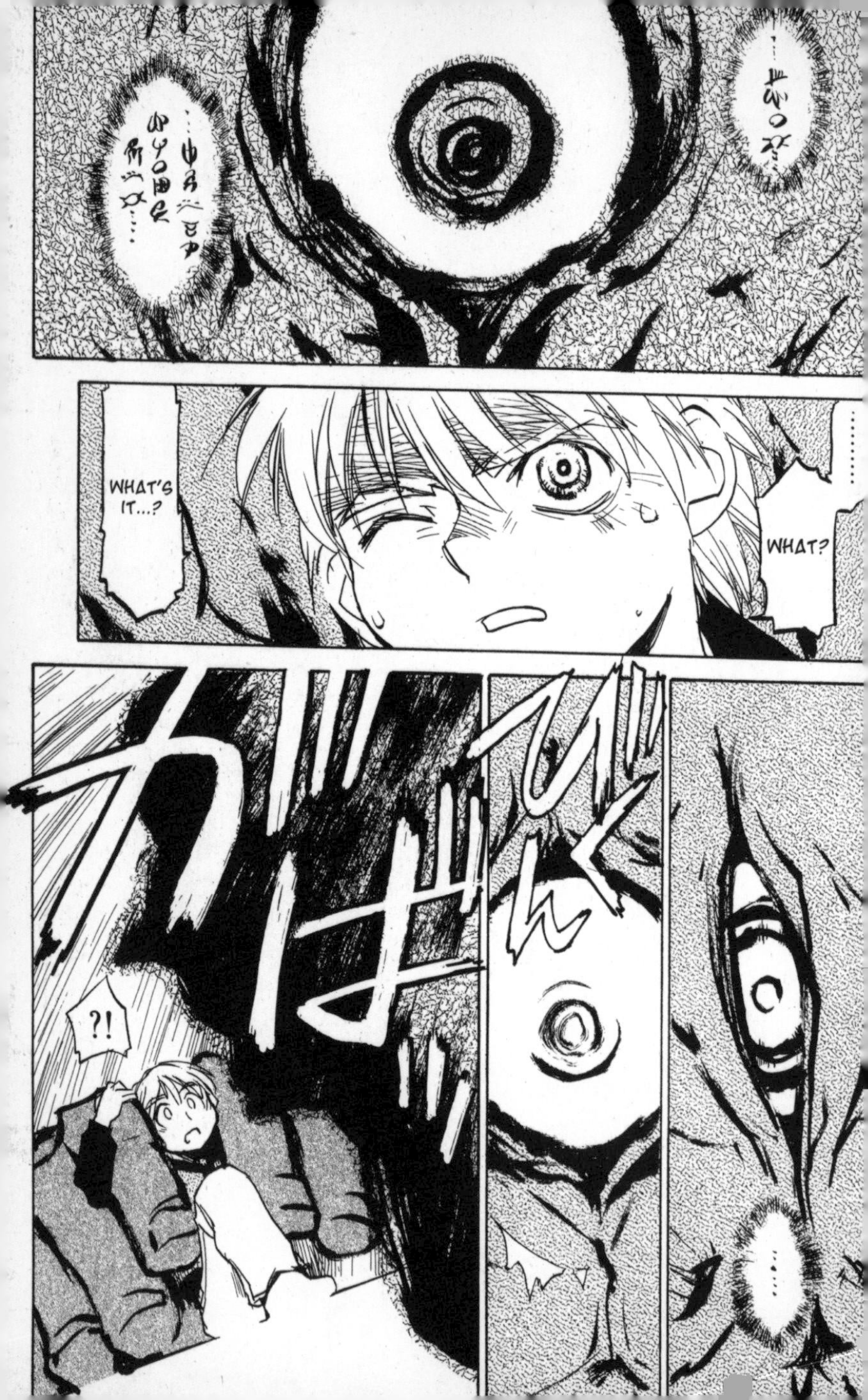
......
WHAT?
WHAT'S IT...?
......
?!

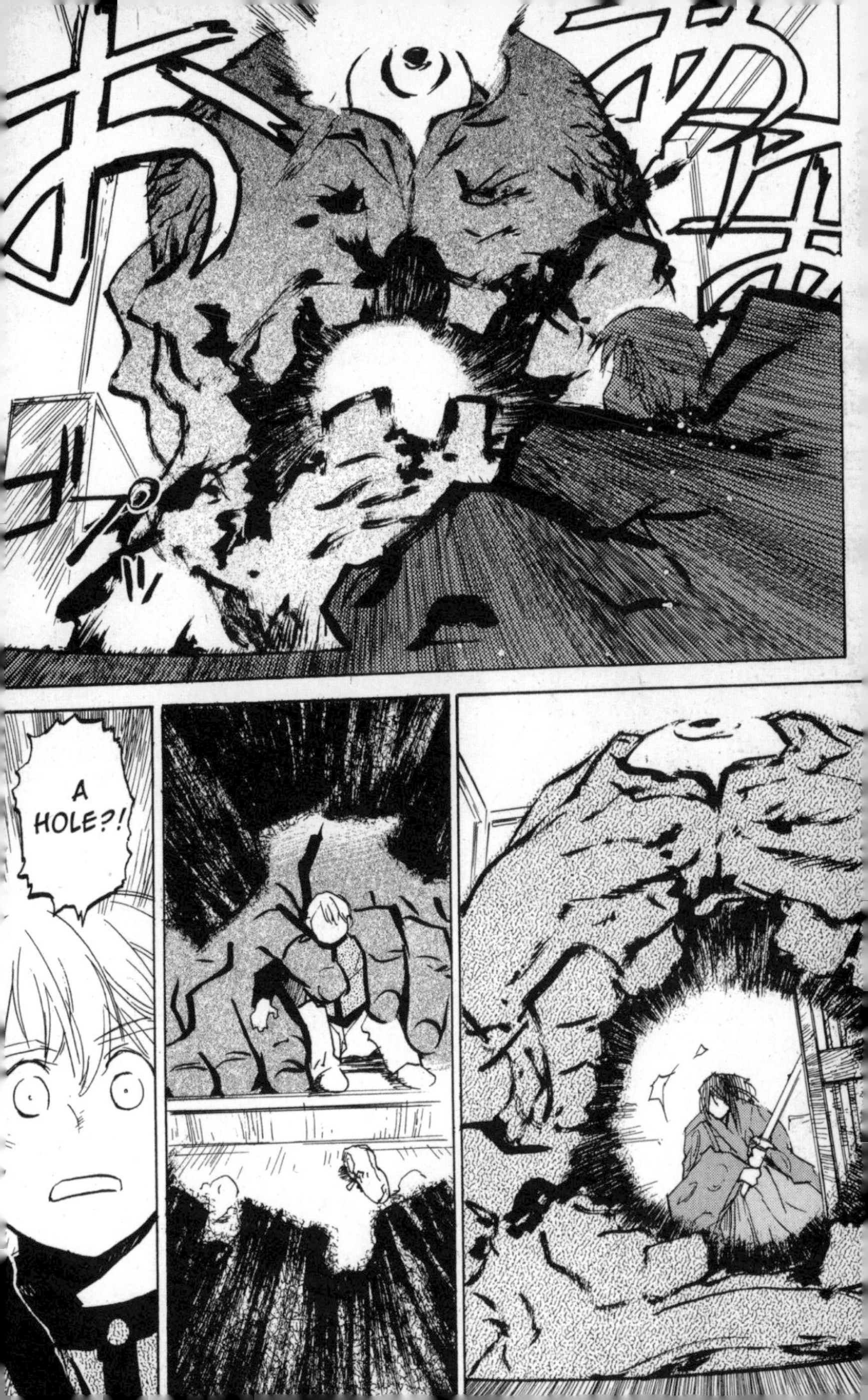
A HOLE?!

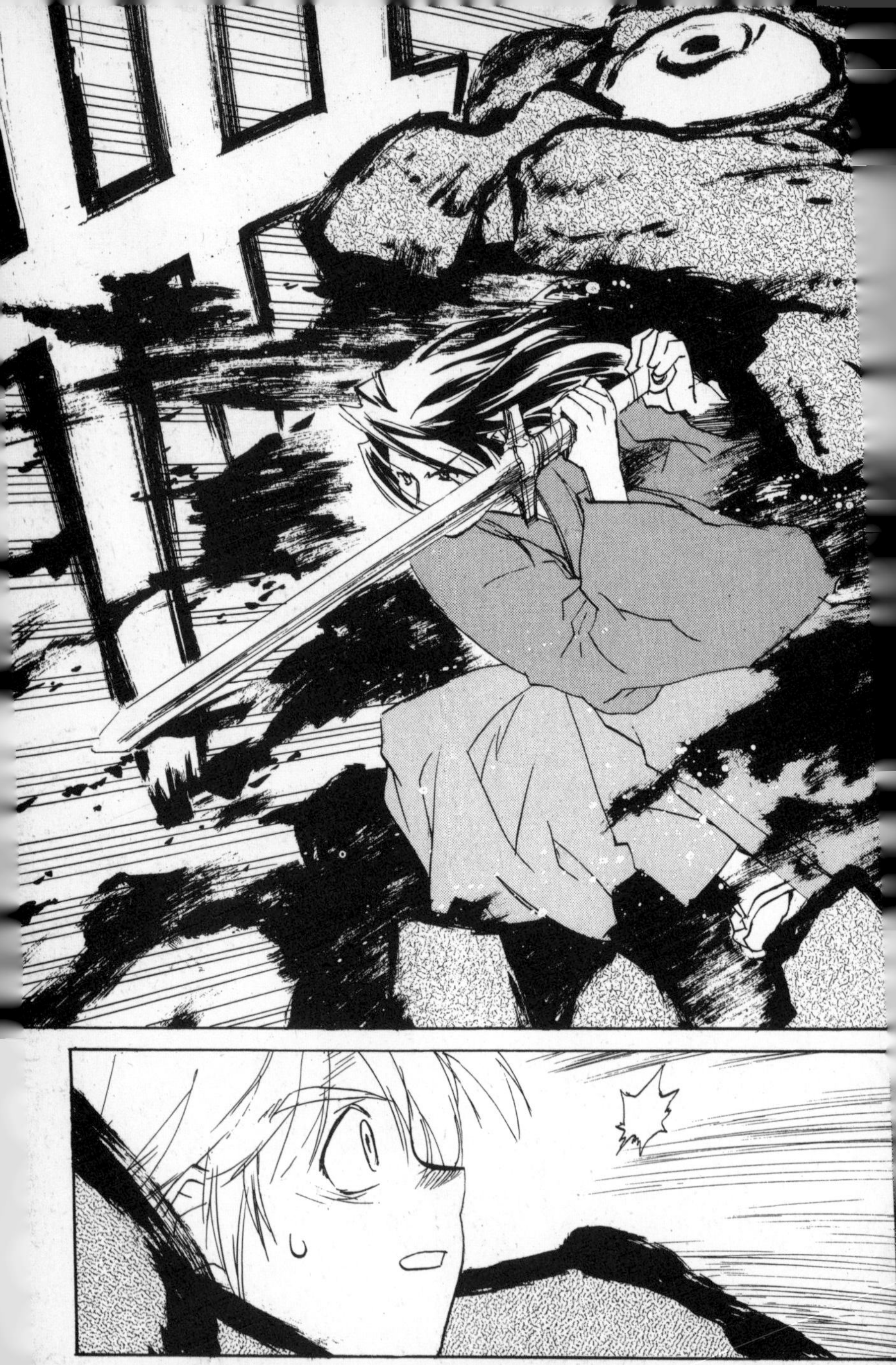

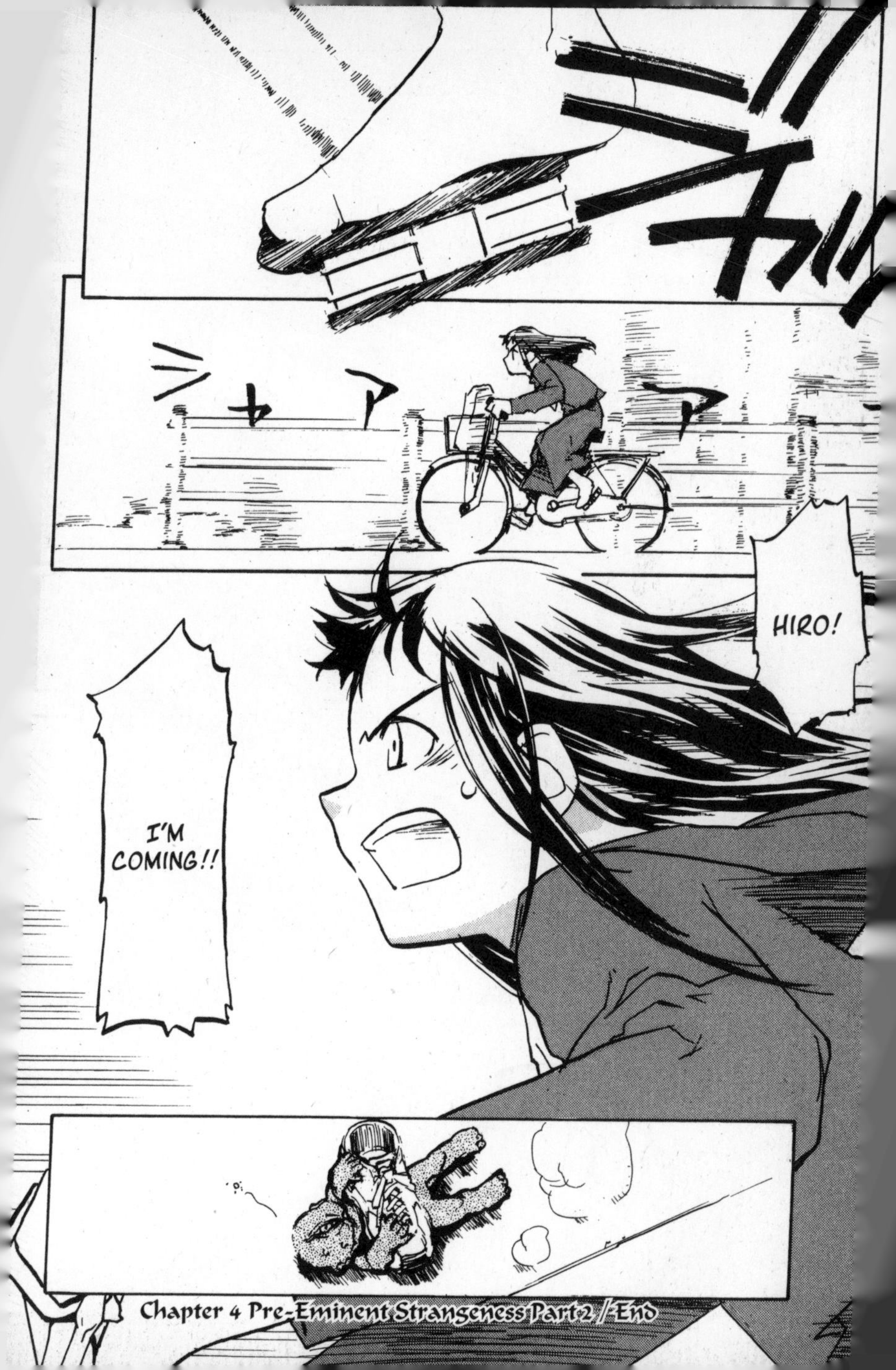
HIRO!
I'M COMING!!

Chapter 4 Pre-Eminent Strangeness Part 2 / End

Chapter 4 Pre-Eminent Strangeness Part 3

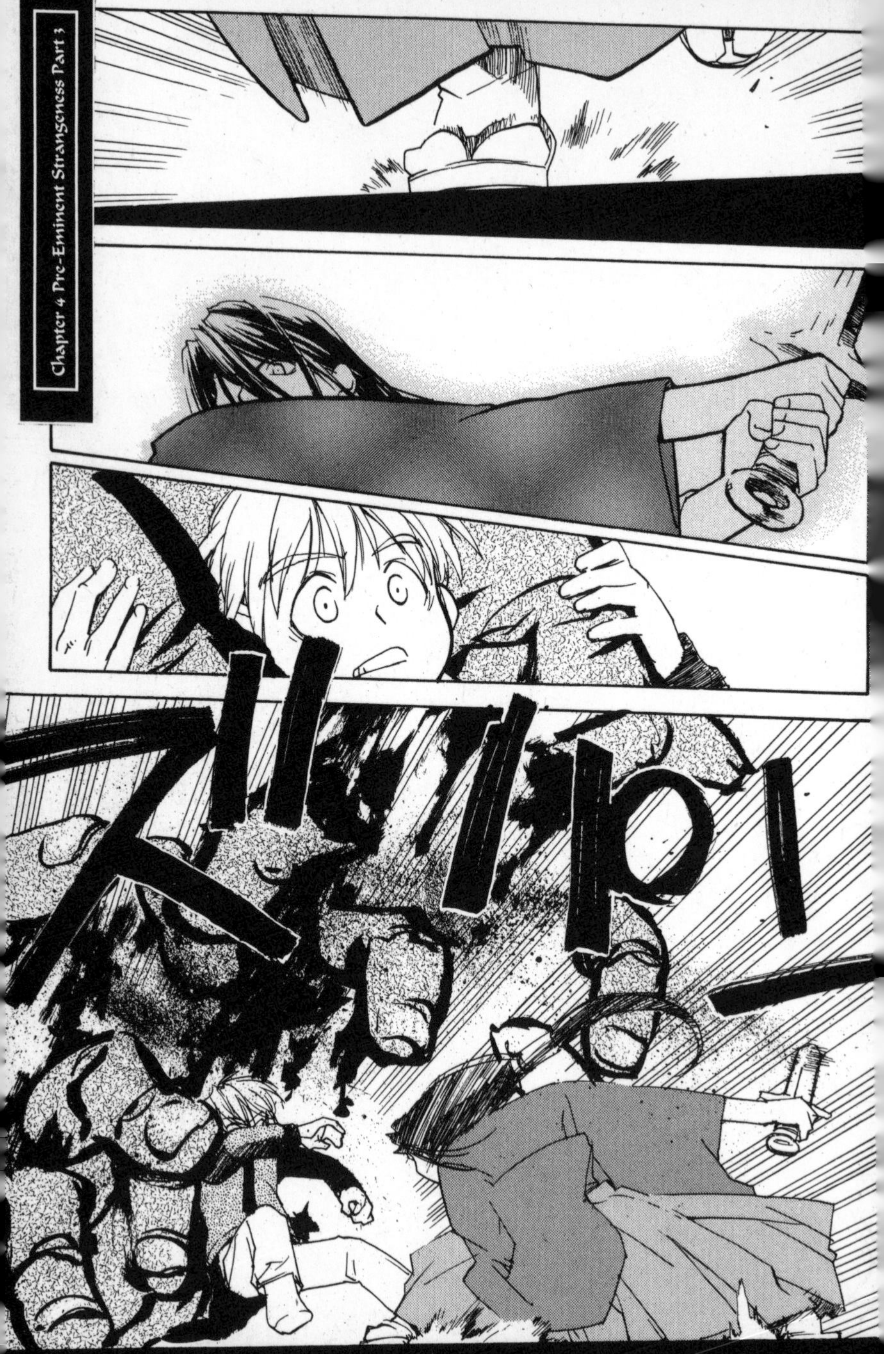

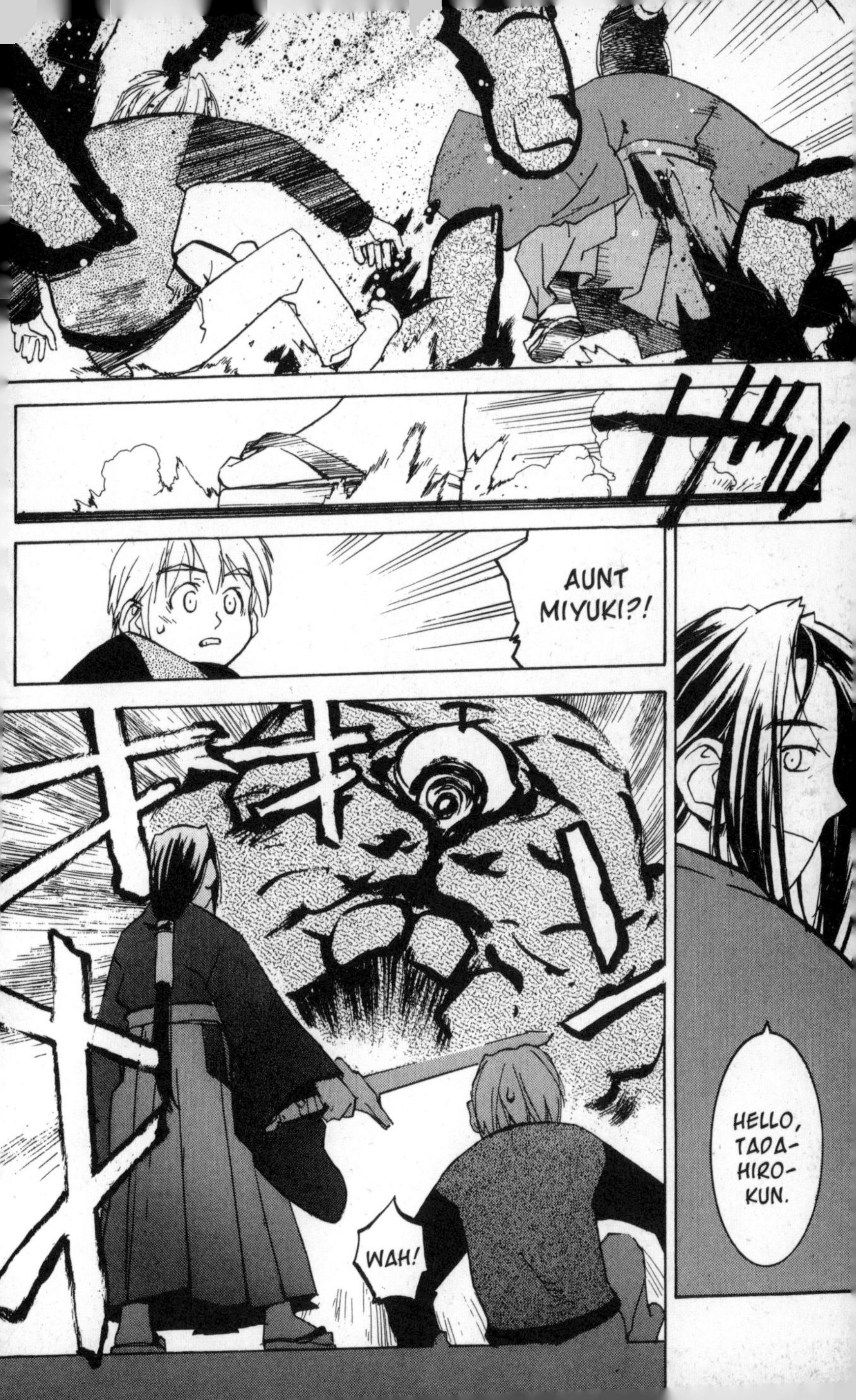
HELLO, TADA-HIRO-KUN.
AUNT MIYUKI?!
WAH!

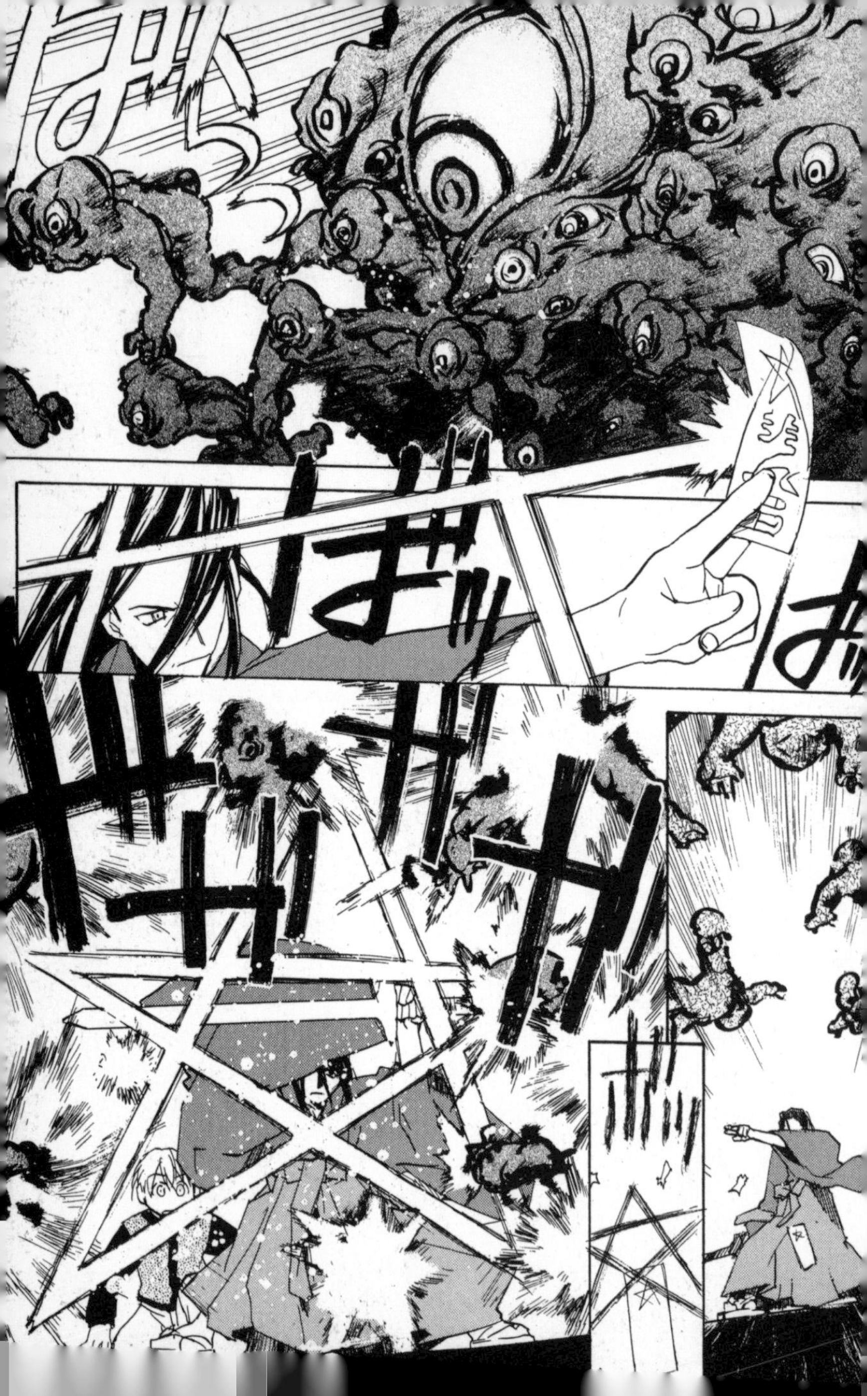

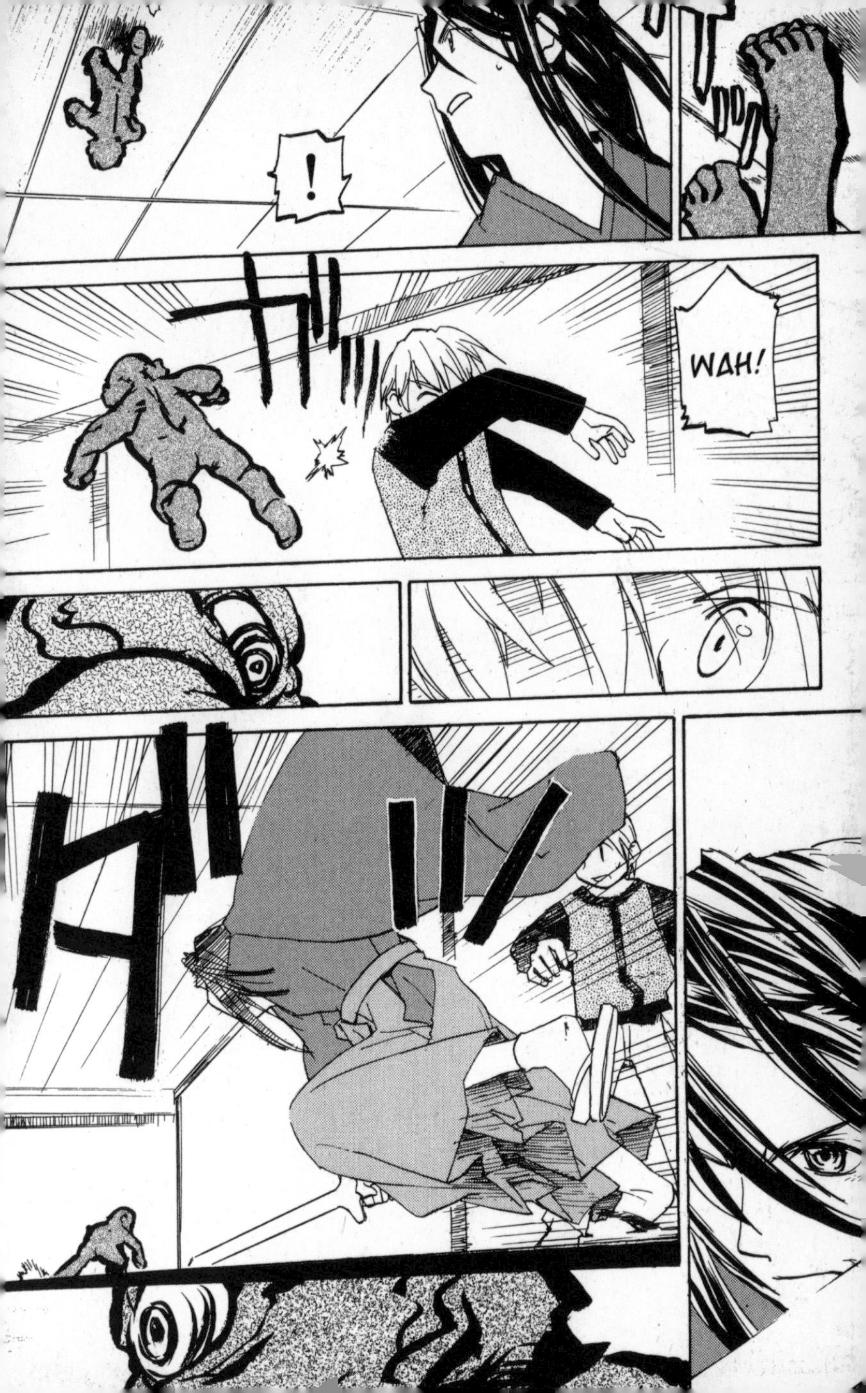
!
WAH!

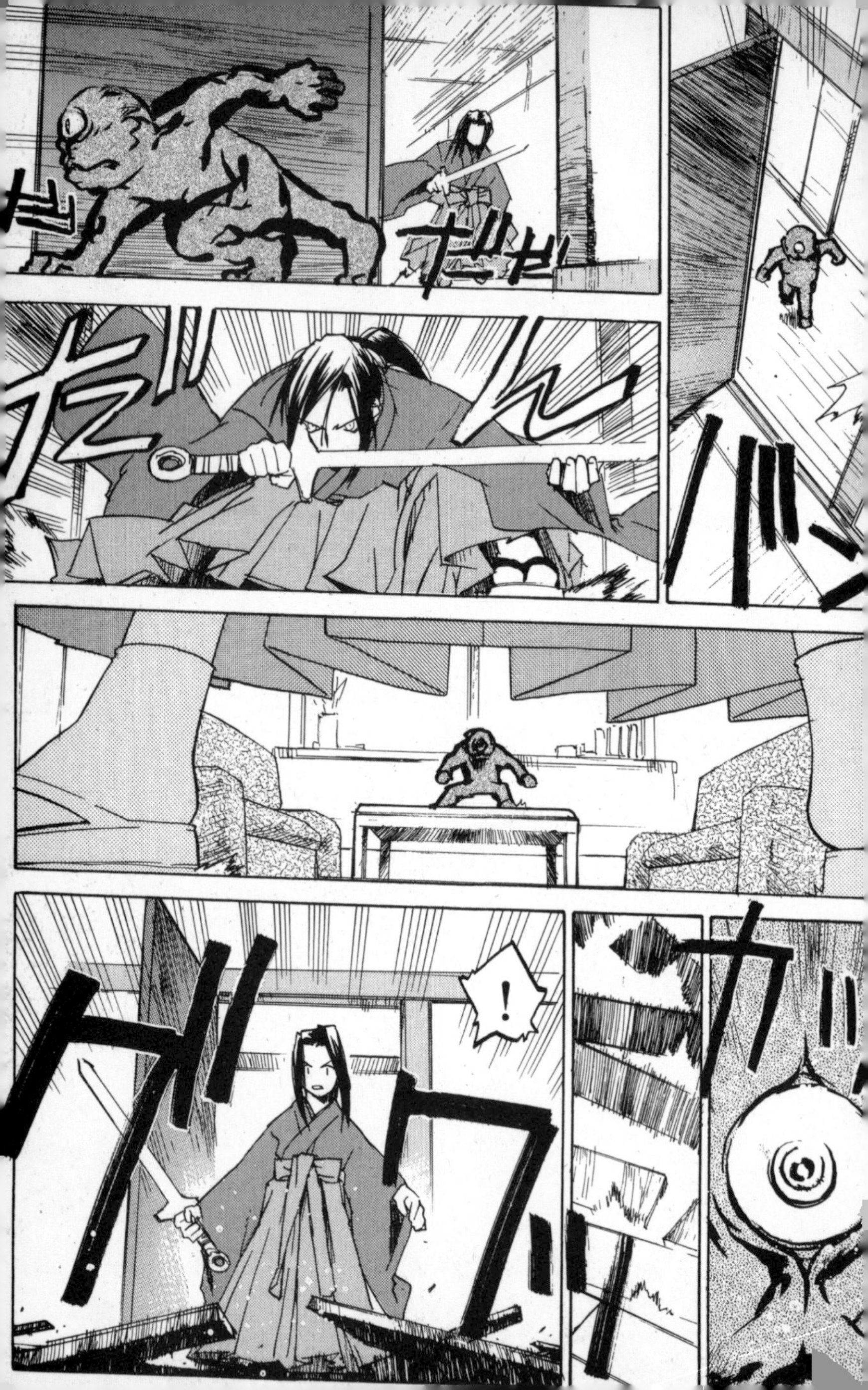
!

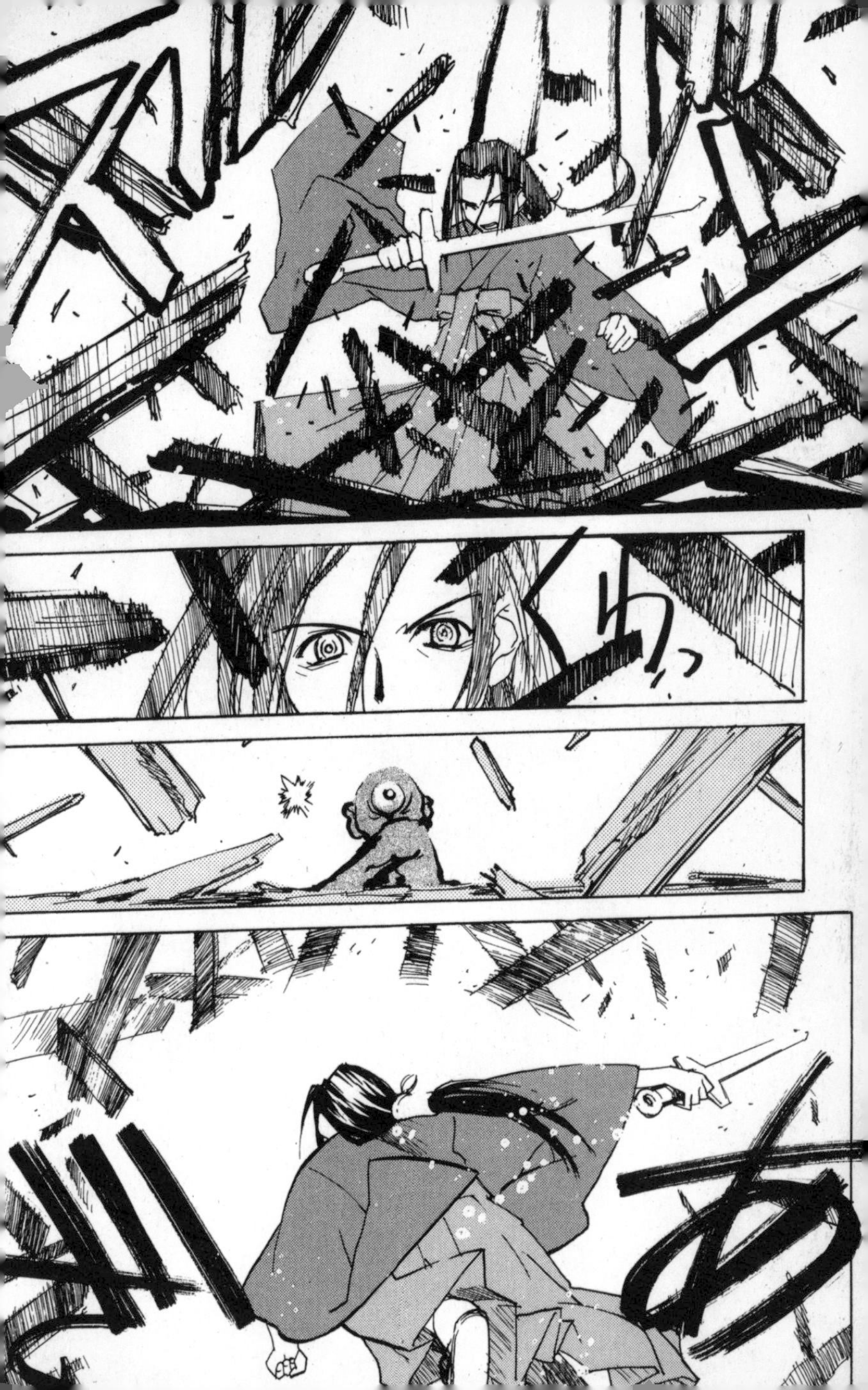
くわっ

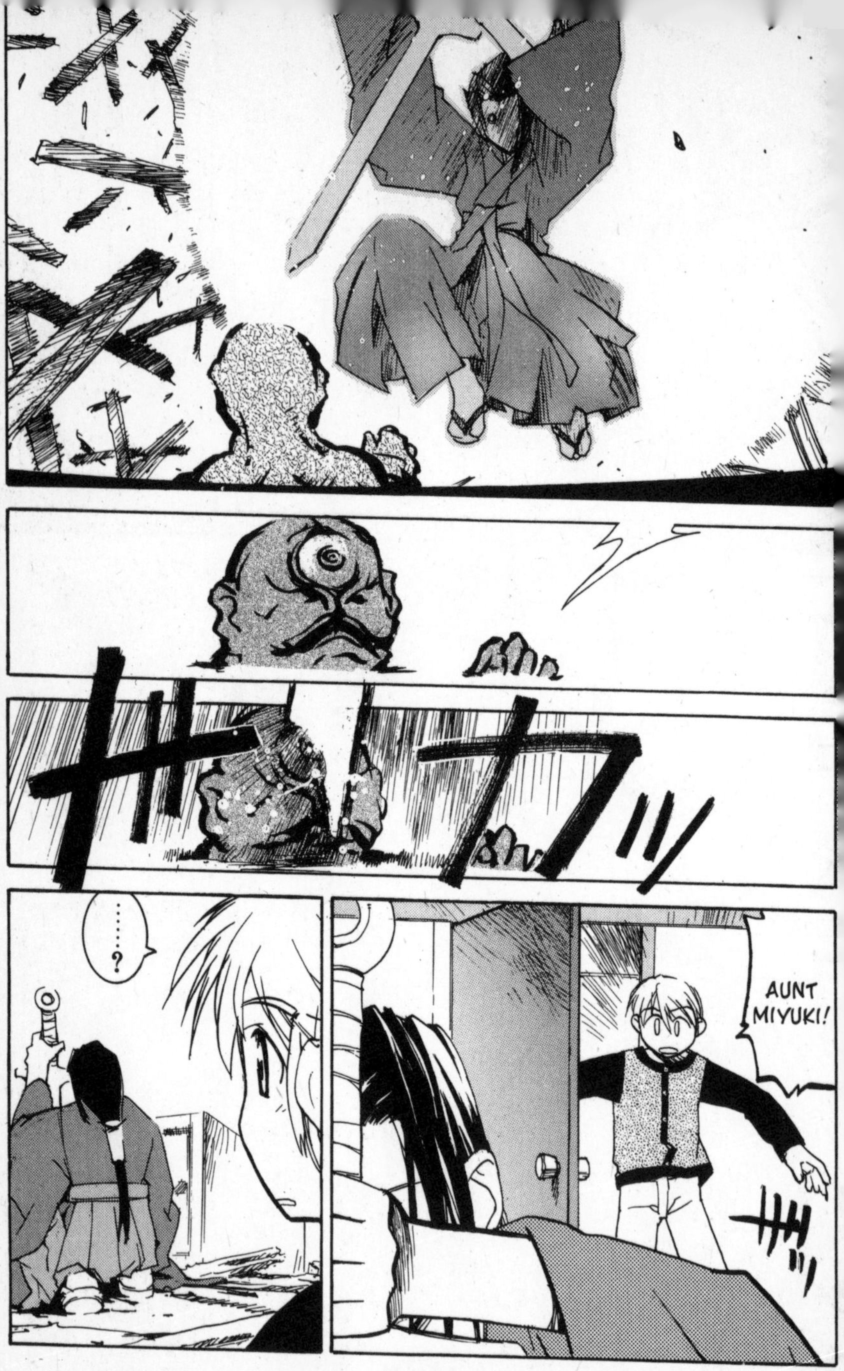
AUNT MIYUKI!
......?

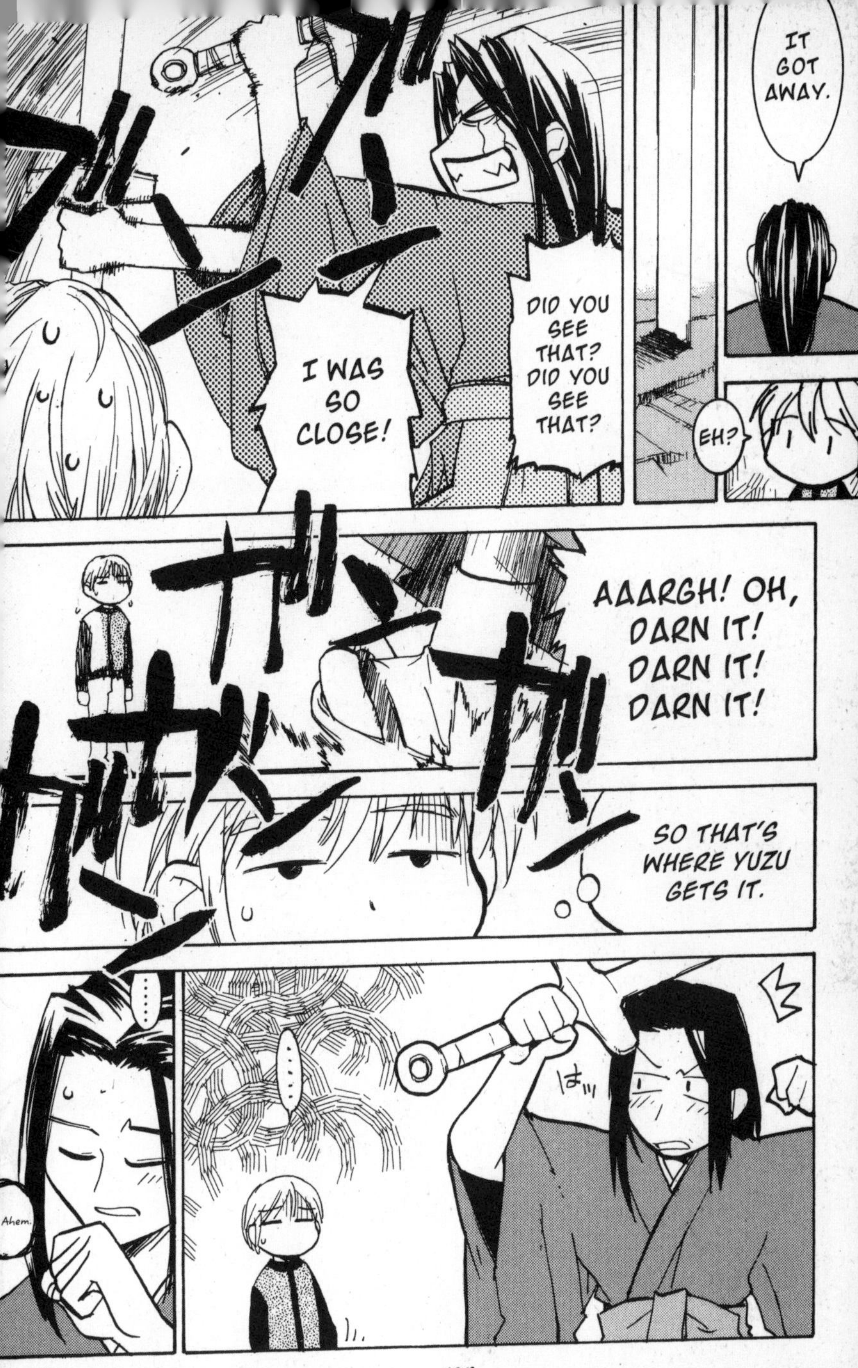
IT GOT AWAY.
EH?
DID YOU SEE THAT? DID YOU SEE THAT?
I WAS SO CLOSE!
AAARGH! OH, DARN IT! DARN IT! DARN IT!
SO THAT'S WHERE YUZU GETS IT.
はッ
......
......
Ahem.

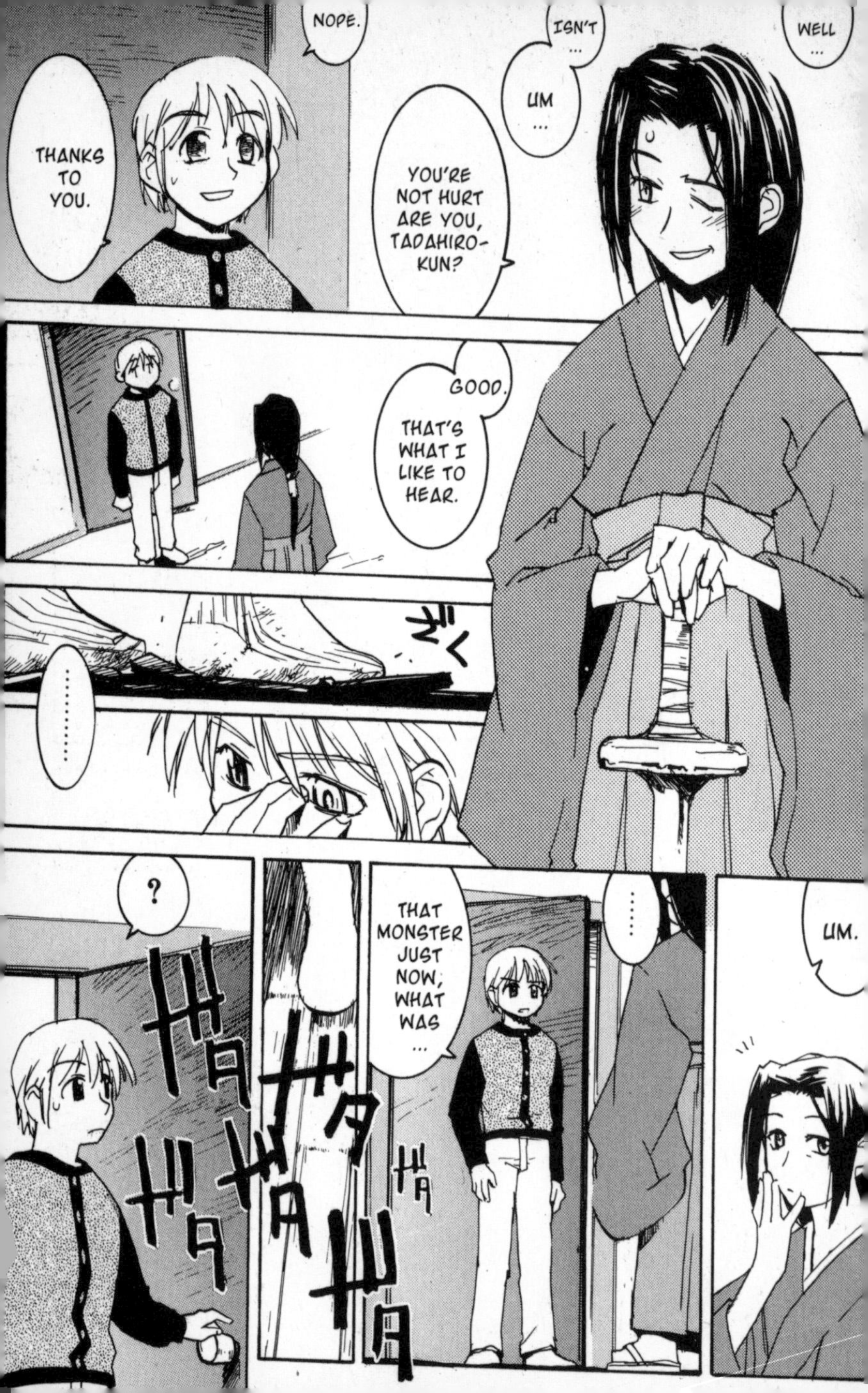
WELL ...
ISN'T ...
UM ...
YOU'RE NOT HURT ARE YOU, TADAHIRO-KUN?
NOPE.
THANKS TO YOU.
GOOD.
THAT'S WHAT I LIKE TO HEAR.
ざく
....
UM.
......
THAT MONSTER JUST NOW, WHAT WAS ...
?
HA HA HA HA HA HA HA

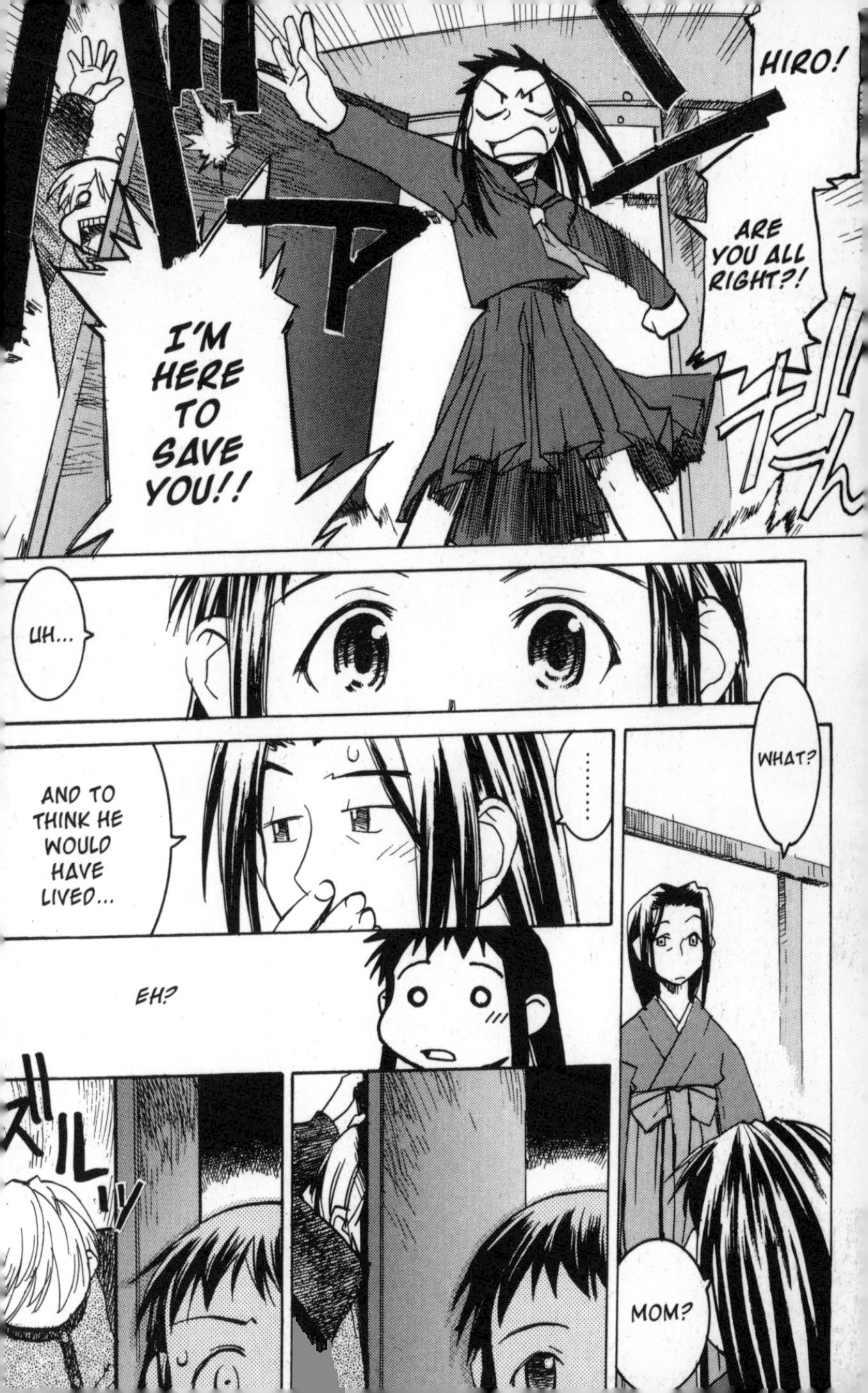
HIRO!
ARE YOU ALL RIGHT?!
I'M HERE TO SAVE YOU!!
UH...
WHAT?
MOM?
......
AND TO THINK HE WOULD HAVE LIVED...
EH?
ズルッ

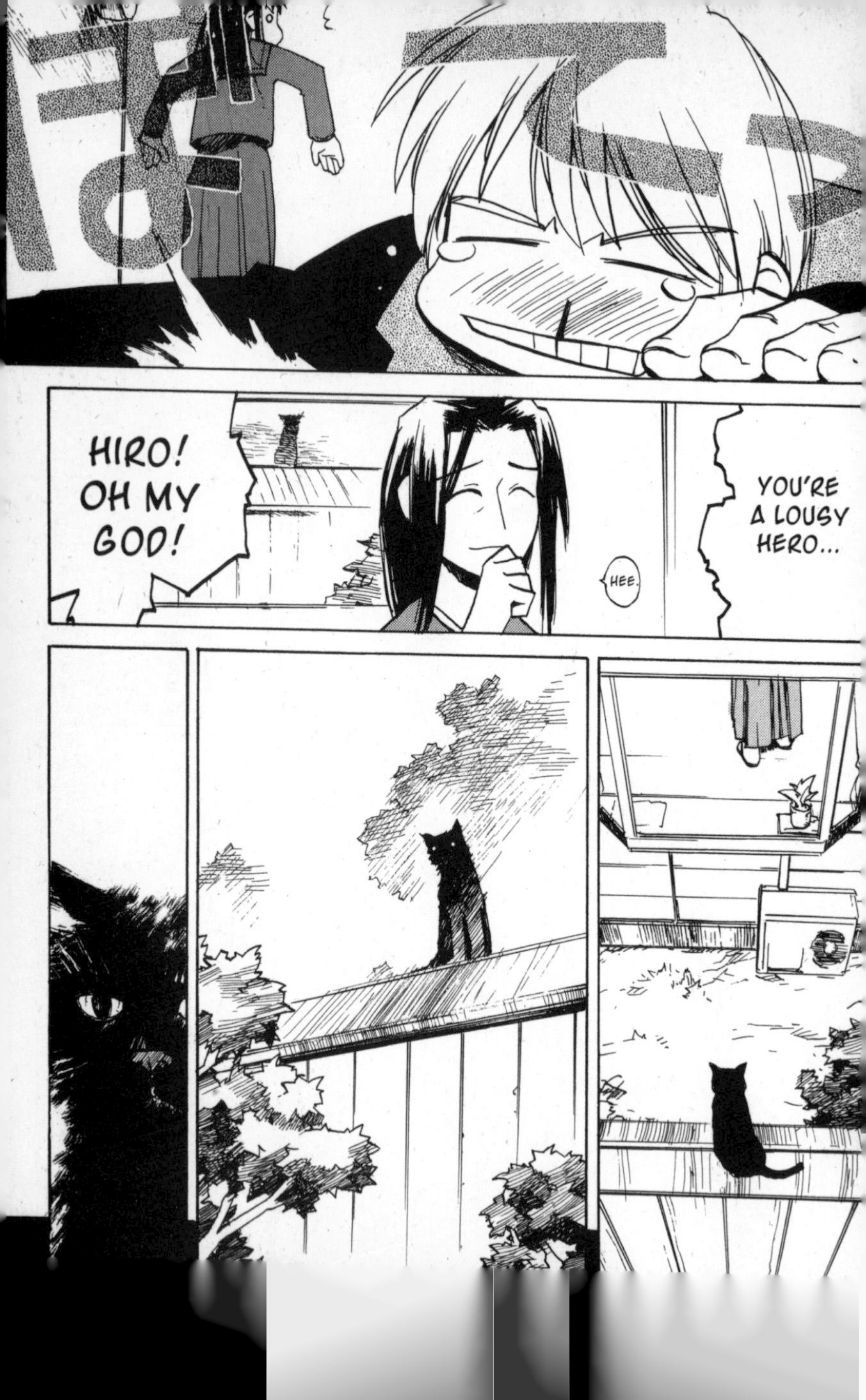
YOU'RE A LOUSY HERO...
HEE.
HIRO! OH MY GOD!

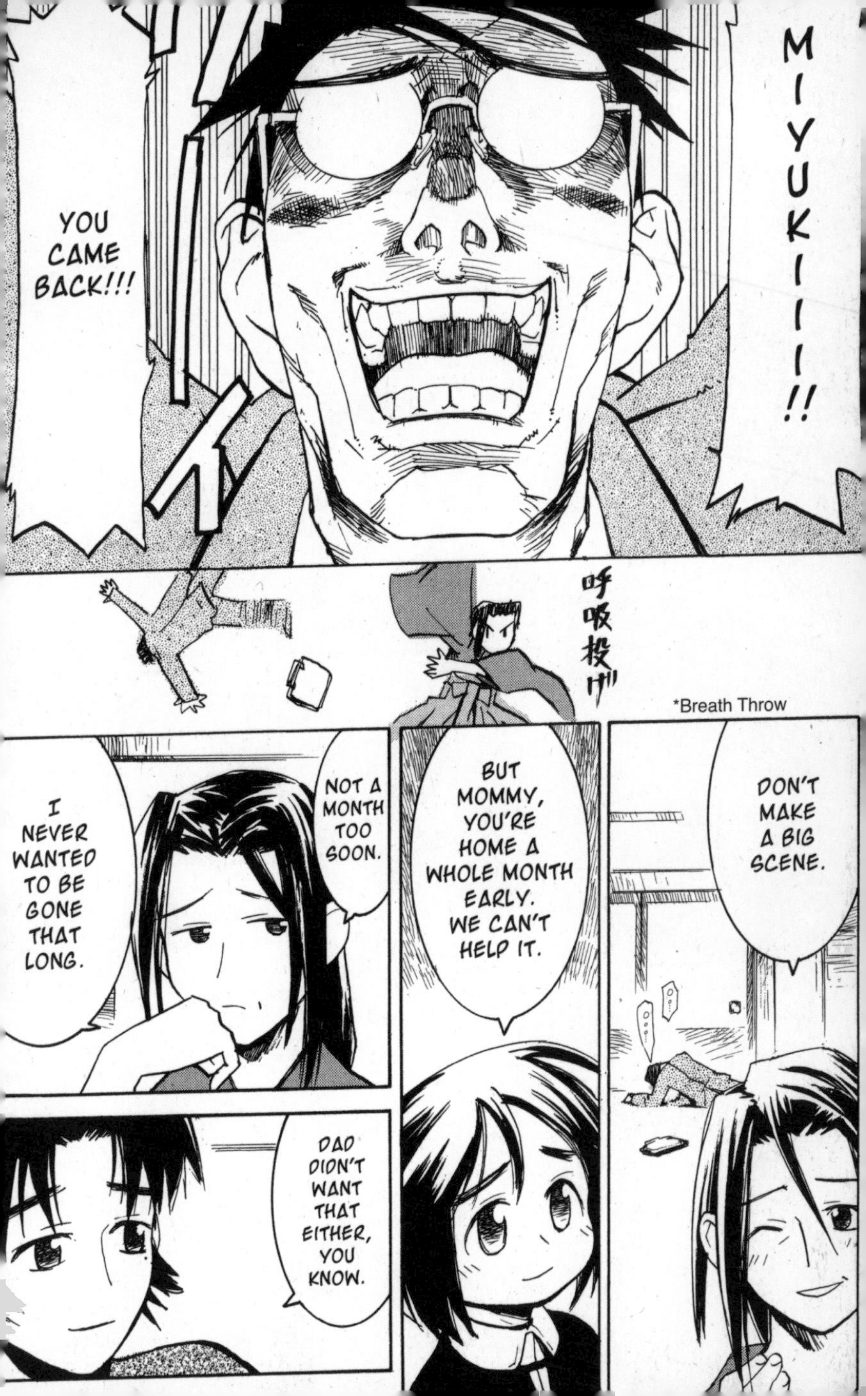
MIYUKIII!!
YOU CAME BACK!!!
呼吸投げ
*Breath Throw
DON'T MAKE A BIG SCENE.
BUT MOMMY, YOU'RE HOME A WHOLE MONTH EARLY. WE CAN'T HELP IT.
NOT A MONTH TOO SOON.
I NEVER WANTED TO BE GONE THAT LONG.
DAD DIDN'T WANT THAT EITHER, YOU KNOW.

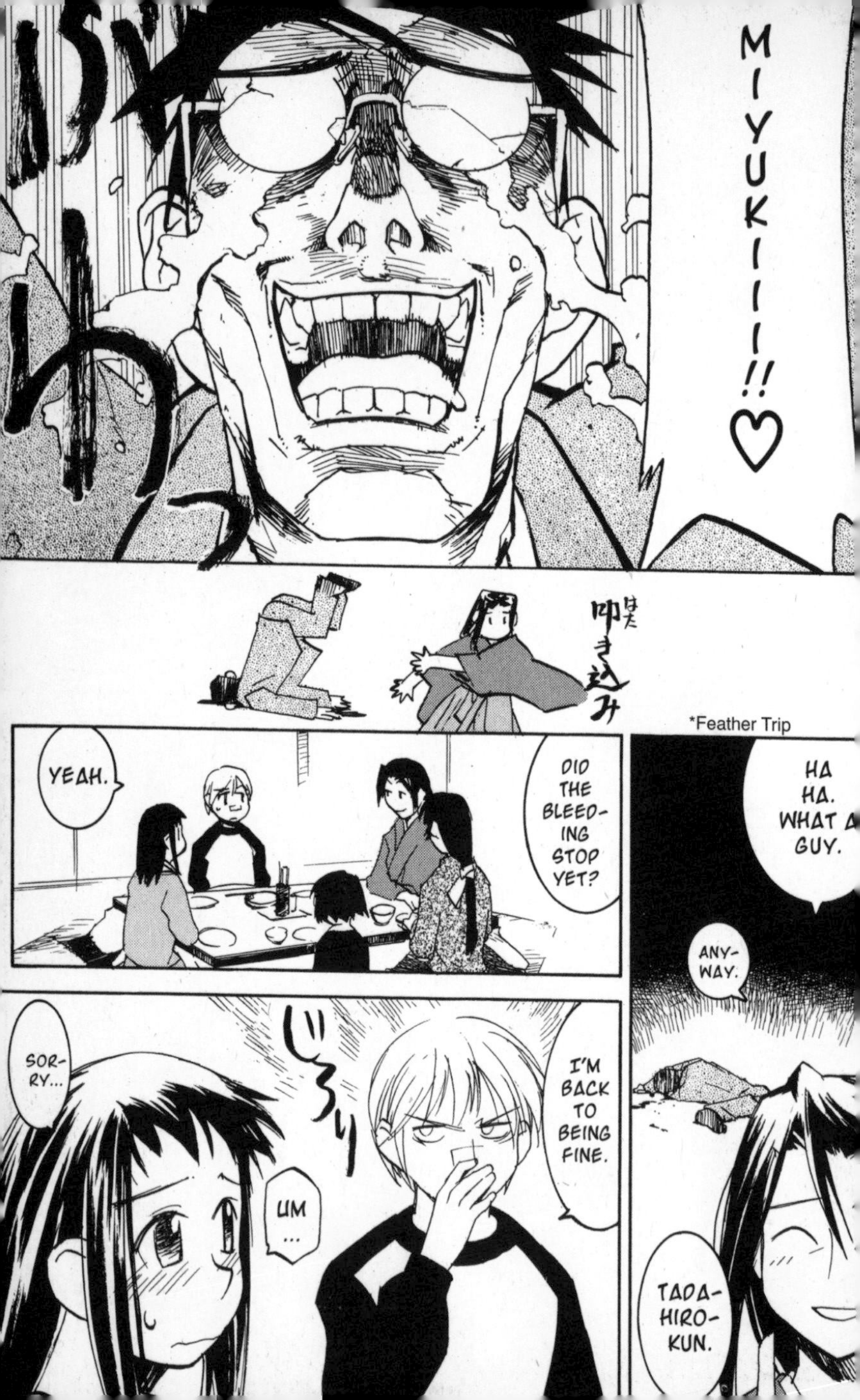
MIYUKIIII!!♡
叩き込み
*Feather Trip
HA HA. WHAT A GUY.
ANY-WAY.
TADA-HIRO-KUN.
DID THE BLEED-ING STOP YET?
YEAH.
I'M BACK TO BEING FINE.
UM ...
SOR-RY...

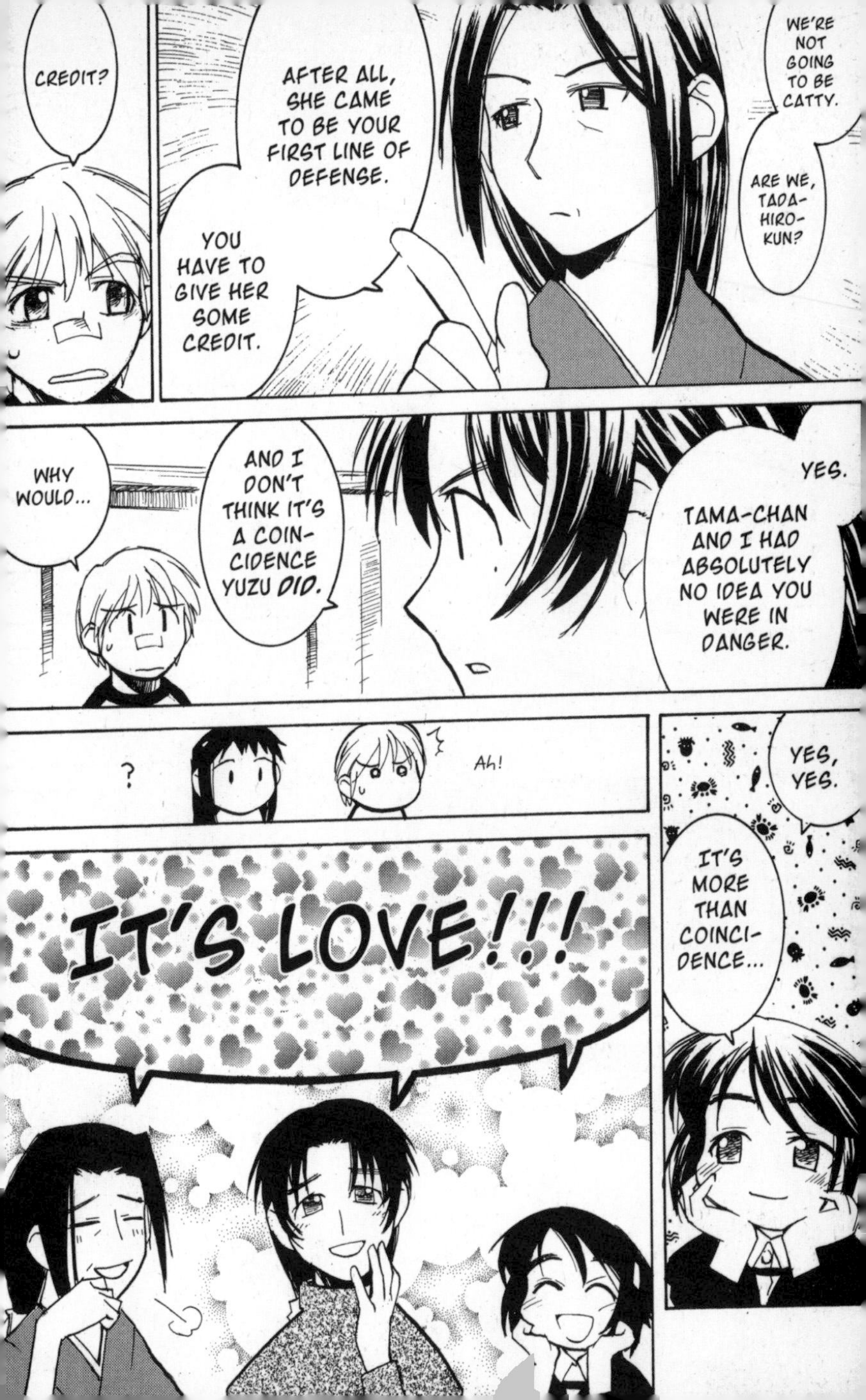
WE'RE NOT GOING TO BE CATTY.
ARE WE, TADA-HIRO-KUN?
AFTER ALL, SHE CAME TO BE YOUR FIRST LINE OF DEFENSE.
YOU HAVE TO GIVE HER SOME CREDIT.
CREDIT?
YES.
TAMA-CHAN AND I HAD ABSOLUTELY NO IDEA YOU WERE IN DANGER.
AND I DON'T THINK IT'S A COINCIDENCE YUZU DID.
WHY WOULD...
YES, YES.
IT'S MORE THAN COINCIDENCE...
Ah!
?
IT'S LOVE!!!

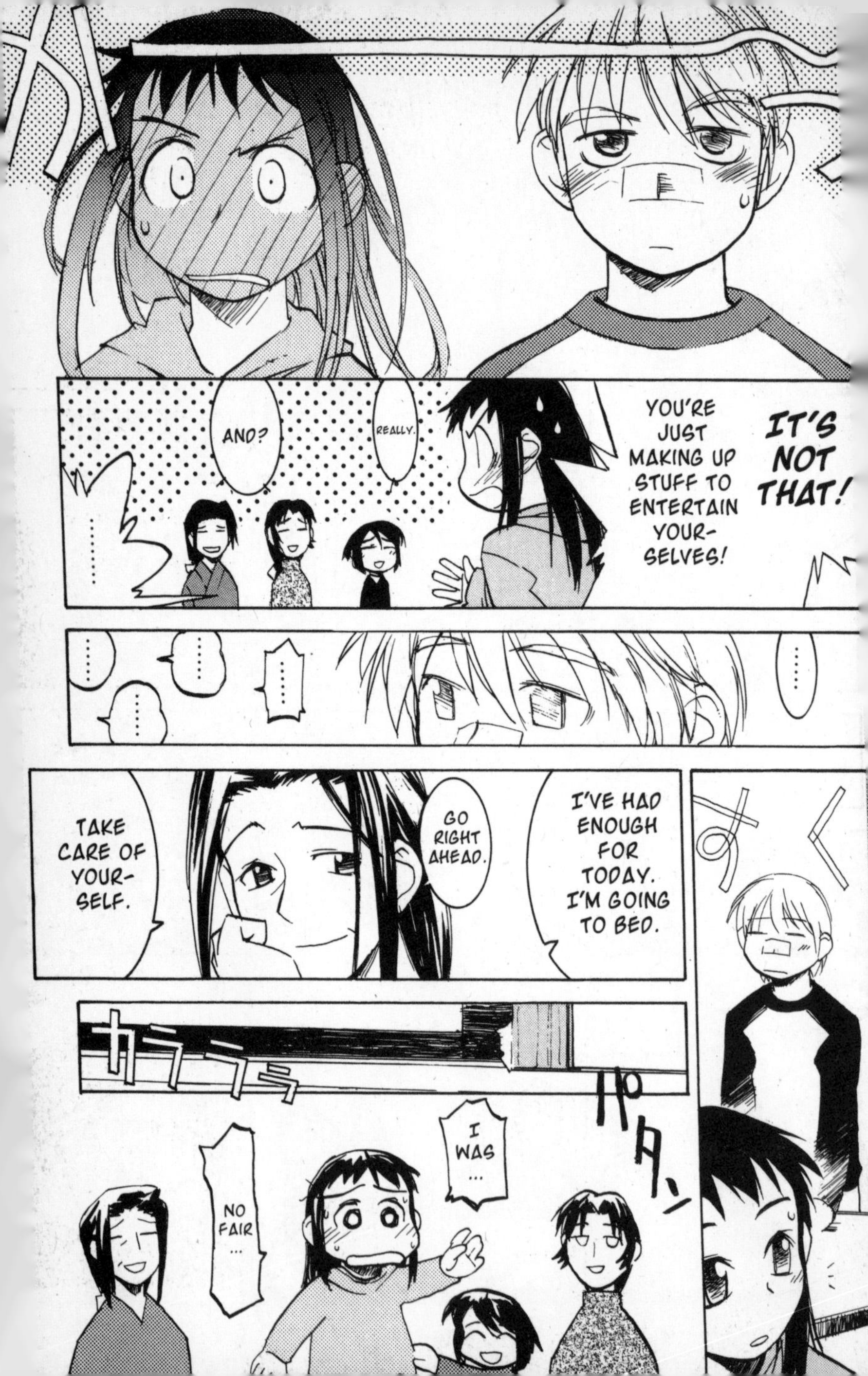
IT'S NOT THAT!
YOU'RE JUST MAKING UP STUFF TO ENTERTAIN YOURSELVES!
REALLY.
AND?
......
......
......
......
......
......
I'VE HAD ENOUGH FOR TODAY. I'M GOING TO BED.
GO RIGHT AHEAD.
TAKE CARE OF YOURSELF.
カラララ
パタン
I WAS ...
NO FAIR ...

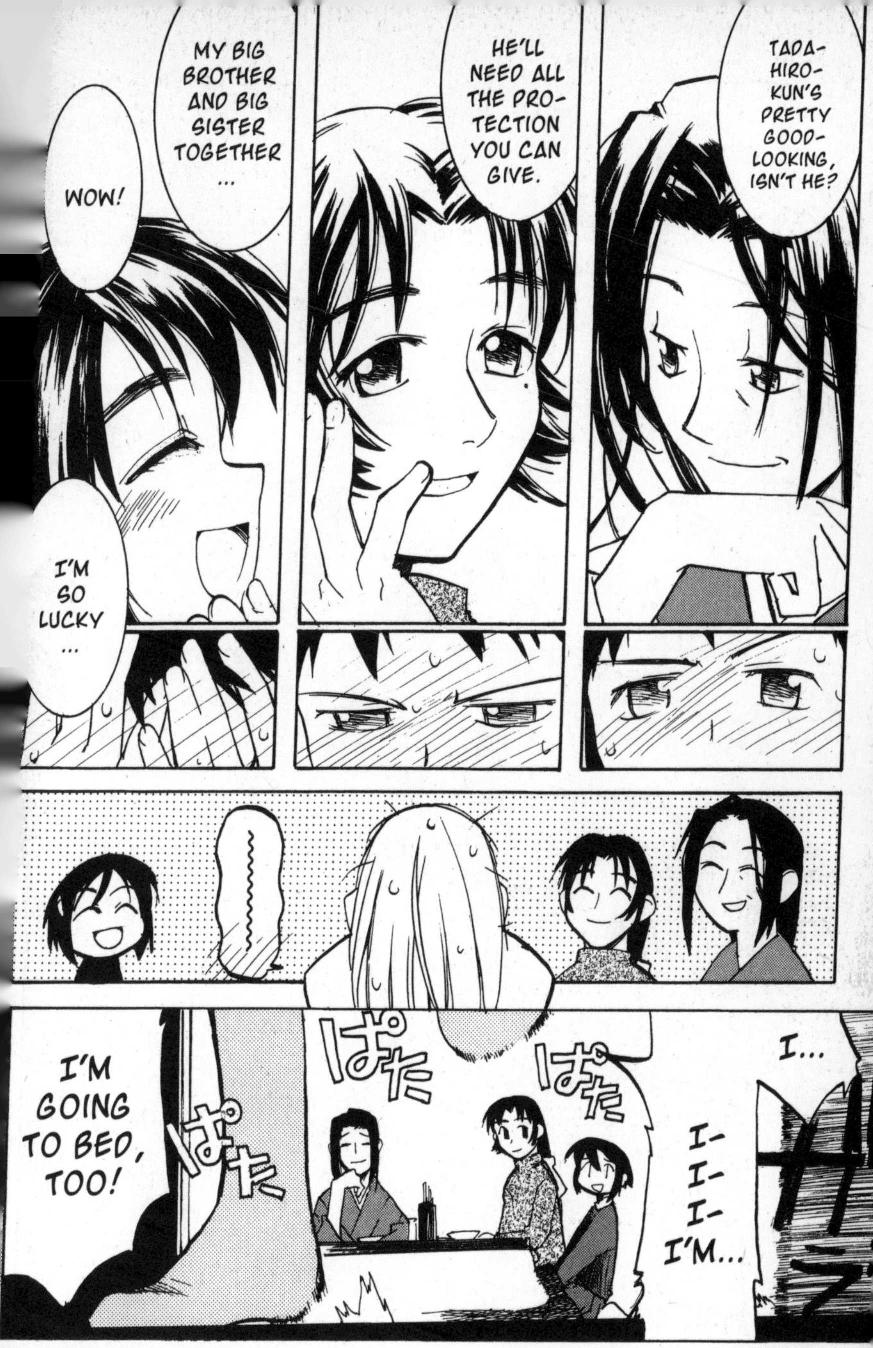
TADA-HIRO-KUN'S PRETTY GOOD-LOOKING, ISN'T HE?
HE'LL NEED ALL THE PROTECTION YOU CAN GIVE.
MY BIG BROTHER AND BIG SISTER TOGETHER ...
WOW!
I'M SO LUCKY ...
I...
I-I-I-I'M...
ぱた
ぱた
ぱた
I'M GOING TO BED, TOO!

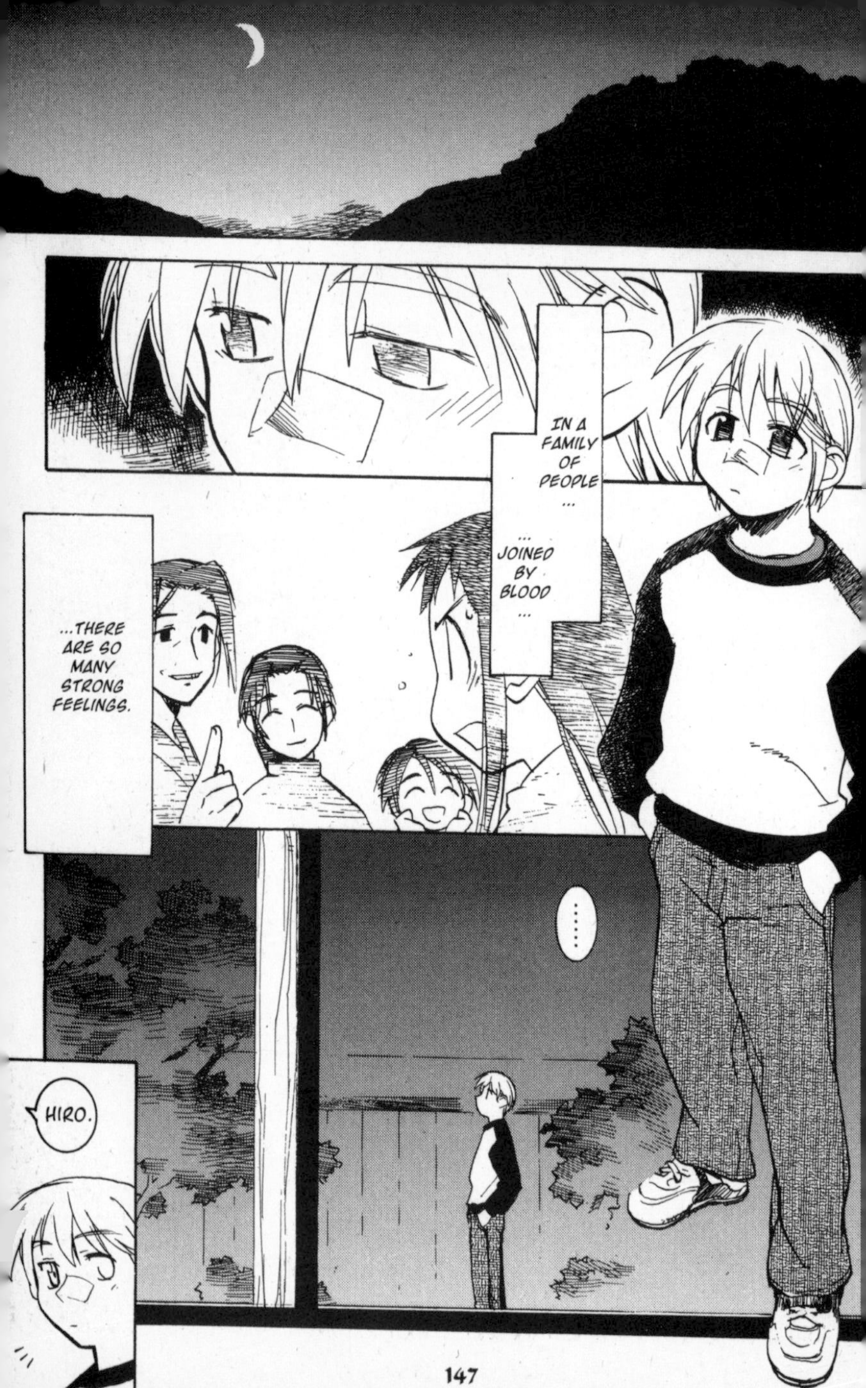
IN A FAMILY OF PEOPLE ...
... JOINED BY BLOOD ...
...THERE ARE SO MANY STRONG FEELINGS.
......
HIRO.

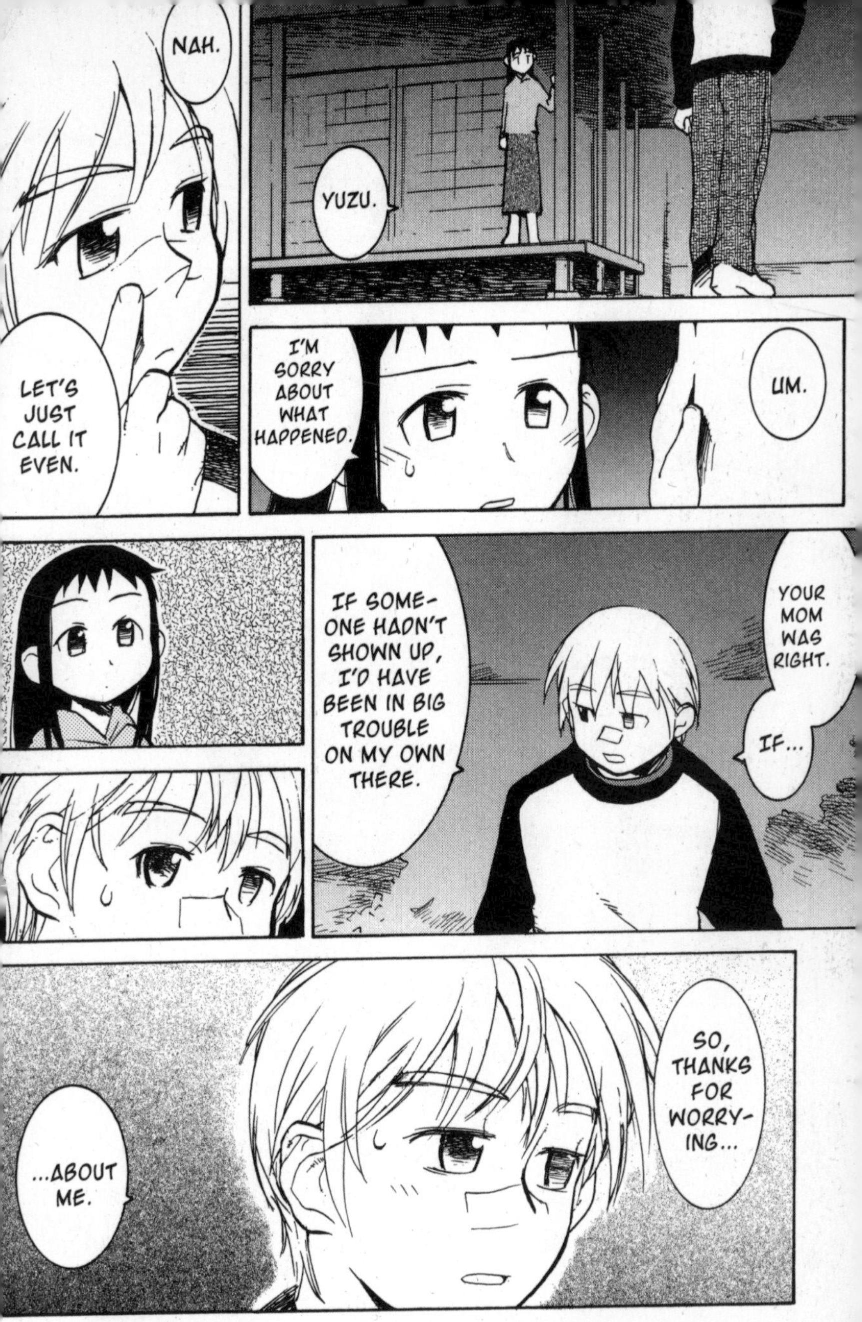
YUZU.
UM.
I'M SORRY ABOUT WHAT HAPPENED.
NAH.
LET'S JUST CALL IT EVEN.
YOUR MOM WAS RIGHT.
IF...
IF SOME-ONE HADN'T SHOWN UP, I'D HAVE BEEN IN BIG TROUBLE ON MY OWN THERE.
SO, THANKS FOR WORRY-ING...
...ABOUT ME.

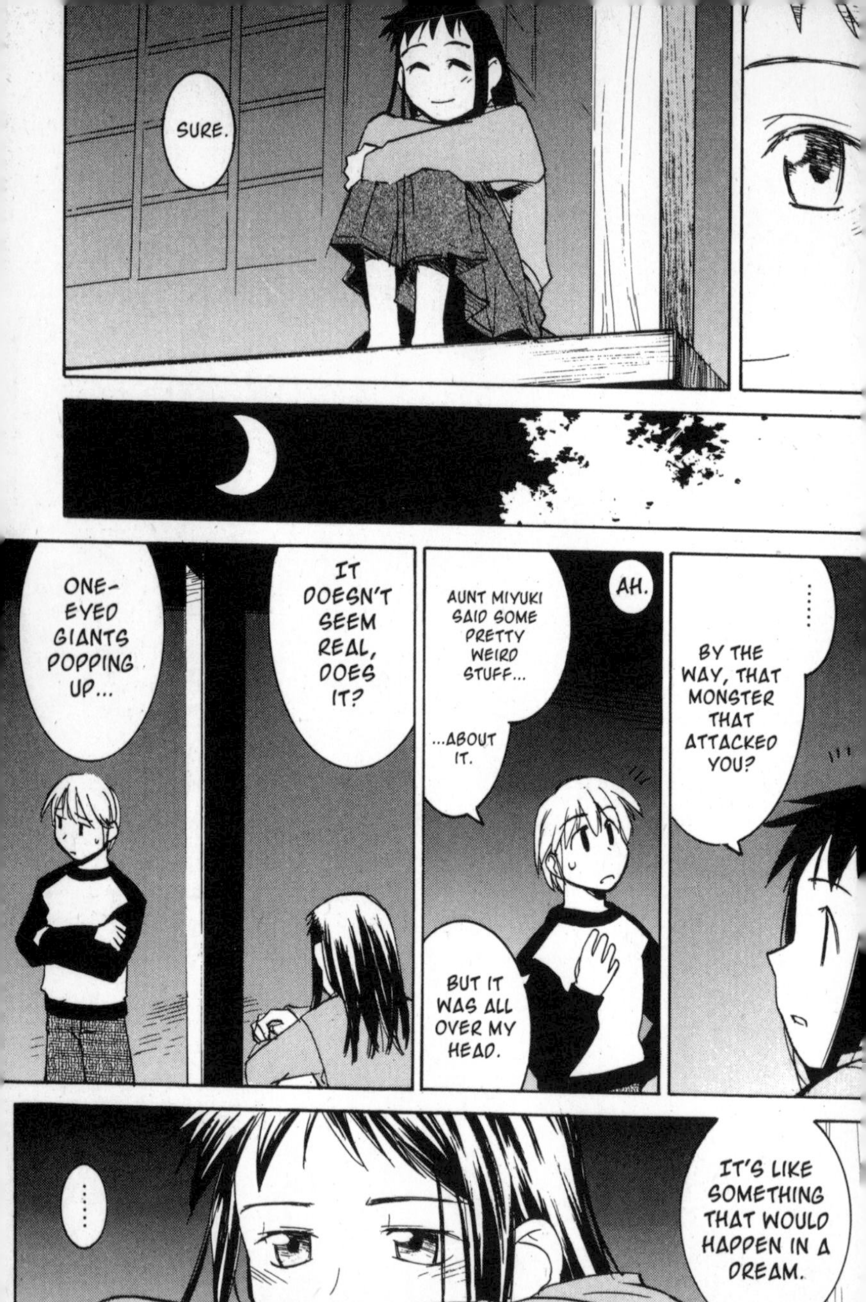
SURE.
......
BY THE WAY, THAT MONSTER THAT ATTACKED YOU?
AH.
AUNT MIYUKI SAID SOME PRETTY WEIRD STUFF...
...ABOUT IT.
BUT IT WAS ALL OVER MY HEAD.
IT DOESN'T SEEM REAL, DOES IT?
ONE-EYED GIANTS POPPING UP...
IT'S LIKE SOMETHING THAT WOULD HAPPEN IN A DREAM.
......

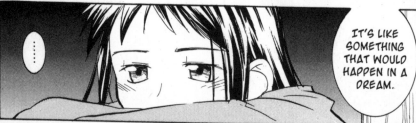

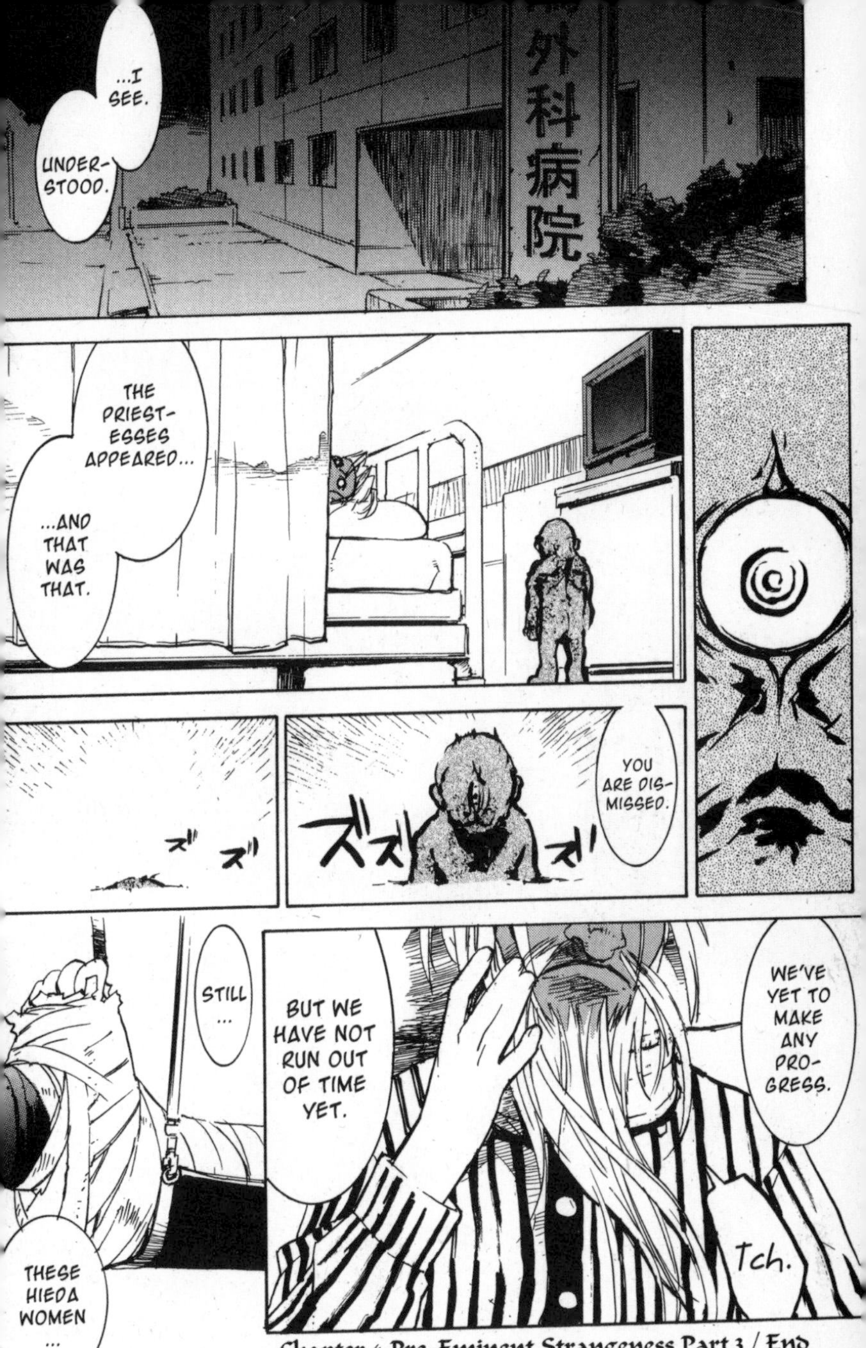
外科病院
...I SEE.
UNDER-STOOD.
THE PRIEST-ESSES APPEARED...
...AND THAT WAS THAT.
YOU ARE DIS-MISSED.
ズズ ズ
ズ ズ
WE'VE YET TO MAKE ANY PRO-GRESS.
BUT WE HAVE NOT RUN OUT OF TIME YET.
Tch.
STILL ...
THESE HIEDA WOMEN ...

Chapter 4 Pre-Eminent Strangeness Part 3 / End

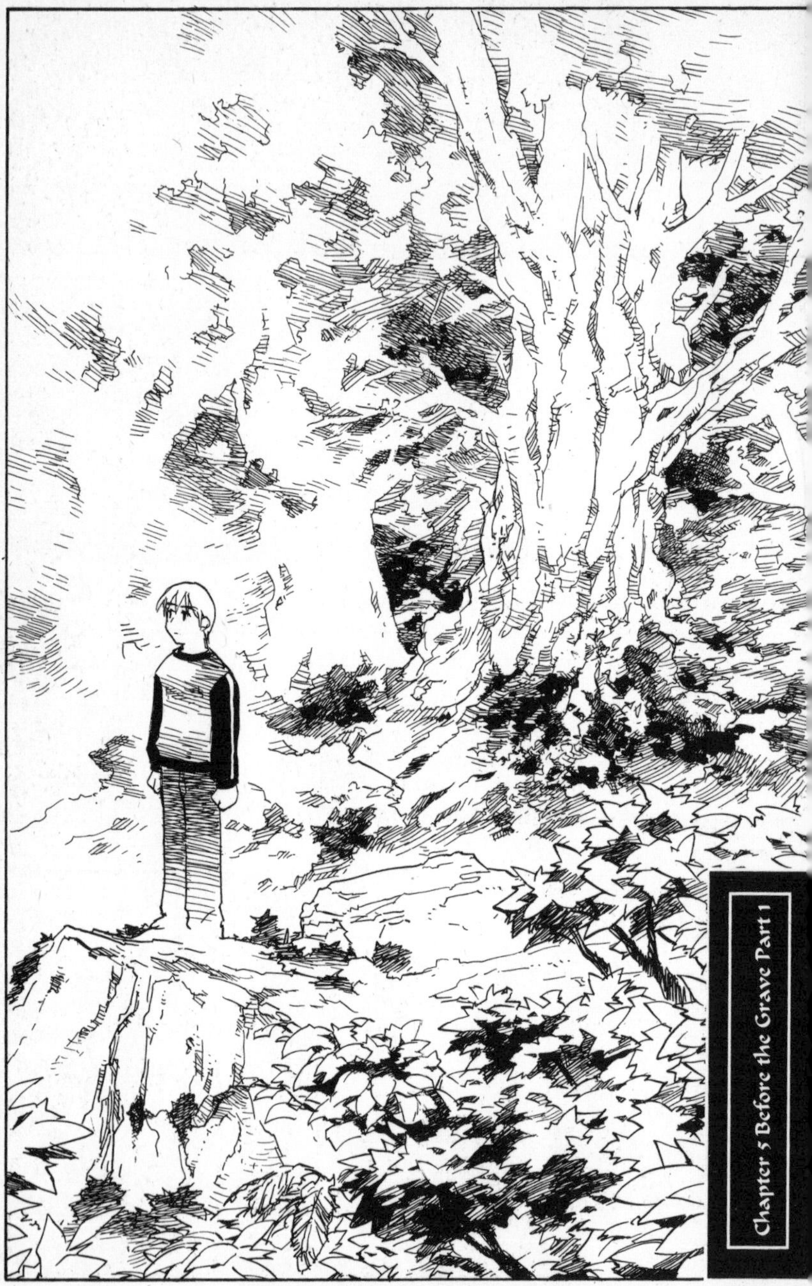

Chapter 5 Before the Grave Part 1

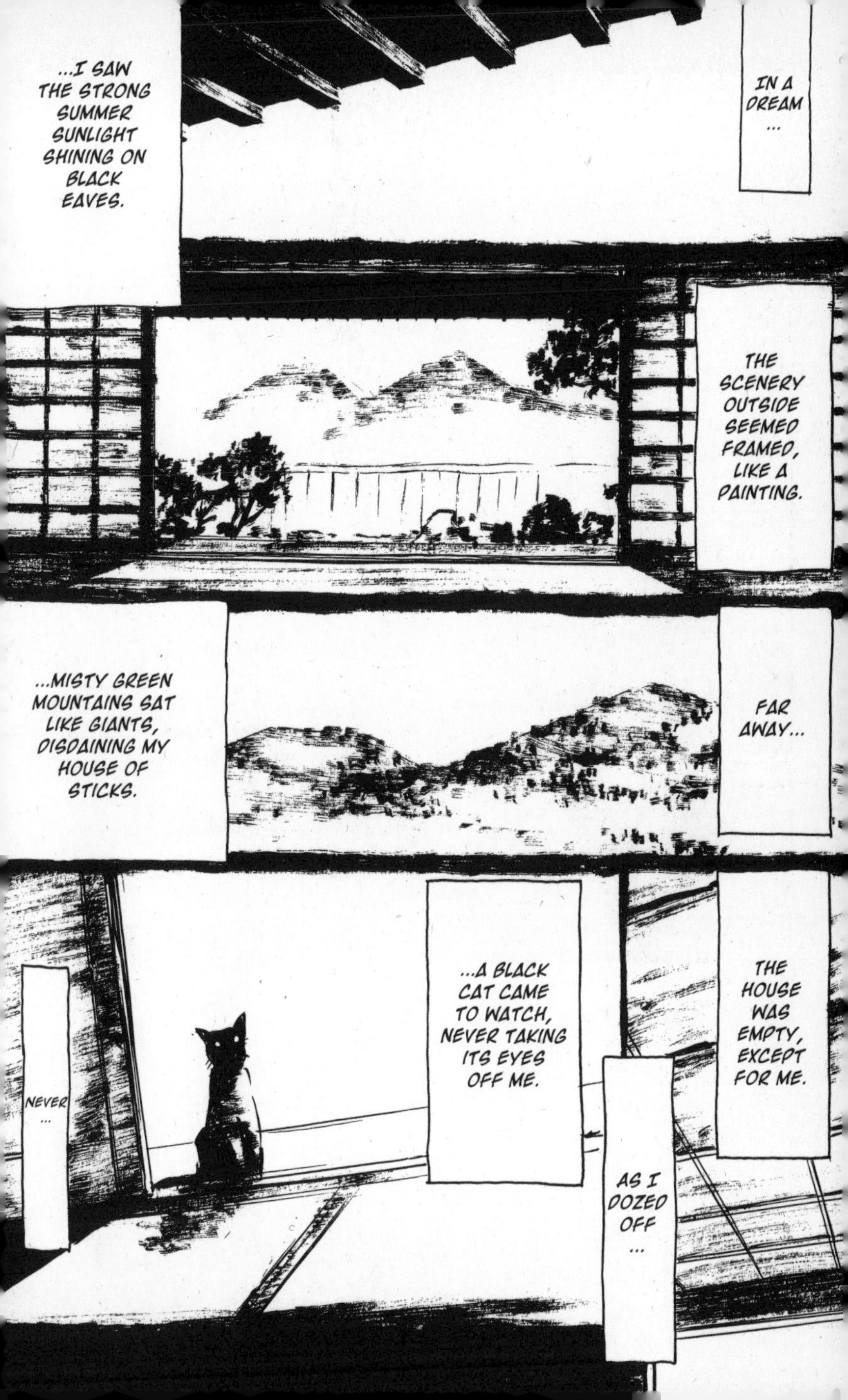
IN A DREAM...
...I SAW THE STRONG SUMMER SUNLIGHT SHINING ON BLACK EAVES.
THE SCENERY OUTSIDE SEEMED FRAMED, LIKE A PAINTING.
FAR AWAY...
...MISTY GREEN MOUNTAINS SAT LIKE GIANTS, DISDAINING MY HOUSE OF STICKS.
THE HOUSE WAS EMPTY, EXCEPT FOR ME.
AS I DOZED OFF...
...A BLACK CAT CAME TO WATCH, NEVER TAKING ITS EYES OFF ME.
NEVER...

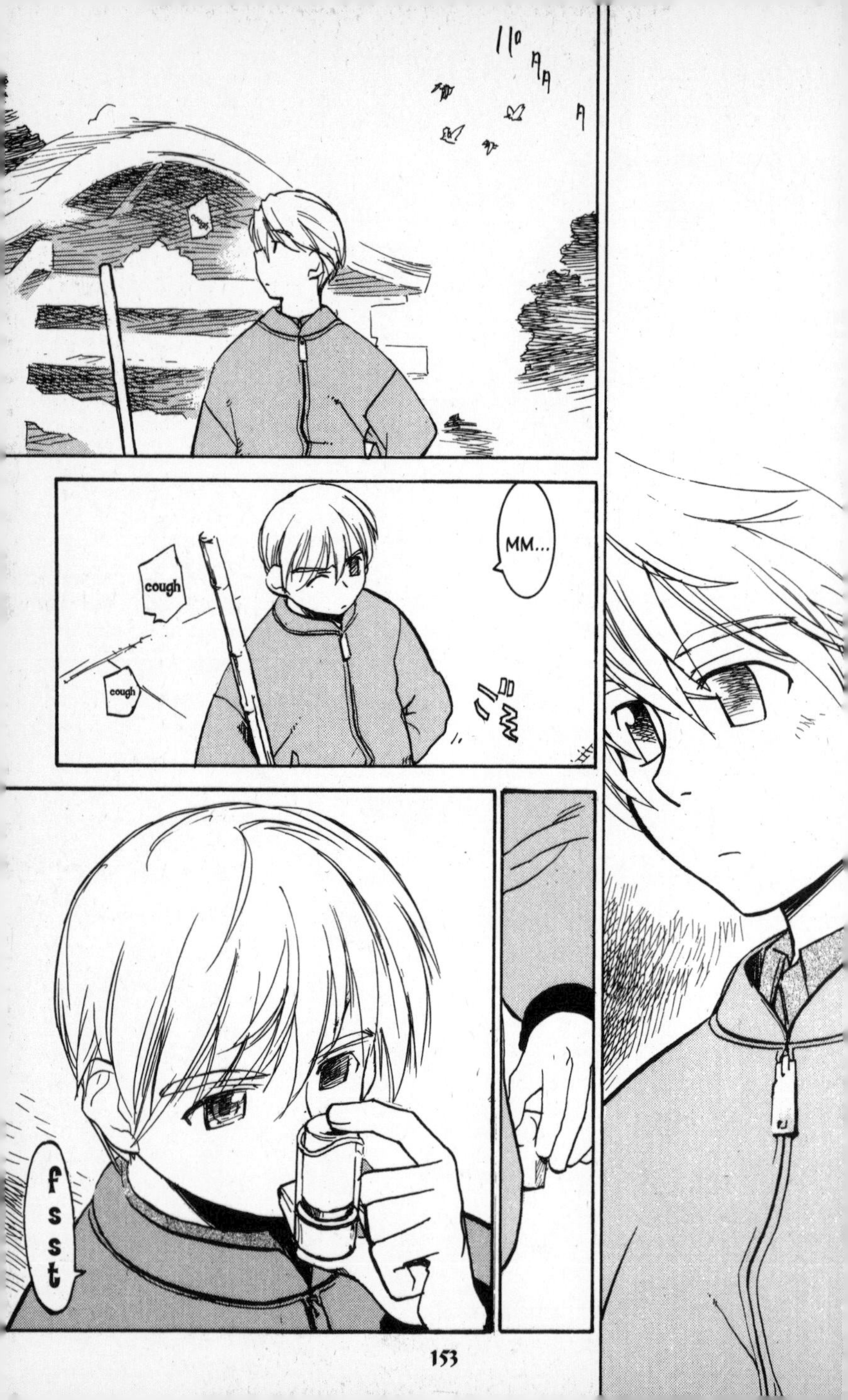
cough
MM...
cough
cough
fsst

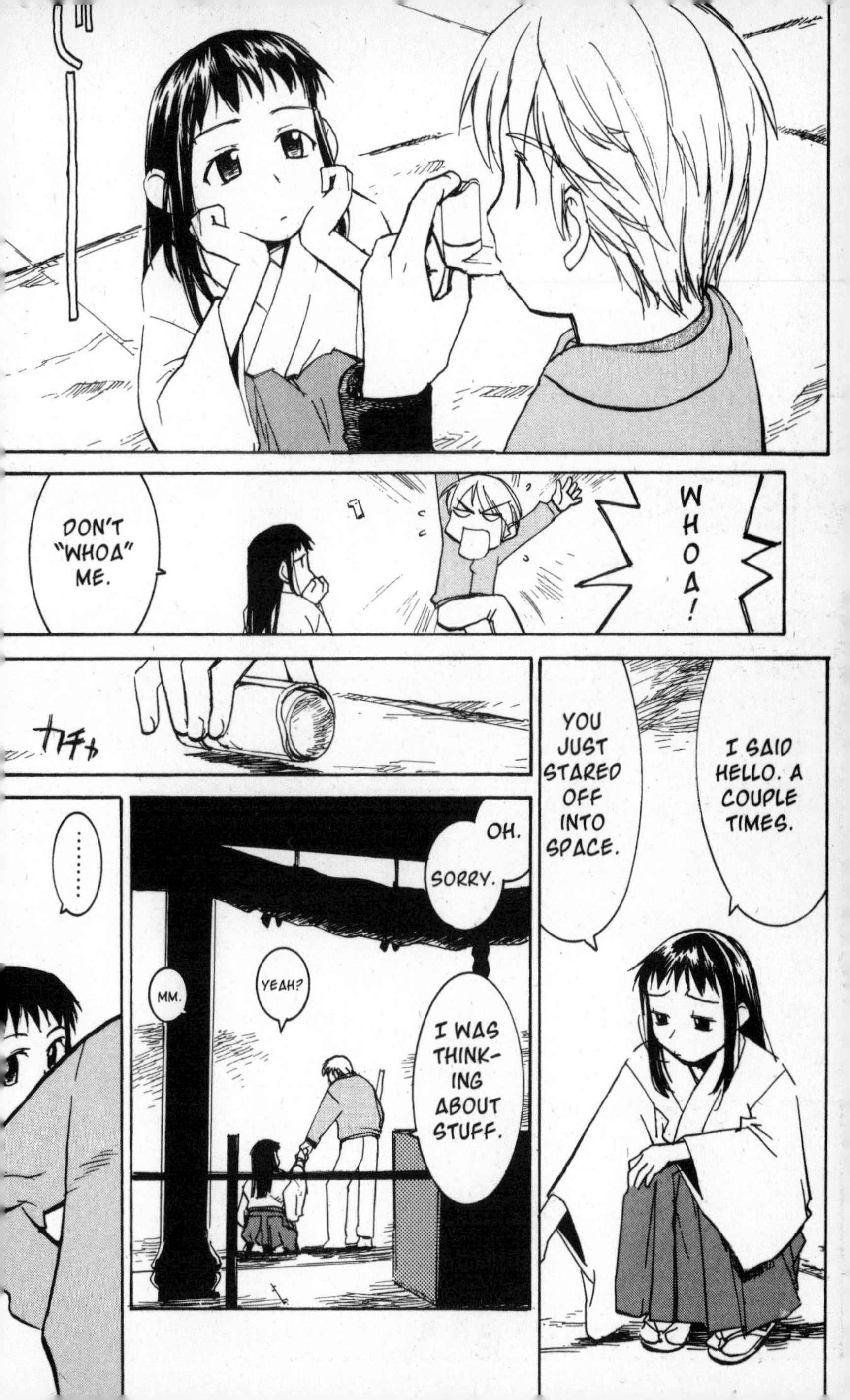
WHOA!
DON'T "WHOA" ME.
I SAID HELLO. A COUPLE TIMES.
YOU JUST STARED OFF INTO SPACE.
カチャ
OH.
SORRY.
I WAS THINKING ABOUT STUFF.
YEAH?
MM.
....

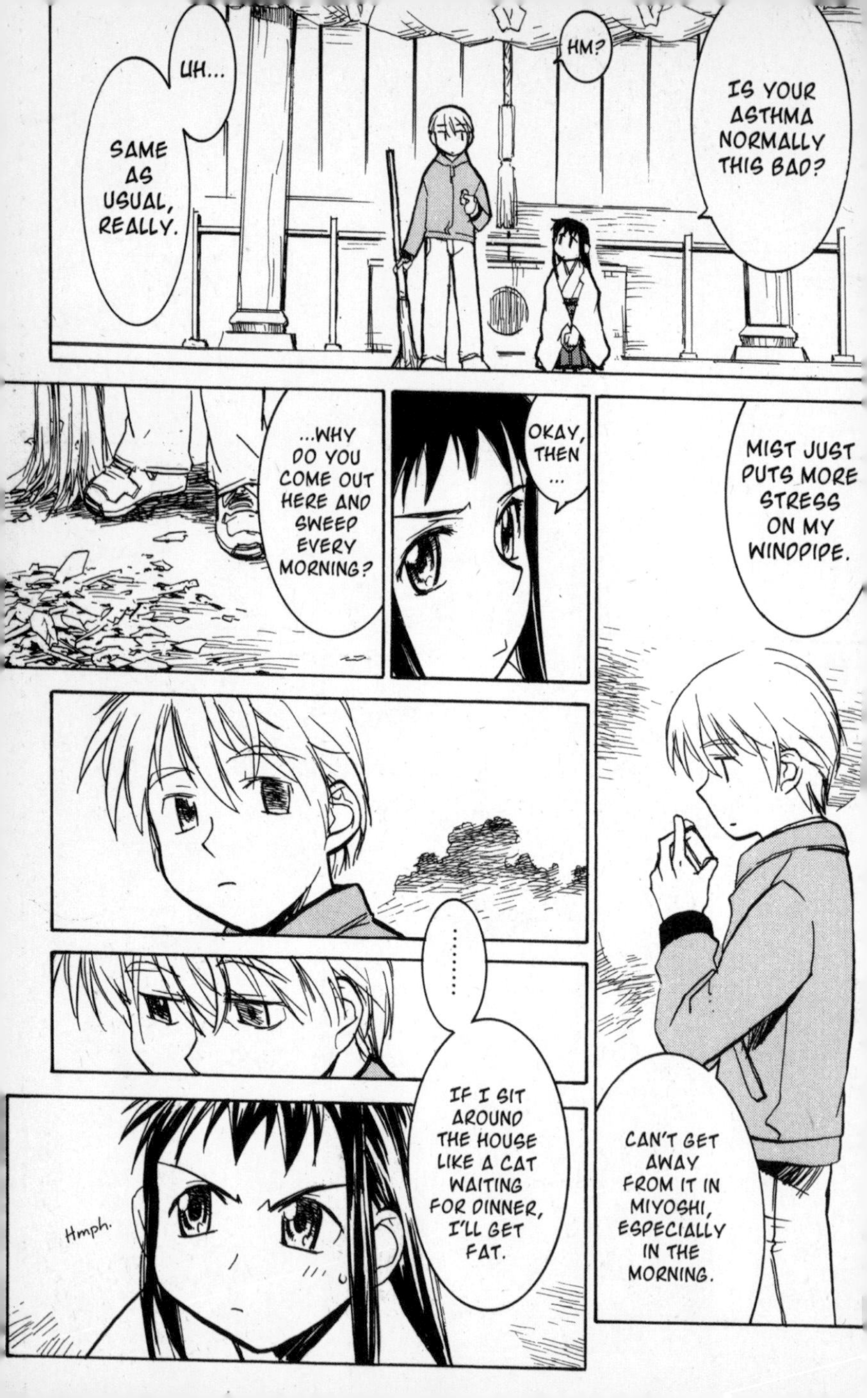
IS YOUR ASTHMA NORMALLY THIS BAD?
HM?
UH...
SAME AS USUAL, REALLY.
MIST JUST PUTS MORE STRESS ON MY WINDPIPE.
CAN'T GET AWAY FROM IT IN MIYOSHI, ESPECIALLY IN THE MORNING.
OKAY, THEN ...
...WHY DO YOU COME OUT HERE AND SWEEP EVERY MORNING?
....
IF I SIT AROUND THE HOUSE LIKE A CAT WAITING FOR DINNER, I'LL GET FAT.
Hmph.

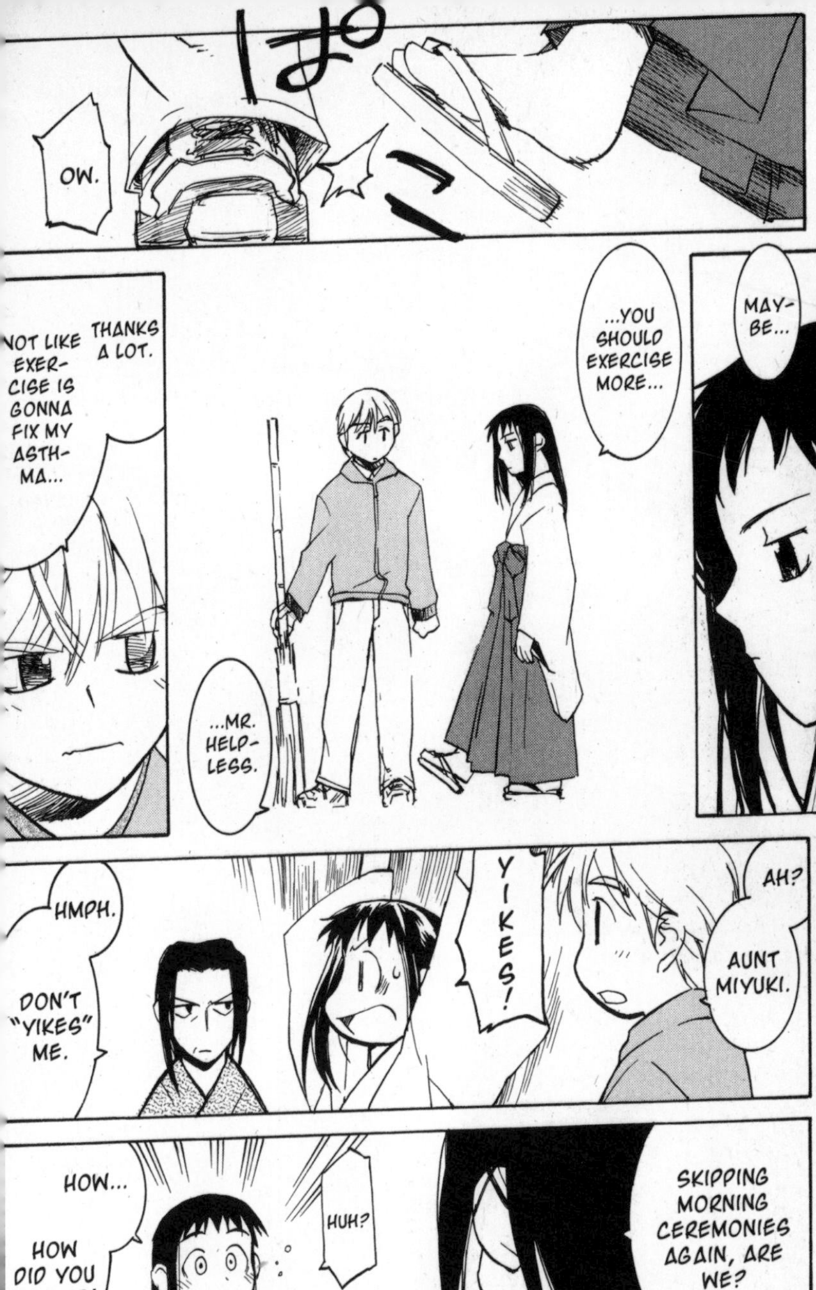

ぱ
OW.
MAY-BE...
...YOU SHOULD EXERCISE MORE...
...MR. HELPLESS.
THANKS A LOT.
NOT LIKE EXER-CISE IS GONNA FIX MY ASTH-MA...
AH?
AUNT MIYUKI.
YIKES!
HMPH.
DON'T "YIKES" ME.
SKIPPING MORNING CEREMONIES AGAIN, ARE WE?
HUH?
HOW...
HOW DID YOU KNOW?!

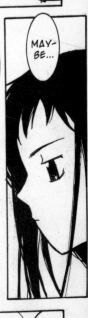

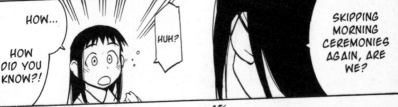

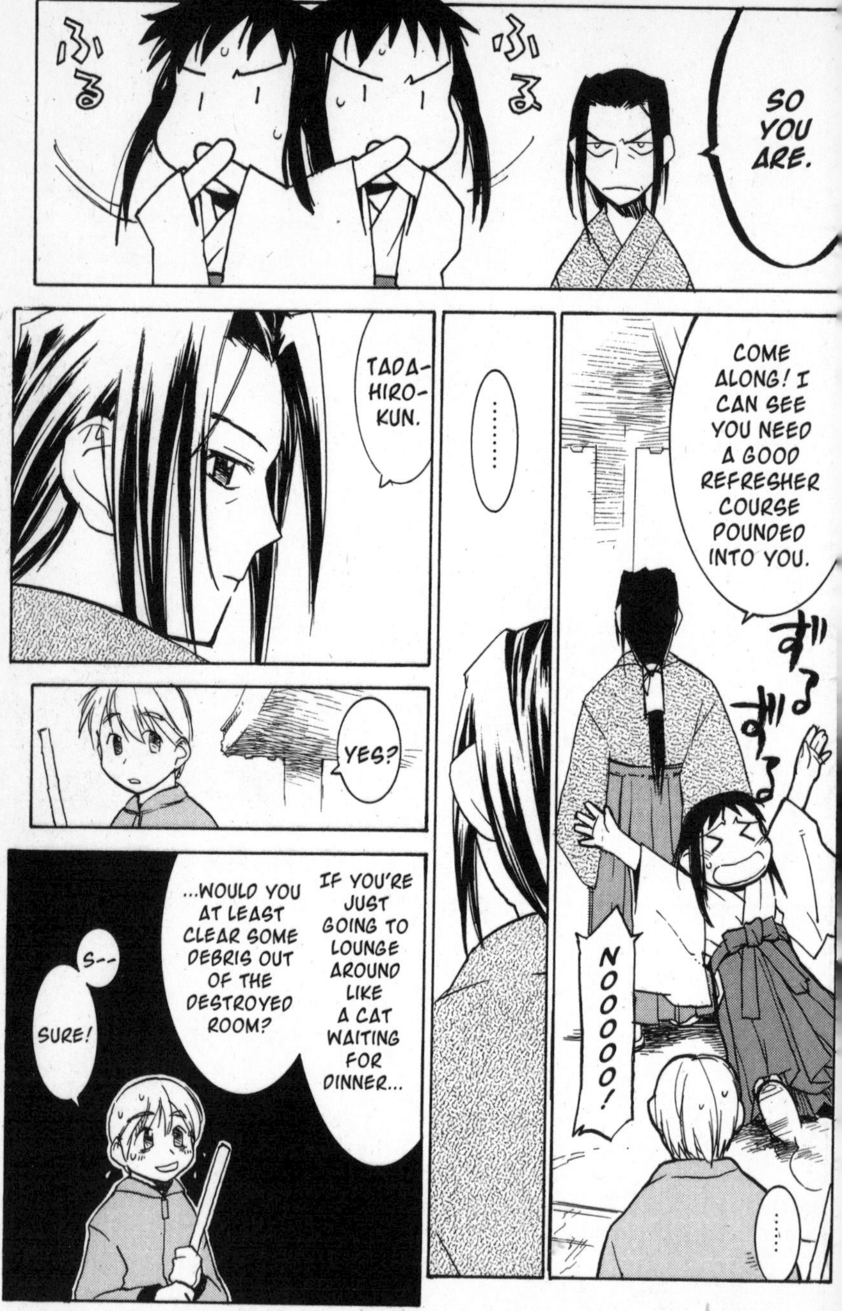
SO YOU ARE.
ふる
ふる
COME ALONG! I CAN SEE YOU NEED A GOOD REFRESHER COURSE POUNDED INTO YOU.
ずる
ずる
NOOOOOO!
......
....
TADA-HIRO-KUN.
YES?
IF YOU'RE JUST GOING TO LOUNGE AROUND LIKE A CAT WAITING FOR DINNER...
...WOULD YOU AT LEAST CLEAR SOME DEBRIS OUT OF THE DESTROYED ROOM?
S--
SURE!

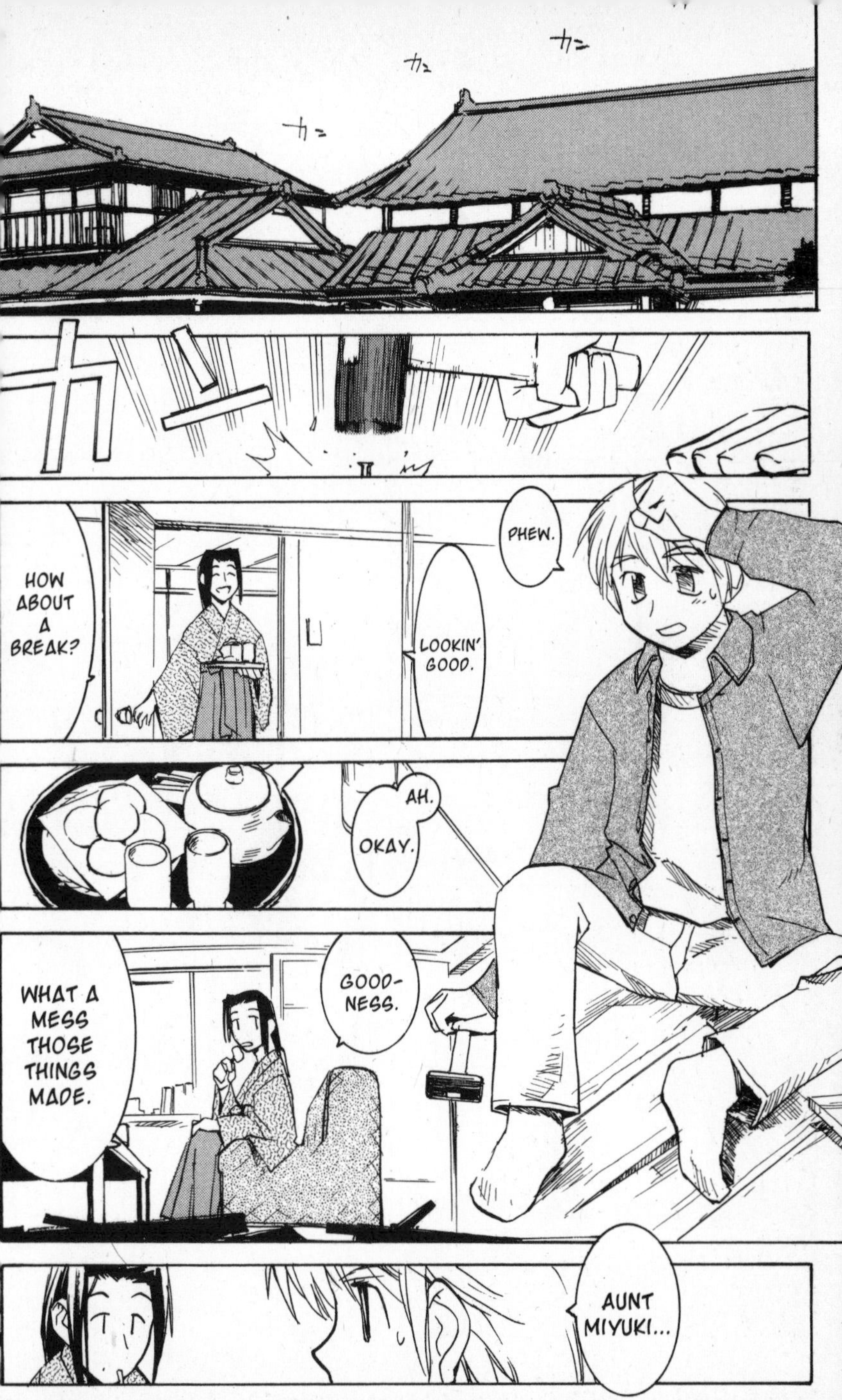
PHEW.
LOOKIN' GOOD.
HOW ABOUT A BREAK?
AH.
OKAY.
GOOD-NESS.
WHAT A MESS THOSE THINGS MADE.
AUNT MIYUKI...

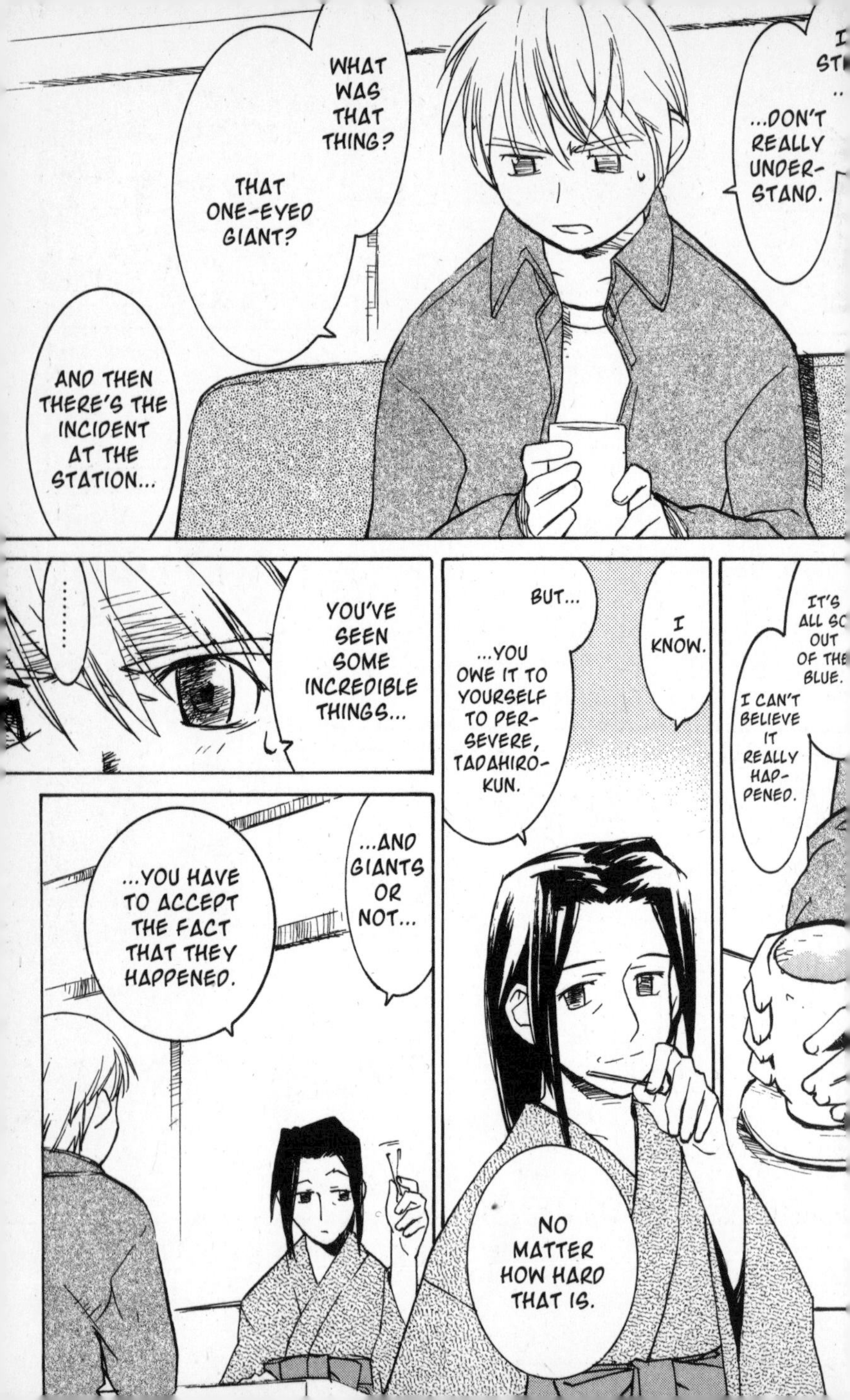
I ST..
...DON'T REALLY UNDER-STAND.
WHAT WAS THAT THING?
THAT ONE-EYED GIANT?
AND THEN THERE'S THE INCIDENT AT THE STATION...
IT'S ALL SO OUT OF THE BLUE.
I CAN'T BELIEVE IT REALLY HAP-PENED.
I KNOW.
BUT...
...YOU OWE IT TO YOURSELF TO PER-SEVERE, TADAHIRO-KUN.
NO MATTER HOW HARD THAT IS.
YOU'VE SEEN SOME INCREDIBLE THINGS...
......
...AND GIANTS OR NOT...
...YOU HAVE TO ACCEPT THE FACT THAT THEY HAPPENED.

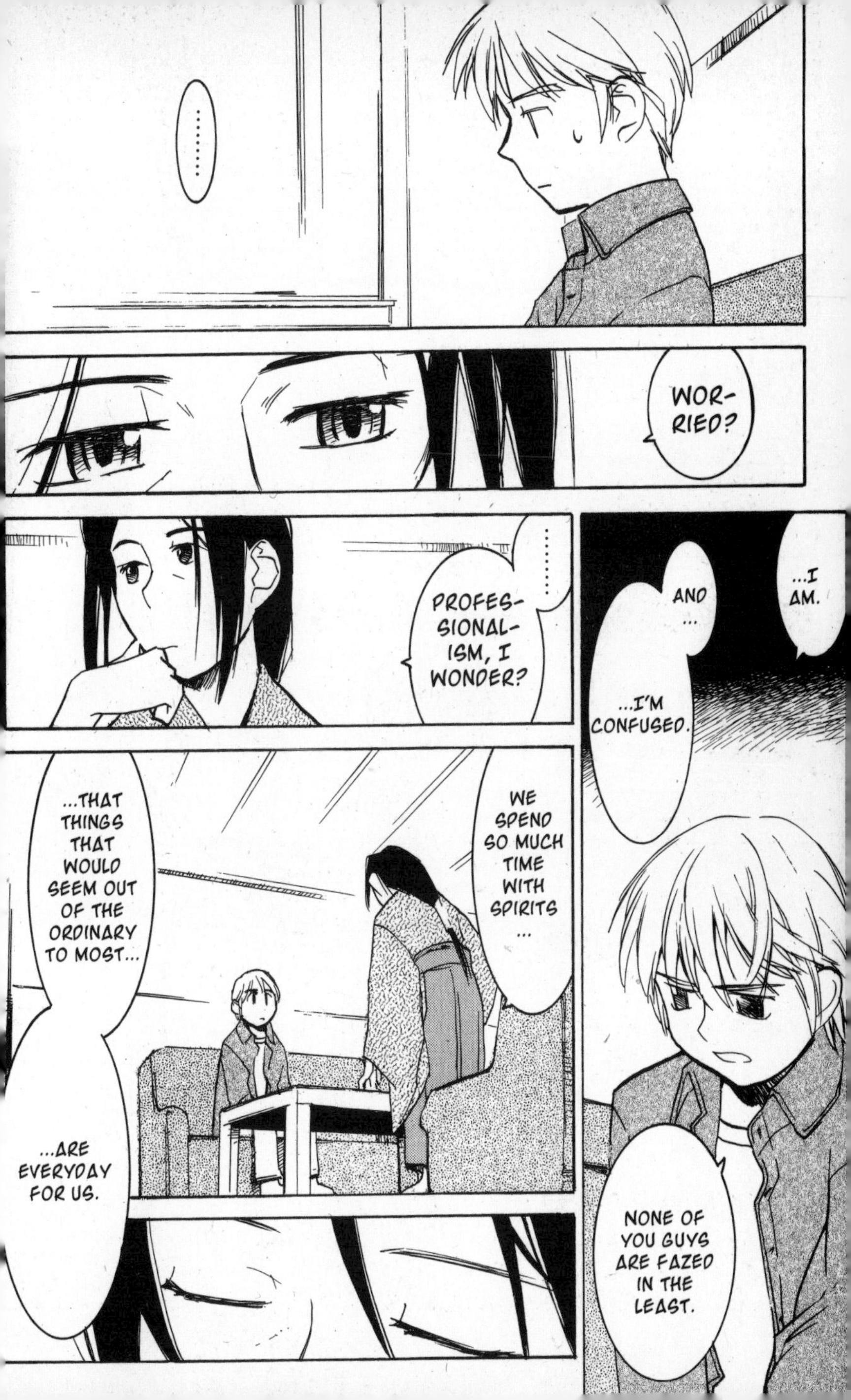
……
WOR-RIED?
...I AM.
AND ...
...I'M CONFUSED.
NONE OF YOU GUYS ARE FAZED IN THE LEAST.
......
PROFES-SIONAL-ISM, I WONDER?
WE SPEND SO MUCH TIME WITH SPIRITS ...
...THAT THINGS THAT WOULD SEEM OUT OF THE ORDINARY TO MOST...
...ARE EVERYDAY FOR US.

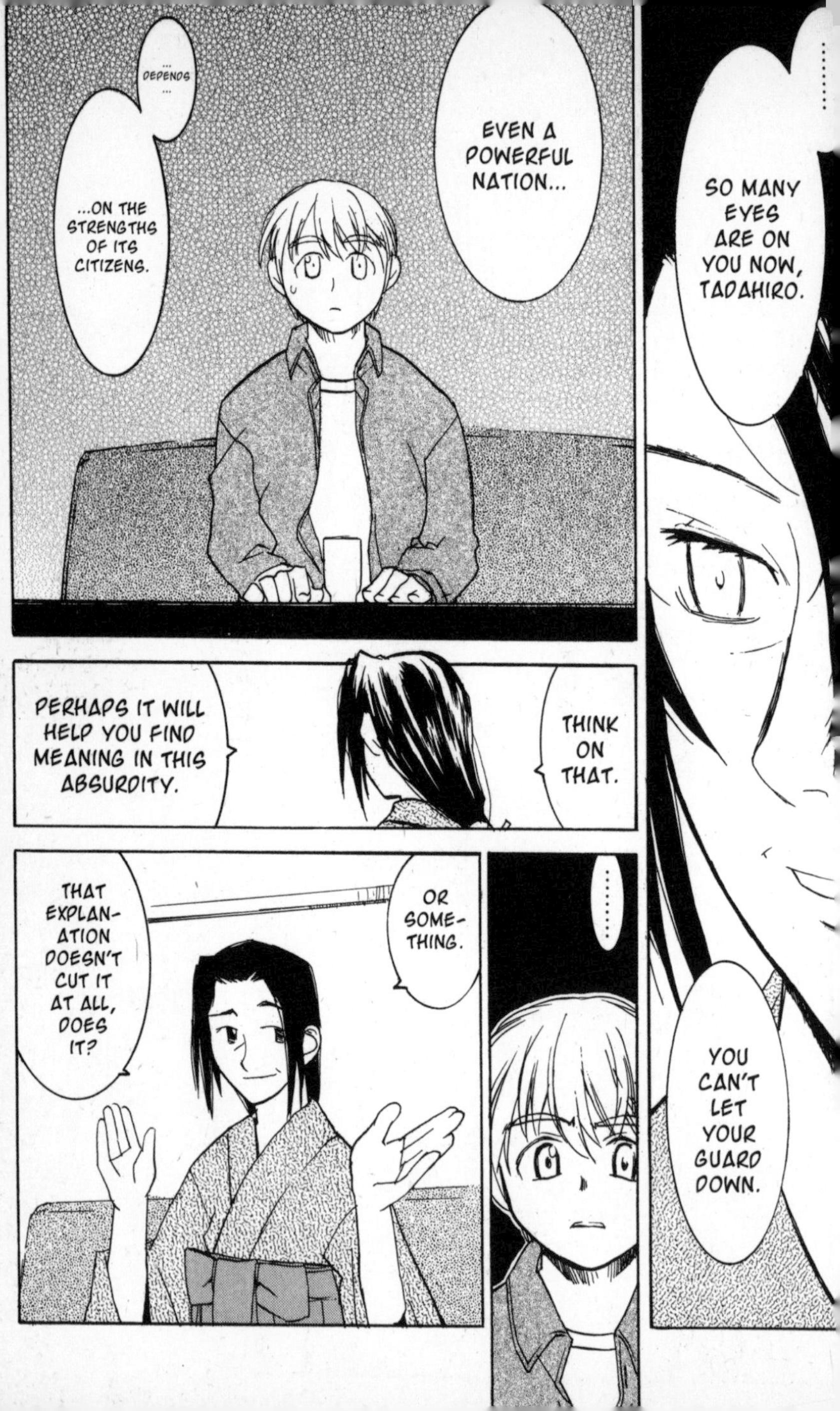
SO MANY EYES ARE ON YOU NOW, TADAHIRO.
YOU CAN'T LET YOUR GUARD DOWN.
EVEN A POWERFUL NATION...
...DEPENDS...
...ON THE STRENGTHS OF ITS CITIZENS.
THINK ON THAT.
PERHAPS IT WILL HELP YOU FIND MEANING IN THIS ABSURDITY.
......
OR SOMETHING.
THAT EXPLANATION DOESN'T CUT IT AT ALL, DOES IT?

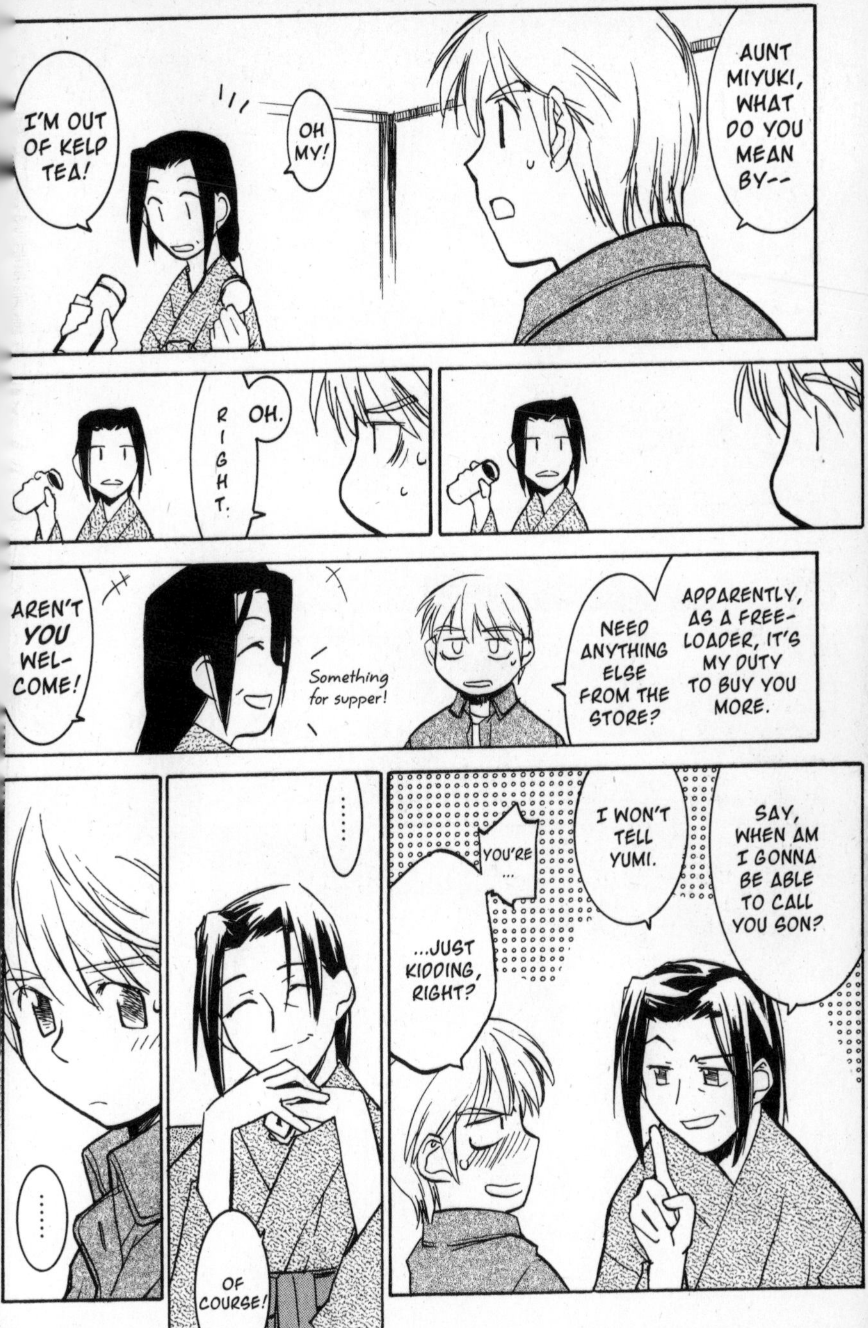
AUNT MIYUKI, WHAT DO YOU MEAN BY--
OH MY!
I'M OUT OF KELP TEA!
OH. RIGHT.
APPARENTLY, AS A FREE-LOADER, IT'S MY DUTY TO BUY YOU MORE.
NEED ANYTHING ELSE FROM THE STORE?
Something for supper!
AREN'T YOU WEL-COME!
SAY, WHEN AM I GONNA BE ABLE TO CALL YOU SON?
I WON'T TELL YUMI.
YOU'RE ...
...JUST KIDDING, RIGHT?
......
OF COURSE!
......

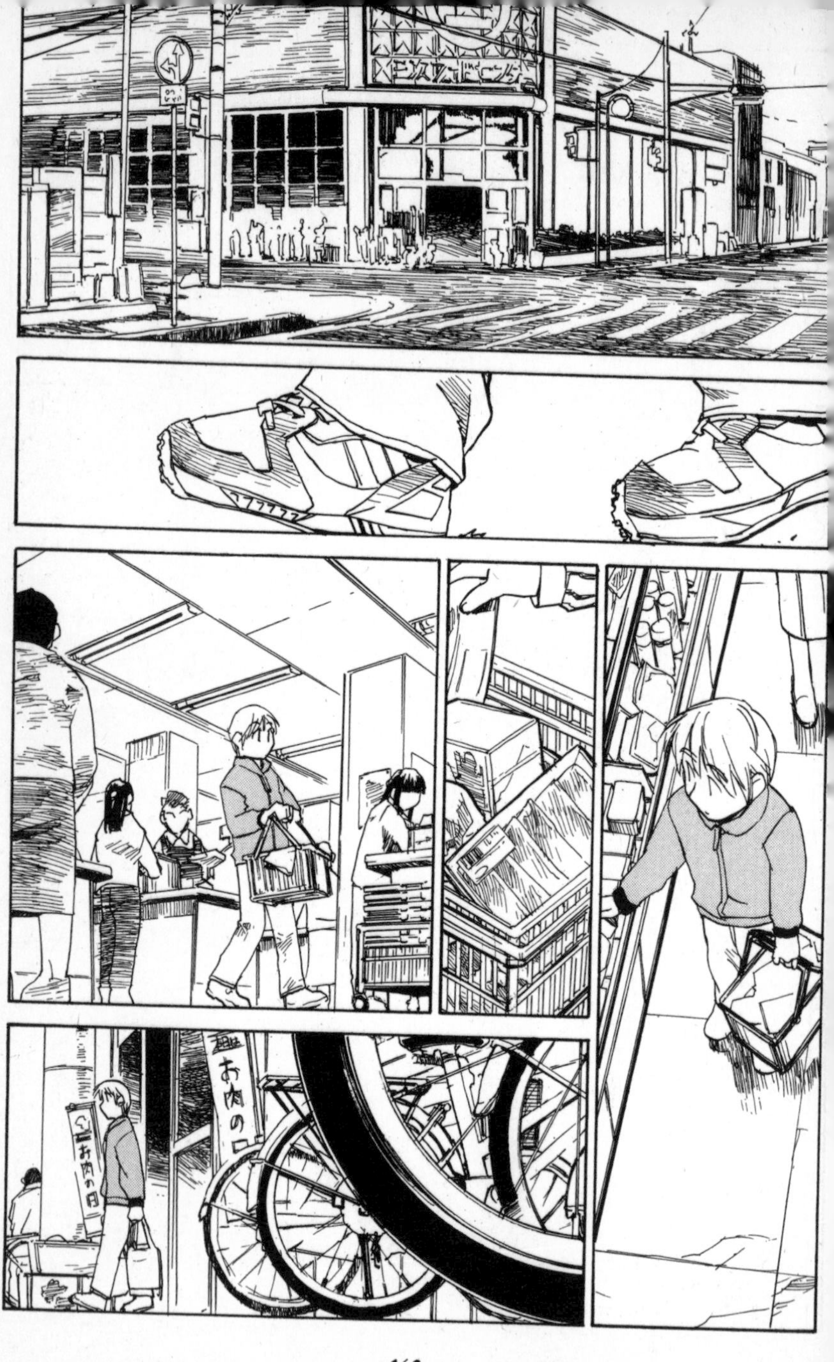
お肉の
お肉の日

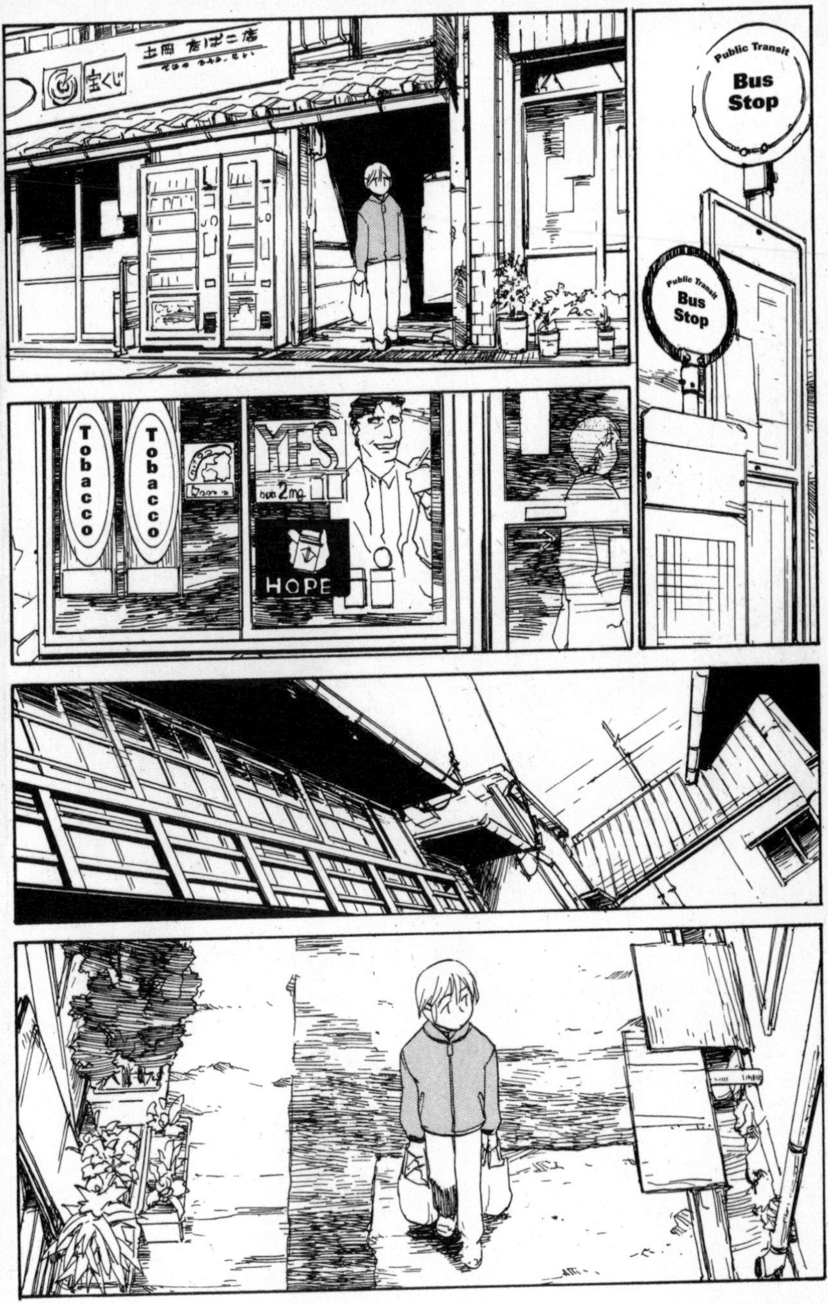
Public Transit
Bus Stop
Public Transit
Bus Stop
土岡 たばこ店
宝くじ
YES
2mg
Tobacco
Tobacco
HOPE

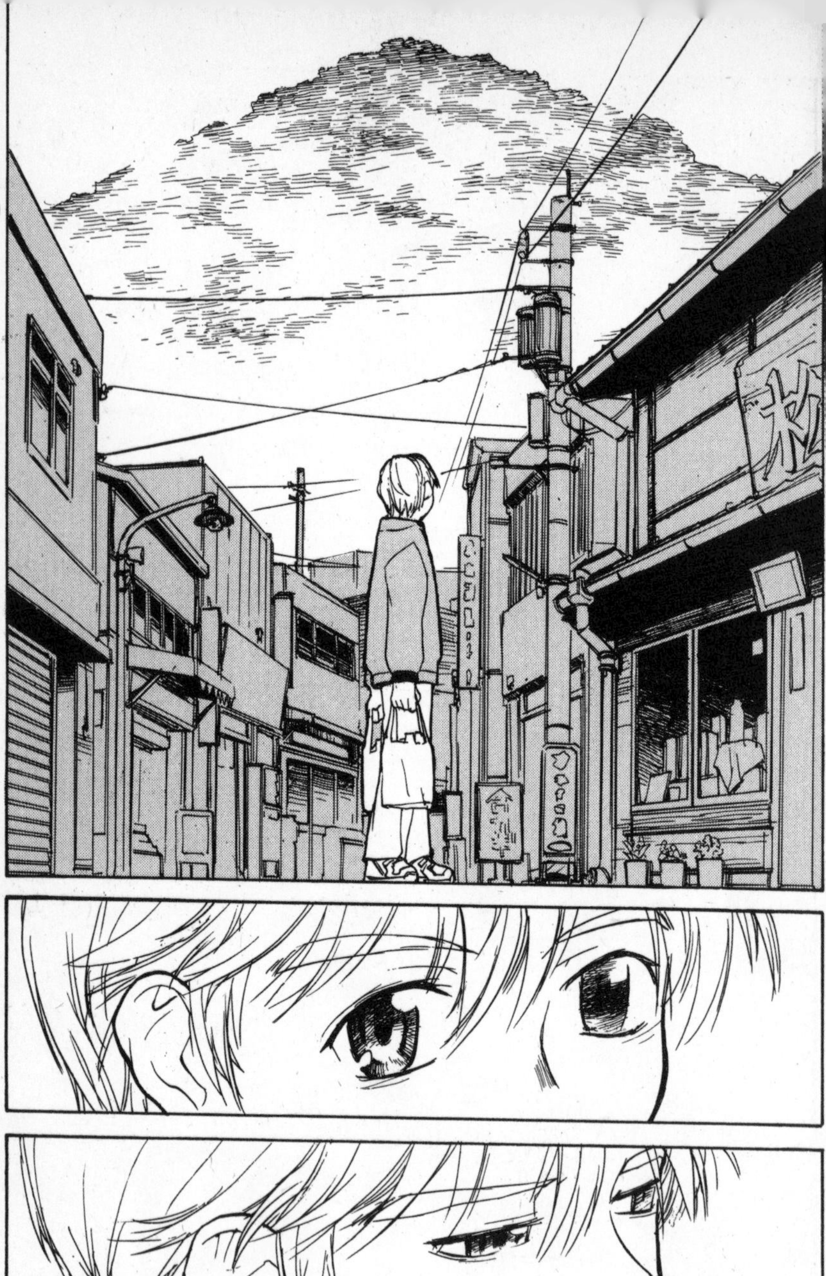

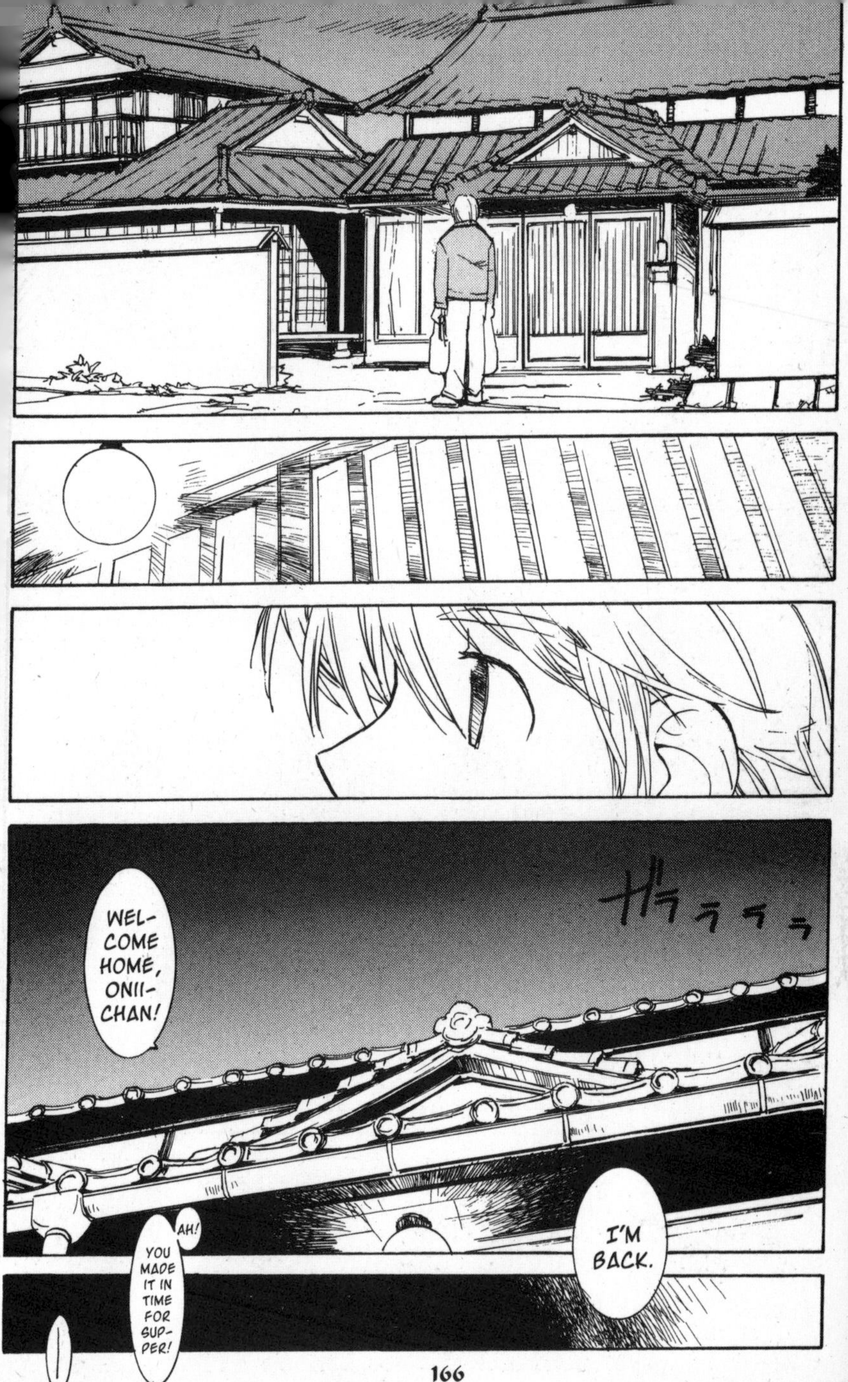
ガラララ
I'M BACK.
WEL-COME HOME, ONII-CHAN!
AH!
YOU MADE IT IN TIME FOR SUP-PER!

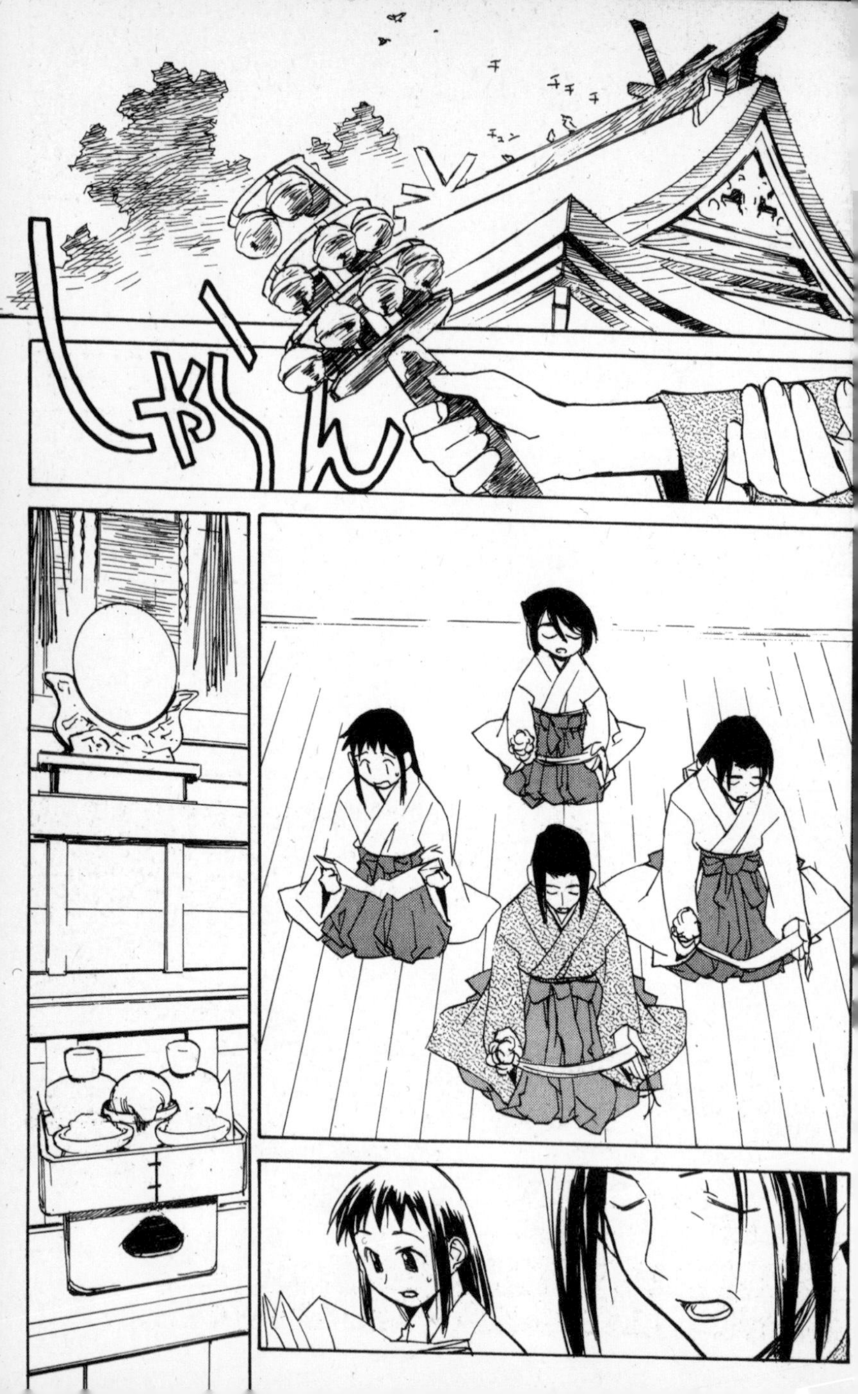
チチチ
チ
チュン
しゃーん

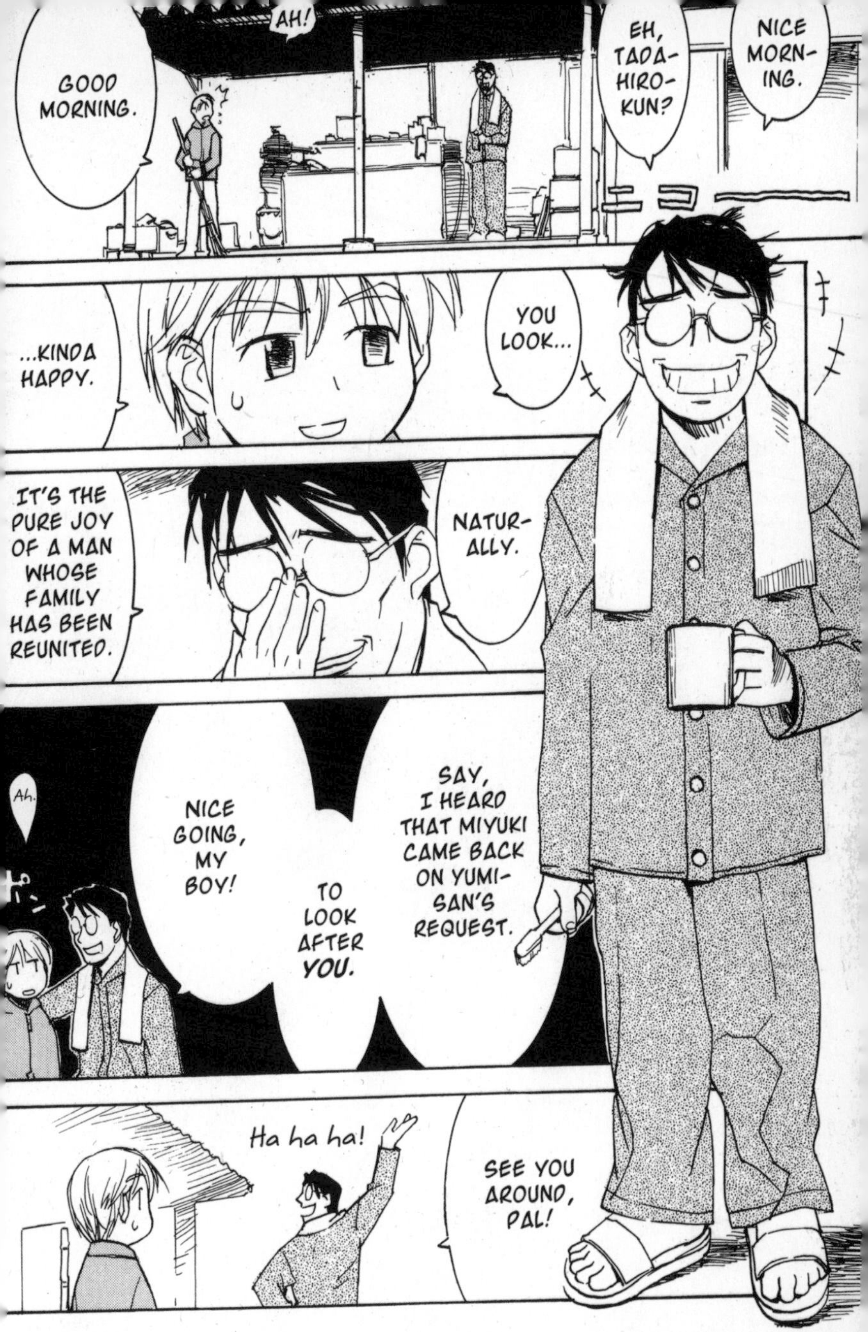
NICE MORN-ING.
EH, TADA-HIRO-KUN?
AH!
GOOD MORNING.
YOU LOOK...
...KINDA HAPPY.
NATUR-ALLY.
IT'S THE PURE JOY OF A MAN WHOSE FAMILY HAS BEEN REUNITED.
SAY, I HEARD THAT MIYUKI CAME BACK ON YUMI-SAN'S REQUEST.
TO LOOK AFTER *YOU*.
NICE GOING, MY BOY!
Ah.
SEE YOU AROUND, PAL!
Ha ha ha!

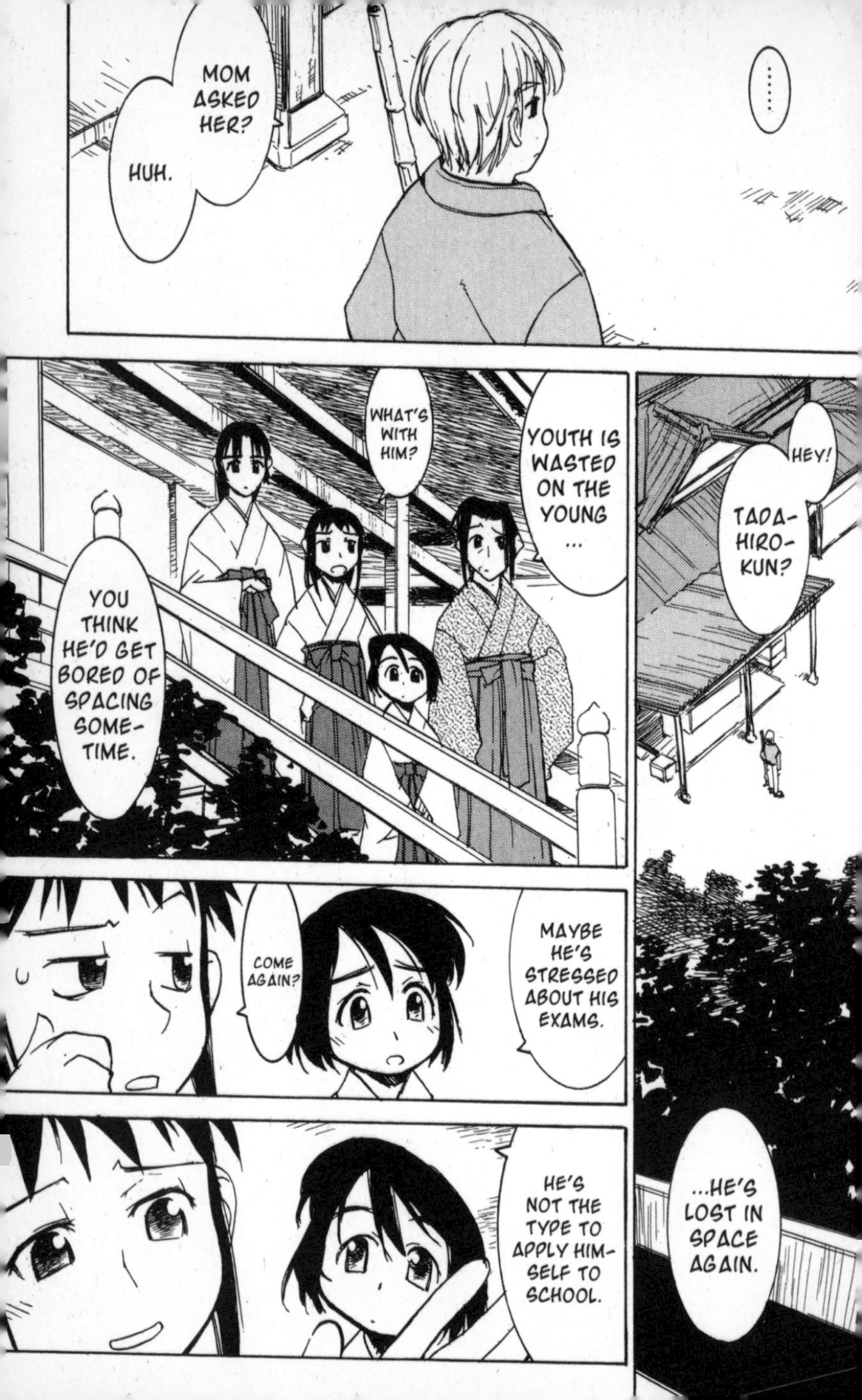
......
MOM ASKED HER?
HUH.
HEY!
TADAHIRO-KUN?
...HE'S LOST IN SPACE AGAIN.
YOUTH IS WASTED ON THE YOUNG...
WHAT'S WITH HIM?
YOU THINK HE'D GET BORED OF SPACING SOMETIME.
MAYBE HE'S STRESSED ABOUT HIS EXAMS.
COME AGAIN?
HE'S NOT THE TYPE TO APPLY HIMSELF TO SCHOOL.

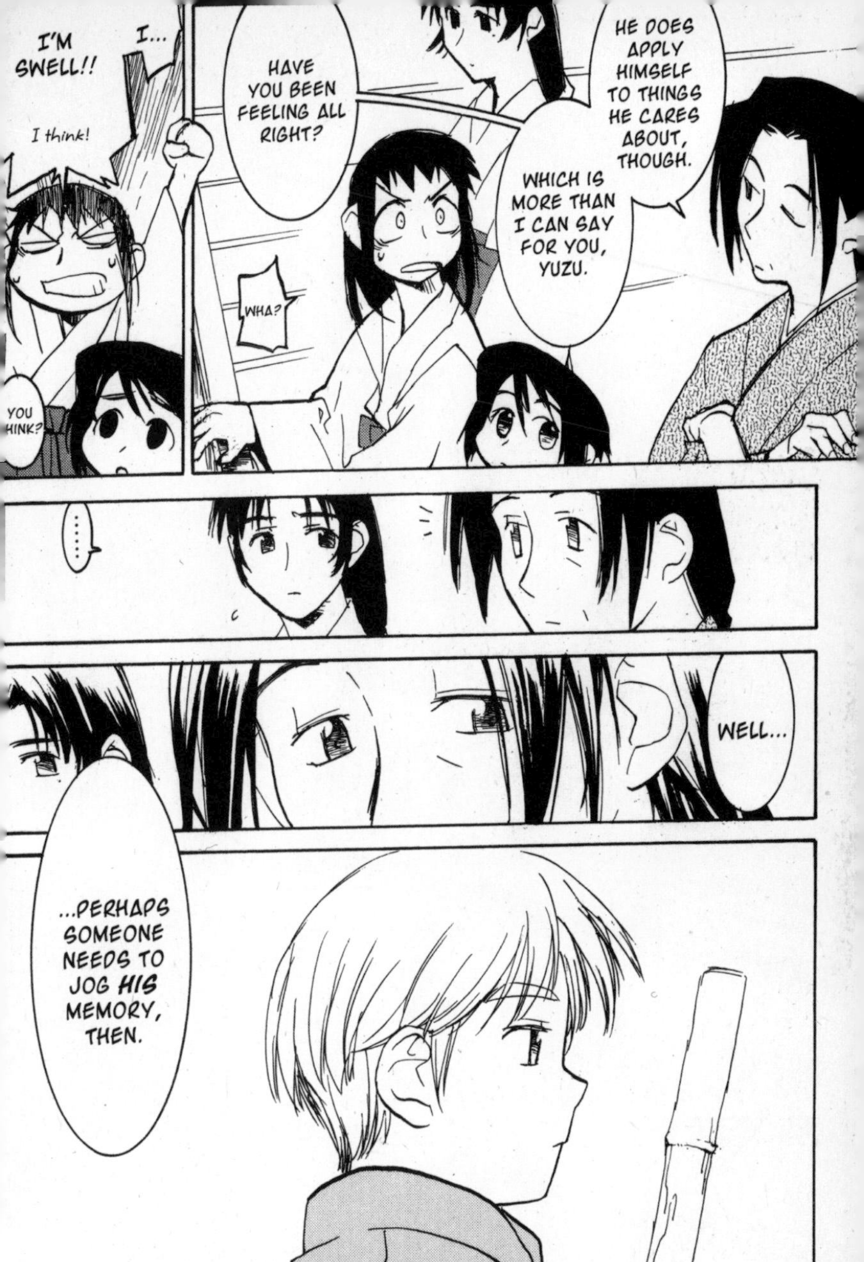
HE DOES APPLY HIMSELF TO THINGS HE CARES ABOUT, THOUGH.
WHICH IS MORE THAN I CAN SAY FOR YOU, YUZU.
HAVE YOU BEEN FEELING ALL RIGHT?
WHA?
I...
I'M SWELL!!
I think!
YOU HINK?
......
WELL...
...PERHAPS SOMEONE NEEDS TO JOG *HIS* MEMORY, THEN.

Chapter 5 Before the Grave Part 1 / End

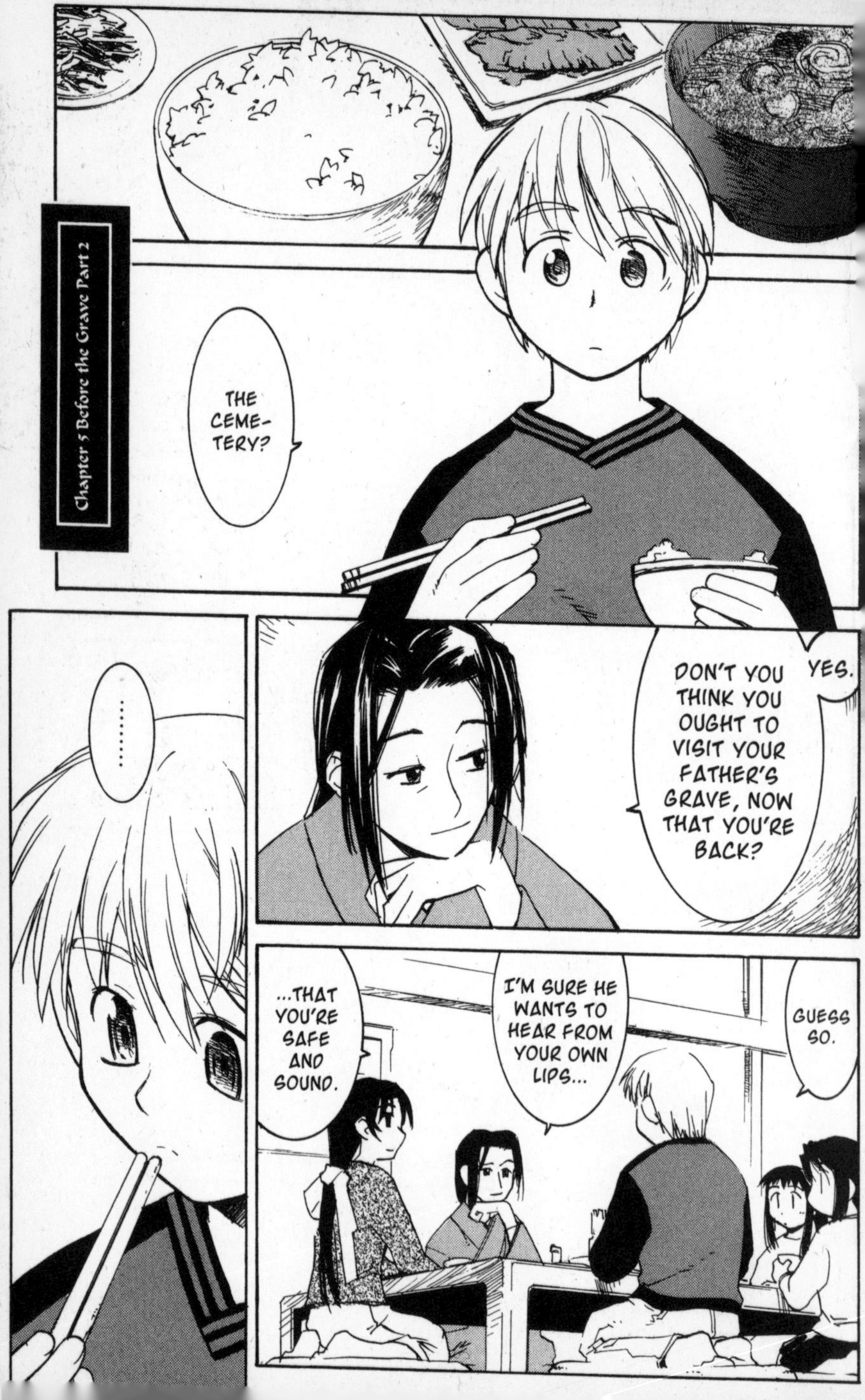
Chapter 5 Before the Grave Part 2
THE CEME-TERY?
YES.
DON'T YOU THINK YOU OUGHT TO VISIT YOUR FATHER'S GRAVE, NOW THAT YOU'RE BACK?
GUESS SO.
I'M SURE HE WANTS TO HEAR FROM YOUR OWN LIPS...
...THAT YOU'RE SAFE AND SOUND.
......

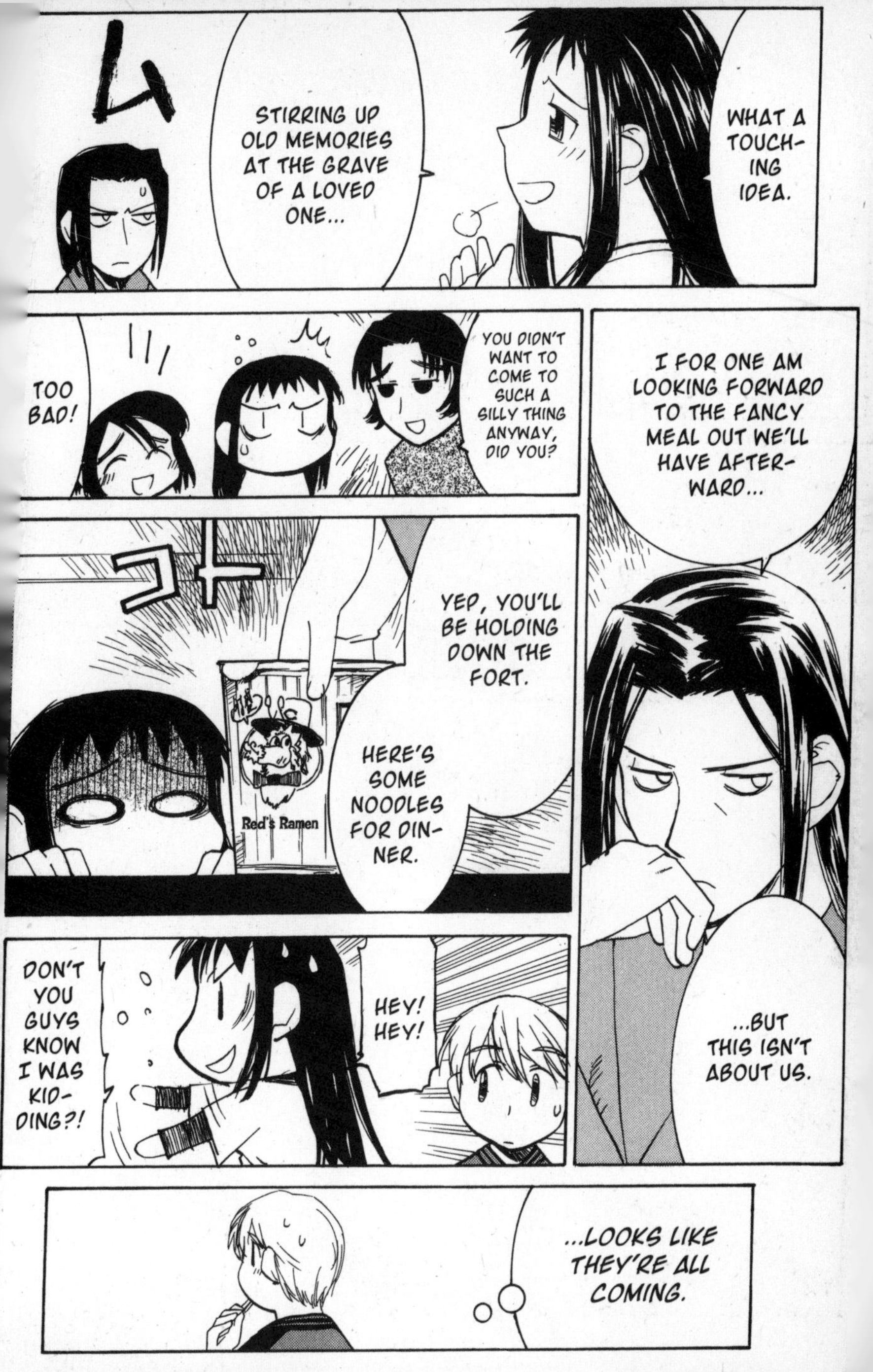
WHAT A TOUCHING IDEA.
STIRRING UP OLD MEMORIES AT THE GRAVE OF A LOVED ONE...
ム
I FOR ONE AM LOOKING FORWARD TO THE FANCY MEAL OUT WE'LL HAVE AFTERWARD...
...BUT THIS ISN'T ABOUT US.
YOU DIDN'T WANT TO COME TO SUCH A SILLY THING ANYWAY, DID YOU?
TOO BAD!
YEP, YOU'LL BE HOLDING DOWN THE FORT.
HERE'S SOME NOODLES FOR DINNER.
コト
Red's Ramen
HEY! HEY!
DON'T YOU GUYS KNOW I WAS KIDDING?!
...LOOKS LIKE THEY'RE ALL COMING.

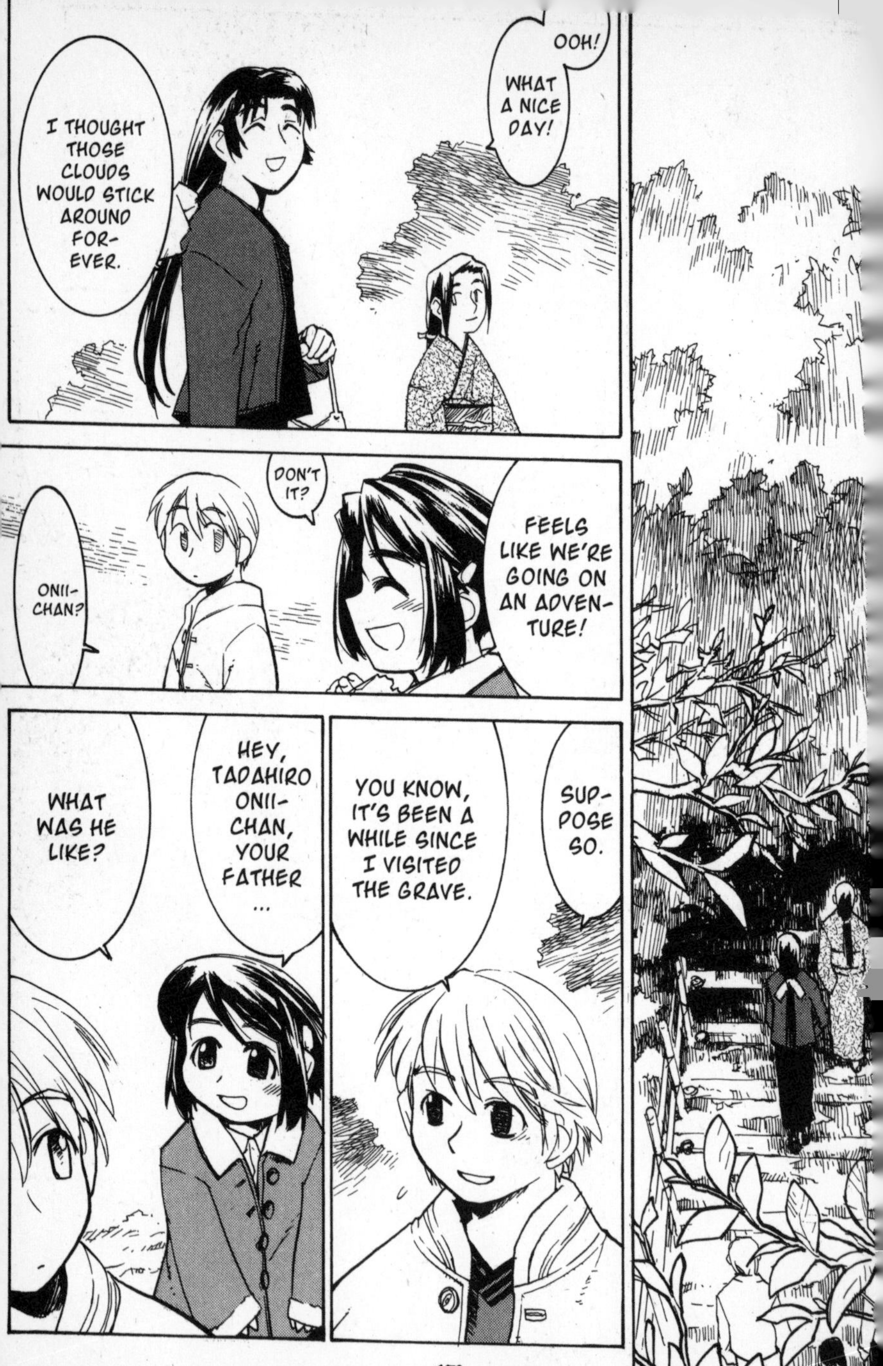
OOH! WHAT A NICE DAY!
I THOUGHT THOSE CLOUDS WOULD STICK AROUND FOR-EVER.
FEELS LIKE WE'RE GOING ON AN ADVEN-TURE!
DON'T IT?
ONII-CHAN?
SUP-POSE SO.
YOU KNOW, IT'S BEEN A WHILE SINCE I VISITED THE GRAVE.
HEY, TADAHIRO ONII-CHAN, YOUR FATHER ...
WHAT WAS HE LIKE?

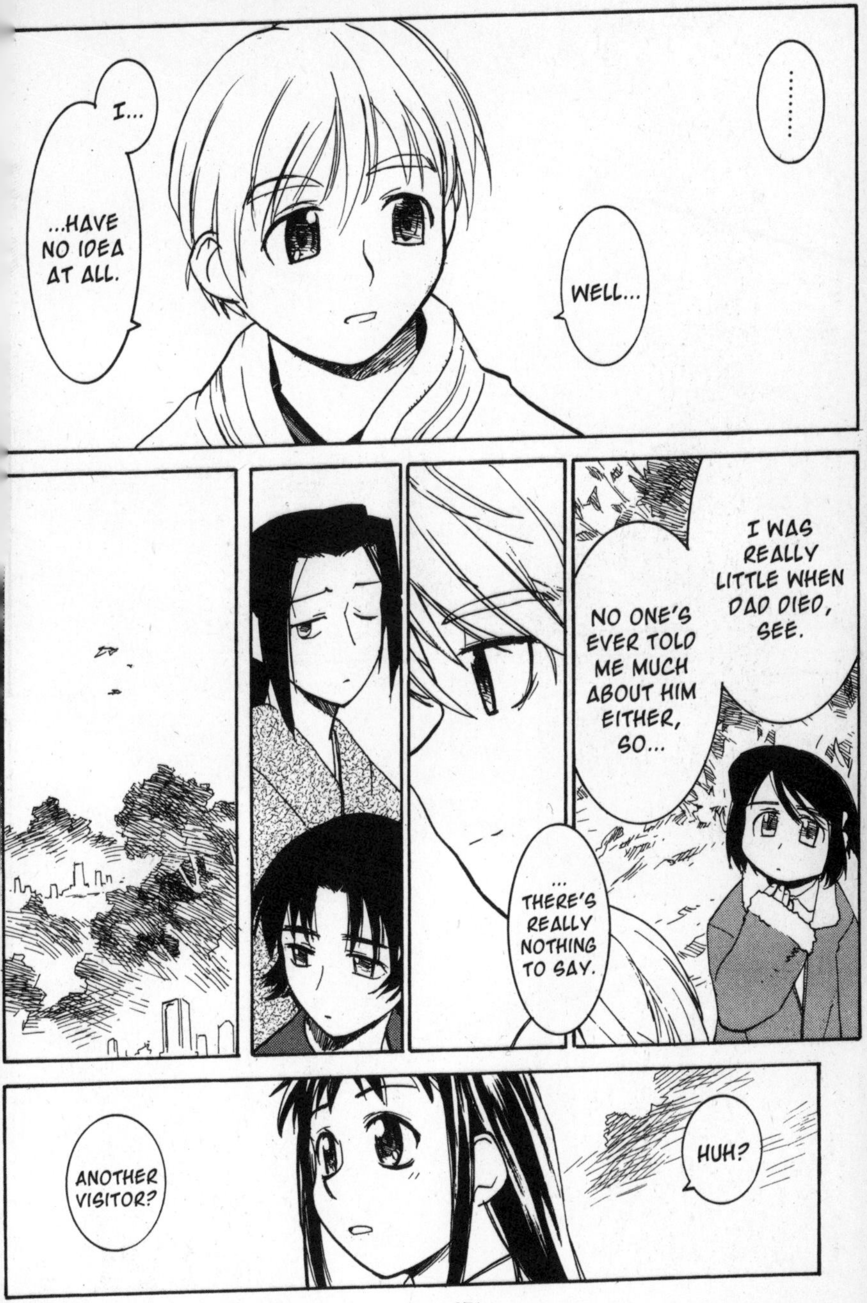
......
I...
...HAVE NO IDEA AT ALL.
WELL...
I WAS REALLY LITTLE WHEN DAD DIED, SEE.
NO ONE'S EVER TOLD ME MUCH ABOUT HIM EITHER, SO...
... THERE'S REALLY NOTHING TO SAY.
HUH?
ANOTHER VISITOR?

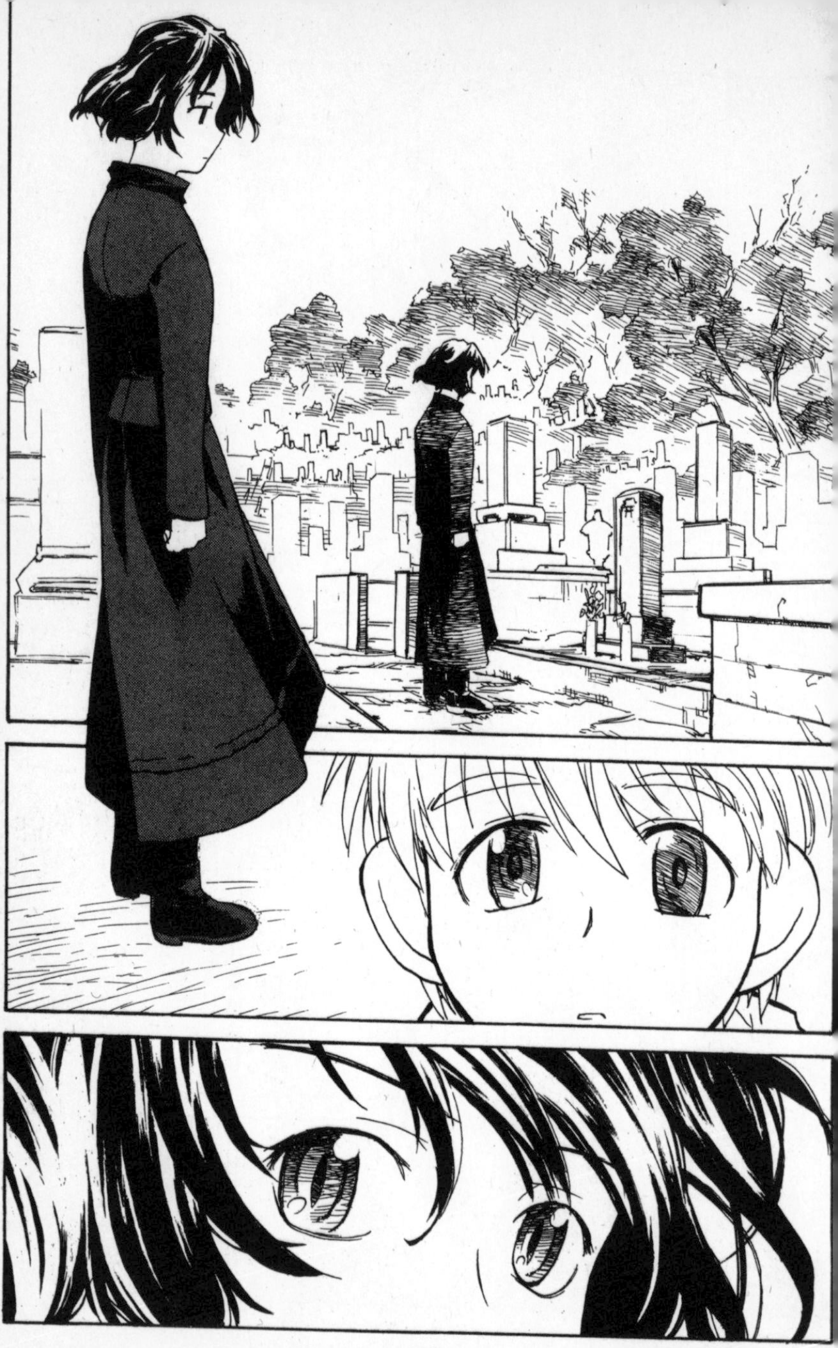

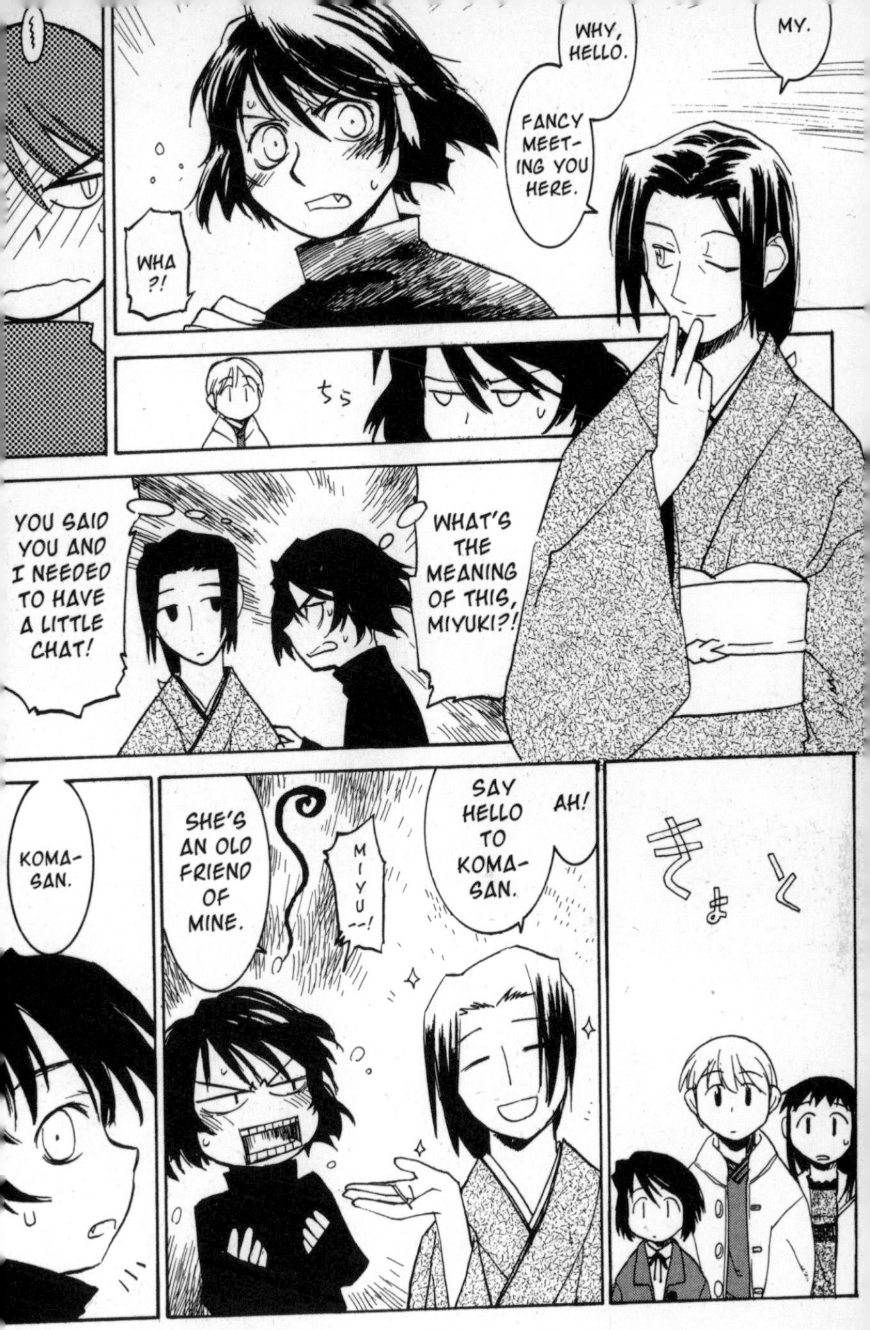
MY.
WHY, HELLO.
FANCY MEETING YOU HERE.
WHA ?!
ちら
WHAT'S THE MEANING OF THIS, MIYUKI?!
YOU SAID YOU AND I NEEDED TO HAVE A LITTLE CHAT!
きょと
AH!
SAY HELLO TO KOMA-SAN.
MIYU--!
SHE'S AN OLD FRIEND OF MINE.
KOMA-SAN.

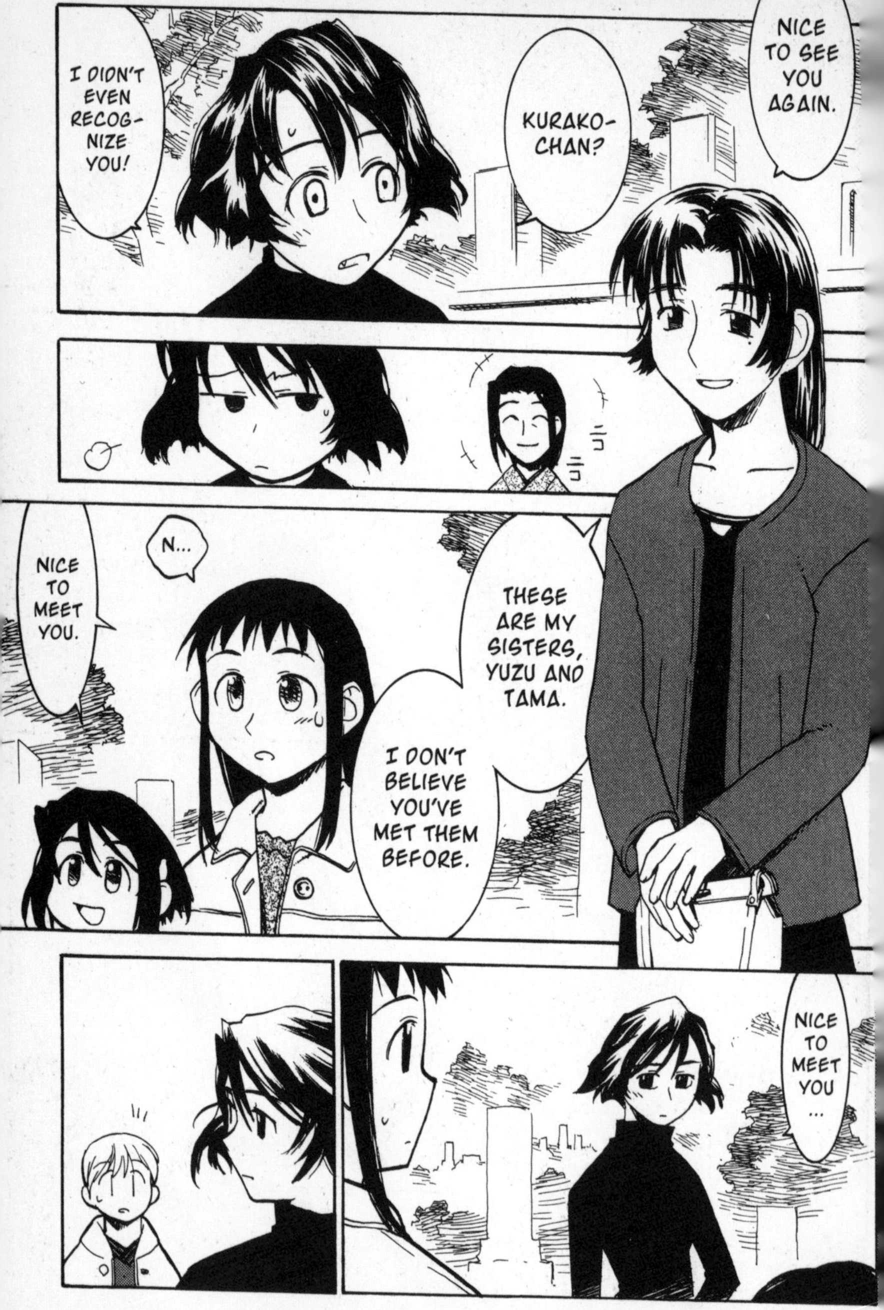
NICE TO SEE YOU AGAIN.
KURAKO-CHAN?
I DIDN'T EVEN RECOG-NIZE YOU!
THESE ARE MY SISTERS, YUZU AND TAMA.
I DON'T BELIEVE YOU'VE MET THEM BEFORE.
N...
NICE TO MEET YOU.
NICE TO MEET YOU ...

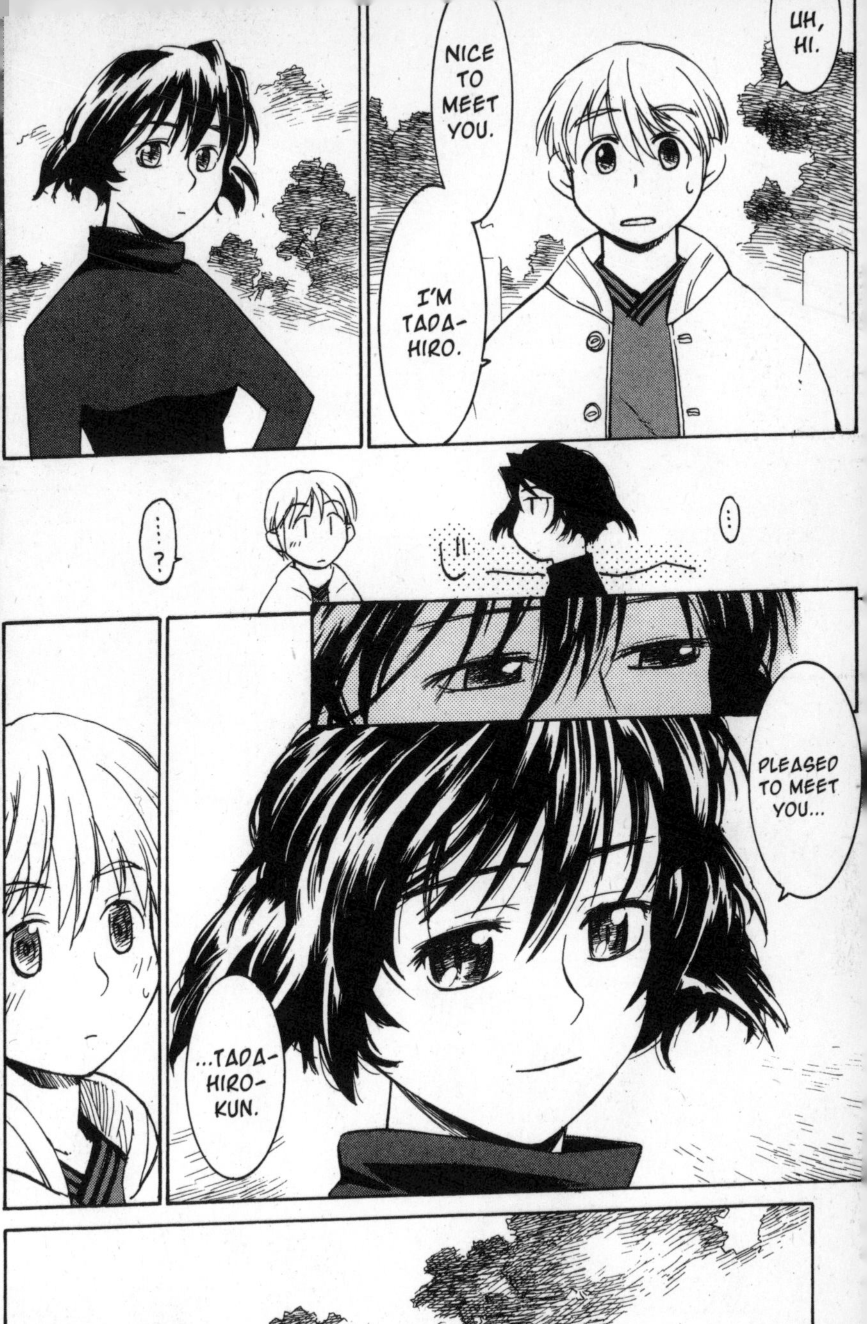
UH, HI.
NICE TO MEET YOU.
I'M TADA-HIRO.
...
...?
PLEASED TO MEET YOU...
...TADA-HIRO-KUN.

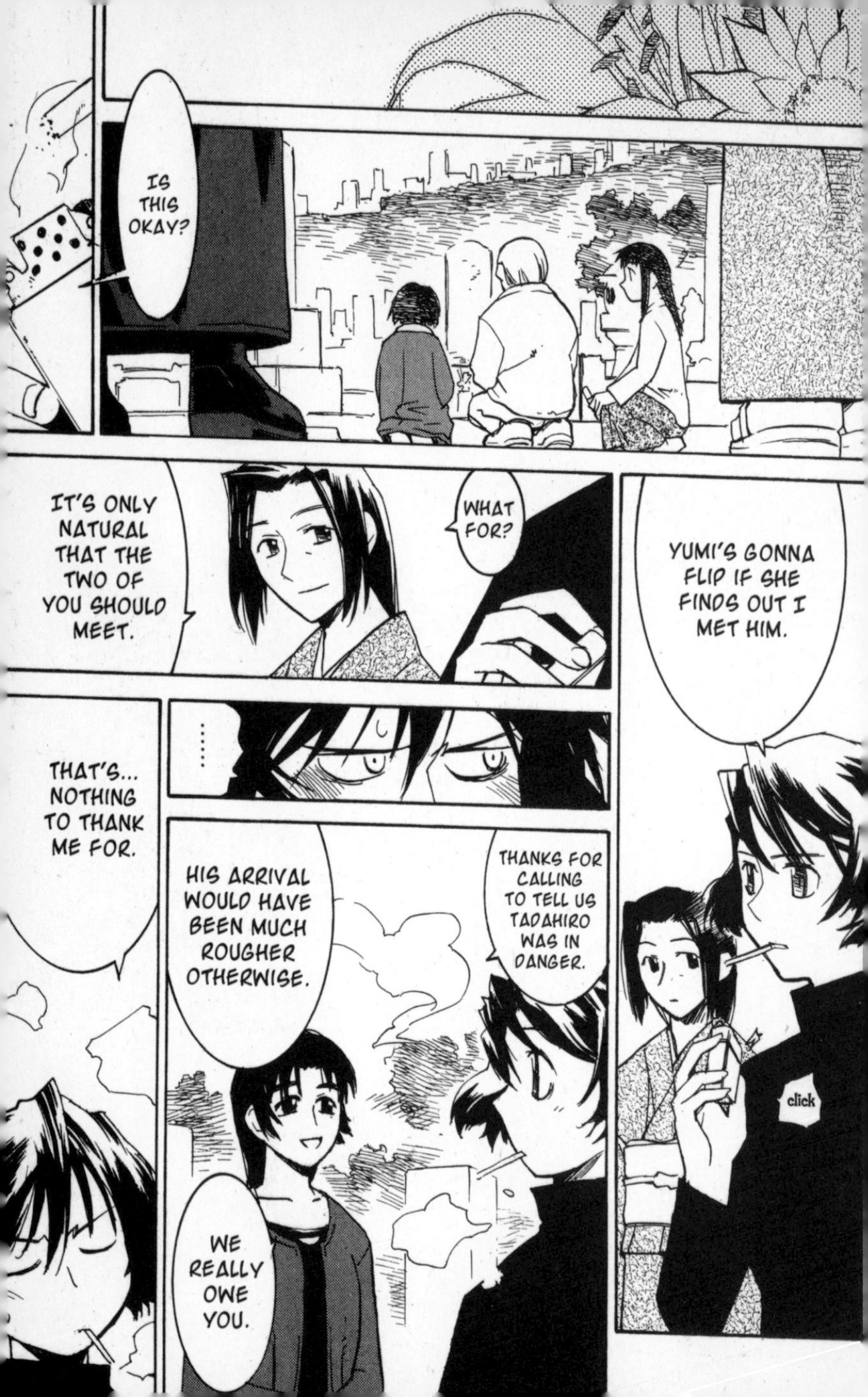
IS THIS OKAY?
YUMI'S GONNA FLIP IF SHE FINDS OUT I MET HIM.
click
WHAT FOR?
IT'S ONLY NATURAL THAT THE TWO OF YOU SHOULD MEET.
......
THANKS FOR CALLING TO TELL US TADAHIRO WAS IN DANGER.
HIS ARRIVAL WOULD HAVE BEEN MUCH ROUGHER OTHERWISE.
WE REALLY OWE YOU.
THAT'S... NOTHING TO THANK ME FOR.

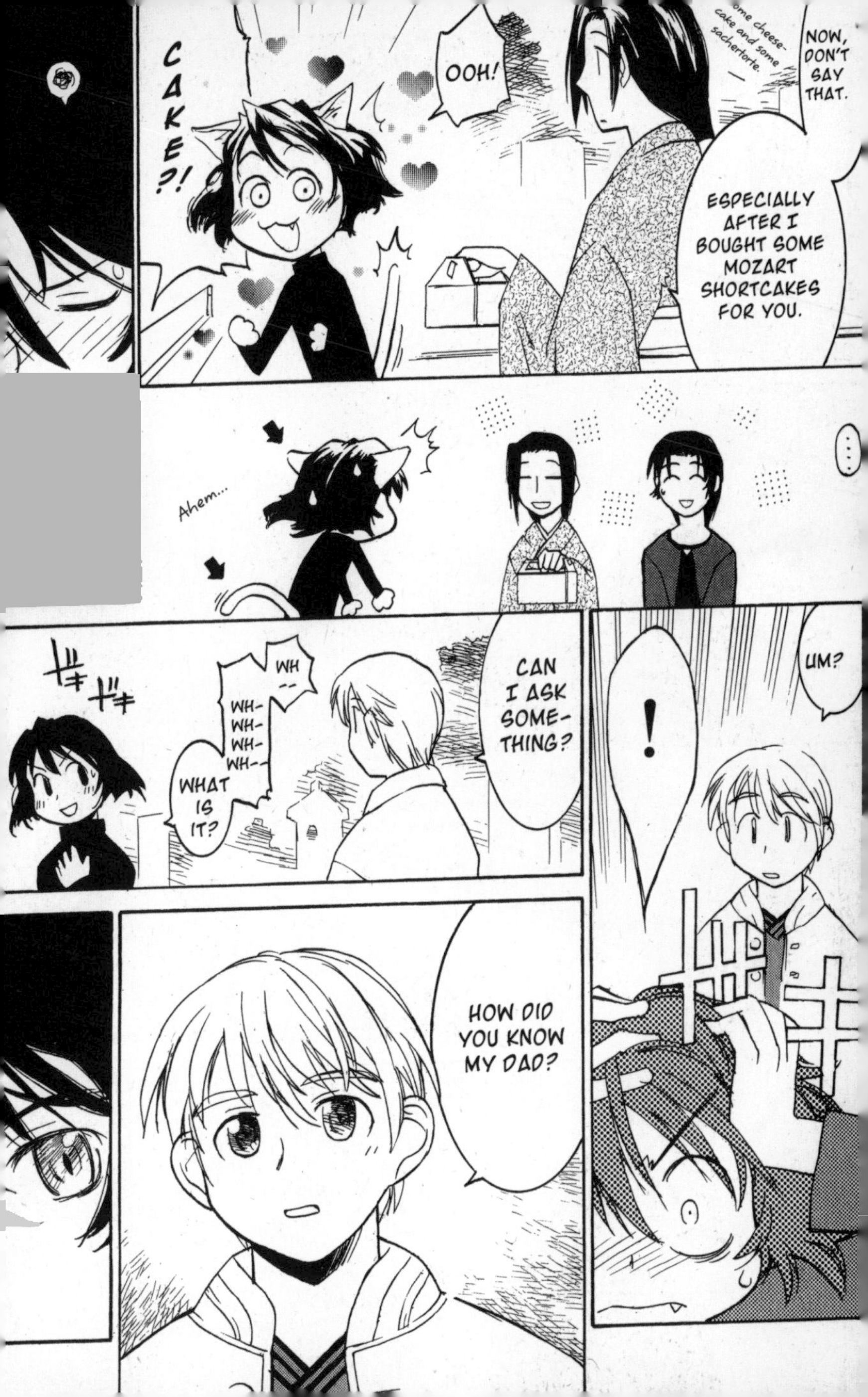
NOW, DON'T SAY THAT.
ome cheese-cake and some sachertorte.
ESPECIALLY AFTER I BOUGHT SOME MOZART SHORTCAKES FOR YOU.
OOH!
CAKE?!
...
Ahem...
UM?
!
CAN I ASK SOMETHING?
WH--
WH-WH-WH-WH--
WHAT IS IT?
ドキドキ
HOW DID YOU KNOW MY DAD?

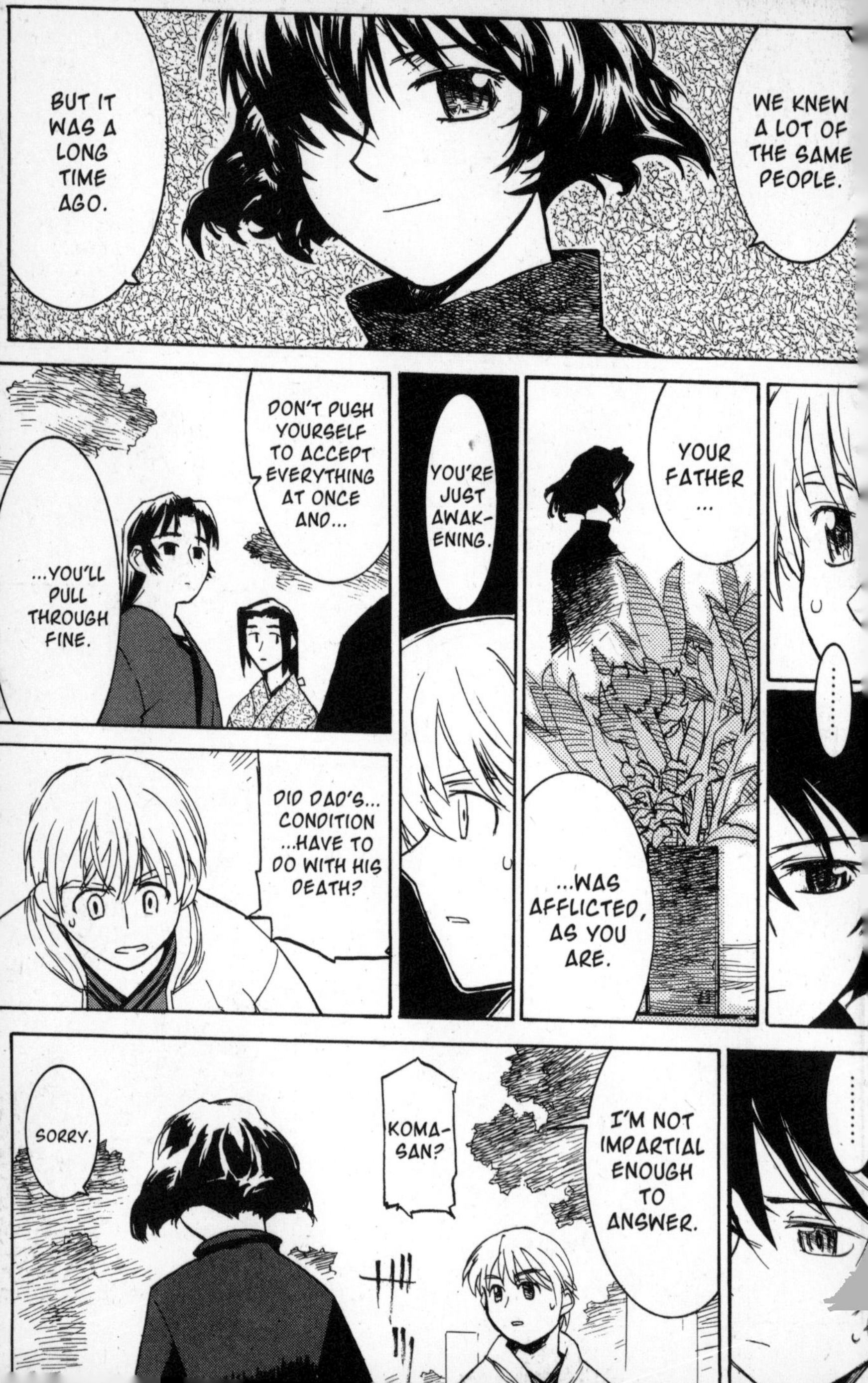
WE KNEW A LOT OF THE SAME PEOPLE.
BUT IT WAS A LONG TIME AGO.
......
YOUR FATHER ...
...WAS AFFLICTED, AS YOU ARE.
YOU'RE JUST AWAKENING.
DON'T PUSH YOURSELF TO ACCEPT EVERYTHING AT ONCE AND...
...YOU'LL PULL THROUGH FINE.
DID DAD'S... CONDITION ...HAVE TO DO WITH HIS DEATH?
......
I'M NOT IMPARTIAL ENOUGH TO ANSWER.
KOMA-SAN?
SORRY.

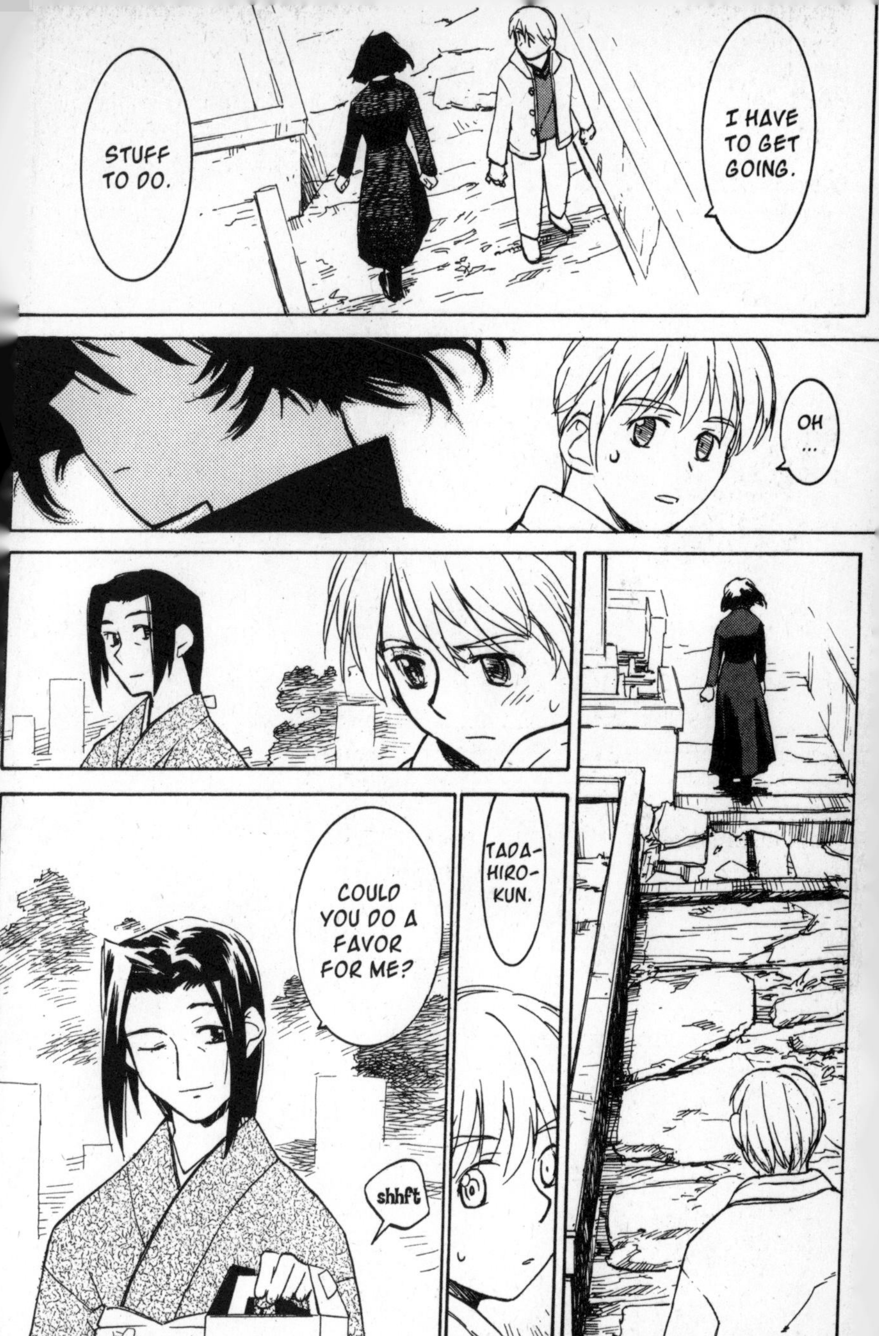
I HAVE TO GET GOING.
STUFF TO DO.
OH ...
TADA-HIRO-KUN.
COULD YOU DO A FAVOR FOR ME?
shhft

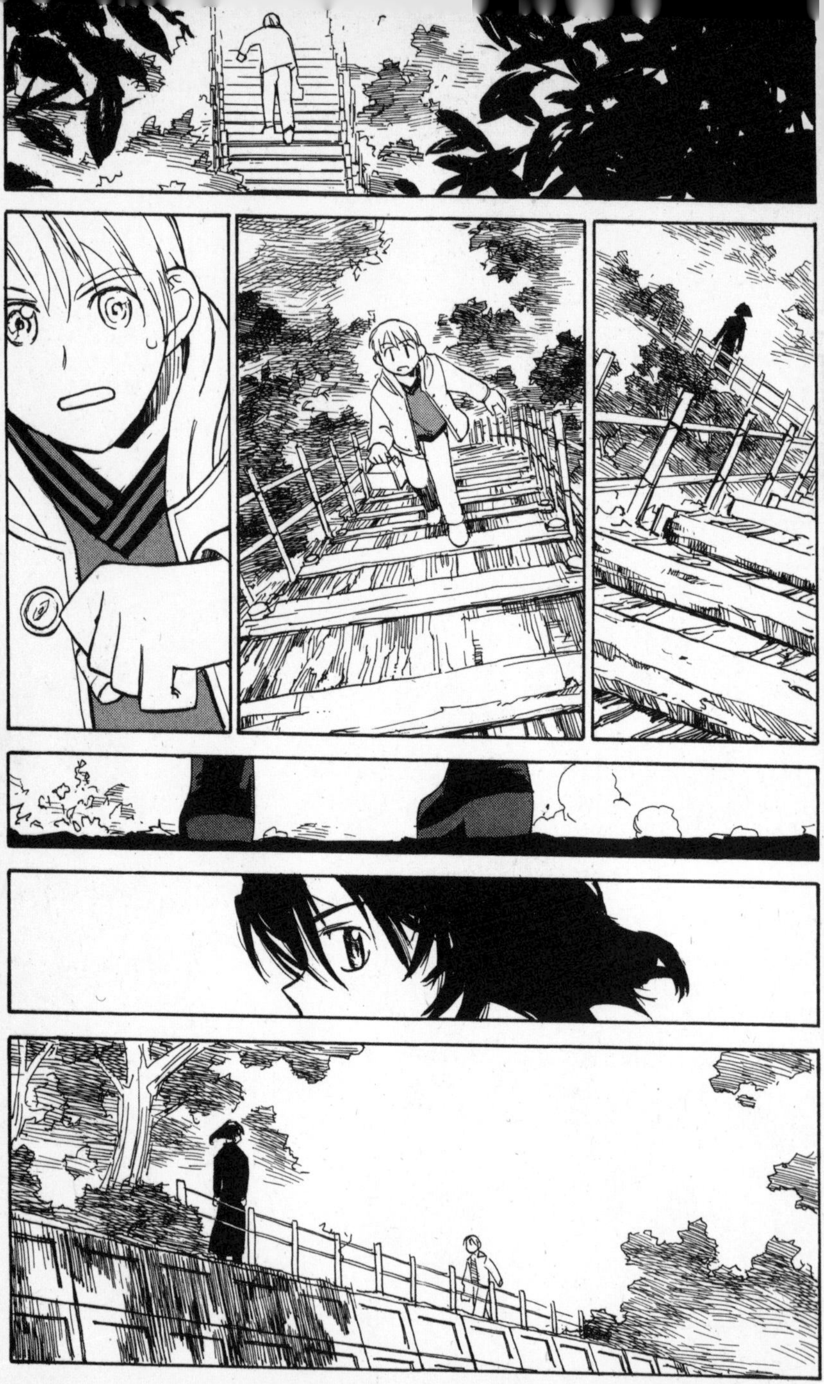

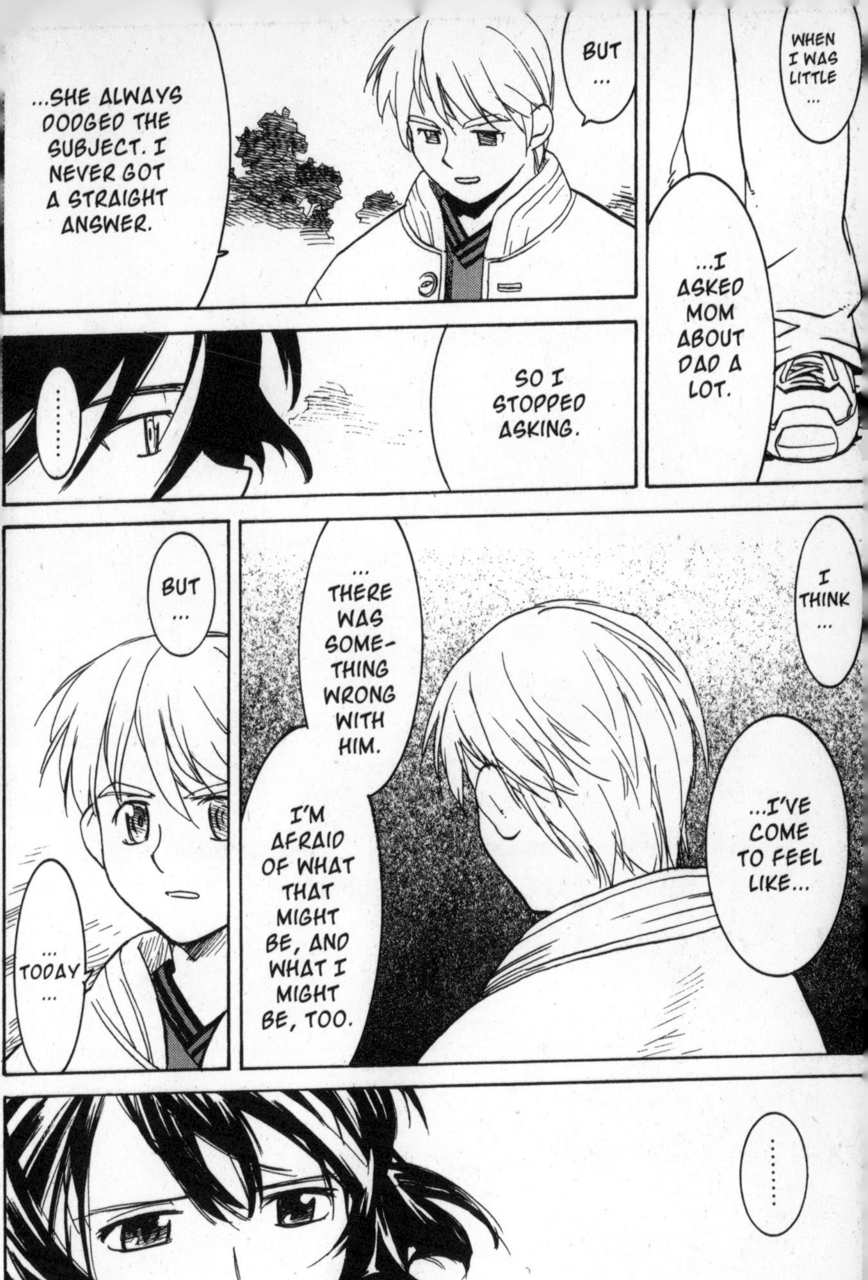

WHEN I WAS LITTLE ...
...I ASKED MOM ABOUT DAD A LOT.
BUT ...
...SHE ALWAYS DODGED THE SUBJECT. I NEVER GOT A STRAIGHT ANSWER.
SO I STOPPED ASKING.
......
I THINK ...
...I'VE COME TO FEEL LIKE...
... THERE WAS SOME-THING WRONG WITH HIM.
I'M AFRAID OF WHAT THAT MIGHT BE, AND WHAT I MIGHT BE, TOO.
BUT ...
... TODAY ...
......

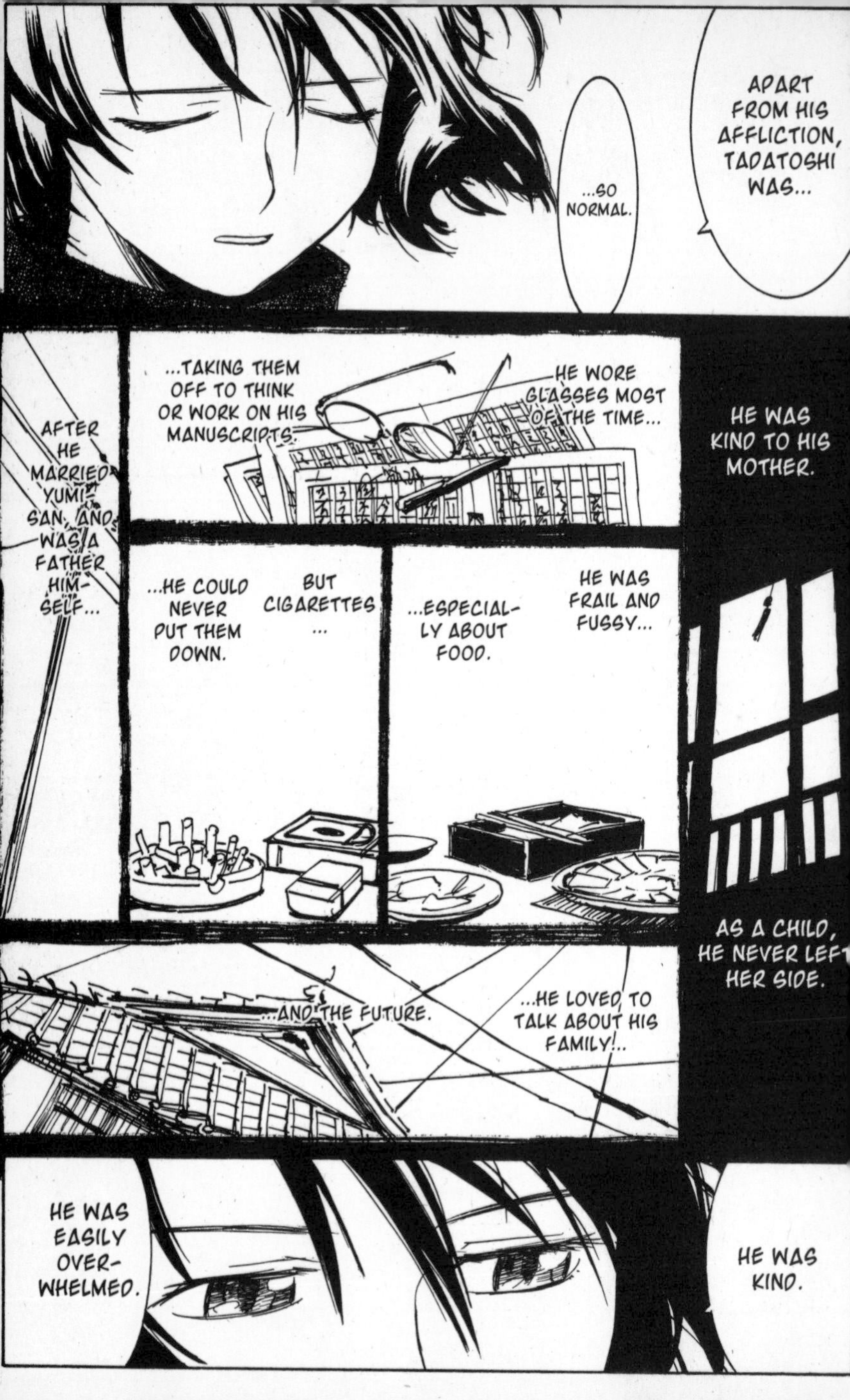
APART FROM HIS AFFLICTION, TADATOSHI WAS...
...SO NORMAL.
HE WAS KIND TO HIS MOTHER.
AS A CHILD, HE NEVER LEF HER SIDE.
HE WORE GLASSES MOST OF THE TIME...
...TAKING THEM OFF TO THINK OR WORK ON HIS MANUSCRIPTS.
HE WAS FRAIL AND FUSSY...
...ESPECIAL-LY ABOUT FOOD.
BUT CIGARETTES...
...HE COULD NEVER PUT THEM DOWN.
AFTER HE MARRIED YUMI-SAN, AND WAS A FATHER HIM-SELF...
...HE LOVED TO TALK ABOUT HIS FAMILY...
...AND THE FUTURE.
HE WAS KIND.
HE WAS EASILY OVER-WHELMED.

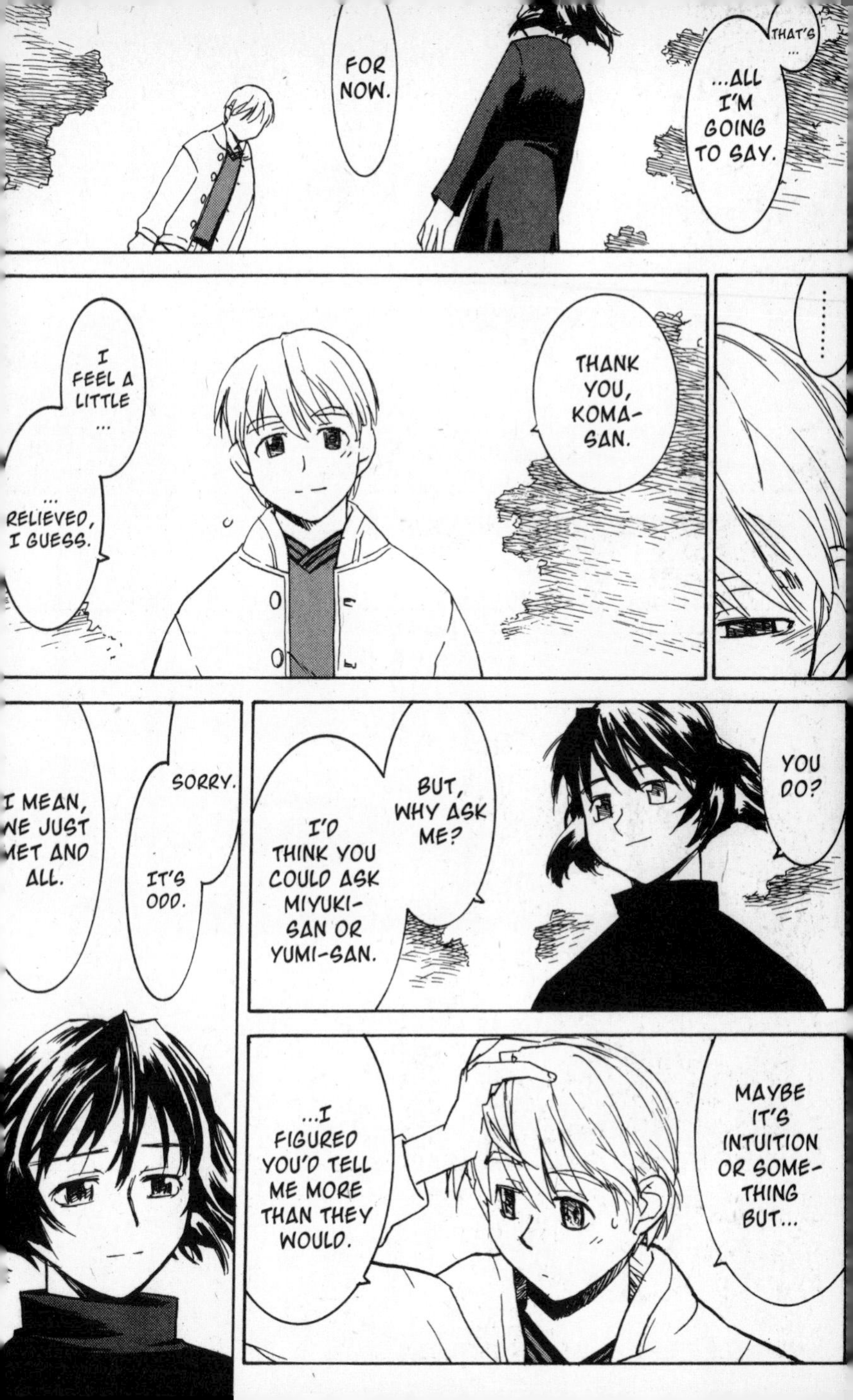

THAT'S ...
...ALL I'M GOING TO SAY.
FOR NOW.
......
THANK YOU, KOMA-SAN.
I FEEL A LITTLE ...
... RELIEVED, I GUESS.
YOU DO?
BUT, WHY ASK ME?
I'D THINK YOU COULD ASK MIYUKI-SAN OR YUMI-SAN.
MAYBE IT'S INTUITION OR SOME-THING BUT...
...I FIGURED YOU'D TELL ME MORE THAN THEY WOULD.
SORRY.
IT'S ODD.
I MEAN, WE JUST MET AND ALL.

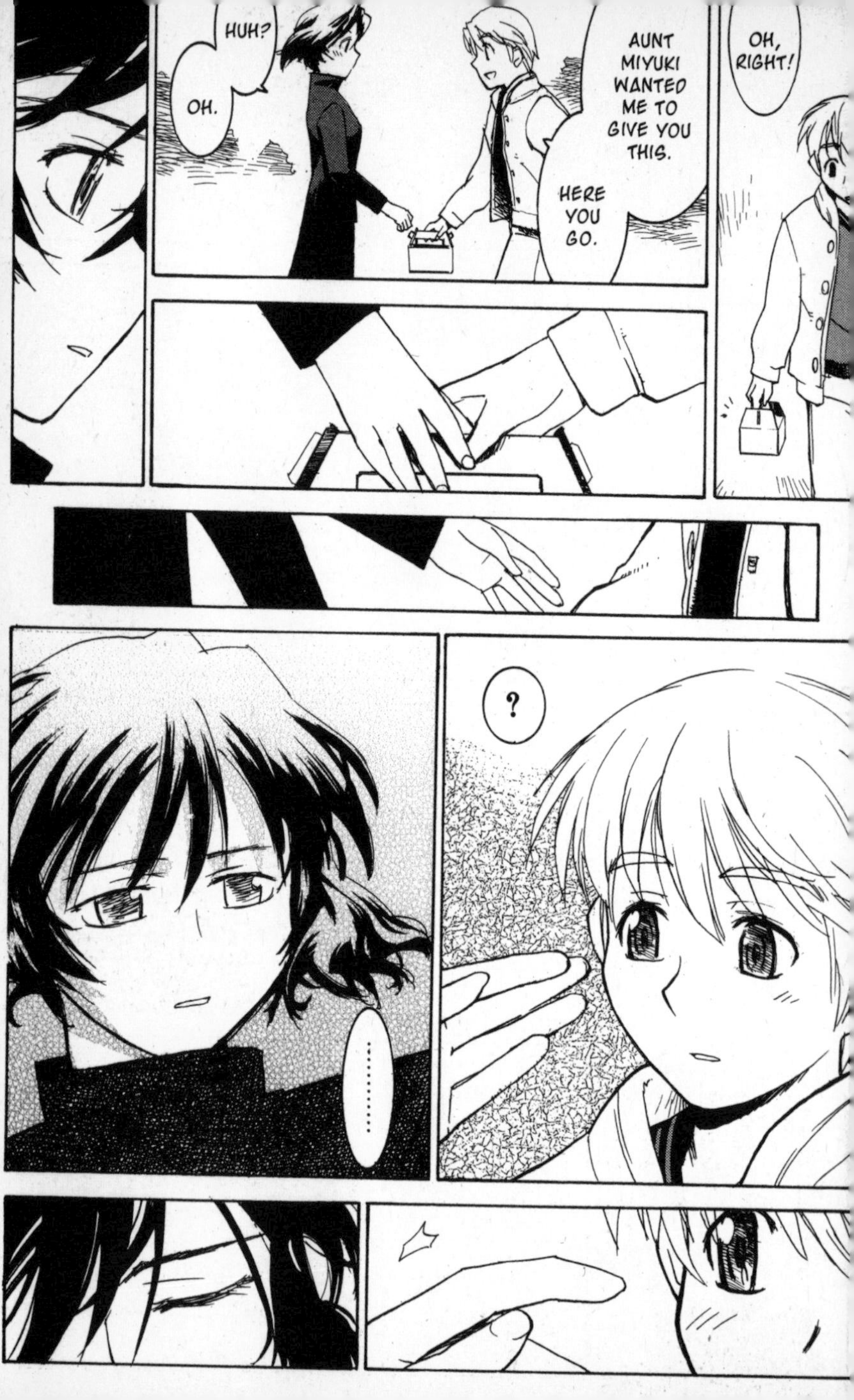
OH, RIGHT!
AUNT MIYUKI WANTED ME TO GIVE YOU THIS.
HERE YOU GO.
HUH?
OH.
?
......

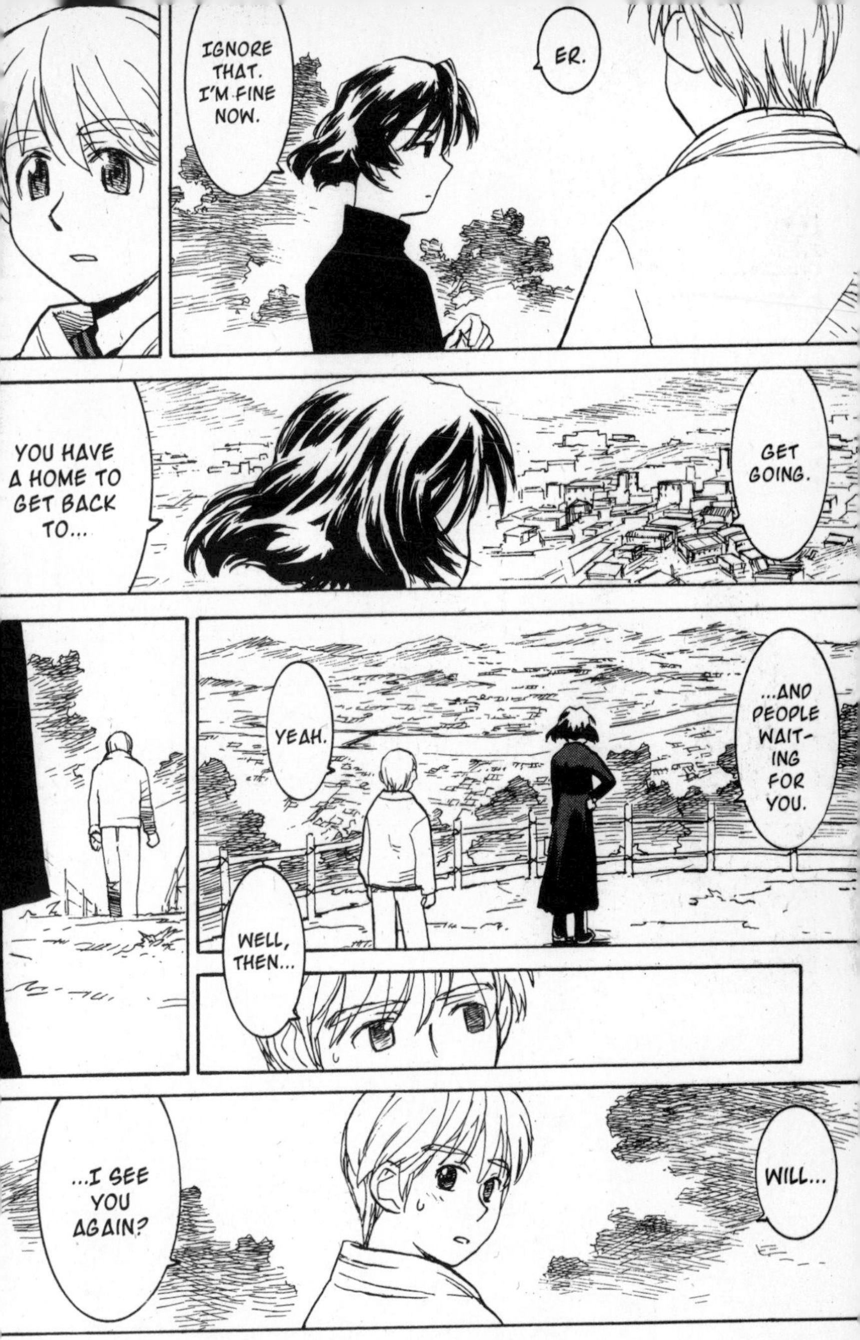
ER.
IGNORE THAT. I'M FINE NOW.
GET GOING.
YOU HAVE A HOME TO GET BACK TO...
...AND PEOPLE WAIT-ING FOR YOU.
YEAH.
WELL, THEN...
WILL...
...I SEE YOU AGAIN?

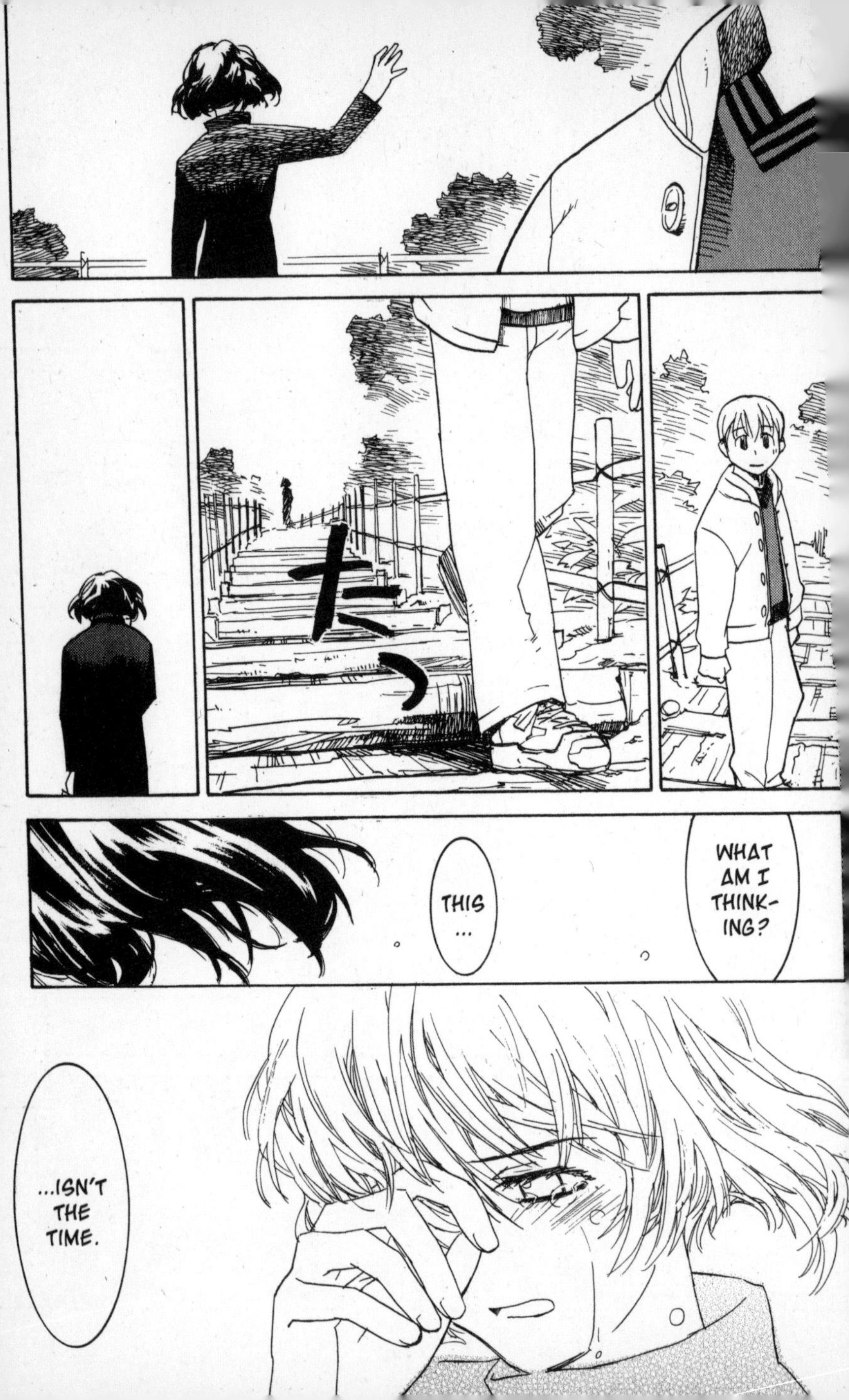
たっ
WHAT AM I THINKING?
THIS ...
...ISN'T THE TIME.

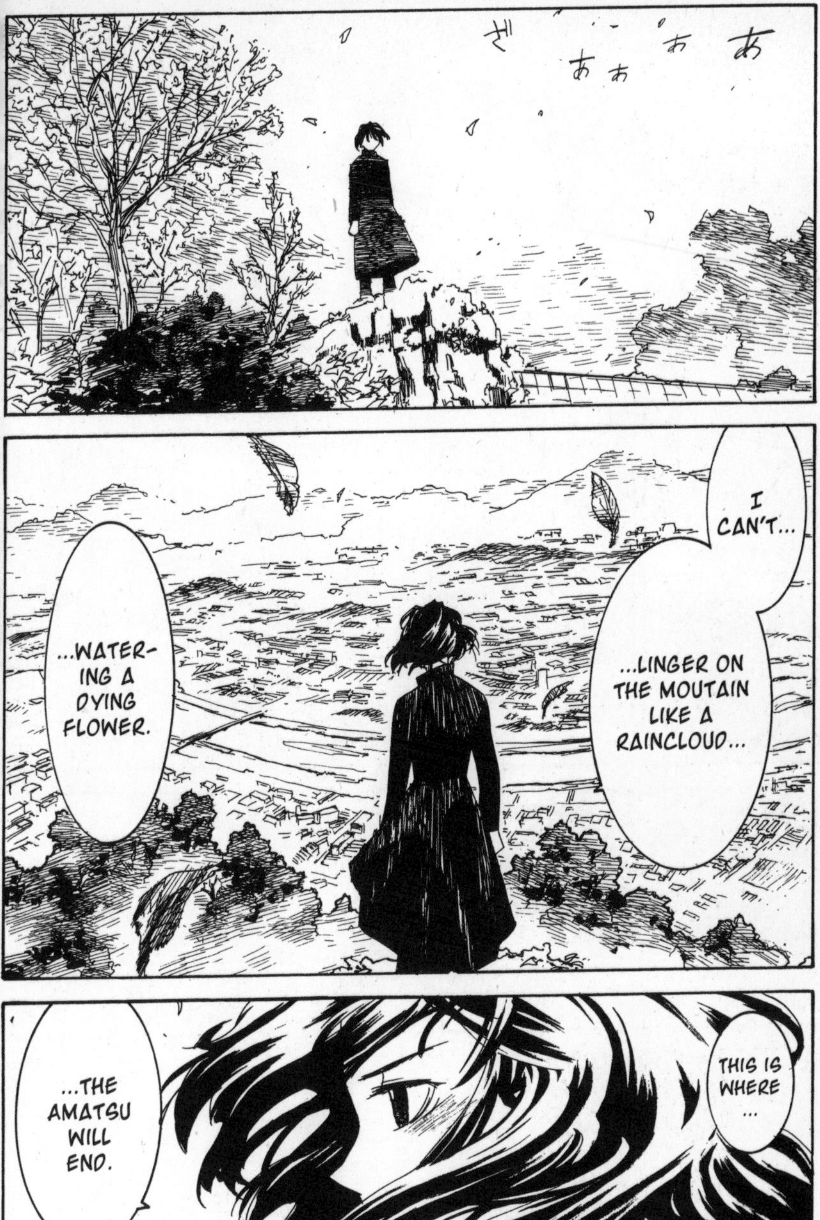
ざあぁああ
I CAN'T...
...LINGER ON THE MOUTAIN LIKE A RAINCLOUD...
...WATER-ING A DYING FLOWER.
THIS IS WHERE ...
...THE AMATSU WILL END.

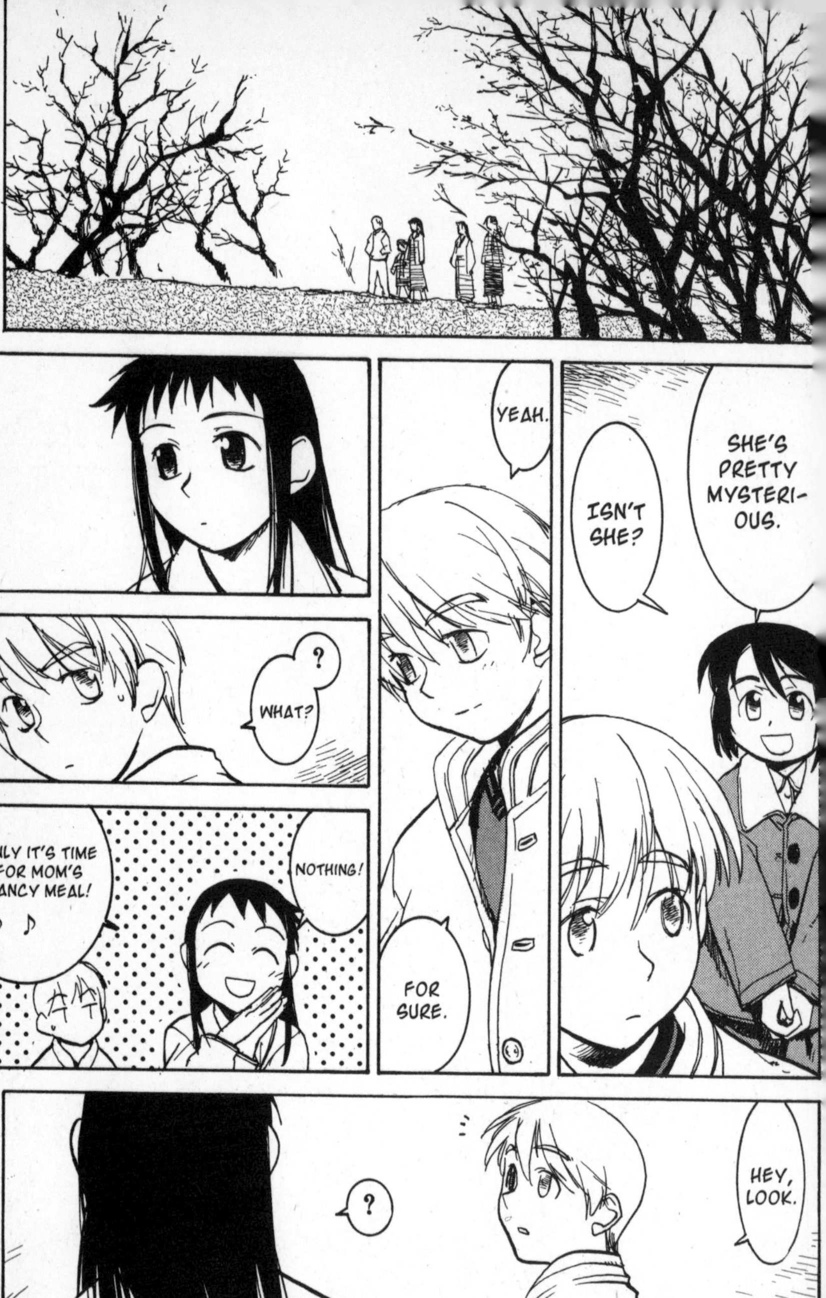

SHE'S PRETTY MYSTERI-OUS.
ISN'T SHE?
YEAH.
FOR SURE.
?
WHAT?
NOTHING!
ONLY IT'S TIME FOR MOM'S FANCY MEAL! ♪ ♪
HEY, LOOK.
?

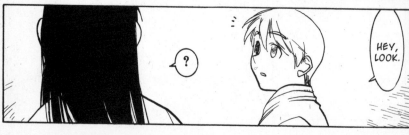

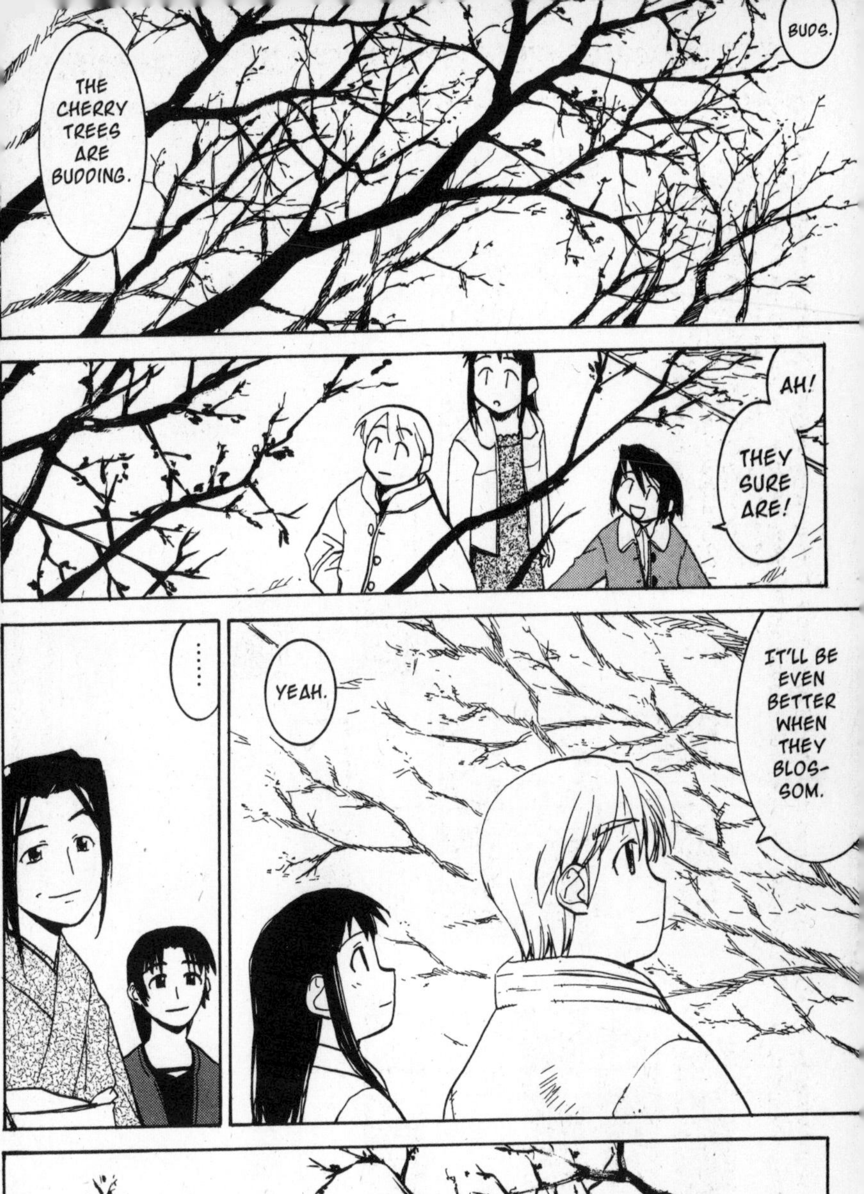
BUDS.
THE CHERRY TREES ARE BUDDING.
AH!
THEY SURE ARE!
IT'LL BE EVEN BETTER WHEN THEY BLOS-SOM.
YEAH.
......

Continued in Vol. 2

Genealogy Chart

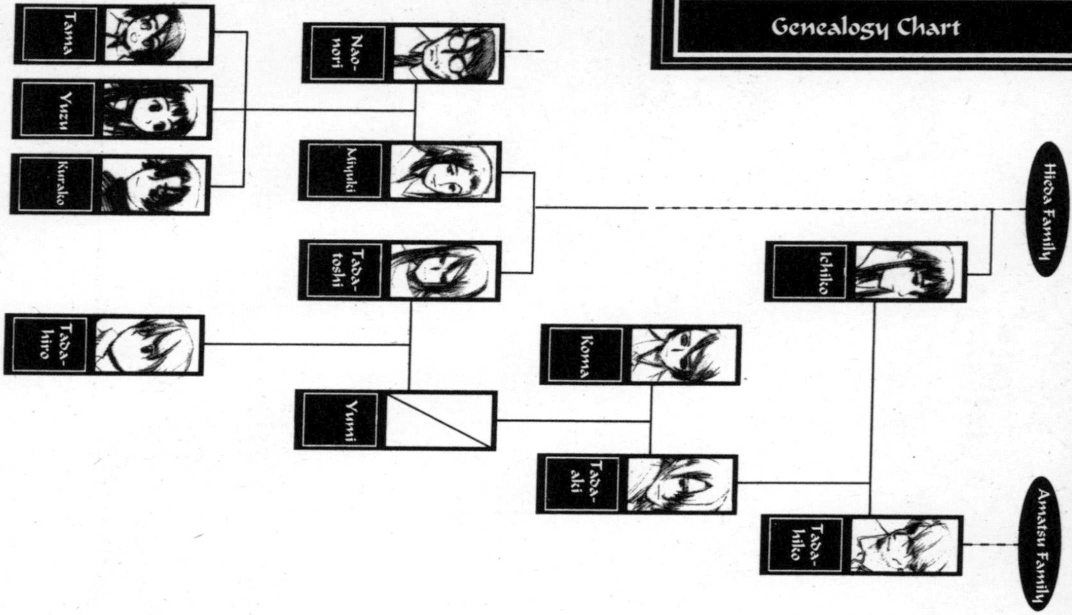

Hieda Family
Amatsu Family
Ichiko
Tada-hiko
Koma
Tada-aki
Nao-nori
Miyuki
Tada-toshi
Yumi
Tama
Yuzu
Kurako
Tada-hiro

Appendix

IN THE NEXT INSTALLMENT OF

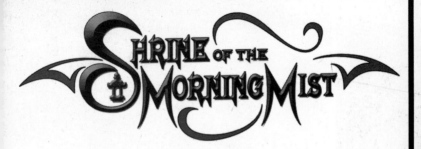

SHRINE OF THE MORNING MIST

When Tadahiro starts his classes, it seems he's brought some uninvited guests with him! During his admittance ceremony, the school is inundated with apparitions, the most dangerous of which have their sights set on Tadahiro. In an effort to combat these ghostly attacks, Kurako-sensei enlists a team of students to ward off the spirits. Also making an appearance is Kusugi, a handsome new student, who comes to Tadahiro's rescue in the nick of time.

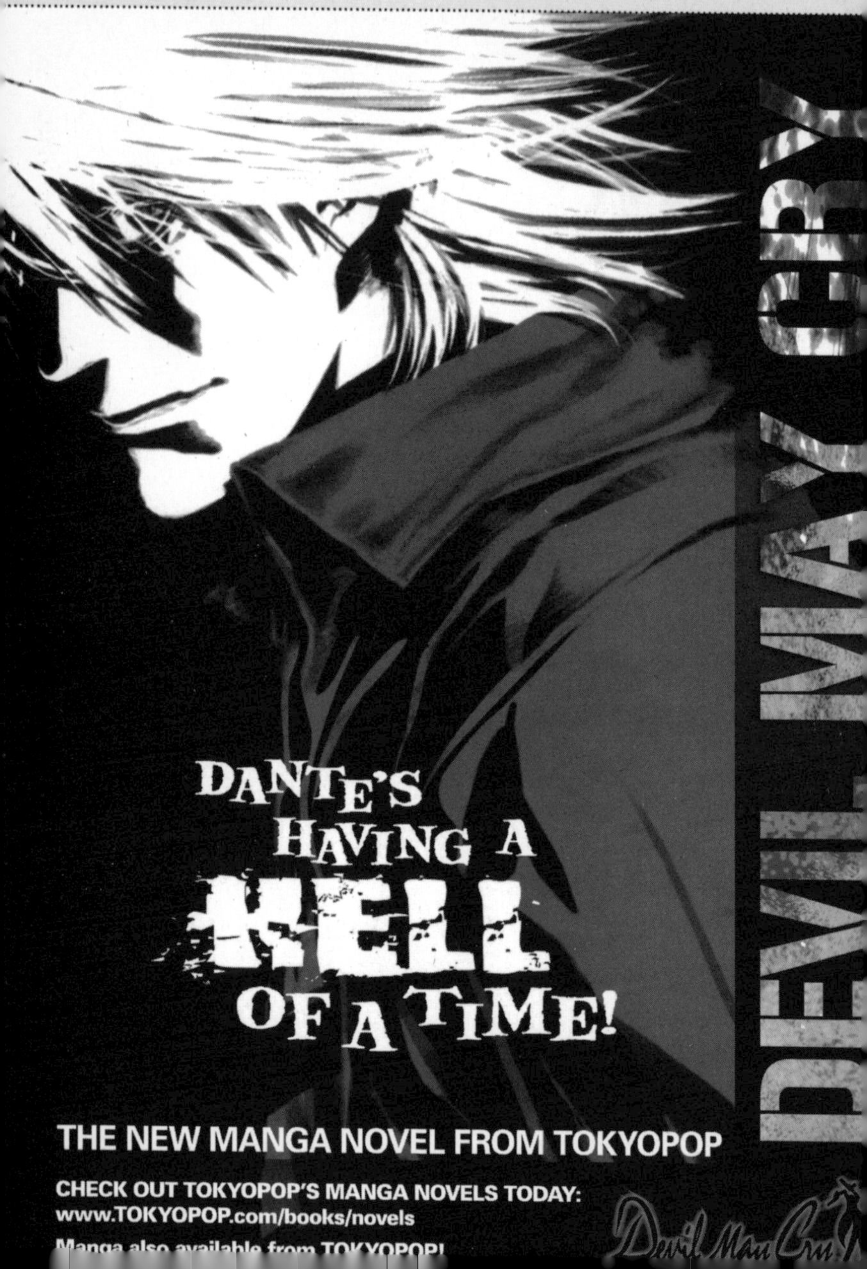
DEVIL MAY CRY
DANTE'S HAVING A HELL OF A TIME!
THE NEW MANGA NOVEL FROM TOKYOPOP
CHECK OUT TOKYOPOP'S MANGA NOVELS TODAY:
www.TOKYOPOP.com/books/novels
Manga also available from TOKYOPOP!
Devil May Cry

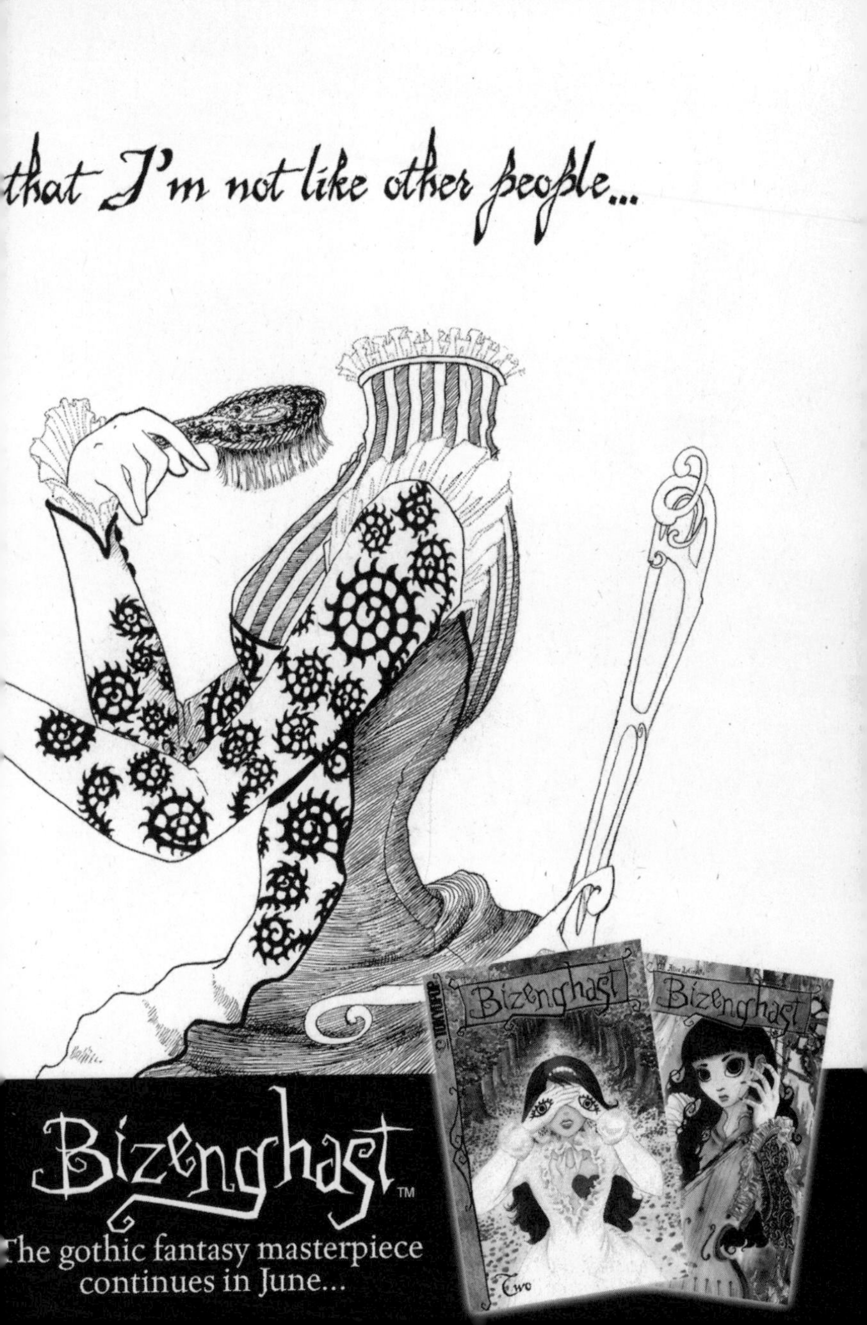
that I'm not like other people...
Bizenghast
Bizenghast
Two
Bizenghast™
The gothic fantasy masterpiece
continues in June...

BIZENGHAST

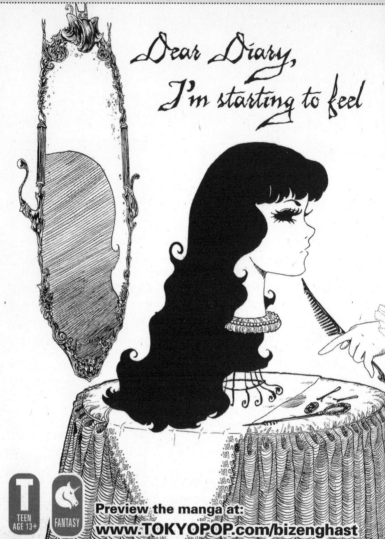

Dear Diary,
I'm starting to feel

THIS FALL, TOKYOPOP CREATES A FRESH, NEW CHAPTER IN TEEN NOVELS...

For Adventurers...

Witches' Forest: The Adventures of Duan Surk

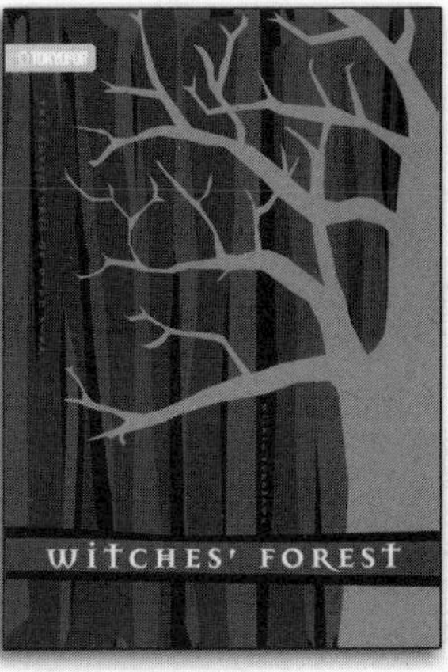
TOKYOPOP
witches' forest

By Mishio Fukazawa

Duan Surk is a 16-year-old Level 2 fighter who embarks on the quest of a lifetime—battling mythical creatures and outwitting evil sorceresses, all in an impossible rescue mission in the spooky Witches' Forest!

BASED ON THE FAMOUS *FORTUNE QUEST* WORLD

For Dreamers...

Magic Moon

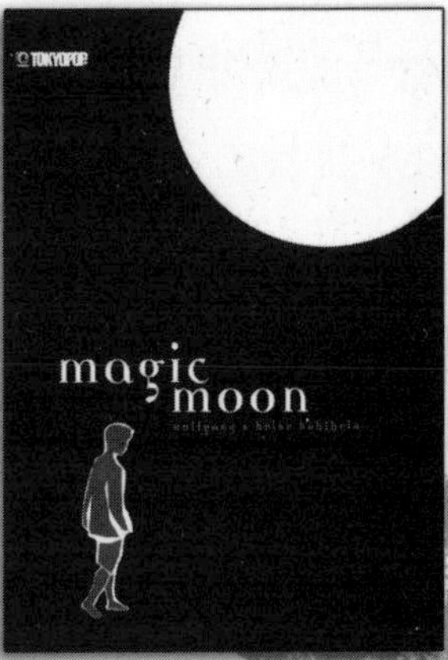
TOKYOPOP
magic moon

By Wolfgang and Heike Hohlbein

Kim enters the engimatic realm of Magic Moon, where he battles unthinkable monsters and fantastical creatures—in order to unravel the secret that keeps his sister locked in a coma.

THE WORLDWIDE BESTSELLING FANTASY *THRILL*OGY ARRIVES IN THE U.S.!

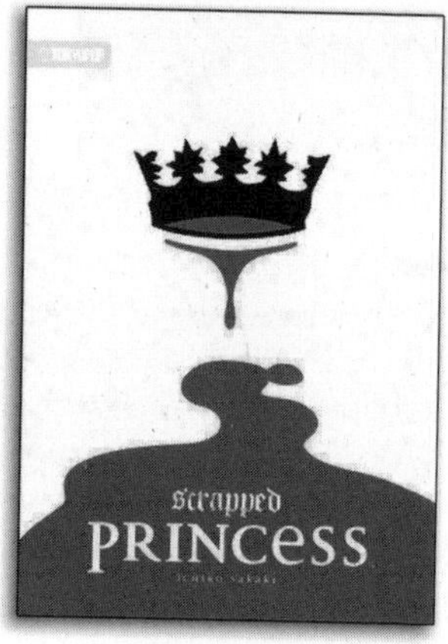
TOKYOPOP
Scrapped
PRINCESS
Ichiro Sakaki

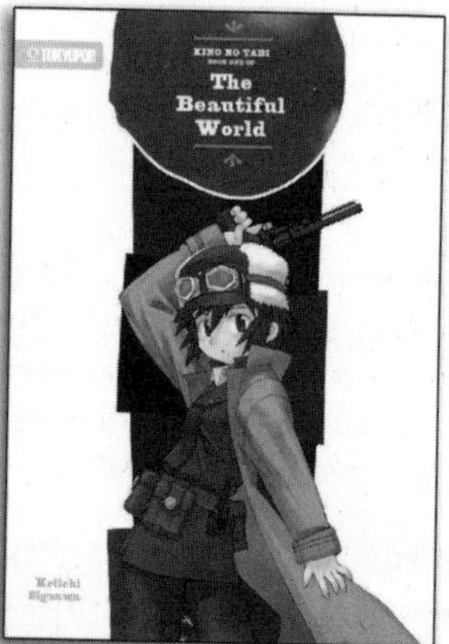
TOKYOPOP
KINO NO TABI
The Beautiful World
Keiichi Sigsawa

STOP!

This is the back of the book.
You wouldn't want to spoil a great ending!

This book is printed "manga-style," in the authentic Japanese right-to-left format. Since none of the artwork has been flipped or altered, readers get to experience the story just as the creator intended. You've been asking for it, so TOKYOPOP® delivered: authentic, hot-off-the-press, and far more fun!

DIRECTIONS

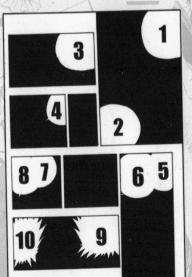

If this is your first time reading manga-style, here's a quick guide to help you understand how it works.

It's easy... just start in the top right panel and follow the numbers. Have fun, and look for more 100% authentic manga from TOKYOPOP®!

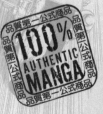